Fighting for Dignity

CONTEMPORARY ETHNOGRAPHY

Kirin Narayan and Alma Gottlieb, Series Editors

A complete list of books in the series is available from the publisher.

Fighting for Dignity

Migrant Lives at Israel's Margins

Sarah S. Willen

PENN

UNIVERSITY OF PENNSYLVANIA PRESS

PHILADELPHIA

Published by
University of Pennsylvania Press
Philadelphia, Pennsylvania 19104-4112
www.upenn.edu/pennpress

Printed in the United States of America
on acid-free paper

1   3   5   7   9   10   8   6   4   2

A catalogue record for this book is available from the
Library of Congress.

ISBN 978-0-8122-5134-0

For the generations before me,
and for Dassi and Adin,
and—in between and especially—for Sebastian

Contemporary Israel is one big bundle of contradictions: it is often as uplifting as it is off-putting; as compassionate as it is oppressive; as humane as it is cruel. Its people display amazing kindness and warmth, yet constantly exhibit reprehensible intolerance and xenophobia. They selflessly tender care to the needy while they close their doors to the dispossessed. And they sustain untenable policies at odds with the basic principles of human dignity which they claim to hold so dear.

—Naomi Chazan

We are *free* to change the world and start something new in it.

—Hannah Arendt

CONTENTS

NOTE ON NAMES AND TERMS

Unless otherwise indicated, all names and identifying details have been changed to protect confidentiality, even in cases where proper names were published by the media, and all translations from the Hebrew are my own. In an effort to render Hebrew terms pronounceable by readers unfamiliar with the language, I have taken the (admittedly unconventional) step of using diacritical marks to clarify emphasis within words. The Hebrew letters ח and כ, sometimes transliterated into English as *ch* or, less commonly, *kh*, are both transliterated as *ḥ*.

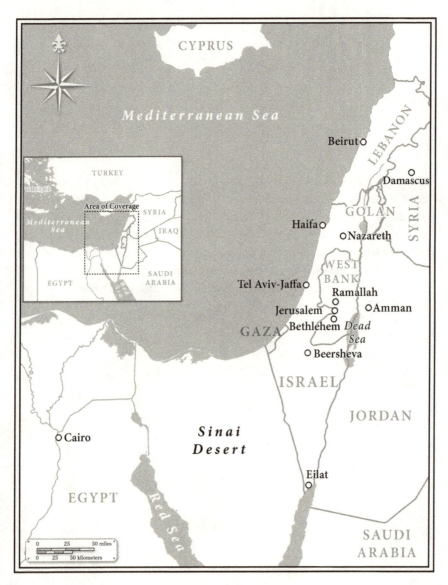

Map 1. Israel and Its Neighbors

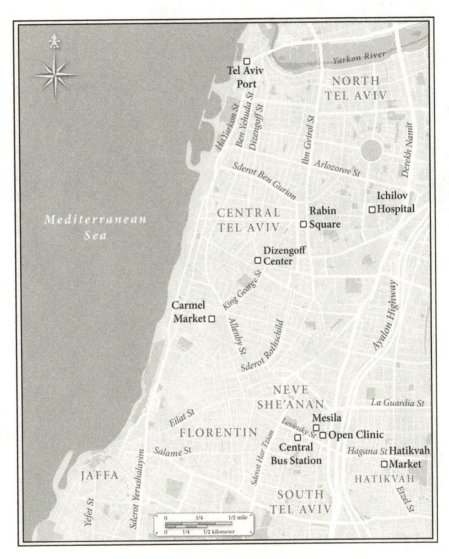

Map 2. Tel Aviv

Introduction

At least five people were killed Monday, including a
five-year-old girl, when a canister of household cooking
gas exploded, causing a two-story house in Tel Aviv's
blue-collar HaTikvah neighborhood to collapse. Among
those killed [were] . . . a man and his pregnant wife—
both foreign workers from Nigeria. Rescue workers were
unsuccessful in saving their unborn child.

Another resident of the collapsed building, a Nigerian man named Elijah,
was spared. Instead of coming home for the night, he had slept in a public
park while his pregnant wife, Pauline, stayed in the flat they shared with
Pauline's sister Rose and brother-in-law Reuben—the couple who had lost
their lives. From his makeshift bed in the bushes, Elijah had heard the explosion at 4:30 A.M., not knowing their two-story building had been struck
and his relatives killed—or, for that matter, that his own wife had survived.
In the media flurry that followed the explosion, one detail caught local
journalists' attention: Elijah's newly acquired habit of sleeping outdoors.
"'Since the police increased the patrols I barely ever sleep at home,' he explained in English. 'All the black men hide out at night and sleep in the
bushes.' In the mornings, he would come home to shower and go to his work
as a housecleaner."[1]

A year before the building collapse, in late summer 2002, the Israeli authorities had kicked off a mass deportation campaign grounded in a catchy if
flawed populist sound bite: 300,000 migrant workers were living in the country, and 300,000 Israelis were unemployed.[2] In recent months, the government's
newly created Immigration Administration (*Minhélet haHagirá*)[3]—equipped
with more than 450 new officers, four new detention centers, and high monthly
arrest quotas—had begun breaking down doors in the late-night hours, pulling people from their beds, and carting them off for swift deportation. A

month earlier, Elijah had been the target of one such late-night raid. Like many migrants who narrowly escaped arrest, he and his wife packed up immediately in search of new accommodations. For now, Pauline was staying with Rose and Reuben—and Elijah had taken to sleeping outside. For a while Reuben did the same, but as Rose's due date approached, he returned home to spend nights at his wife's side.

On that summer morning, by the time Elijah normally would have been at the apartment preparing for work, their building on Natan Street had collapsed in a pile of rubble: crumbled concrete, tangles of steel and wire, pulverized mortar hanging heavy in the air. Trapped in the rubble were not just Pauline, one of six people injured, but also their flatmates and five others who didn't make it: a woman with twenty-six years of state service; an eighty-year-old grandmother; a couple in their late forties who had moved in just three months earlier; and a five-year-old girl, born in Israel to Filipino parents, whose cries could be heard as rescue workers pulled her—still alive, momentarily—from the rubble.

Three hours later, at 7:30 A.M., my cell phone rang. Ayelet, a social worker at the Mesila Aid and Information Center for the Foreign Community, a small municipal agency in South Tel Aviv where I regularly volunteered, was calling to tell me what had happened, and to ask if I could come help. An unusual agency of professional social workers supported by teams of volunteers, Mesila followed an unwritten motto that revealed its delicate position: *We will not interfere with government policies—but as long as migrants are here, they are entitled to a basic standard of respect and support which it is our duty to provide.*

By 8:00 A.M., I had cycled across South Tel Aviv to the site of the explosion in Shḥunat HaTikvah, a lively, hardscrabble neighborhood whose name— literally, "Neighborhood of Hope"—belies visible signs of residents' daily struggles: weedy vacant lots, overflowing trash bins, mangy street cats, market smells of fish and slaughtered poultry sitting out in the summertime heat. Until global migrants like Elijah and his wife began arriving in the late 1990s, most of the neighborhood's residents—unlike Mesila's predominantly Ashkenazi volunteers—were Mizraḥim, or Jews of Middle Eastern and North African descent.

All looked peculiarly normal as I sped down narrow streets lined with aging two-story buildings and through the neighborhood's tight intersections, Ayelet's words echoing in my head. Rounding the corner onto Natan Street,

I was wholly unprepared for the raw devastation that had already attracted a sea of onlookers. Hundreds of people—Israelis, Nigerians, Ghanaians, Filipinos—crowded shoulder-to-shoulder along the main road and cross streets, peering behind the police barriers and toward the gaping hole where, just hours earlier, a building had stood, filled with people asleep in their beds. The crowd stayed eerily quiet as uniformed soldiers, police officers, rescue crews with heavy equipment, and emergency personnel teemed about the live wreckage (Figure 1). Journalists scampered freely, snapping photos and thrusting microphones into people's faces without invitation, eager to package the rawness of individual trauma into media ephemera for consumption at a distance, soon to be forgotten. From a nearby rooftop, a few neighbors peered down into the rubble.

When I arrived on the scene, Mesila's director guided me past the crowds and brought me behind the police barrier. At that point, with an active rescue operation under way, no clear mandate for action had been established.

An African woman, her body contorted and eyes wild, sat in a huddle of women on a narrow stairway across from the rubble, weeping and praying. "Her daughter and son-in-law are trapped inside the building," Ayelet told me as we walked by. I immediately recognized her as Comfort, a woman who had welcomed me three years earlier to the apartment she and her husband shared with several flatmates, including Yvonne, the Nigerian woman and single mother I had come by to interview. On that evening, we had all swapped family stories. Comfort, poking at me playfully and calling me "skin and bones," had insisted I eat a towering plate of food she had prepared. Since then we greeted each other warmly, and regularly, at the NGO-run Open Clinic for migrant workers, where she was a patient and I spent my afternoons as a volunteer and participant-observer. In that protected space, cast in familiar roles of patient and volunteer clinic staffer, we had always exchanged news, and hugs. But when I saw Comfort on Natan Street that morning, my own limbs shaking and pulverized concrete invading my nostrils, I could barely recognize the hysterical woman on the steps.

Unsure of how to make myself useful, I suggested to Mesila's director I might pass those anxious hours with Comfort and the women who had flocked to her. As the sun rose in the sky, an emergency worker coaxed us all out of the heat and into a small shaded courtyard, where an Israeli woman with a kerchief on her head and a mouthful of black stubs for teeth took down

Figure 1. Building collapse in South Tel Aviv. Photo: Mati Milstein.

laundry while tending to an infant. Another woman arrived: the stout land-lady, dressed fashionably in black, hair dyed blond. Her cousin was also trapped, she told us. We were welcome to use the bathroom.

The pace of the rescue operation was excruciatingly slow. At one point, a soldier approached the courtyard with a plea for patience. "We're working slowly and carefully," he told Comfort in English, "because it's the only way we can work." He promised to return with an update. We didn't see him again.

Later a rescue worker arrived with a stack of photo albums taken from the rubble, which made their way into a canvas tote bag offered by the woman with the kerchief.

Eventually a police officer approached me with a request. Could I clarify the names of the couple, and of the woman who had been taken to the hospital? I took care to convey his questions in the present tense.

Then, an announcement: the rescue teams requested silence from the crowds as they prepared to enter with search dogs. Comfort, hearing this news, flew from her seat and toward the rubble; several of us held her back. A television crew forced their way toward us angling for a better shot, and I found myself shouting and shooing them away. "We have a right!" the journalists yelled at me. "Don't they want this to be on the evening news?"

The canine team surveyed the building in silence. Comfort, now swaying on a plastic lawn chair, prayed and cried. At one point, the Nigerian woman beside her interrupted: "No, don't take your life. . . . This is God's land, you know, this is His land. He can do anything, and especially here, here He can do anything. Have faith. He'll prove himself. . . . He will come through."

Time was slow, the heat heavy beneath a preternaturally clear blue sky. Late in the morning, rescue workers emerged from the rubble, a black body bag in tow. "It's Reuben, it's Reuben!" someone cried.

A crowd surged toward the police barrier, and a scuffle ensued as several officers tried to hold people back. A Nigerian man fell to the ground; an instant later, word reached Comfort. And then, chaos. As she let out a piercing wail, crowds swarmed: Mesila social workers trying to calm her down and offer her water, journalists shoving cameras in her face. One woman even tried to dump water on her head, for reasons I couldn't understand. *It was horrible*, I scribbled in a notebook later that morning. *Just horrible.*

Only hours later did we learn the crowd had been mistaken. The body in the black bag, one of Mesila's social workers told us, was not Reuben's. It was Rose, his pregnant wife. Her near-term fetus could not be saved.

Rupture

The building collapse on Natan Street was no commonplace event in South Tel Aviv. Yet much about that fateful morning followed disaster routine. Immediately after the explosion, curious onlookers poured into the streets, horrified but enraptured by the unfolding calamity. A high-tech, organizationally complex emergency operation—much like those Israel deploys in response to suicide bombings, and exports overseas on humanitarian missions—kicked rapidly into gear. For just a moment, the tensions and antipathies that usually coursed through the streets and alleyways of this struggling urban neighborhood gave way to a different logic altogether: a logic that put human life—bare, vulnerable, unmarked by social distinctions—above all else.

Yet there was nothing redemptive about this momentary erasure of social boundaries, especially since another, darker tale lurked in plain sight. However authentic the Israeli authorities' momentary solicitude toward unauthorized migrant victims and their relatives, it contrasted starkly with the manhunt mentality that preceded it, and that would quickly resurface in its wake.

As for Elijah, he owed his own survival to a deeply unsettling paradox. What saved his life, above all, was precisely the aggressive deportation campaign that had hounded him out of his home and sown fear and panic among the migrant men, women, and children, numbering between 60,000 and 80,000, who had recently taken up residence in Tel Aviv on an unauthorized basis. For some, including Elijah, this fear was strong enough to drive them from their beds at night, into the bushes.

*   *   *

This book is a story of dignity, indignity, and indignation. Drawing on over eighteen years of ethnographic engagement (2000–2018), including more than thirty nonconsecutive months of ethnographic fieldwork in Tel Aviv, it explores the rhythm, texture, and existential demands of everyday life for a relatively new population of excluded Others in the charged sociopolitical space of contemporary Israel/Palestine: global migrants who have been illegalized and, I argue, "abjected" by the Israeli state and Israeli society. The country's ethnonational migration regime, described more fully below, and the simmering Palestinian-Israeli conflict form the backdrop to the story I aim to tell. As we will see, the abjection of migrants is not a one-time event. It is a "lived social process," as sociologist Imogen Tyler puts it, and the "consequences of 'being abject' [vary] within specific social and political locales."[4]

At the center of the book is an expensive, heavily publicized, mass deportation campaign initiated by the Israeli government in late summer 2002 that I describe in this book as the gerush (pronounced *gerúsh*)—Hebrew for "deportation" or "expulsion." During the most intensive period of the gerush (2002–5), which coincided with my longest consecutive stint of fieldwork in Tel Aviv, over 150,000 migrants were "distanced" from Israel, to employ the Immigration Police's sanitizing euphemism.[5] Among them, over 40,000 were arrested and forcibly deported, and tens of thousands more were "encouraged"—essentially, regularly and systematically intimidated—into leaving "voluntarily." This was not the first period of heightened arrest and deportation targeting global migrants in Israel, nor was it the last. Earlier, smaller waves of expulsion had taken place late in the preceding decade, and additional campaigns took place in subsequent years. But this deportation campaign was unprecedented in both scope and scale, and it marked a definitive moment in Israel's treatment of global migrants, who had begun arriving in the mid-1990s in response to the same array of "push" and "pull" factors that spur transnational migration the world over.

One "pull" factor bears particular mention: the labor vacuum that emerged following the first intifada, or Palestinian national uprising, to protest Israel's protracted military occupation of Palestinian people and lands. Since Israel first occupied the West Bank and Gaza in 1967, Palestinian workers had become an indispensable source of labor for the Israeli economy. When Israel imposed closures in the West Bank and Gaza in response to the intifada, nearly every aspect of Palestinian civilians' lives was affected, among them their ability to attend school, access health care, and travel freely to see relatives and friends. The closures also had profound economic effects. In addition to clamping down on commerce within the Occupied Palestinian Territories (OPT), the closures also cut off job opportunities in Israel that had long provided livelihoods to Palestinian families, households, and entire communities.[6] The exclusion of Palestinian workers was also a problem from the standpoint of Israeli industry: it produced major labor shortages. Although the Israeli government was initially reluctant to grant approval, migrants from overseas—most arriving, at least initially, with legal authorization—were eager to fill jobs in agriculture, construction, and restaurant work that Palestinians could no longer access.

Although the ostensible goal of the gerush was to reduce Israeli unemployment, its barely disguised secondary goal was to preserve the country's "Jewish character" or, more bluntly, its Jewish demographic majority. In the Knesset, Israel's parliament, a single committee held responsibility for all matters involving these new arrivals, and its name clearly captured this governmental disposition: the "Special Committee on the Problem of Foreign Workers" (*haVaadá haMeyuḥédet leBaayát haOvdím haZarím*). From the standpoint of the state, migrants' presence in the country was itself a problem—and the gerush was supposed to be part of the solution. From my ethnographic vantage point, this campaign held little promise of solving any such "problem." It did, however, create new ones, including the rapid collapse of Tel Aviv's newly formed migrant communities, the disintegration of migrants' already precarious individual and group lifeworlds, and a whole host of indignities outlined in the following pages. At the same time, the gerush also laid the foundation for an even more aggressively nationalist and more violently exclusionary agenda that would prevail in the years to come—an agenda that has found parallel in other world regions, including western Europe and North America. In the concluding chapter, I turn briefly to the government's effort to launch a new deportation campaign in 2018, when the events chronicled here came full circle, albeit with a new group of excluded Others as target: African asylum seekers from Eritrea and Sudan, many of them living in the same parts of South Tel Aviv in which Elijah, Comfort, and other migrant workers had taken up residence two decades earlier.

Alongside these mounting changes, something else emerged in immediate response to the gerush: a burgeoning, often burning, sense of indignation among a small but expanding group of Israeli citizens who flatly rejected both the logic of the deportation campaign and its tactics. Over the course of my fieldwork, I met, interviewed, and volunteered alongside dozens of these advocates and activists. Although they differ in many ways, most have one thing in common: they reject state arguments that migrants are "the problem." Similarly, most reject the government's invocation of vague demographic concerns to justify policies and policing strategies that harm migrants, their families, and their communities. Instead, advocates and activists tend to see Israel's status as a host country through a different frame altogether—a frame that accounts for the interplay of "push" and "pull" factors, including the global demand for unskilled labor as well as the economic and political instabilities that often push people to leave their homes and communities in the first place. So, too, do advocates and activists recognize that successive Israeli governments have enabled private employment companies to amass billions of dollars in wealth through the recruitment of migrant labor.[7] In short, their greatest concern is not what the government calls "the problem of migrant workers," but instead the myriad problems faced by migrant workers themselves, ranging from practical everyday predicaments to grave violations of their human rights and bodily integrity.

Beyond the gerush itself, this shifting landscape of migrant advocacy constitutes the book's second core theme. Longtime volunteer involvement and in-depth interviews with more than forty Israeli advocates and activists helped me appreciate the wide range of variation in this group and what we might call the disparate *idioms of social justice mobilization*[8] to which they gravitate. For example, some framed their commitment to migrant advocacy in terms of humanitarianism, while others invoked human rights, Jewish values, or professional ethics (e.g., Hippocratic obligations, journalistic ethics, or ethical mandates as social workers). Although their motives were varied, most shared two commitments: a sense of indignation at their government's treatment of global migrants and a refusal to be complicit in what I characterize in this book as migrants' sociopolitical abjection—their clear and categorical exclusion from the political and moral community.

A central aim of this book is to explore what happened when the Israeli government took the aggressive step of criminalizing, then expelling large numbers of people who had arrived in search of work (in the short term) and a more stable and secure future for themselves and their families (in the longer term). We cannot understand this turn of events without engaging questions of history, politics, and ideology. Yet these contextual concerns ultimately are supplemental to the book's overall goal. In these pages, I aim to show how the gerush was *lived*—how it affected the rhythm, texture, and dynamics of everyday life for the migrants I came to know, and for their Israeli-born children. As we will see, the sociopolitical abjection of global migrants was not a single event, but an ongoing and evolving process. This is a descriptive, not a moral claim; as the evidence marshaled in these pages will show, various national leaders and branches of state power took discrete steps to shore up migrants' exclusion in order to facilitate their criminalization and forcible removal from Israeli sociopolitical space.

In advancing this claim, I draw on Tyler's "conceptual paradigm of social abjection."[9] Not only does Tyler call for greater attention to "abjection as a lived social *process*," but she shows how the very idea of abjection "hovers on the threshold of body and body politic." From her standpoint, abjection describes not only "the action of casting out or down, but [also] the condition of one cast down—that is, the condition of *being abject*. In this sense abjection allows us to think about forms of violence and social exclusion on multiple scales and from multiple perspectives." At the same time, Tyler takes care to distinguish her own project from the better-known work on abjection by French psychoanalyst Julia Kristeva, which has been critiqued for its inclinations toward Eurocentric nationalism and xenophobia—critiques I share. Describing herself as an "unfaithful reader of Kristeva," Tyler explains that she is "not concerned about remaining obedient to the orthodox psychoanalytic logic and conservative political agenda that inform . . . [Kristeva's] writing. Rather, my intention is to prise abjection out of the theoretical and political frames in which it is positioned in her work." In deliberately "twisting and redefining Kristeva's conceptual paradigm" and turning it "against itself," Tyler's approach resonates with my own long-standing interest in *abjectivity*, or the intimate entanglements of law and state power in the lives of people consigned to abject spaces and sociopolitical positions.[10]

If abjection is "a design principle of British citizenship,"[11] it is by no means a uniquely British feature. Tyler's empirical focus on Britain leads her to foreground a local set of "figurative scapegoats," whom she calls "national abjects." These include "the underclass," "the Gypsy," "the bogus asylum seeker," and "the illegal immigrant," among others. Israel has its own evolving list of "national abjects," as we will soon see, including Palestinians as well as the so-called "foreign workers" (*ovdím zarím*) at the center of this book. Israel's newest category of "national abjects," asylum seekers from Eritrea and Sudan, are officially and disparagingly labeled "infiltrators" (*mistanením*), a term first used in the early years of Israel's statehood to describe *fedayeen*,[12] Palestinians who crossed borders illicitly in an effort to wrest back control of land that had become part of Israel.

There are, of course, major differences between Israel and the United Kingdom. Yet their similarities raise common themes and comparative questions about the impact of aggressive anti-immigrant attitudes and policies on migrants' lives and on the "lived social process" of sociopolitical abjection. Much can be learned by approaching these matters with an ethnographic sensibility, and a comparative eye.

Two parallel narratives are entwined in this book's account of what Tyler calls "abjection as lived." First is the complex story of Otherness in Israel, where prevailing (i.e., Jewish Israeli) attitudes toward global migrants are always inflected by the systematic Othering of Palestinians, a theme I explore in Chapter 3. A second, contrapuntal narrative involves that strong current of indignation that has electrified a vocal minority of Israeli citizens who, invoking various idioms of social justice mobilization, have fashioned themselves as migrant advocates and activists. By paying ethnographic attention to the different idioms they invoke—human rights, humanitarian sentiment, professional ethics, and Jewish values, among others—we gain unique insight into the messy and tangled ways in which competing ideologies of justness and fairness inform political life, moral commitments, and civic participation.

I view these issues through the lens of critical medical anthropology, a lens that demands careful attention to economics, ideology, and power. As a critical project, this book is concerned with how certain people—global migrants and others—are cast as "national abjects," then strategically deployed as "ideological conductors" to do various kinds of "dirty work."[13] As a work of medical anthropology, it remains ever attuned to the ways in which illegalization and sociopolitical abjection become embodied in ways that impinge upon migrants' health, well-being, and ability to access needed services and supports.[14]

Yet the book's overarching questions emerge from another, rather different anthropological tradition, as explained below. How might the experience of sociopolitical abjection—in this case, the process of being rendered "illegal"—shape the rhythm, texture, and dynamics of everyday life? How might it reach people's "inward parts"—including both their embodied experience and their sense of self, personhood, and interconnection with others? How might it affect a person's capacity to follow through on the moral and ethical commitments that define who one is—those commitments that frame one's goals, and purpose, in life? How might it harm one's sense of dignity?

The Lens of Experience: Existential Anthropology and Critical Phenomenology

To engage these questions, I adopt an anthropological mode of inquiry that pays careful attention to matters of existential concern, including the basic cravings for groundedness, connectedness, and dignity that so many of us share. This vigorously heterogeneous tradition—sometimes described as the anthropology of experience, or as phenomenological, existential, or person-centered anthropology—explores how dynamics of history and biography, subjectivity and intersubjectivity, power and materiality, arise and intersect in the zones of encounter that ethnographers describe as fieldwork.[15] Ethnographers working in this tradition cultivate multiple channels of attentiveness, but try especially hard to tune themselves to the pitch of human voices, relationships, and predicaments. The conceptual language of this book—of lifeworlds, moral struggles, and existential pursuits—and the key concepts it introduces—the notions of inhabitable spaces of welcome and local moral economies, for instance—emerge from, and aim to contribute to, this lively tradition.

To take human experience seriously, anthropologist Michael Jackson argues, is "to give issues of *existential* power the same value as issues of political power."[16] What might this mean? Shelf upon shelf of social science research has explored questions of political power and social control, yet much of this work exhibits a troubling blind spot. We can frame the question thus: Why should we assume that questions of social domination are more important, or worthier of study, than people's efforts to pursue meaningful, dignified, flourishing lives regardless of the circumstances into which they are thrown?

In training our gaze on people's efforts to respond to this and other "existential imperatives,"[17] a related tradition proves equally vital: the anthropological tradition of critical phenomenology, which asks how particular modes of being in the world are configured, and how they are experienced. To explore migrants' lives, especially those whose formal status is irregular or precarious, is to see these dynamics in action. Migration scholars long ago distinguished between two facets of migrant "illegality": It is both a juridical (legal) status and a distinct sociopolitical condition. Yet this form of sociopolitical abjection cuts deeper still. As many migrants in Israel helped me understand, "illegality" bears not two, but three dimensions. It is undoubtedly a legal status and a sociopolitical condition—but it is also a way of being-in-the-world: a particular way of orienting oneself in time and space, to other people, and to one's moral commitments and life aims.

A critical phenomenological approach[18] invites us to pursue two very different sets of questions, as well as the links between them. First are sociopolitical questions about human value and belongingness. Who is deemed worthy of inclusion in the moral community—the collective "we"—and who is excluded? How is the deservingness—or undeservingness—of different groups reckoned? Once sociopolitical lines are drawn, how are the boundaries of the moral community patrolled? And what about the relationship between public discourse and governmental practice? Do exclusionary moves by politicians or policymakers align with broader currents of public sentiment, or do they diverge—and, in either case, why?

From the angle of experience, we face a very different set of questions. How do the dynamics of sociopolitical abjection reverberate in individual and group lifeworlds? What existential harms, or indignities, do they impose? How might the experience of abjection influence what anthropologist Robert Desjarlais calls the "intimacies" and "felt immediacies"[19] of everyday life? And, crucially, how do people facing sociopolitical abjection find ways to reclaim or remake their worlds—even, perhaps, to flourish—despite these incursions?

In a pioneering ethnography that laid the groundwork for the critical phenomenological approach advanced here, Desjarlais observed:

> Many politically attuned studies of social life neglect the finer questions of human agency and subjectivity, while many "experience-near" approaches are bereft of serious analyses of the political and economic forces that contribute to the apparent reality or nearness of experience. Anthropology is in dire need of theoretical frames that link the phenomenal and the political . . . especially [studies] that convincingly link modalities of sensation, perception, and subjectivity to pervasive political arrangements and forms of economic production and consumption. Such work can offer insights into how political, economic, biological, and cultural forces intersect in constituting a person's or a group's lifeworld, as well as address the perennial critique that phenomenological approaches tend to neglect broader social and political dynamics in accounting for subjective realities.

In other words, we need an ethnographic lens wide enough to capture these entwined dimensions of sociopolitical abjection: not only its historical roots and political dynamics but also its everyday consequences as well as the moral challenges it poses for individuals, families, and communities whose lives are gridded by constraint and tainted by degradation and humiliation—yet who struggle to make life bearable, even livable, nonetheless.

To Flourish

Illegalization and other forms of sociopolitical abjection tend to beget harsh indignities, sometimes even violence, yet we cannot assume they will crush the human spirit. As anthropologist Cheryl Mattingly points out, "even in the most blighted and unpromising circumstances,"[20] powerful imperatives push most human beings to pursue not merely a life that is tolerable but a meaningful and dignified life: a life of *flourishing*.

In recent decades, anthropologists have demonstrated a strong, at times overwhelming, tendency to explore suffering in its many forms. Certainly there is no shortage of suffering in the world. Some suffering is of human design, but often it is the unintended result of structural arrangements that worsen social, political, and economic inequities and precipitate what medical anthropologists describe as "structural violence."[21] Yet a myopic focus on suffering misrepresents the human condition. It occludes our view of what the political theorist Hannah Arendt calls "natality": that open quality of action that allows us, even under circumstances of violation, loss, or despair, to set new things in motion, perhaps to create something entirely new. Such myopia obscures the myriad, often experimental ways in which people hew to what Mattingly calls "ground projects": those orienting commitments "that people find so deep to who they are that they might not care to go on with their lives without them, or would not know themselves if they no longer had them."[22]

In foregrounding these concerns, I join those who argue that anthropology has been preoccupied with human suffering for too long. Some have proposed a different focus for the discipline altogether, variously conceptualized as an anthropology of morality and moral experience or, alternatively, as an anthropology of the good, happiness, or well-being.[23] Certainly it would be foolish to walk away from the task of illuminating the causes and consequences of human suffering altogether, especially in a historical moment of profound instability and political turmoil. At the same time, we do greater justice to the complexity of human life if we employ a lens that can capture not just suffering but also the gestures, imperatives, and projects that make it possible to anchor, or reanchor, individual and common lifeworlds when they have become untethered.

Threading through recent efforts to recalibrate the ethnographic project is Aristotle's classical notion of *eudaimonia*, often rendered in English as "happiness" or "the good life." Admittedly, these terms carry distracting connotations—for instance, of superficial contentment or hedonism—but Mattingly offers a different interpretation: "The good life for humans is not merely about surviving but concerns *flourishing*, Aristotle argued. This notion is sometimes translated as 'happiness,' but problematically so because it cannot be equated with a mere subjective feeling of pleasure or contentment. Rather, happiness or human flourishing is better understood as something like leading a 'life worth living' or a 'good life.'"[24] Not only have philosophers found the notion of flourishing "good to think" with, as Claude Lévi-Strauss might have said, but psychologists and health researchers have as well.[25] From an anthropological standpoint, each of these disciplinary approaches brings its own menu of strengths, limitations, and valuable provocations. Yet these accounts of flourishing often struggle to accommodate the basic ethnographic insight that different people, and different human groups, can hold dramatically different ideas about what a flourishing life entails.[26]

Even if conceptions of flourishing or the good life vary widely, Mattingly is undoubtedly right in suggesting that a basic sense of "moral striving seems to matter a great deal to people in all sorts of societies."[27] By exploring the tension between sociopolitical abjection and migrants' existential and moral strivings, this book aims to help broaden our gaze beyond suffering to consider how human beings—even in moments and places that appear overdetermined by abjection or abandonment, hopelessness or despair—so often feel compelled to become otherwise: to dwell in the world fully and intimately, without feeling diminished, or trapped.[28] To ground ourselves by cultivating relations of care. To forge ahead into a "nonprojected future."[29] Although such efforts may not succeed, many of us remain tenaciously committed to their pursuit. Of course, such pursuits are by no means limited to those who have been abandoned by the societies in which they live. As Arthur Kleinman observes in a more general vein, "Given the manifest shakiness of our lives, what is surprising is that we act, think, and write as if we were in control of ourselves and our world."[30]

If these strivings are fundamental to the notion of human flourishing, then anthropological inquiry can provide a valuable array of "ethnographically grounded depictions of struggles for the good life,"[31] as Mattingly puts it. Our efforts to depict these struggles must take full account of constraints on these human pursuits, among them "the fragility of life, the sociality of being, and the vulnerability of action in the face of circumstances very often out of human control and certainly out of control of any one person."[32] In light of these constraints, everyday life is what Mattingly describes as a kind of "moral laboratory": a space for everyday experimentation with the question of what it would mean to live a meaningful, flourishing life. A life, some might say, of dignity.

An Anthropology of Dignity?

> True, the recognition of dignity does not exhaust the conditions of human flourishing; yet, without its recognition, the ability for humans to flourish tends to be extremely limited.
>
> —John Kleinig and Nicholas G. Evans

The image of Elijah sleeping in a Tel Aviv park to avoid late-night arrest raises profound questions about the relationship between sociopolitical abjection and dignity. But what, exactly, is dignity? According to philosopher Martha Nussbaum, it is "an intuitive notion that is by no means utterly clear" and a "vague idea that needs to be given content by placing it in a network of related notions."[33] Despite this vagueness, the notion of dignity has captured an unusually high level of interest in recent years, especially in political theory, philosophy, and law. Scholars across disciplines grapple with thorny questions: How ought dignity be defined, and what is its genealogy? How is it linked to other domains of scholarship and practice? How is dignity related to other basic concepts like inequality, justice, or recognition? How is it entangled with ethical projects like bioethics and human rights? For most scholars pursuing these questions, dignity remains an abstraction, untethered to empirical realities or everyday predicaments and constraints. For the most part, anthropological voices have remained few and far between.[34]

Anthropologists' relative muteness is perplexing. Doesn't anthropology presume an incipient link among all ἄνθρωποι (Greek: *anthropoi*), whether wealthy or indigent, modal or transgressive, living or dead? And if so, might dignity name that link? We can pose the question differently: Why has dignity played so negligible a role in anthropological scholarship—or might something akin to dignity appear to anthropologists in other guises? What, in short, might an anthropology of dignity entail?

The core of my argument is straightforward. It is not the ethnographer's task to hammer out a precise definition of dignity, or to collect and compare conceptual correlates across languages and cultural settings. Neither should anthropologists simply jump feet first into conversations and debates raging in other fields, most of them untethered to empirical observation or ethnographic realities. Reified or abstract conceptions of dignity, whatever their genealogy, would seem to hold little anthropological value, especially those ripped from the intersubjective matrix of human being-in-the-world. Instead, I argue, the notion of dignity becomes ethnographically visible, and anthropologically meaningful, only *in motion*: as dignity harmed, denied, violated, or stripped away—or, conversely, as dignity pursued, safeguarded, recuperated, reclaimed. As indignity, for example—or indignation. If abjection violates dignity, then its flip side—what Jackson calls the existential imperative to "convert givenness into choice" by living "*decisively*, on one's own terms"[35]—would seem to bolster dignity's pursuit.

Understood in this way, the notion of *a sense of dignity* helps illuminate a powerful cluster of desires that most humans have in common. Most people want to be "recognized as a person in [one's] own right," rather than be "reduced to an object of other people's wills, a slave to their desires."[36] To feel meaningfully connected to others rather than forcibly excluded, alienated, or abjected from communal life. To feel grounded and secure in a world that can be frightening, disordered, and unstable. To feel that our life circumstances, whatever they may be, do not define us. To live in keeping—or at least in conversation—with the values, ideals, and moral commitments that define our sense of who we are in relation to ourselves, our loved ones, and the communities to which we feel connected. To approach dignity as lodestar, and the pursuit of dignity as an existential imperative, is to gather together these widely held hopes and desires.

Dignity is necessarily elusive, and not only because it eludes precise definition. Like our bodies, which often remain invisible to us until we feel discomfort or pain,[37] our sense of dignity may be eclipsed by more pressing concerns until it becomes present to us in a moment of violation. Yet unlike bodily injuries, which can have solitary dimensions, violations of dignity are inherently relational and intersubjective. We may experience such violations in our bodies, but they transpire in the spaces between us.

For ethnographers, the empirical challenge is to explore how this sense of dignity, however elusive, is lived—not just in the breach, as something that can be violated, but also as a powerful drive to make life bearable, or remake it as livable. One path forward is to consider how people facing sociopolitical abjection find, or create, what we can call *inhabitable spaces of welcome*: zones of familiarity and comfort, meaning and solidarity in the shadow of laws, policies, and practices that are explicitly designed to make certain people, and certain groups, feel unwelcome.[38] I offer the notion of inhabitable spaces of welcome as an intentionally open-ended, flexible way of illuminating how people living in deep precarity can break through the constraints of an oppressive everyday to pursue a bearable, if not livable, way of being-in-the-world. Such spaces can vary widely in shape and form. They may involve physical places like one's apartment (or a friend's or relative's), the office of an advocacy organization, or an open-air market redolent with familiar smells. They may emerge in social spaces like a soccer club, ethnic association, or church congregation. Alternatively, an inhabitable space of welcome might be a grounding relationship with a neighbor, an employer, a spouse—or even a young, dependent child. An ethnographic focus on inhabitable spaces of welcome can help illuminate how, and why, humans strive to feel existentially and morally grounded, supported, and safe even under fraught and rapidly changing sociopolitical circumstances.[39] Of course it is one thing to *feel* welcomed and quite another to have the capacity to follow what Jackson describes as "protocols of hospitality and reciprocity"[40]—to be welcoming toward others. Attending ethnographically to such transgressive spaces can shed light on the dynamics of creativity and constraint that give shape and contour to what some call moral experience—and to the pursuit of a dignified, flourishing life.

Local Moral Economies

> Thinking of moving to Israel? Here's all the information
> you need for a successful homecoming.
> —Web page of the Jewish Agency for Israel

> Israel is not an immigration country.
> —Senior official in the Israeli Ministry of Labor
> and Social Welfare

When this project began, I had lived in Israel for two years—and benefited, in ways large and small, from the country's national self-understanding, which bolsters the existential strivings of some people while undercutting others'.

I first moved to Jerusalem in 1996, in the heady days of the Oslo "peace process," for a university fellowship that brought ten freshly minted American college graduates of diverse backgrounds—Jewish and Muslim, Catholic, Protestant, and Mormon—to Jerusalem for an intensive meditation on "the role of leadership in democracies." As Raoul Wallenberg Fellows at the Hebrew University of Jerusalem, our year included academic and language study, individual internship opportunities, and, on occasion, private meetings with diplomats, political leaders, and activists in Jerusalem, Ramallah, Cairo, and Tel Aviv and at the United Nations in New York. Several of us rented apartments in West Jerusalem's tony Reḥavia neighborhood, including me (a Jew) and the two women who became my close friends and flatmates—a Catholic New Yorker and an Egyptian-American Muslim. During our year together, we often laughed that our everyday lives were the premise of a bad joke: A Catholic, a Muslim and a Jew—go grocery shopping. Throw a dinner party. Make soup.

All jokes aside, the dynamics of Israeli society and its underlying fissures often crossed our doorstep. On many occasions, and despite our comparable passports, it was palpably evident that Israel's national myths and narratives militated strongly not just in favor of my rights and opportunities—in particular, to obtain Israeli citizenship and carve out a future in what I had been raised to see as the "Jewish national homeland"—but also against their ability even to feel comfortable or welcome.

One of our first experiences as a group cast Israel's open-armed embrace of the Jews among us, and concomitant suspiciousness toward others, into sharp relief. When the ten of us arrived at New York's JFK Airport for our flight to the Middle East, some of us sailed through security with ease while others faced heightened scrutiny. The woman with the Arabic name who would soon become my friend and flatmate saw her luggage meticulously inspected—each shampoo bottle opened, each lipstick tube uncapped and fully unscrewed. She was prevented from boarding, only to be rebooked, then subjected once again to extraordinary scrutiny before boarding a later flight. Even then, her laptop lagged behind.

During my years in Jerusalem, it was the rare Israeli I met who failed to ask: "So, are you making *aliyá*?" For a Jew living outside Israel to relocate and choose Israeli citizenship—to "make aliyá," as some of my closest childhood friends had chosen to do—was not simply a matter of acquiring a new passport. Etymologically, and ideologically, it signified a desire, whether political or religious or both, to "ascend" (*la'alót*) to a higher place, perhaps a higher condition of Jewish being-in-the-world. My Catholic roommate found her interlocutors crestfallen whenever she faced this question and divulged, often to great surprise, that she wasn't Jewish. As for my Muslim roommate, Jewish Israelis didn't dare ask—and Palestinians we met tended to approach her with intense curiosity, if not overt suspicion.

The Israeli state's open-armed embrace of all Jews, including me, and its concomitant refusal to assimilate nearly anyone else, reflect core elements of what I call its *local moral economy*. The notion of local moral economies, developed more fully in Chapter 3, melds and recasts two influential ideas in contemporary anthropology, each calibrated to a different social scale: moral economies[41] (at the collective level) and local moral worlds[42] (at the level of subjective experience and intersubjective engagement). We can define a local moral economy as that shared matrix of historically and culturally particular memories and emotions, values and expectations that outline the parameters of everyday discourse and collective moral reflection. An ethnographic window onto a given local moral economy thus provides a kind of societal X-ray: a penetrating view of how history, affect, and morality become crystallized in particular principles, sentiments, and concerns that repeat and reappear in different domains.

Importantly, local moral economies are dynamic and messy, and they can give rise to radically different, even contradictory interpretations of a particular political phenomenon or social concern. For instance, competing perspectives on inclusion and exclusion, deservingness and undeservingness, may draw on shared sources of emotion, memory, and moral value, but invoke and admix them in substantially different ways. The core components of a given local moral economy can tug and pull people in different directions and spark lively, even acrimonious, public debate. Often such disputes hinge on competing interpretations of the same historical moment, experience, or cultural resource. However radical their differences, stakeholders on opposing sides of any given issue—a country's most indignant migrant rights activists and most outspoken xenophobes, for example—are nonetheless embedded in the same local moral economy. Deviating from mainstream interpretations can come with a steep price.

Occupation(s)

To begin deepening our understanding of Israel's fractious local moral economy, we need to think back to the 1990s, before global migrants had begun arriving en masse. In that decade, the region of Israel and Palestine was undergoing dramatic change. Memories of the first intifada were fresh on all sides, but a legendary Rabin-Clinton-Arafat handshake on the White House lawn in 1993 had marked a potential turning point: the signing of a major peace agreement, the Oslo Accords. Although many on both sides were deeply skeptical about its terms and prospects, this agreement, along with the 1994 treaty between Israel and Jordan, led some to dream of an interconnected, peaceful "new Middle East."[43] Even after the assassination of Israeli prime minister Yitzhak Rabin by a radical right-wing Jewish Israeli in 1995, talk of peace—or at least a "peace process" between the Israelis and the Palestinians—lingered in the air.

On the ground, however, tensions simmered. In the economic sphere, the Israeli military continued to block tens of thousands of workers in the Occupied Palestinian Territories (OPT) from returning to their jobs across the Green Line in Israel.[44] Most of these jobs were in agriculture, construction, and restaurant work, all sectors occupied predominantly by Palestinian workers since Israel's occupation of the West Bank and Gaza during the Six-Day War in 1967. As a result of these military closures, Palestinian unemployment skyrocketed, with devastating consequences for the Palestinian economy and for Palestinian individuals, families, and social institutions.[45]

On the other side of the Green Line, Palestinians' exclusion from the Israeli labor market left contractors and other large-scale employers, who had long depended on Palestinians as a cheap and exploitable noncitizen labor force, clamoring for an alternative. In effect, the employment conditions faced by Palestinian workers between 1967 and the first intifada in the late 1980s anticipated the circumstances of their transnational migrant replacements, albeit with one key difference. At the end of each working day, Palestinian workers returned to their homes in the OPT, thereby enabling Israel "to reap the benefits of employing foreign labor without experiencing the full social burden of incorporating them residentially and institutionally into society."[46]

After a period of heated political debate, the Israeli government reluctantly conceded to employers' demands. By permitting the recruitment of "foreign workers" (ovdím zarím) overseas—for example, agricultural workers from Thailand and construction workers from Romania, Turkey, and eventually China—one source of disposable, exploitable labor was exchanged for another. Most of these migrants paid dearly for the chance to work in Israel with legal authorization. Although Israeli law forbade the collection of recruitment fees by "manpower agencies" working overseas, such agencies nonetheless charged large sums, ranging from US$3,000 to upward of US$30,000, for the oppor-

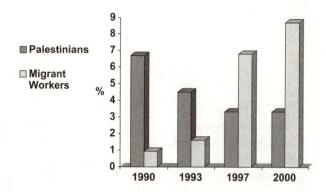

Figure 2. Noncitizen workers in the Israeli labor market, 1990–2000. Source: Data published by the Israeli Central Bureau of Statistics and analyzed in Kemp and Raijman 2001, 8.

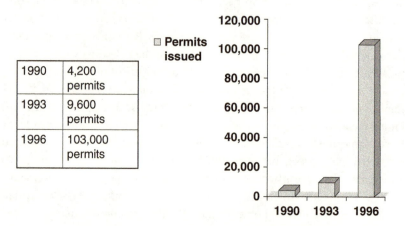

1990	4,200 permits
1993	9,600 permits
1996	103,000 permits

Figure 3. Permits issued to authorized migrant workers, 1990–96. Source: Bartram 1998.

tunity. This pattern of transnational recruitment—sometimes described as a form of human trafficking—quickly ballooned into an extraordinarily lucrative, and highly underregulated, industry generating billions of dollars in revenue, often for entrepreneurs with close ties to well-placed public and political figures.[47] Nearly a decade passed before the government moved to curb these arrangements, and then only in response to pressure from the U.S. Department of State.

As Figures 2 and 3 make clear, the rapid drop in Palestinians' participation in the Israeli labor market paralleled an equally precipitous increase in the participation of migrant workers from overseas. Between 1990 and 1996, the number of authorized workers recruited abroad skyrocketed from a negligible 4,200 in 1990 to 103,000 in 1996. Meanwhile, the number of Palestinians in the Israeli labor market plummeted from 108,000 in 1990 to well under 40,000 by 1996, then further dwindled as the decade wore on.[48]

Despite initial government opposition, the state-authorized recruitment of transnational laborers quickly garnered support as a politically desirable solution to the needs of Israel's large-scale employers. What motivated this rapid change of heart? Potential overseas workers were abundant in supply, and—due in no small measure to the vulnerability of their work conditions and the precariousness of their contracts—they were presumed to be as "flexible"—that is, exploitable—as the noncitizen workers they were hired to replace. Yet their greatest value, from the standpoint of most policymakers and employers, stemmed from their presumed disinterest in the simmering Palestinian-Israeli conflict. Despite the added effort and expense involved in their recruitment, migrant workers' presumed political neutrality in this highly volatile region was viewed as their greatest asset. Some government officials even looked favorably on the recruitment of overseas workers as a form of collective punishment targeting Palestinians.[49]

In the corridors of power, the importation of foreign labor was touted as a temporary solution to a temporary problem, not a permanent solution to the needs of the labor market. In this regard, Israel was repeating overseas recruitment strategies that other countries had tried decades earlier (Germany and Switzerland, for instance),[50] while expecting different results. Unsurprisingly, a high proportion of authorized workers stayed on after the expiration or loss of their legal work authorization. In many cases, they became "illegal workers generated by the system,"[51] having lost their status through no fault of their own but, instead, as a result of systematic state- and industry-level policies and practices. Most of the unauthorized Filipino migrants I came to know in Israel fit this description.

Most of my West African friends and interlocutors, in contrast, reached Israel via another route. In addition to government-authorized workers recruited in their home countries, growing numbers of unauthorized migrants also began arriving in the 1990s, but by a different pathway: the "tourist loophole" in the country's otherwise rigid migration regime. Given its profound archaeological, historical, and spiritual significance for multiple world religions, the "Holy Land" has attracted tourists and religious pilgrims for centuries, and tourism is a core building block of the contemporary Israeli economy. Through the 1990s, the country's liberal tourist visa policy (unintentionally) opened the door to tens of thousands of work-seeking migrants who were unable to access more desirable destinations in North America and Western Europe. By coming as tourists or Christian religious pilgrims, these migrants could enter Israel with short-term visas (of one to three months), then find work in the informal labor market, typically cleaning homes and offices or in other service sector jobs in the Tel Aviv area.

By 2002, migrants from a vast panoply of countries and world regions constituted about 11 percent of the labor force, ranking Israel among the industrialized countries most heavily dependent on migrant labor.[52] Those recruited on an authorized basis included construction workers from Romania, Bulgaria, and China; agricultural workers from Thailand; and elder-care providers from the Philippines. Workers arriving via the tourist loophole hailed from a much wider array of regions including South America (Colombia, Bolivia, Ecuador), Africa (Ghana, Nigeria, and South Africa), Eastern Europe (Romania, Moldova, Poland, Ukraine, Russia), Central Asia and the Caucasus (Mongolia, Georgia, Kyrgyzstan), and South and Southeast Asia (India, Sri Lanka, the Philippines). Migrants' premigration experiences varied widely, as did their travel routes and strategies, levels of travel debt, labor market experiences, and social opportunities once in Israel. So, too, did they bring divergent expectations of Israel, and of their own futures.

Citizens, "Real" Others, and "Other" Others

Like other countries around the globe, Israel has been eager to employ authorized migrant workers and their unauthorized counterparts on a temporary basis, but conspicuously unwilling to welcome them into the social body or body politic. This reluctance to incorporate global migrants stems from the biopolitical logic undergirding the country's local moral economy and ethnonationally defined migration regime. The legal foundation of this regime is the "explicit and formal demarcation between Jews and non-Jews"[53] encapsulated in the country's Law of Return, which restricts immigration to individuals who possess a bureaucratically legible tie to the Jewish people. Three such ties exist: proven Jewish descent (to the satisfaction of the state's rabbinic authorities); close familial relationship to someone Jewish (e.g., through marriage); or conversion to the Jewish religion via state-approved channels. Any individual who bears one of these ties can "make aliyá" and thus become an *oléh*, a term that literally means "one who ascends"—ascends, that is, to the Jewish homeland (feminine: *oláh*, plural: *olím*). This ideologically laden discursive frame undergirds a broad swath of law, policy, and bureaucratic practice. It affords no smooth path to inclusion for anyone else who hopes to live permanently in Israel, regardless of motive.

Let's be explicit: Given the preeminence of Jewishness as a criterion for citizenship eligibility, it is virtually impossible for most non-Jews to become Israeli citizens. In the nineteenth and twentieth centuries, Jewishness had been racialized to Jews' terrible detriment—especially, but not only, under the Nazis' Nuremberg Laws. In the 1950s, Jewishness was effectively reracialized by the Israeli state in its Law of Return, albeit in the inverse—and, of course, with different motives altogether. For Israel's political leaders, the intent of the Law of Return was salvific; it was designed so that anyone who might have been targeted by the genocidal Nazi regime could find safety in the new Jewish state. Those early intentions notwithstanding, the Law of Return has since become a bureaucratic mechanism for privileging certain expressions of Jewishness, linking it with full citizenship and membership, and ascribing lesser forms of social and political status—or denying recognition and status altogether—to all other citizens, residents, and potential immigrants.

Israel's local moral economy finds expression in two interlinked patterns of sociopolitical distinction: one that juxtaposes Jews and Arabs, and another that differentiates Jews from the broader category of non-Jews. As I discuss more fully in Chapter 3, anyone living under Israeli sovereignty effectively belongs to one of three groups: ratified citizens, "real" Others, and "other" Others.[54] Notably, ratified citizens include native-born Jewish Israelis as well the ideologically celebrated olím described above. Jewish Israeli society is itself deeply heterogeneous in both ethnic and ideological terms. Israeli Jews are a diverse group with ancestral origins around the globe, including not just Eastern and Northern Europe (Ashkenazi Jews) and the Mediterranean and Middle East regions (Mizrahi Jews)[55] but other places as well: Central Asia, the Indian subcontinent, the former Soviet Union, Ethiopia. Israeli society is also riddled with internal tensions, including tensions between earlier and more recent immigrant groups, tensions regarding levels and forms of religious practice, and theological and bureaucratic disputes about who counts as a Jew. For the Israeli government and most Jewish Israelis, however, it is self-evident that Jews are the country's authentic citizens and, moreover, that their interests, and their lives, matter most.

Palestinians, in contrast, are collectively imagined and discursively constructed as the country's primordial adversaries—its "real" Others. For decades, the state has euphemistically described Palestinian citizens as "Israeli Arabs"—a linguistic move that aims to discursively domesticate members of this community and erase their bonds with Palestinian relatives and conationals in the OPT and the broader Palestinian diaspora. Yet this discursive fiction is a flimsy one. By no means has it dissolved the familial, cultural, or national ties that endure across generations. Neither has it neutralized Jewish Israeli concerns about the potential risks that "Israeli Arabs" might pose to the cultivation of a "Jewish and democratic state." I return to the experiences of Palestinian citizens of Israel, as well as Palestinians in the OPT, in Chapter 3.

What about people who live in Israel but are neither Jewish nor Palestinian? This changing array of noncitizen residents forms a third group we can describe as Israel's "other" Others. While some are students, long-term visitors, or romantic partners of Israelis encountered abroad, the vast majority of those who arrived from the 1990s to the first decade of this century were global migrants who came, with or without legal authorization, in search of work. A much smaller number were victims of human trafficking, including women trafficked for purposes of employment in the sex industry.[56]

In the years following the gerush, Israel's other Others came to include another large group as well: the Eritreans and Sudanese mentioned earlier. These African asylum seekers arrived via the Sinai desert, often facing risks of kidnapping, torture, rape, and ransom en route. Although Eritreans and Sudanese who seek asylum in most industrialized countries are granted protection at high rates (nearly 90 percent of Eritreans and over 60 percent of Sudanese), Israel is a clear outlier, with a recognition rate well below one percent for both groups combined.[57] Eritrean and Sudanese asylum seekers in Israel have been widely described both by national leaders and in official government reports as "infiltrators" (mistanením)—or even, using a condemnatory neologism that melds parallel allegations of unlawful entry and unlawful work seeking, as "labor infiltrators" (mistanenéi avodá). For years, the state has refused to accept or review their asylum petitions. Instead, thousands of asylum seekers have been either incarcerated in administrative detention or, in several hundred cases, expelled under circumstances that violate the United Nations' prohibition on "refoulement"—forcible removal to a place where an individual is at risk of persecution. As non-Jews in a state that privileges Jewishness, offers no path to naturalization, and neglects its obligations under the very 1951 UN Refugee Convention it helped compose[58] and quickly ratified, the sociopolitical exclusion of these global migrants—whatever their origin, motive, or path of entry—has, with few exceptions, been categorical and complete.

Despite the relative rigidity of these discursive patterns of inclusion and Othering, successive Israeli governments initially refrained from developing any consistent or long-term policies regarding global migrants. One result in the mid- to late 1990s was a considerable degree of variation in policy and practice among different government ministries and between municipal and national levels of governance. Another result was the emergence of several large, institutionally well-developed migrant communities, including the communities of mostly unauthorized migrants—West Africans, Filipinos, South Americans, and others—that sprang up in HaTikvah and other southern neighborhoods of Tel Aviv, the country's major metropolis, and to a lesser extent in the cities of Jerusalem, Haifa, and Eilat. Other than a few small-scale waves of arrest and deportation in that era, most of these communities grew and flourished—until the gerush.

In the period preceding the mass deportation campaign, global migrants' presence was scarcely palpable in Israeli public life. When the media did take notice, migrants usually were portrayed as a kind of benign curiosity. By the early years of the new century, things had changed. At that point, an estimated 213,000 migrant workers were employed in Israel, including about 72,000 with and 141,000 without work permits.[59] As average Israelis began to encounter migrant workers—or at least representations of migrant workers—in diverse settings, mainstream Israel began struggling to make sense of their changing society. For most, these encounters were limited to occasional media reports and a well-regarded series by journalist Einat Fishbain in *Ha'Ir*, a weekly Tel Aviv newspaper, that piqued public curiosity and fueled political dialogue, citizen activism, and public conversation. In addition to Fishbain's pioneering reportage, which appeared under the overly optimistic tagline "The New Tel Avivians," global migrant characters also began to appear on-screen. As supporting characters, parodic caricatures, or even protagonists in the occasional feature film, these representations of global migrants in Israel offered viewers a new, if largely fictionalized, array of windows onto their own society. Meanwhile, the voices of Israelis whose neighbor-hoods had become home to large numbers of global migrants—including the mostly working-class, predominantly Mizraḥi residents of neighborhoods like HaTikvah—largely went unheard.

As the gerush gathered momentum, the authorities increasingly pushed back against these generally sympathetic media portrayals. The primary instrument of that pushback was a series of radio and newspaper announce-ments that cast unauthorized migrants as expendable, exploitable, and potentially dangerous.

Crackdown

When the government led by then prime minister Ariel Sharon launched the gerush in mid-2002, its ostensible goal was to curb the country's growing ad-diction to imported labor. Framed as a solution to skyrocketing unemploy-ment and related economic woes, the mass deportation campaign reflected politicians' and policymakers' reluctant acknowledgment that simply declar-ing transnational workers' presence temporary would not make it so. In place of previous governments' haphazard policies, Sharon's government reframed those it called "foreign workers" as both a burgeoning threat to the state and a major social and economic problem in need of a concerted, systematic so-lution. Through massive investment of state funds, a new government office was created: an Immigration Administration whose mandate was not to fa-cilitate immigration but rather to facilitate the mass arrest and deportation of those whose long-term presence was now deemed unwelcome. Nearly 500 new police officers were recruited,[60] and four new detention centers were es-tablished. An aggressive media campaign began disseminating anti-immigrant ads in newspapers and on the radio. The crackdown on "illegal" workers quickly evolved into a vast and multi-tentacled deportation apparatus. In ex-ecuting its plan, the government thus recast migrant workers—especially, but not only, those lacking legal authorization—as a threat to the economic and demographic security of the state and to the integrity and future of Israeli society.

Within a few short months, global migrants were reconstituted in offi-cial state discourse as job stealers, tax evaders, dangerous interlopers—and deportable, wanted criminals. The gerush, which mainstream newspapers and human rights activists alike characterized as a "witch hunt," led to the arrest and deportation of over 50,000 global migrants in a period of three years, while an estimated 90,000 others were intimidated into leaving "voluntarily."

Yet this campaign of mass expulsion failed to change the basic structural conditions that had led Israel to become a destination country for work-seeking migrants in the first place. Large-scale employers were determined to continue paying low wages for back-breaking work in vegetable fields and citrus orchards, constructing buildings, and performing the other forms of menial labor that had once sustained tens of thousands of Palestinian families. Despite the country's high unemployment rates, Israeli citizens—like their counterparts in other countries around the globe—proved unwilling to step into the jobs that Palestinians, then global migrants had been forced to vacate. Even after spending nearly US$100 million on the gerush, the large-scale recruitment of tens of thousands more *authorized* workers continued, and continues, apace. In addition to ongoing demand from large-scale employers, private recruitment companies continued to earn billions by illegally charging new recruits thousands of dollars for a visa and the "opportunity" to work in Israel. And like those who preceded them, many newly arriving workers eventually lose their documentation status and, in due time, join the ranks of the "illegal." And so the cycle continues.

Genesis of the Project

When my ethnographic fieldwork began, these changes and transformations were not on the radar of anyone I knew. In fact when I returned to Israel in June 2000 with two years of graduate school under my belt, I had a different set of research plans altogether: I intended to spend the summer studying Arabic and laying the groundwork for an ethnographic study of an unrecognized village, one of dozens of communities in the northern Galilee and southern Negev Desert whose inhabitants—Palestinian citizens of the state—are cut off from such basic infrastructure as bus routes, electric grids, and sewage systems.[61] I spent my mornings studying Arabic at a language institute near the coastal city of Netanya, taught somewhat surrealistically in Hebrew by a team of young teachers, all of them Palestinian citizens of Israel. Some afternoons, when I wasn't conjugating verbs or musing about the unchanging Levantine summer weather in rudimentary Arabic, I would catch a ride to Tel Aviv to meet a friend, or stretch out on a blanket by the sea with a book, or just wander around the city learning its streets and rhythms, all vastly different from the landlocked, hilltop city of Jerusalem where I had made my home before returning to the United States to begin my graduate studies.

It was on these aimless forays into Israel's largest urban metropolis that an entirely different social phenomenon caught my attention. Walking through Shuk HaCármel, the busy open-air market in the heart of Tel Aviv, I was surprised to see market-goers from Southeast Asia, Africa, and South America—in short, people whose presence no one I asked could readily explain. Between Arabic lessons, I started to poke around, ask more questions, and recall similar moments from my years in West Jerusalem. At the number 9 bus stop in Reḥavia, the historically elite, German Jewish Jerusalem neighborhood where my flatmates and I had shared an apartment in the mid-1990s, I had often seen older Ashkenazi men and women walking, shopping, or waiting for the bus with young Filipina women. I remembered greeting such pairs while awaiting the bus that took me from Reḥavia, down into the Valley of the Cross and past its eleventh-century medieval monastery, uphill toward the sprawling Israel Museum, then further on to the Knesset, where I was interning as part of my university fellowship. During a period of heavy construction near the Knesset complex, I remembered pondering a similar puzzle on my homeward route. As I waited for my evening bus, I regularly encountered construction workers speaking not Hebrew, or Arabic, or Russian—but Romanian. I realized in retrospect that these Filipina caregivers and Romanian construction workers were probably among the first global migrants to be legally recruited for jobs in Israel.

Half a decade later, while wandering between parallel rows of merchants hawking fruits and vegetables, hummus and olives, cheeses and freshly caught fish in Tel Aviv's Carmel Market, these images from Jerusalem returned to me. Were Jerusalem and Tel Aviv becoming "global cities" like New York, London, Paris, and Berlin? In the summer of 2000, questions like this puzzled the Israeli friends, scholars, and acquaintances I queried.

For the rest of the summer I made my best effort to learn Arabic, but I was already spending my spare time in libraries and archives, reading the earliest smattering of newspaper articles and scholarly publications about the new patterns of labor migration to Israel, and meeting with the handful of people I could find who might help me answer—or at least begin to formulate—research questions. A young Congolese Embassy staffer, who wrote what was likely the first graduate thesis on migrant labor in Israel,[62] handed me a golden

Figure 4. PHR–IL Open Clinic in South Tel Aviv (first location). Photo by the author.

thread during an afternoon interview in his country's diplomatic offices. "You may be interested in knowing about the clinic for migrant workers in South Tel Aviv," he told me. "Here's the address" (Figure 4).

The next day I found myself lost in a neighborhood I'd never before had occasion to visit, map in hand, searching for the Open Clinic run by a local human rights organization, Physicians for Human Rights–Israel.[63] Among the ground-floor shops and industrial work spaces, most of them topped by crumbling apartment buildings, I found my destination: a small storefront preceded by a narrow stoop. A long line of people—South Americans, Eastern Europeans, Africans, and others—stood, sat, or leaned on the metal railing, all awaiting their chance to see a doctor. I lingered a bit among the patients gathered outside, then struck up a conversation with Philip, a Nigerian man waiting in line. Many of the key themes I would later pursue were on the tip of Philip's tongue: straining physical labor, a tenuous conjugal tie, a health emergency, a subsequent financial crisis, the occasional sympathetic Israeli as foil to unsympathetic systems, marriage as a strategy for accessing mobility and membership despite rigid, bureaucratically fortified nation-state boundaries.

Eventually I worked up the nerve to cross the threshold and try to catch a word with a member of the clinic staff. Hesitant, and keenly aware that patients would likely assume, based on my appearance and comfortable use of Hebrew, that I was Israeli, I tried to squeeze through the crowd and into the cramped reception area. A row of patients sat on white plastic lawn chairs awaiting their turn to receive medical attention. I felt guilty distracting a staff member with my questions, which felt frivolous given the clinic's tight quarters and the apparent magnitude of need. Still, I desperately wanted a chance to come back—and stick around.

Somehow, I caught the clinic director's attention, introduced myself, and rather presumptuously declared my eagerness to volunteer regularly—either until I had learned enough to write a dissertation, I explained, or until they kicked me out. When my odd pledge met with her acceptance, I knew my work had begun. And by the time someone *did* consider kicking me out (late in my fieldwork, and for interpersonal rather than political or ideological reasons),[64] two years had passed, and the thread of my volunteership had become deeply woven into the fabric of the clinic, which had by then relocated and undergone a change in institutional leadership.

On that summer day in 2000, in a nondescript corner of Israel's increasingly globalizing urban metropolis, I set out to understand how global migrants had come to live in and around Tel Aviv; what their lives were like; and what they did when they got sick, or pregnant, or faced moments of difficulty or crisis. But when the gerush kicked into gear in mid-2002, the basic texture and rhythms of migrants' everyday lives were transformed, and the dramatic changes I trace in these pages became my central focus of inquiry.

Following my primary period of fieldwork (2000–2003), I returned to Tel Aviv nearly every summer and winter, typically for a month or more, which further deepened my understanding of Israel's encounter with global migration—and, crucially, of migrants' encounter with Israel. Although these regular visits became more challenging once I had a full-time academic post and a family of my own, I continued making briefer (two- to three-week) trips to Tel Aviv whenever possible, most recently in summer 2017. In total, I have conducted over thirty nonconsecutive months of ethnographic research, during which I have spent most of my time with advocates and activists at three migrant advocacy organizations, and with members of two of the city's migrant communities: Filipinos and West Africans.

Filipinos and West Africans in Tel Aviv

Despite the linguistic and cultural diversity within each group, the Filipino and West African communities that flourished in Tel Aviv in the mid-1990s cohered in meaningful ways, and they offered an ideal opportunity for comparison. In that period, Filipinos and West Africans became two of the city's largest and most institutionally well-organized migrant communities, with the large community of South American migrants from Colombia, Ecuador, and Bolivia constituting a third.[65]

Although most Filipinos in Tel Aviv shared Tagalog and English as common languages, they hailed from various regions and communities in the Philippines (e.g., Tarlac, Pangasinan, Visayas) but predominantly from areas close to metropolitan Manila.[66] The city's West African community was even more diverse, including Ghanaians (Asante, Fante, Ewe, and Ga) and Nigerians (Igbo, Yoruba, and Bini) as well as smaller numbers of South Africans, Ivorians, Sierra Leoneans, and others. Since I am fluent in Hebrew and English but not Spanish, it made most sense to work with Anglophone communities. For similar reasons, I chose not to conduct systematic research with migrants from the former Soviet Union, Eastern Europe, China, or Turkey, although I often encountered members of these groups at the Open Clinic and other migrant advocacy organizations where I volunteered.

Filipinos and West Africans living without legal authorization in Tel Aviv tended to inhabit a common labor niche: housecleaning and other forms of domestic work. In addition, both groups tended to worship—occasionally together, but more often separately—in Christian congregations. Most Filipinos attended either the Catholic church in Jaffa (just south of Tel Aviv) or, less commonly, evangelical Protestant churches. Among the city's West African residents were Catholics (including some Catholic charismatics), Protestants from a range of denominations, and members of African independent churches. Other than the Catholics, for whom dedicated masses were offered at the parish church, all of these Christian migrants worshipped in rented spaces previously used as homes or businesses.

Despite their similarities, these two communities differed in one important way. Nearly all West Africans arrived through the tourist loophole in

Israel's otherwise strict migration regime. Most Filipinos, on the other hand, like Filipino migrant workers in many other countries, were legally recruited in the Philippines to fill a specific labor niche—in the Israeli case, elder care. In other words, most undocumented Filipino residents had worked in Israel with legal authorization, sometimes for years, before losing their status. According to Israel's "binding arrangement" (*hesdér ha'kvilá*), which was declared illegal by the High Court in 2006, each authorized worker was "bound" to a single employer, whose name was printed on the work visa affixed to his or her passport.[67] When an elderly employer passed away, one's visa would be terminated if no new employer could immediately be found. As we will soon see, Filipino caregivers often overstayed expired visas and remained in the country on an unauthorized basis—sometimes while continuing to work for the same employer. In other cases, documented Filipino workers fell out of status following the termination of their relationship to their authorized employer, either of their employer's choosing or, less frequently, their own.

My initial research questions focused on experiences of pregnancy, reproductive health care, and fertility decision making, and I spent my first months in Tel Aviv volunteering at the Open Clinic and two other migrant advocacy organizations, where I met many women who were pregnant or had given birth in Israel. Through PHR-Israel's Open Clinic, Mesila (the municipal agency that called me to duty following the building collapse on Natan Street), and the Hotline for Migrant Workers[68] (a human rights NGO established to assist migrants in detention and their families), I was able to meet and interview more than forty women. With their permission, I accompanied a dozen women as they pursued reproductive health care, including abortions or, alternatively, prenatal checkups and other pregnancy-related services. Most sought care at public clinics and hospitals in the Tel Aviv area, although a few consulted private physicians, including all of the women who sought abortions and a substantial number who received prenatal care from a Palestinian physician in East Jerusalem. Although most of the women who carried their pregnancies to term delivered in Israeli hospitals, a few—including Marina, introduced in Chapter 2—delivered in Palestinian hospitals in the West Bank.

I also had the privilege of accompanying three women—Olivia, Ruby, and Gloria—into the labor and delivery room, each at a different public hospital in the Tel Aviv area. In many respects, these three African women—along with Marina and Lorena, Christina and Marlene, my guides to Filipino Tel Aviv—are the heart and soul of this long-term project, and this book, even in chapters where their names never appear. My dear friend Tanya, from Ukraine, introduced me to yet another community of unauthorized migrants in Tel Aviv: Russian speakers from the former Soviet Union, many of whom developed close ties with Russian-speaking olím with whom they had much in common except their sociopolitical status.

All of these women welcomed me generously into their homes, introduced me to their families and friends, and brought me along as they went about their everyday routines. Together we picked out groceries at HaTikvah's bustling open-air market and prepared meals—*fufu* (pounded yam) with curry at Olivia's and with spicy fish in palm oil at Gloria's; rice and vegetables at Lorena's; borscht with dill, sour cream, and heavy bread at Tanya's. We strolled, or rushed, through narrow streets and alleyways to drop children off or pick them up from day care, or to whisk them to the pediatrician in an emergency. We shared moments of laughter and lightness during shopping trips to the city's massive, labyrinthine Central Bus Station (Figure 5), bad TV movies, and bawdy conversations about our own partners—or about our mutual friends and acquaintances and their partners. My friends even gave me new names: Ngozi, Igbo (Nigerian) for "blessing." Abena, the Akan (Ghanaian) feminine for "Tuesday-born." And in Tanya's classic Russian diminutive, Sarochka.

Saturday, Israel's weekly day off, was typically set aside for social visits and parties—birthday parties, christening parties, rescheduled holiday par-

Figure 5. Tel Aviv Central Bus Station. Photo by the author.

ties when Christmas or New Year's landed inconveniently on a weekday. But earlier in the day, on Saturday mornings, many migrants and I were often in church. Most often I joined Olivia and Ruby at the evangelical church they attended near the Central Bus Station, but over the years I visited many other churches as well: Protestant, Catholic, and independent; Anglophone and bilingual (French/English, Tagalog/English, English/Twi); musically sober, with simple singing or sonorous organ music, and spirited, with live bands, booming sound systems, and extended communal dancing midworship. Some churches were dominated by people from a particular country or cultural community, but most were at least nominally multicultural. With the exception of the Catholic church in Jaffa, whose focal constituency was the city's Palestinian Catholics, rarely if ever did Israeli citizens attend any of these churches. In addition to weekly services and holiday celebrations, I often joined in other church-related events as well. Many were life-cycle events like weddings, baptisms, "dedications" or christenings (Figure 6), or, less frequently, memorial services. Others were communal celebrations, including a multicultural "Silver Jubilee" celebration honoring the ordination anniversary of the Catholic parish priest and attended by hundreds of people from all of the church's constituent national communities: Palestinians, Filipinos, Nigerians, Ghanaians, Romanians, and others. On another, very different occasion, I was invited to the anniversary celebration of a small Filipino evangelical congregation where the featured guest was a prominent Israeli Messianic Jew.

We also shared all manner of stress and sorrow. Pregnancy complications and conjugal crises. Suicide bombings in South Tel Aviv. Tragedies like the building collapse on Natan Street. The lead-up to the 2003 U.S. invasion of Iraq, when Israelis were encouraged to check the status of their government-issued gas masks while migrants wondered how they might protect themselves and their children in the event of a chemical weapons attack. For some of the women I came to know, I became a go-to source of support—sometimes as a friend, sometimes for my strong Hebrew and links to migrant advocacy and activist groups, and often for a mix of reasons. Over the years, many of these women's lives became tightly woven into my own. And as the gerush intensified against this tumultuous backdrop, its scale and stakes became ever more frequent a topic of conversation among us, its damaging effects ever more palpable.

Although the initial focus of my fieldwork involved Nigerian, Ghanaian, and Filipino mothers and their families, my research focus and community of interest shifted and expanded as the gerush gathered steam. By then, a nar-

Figure 6. Christening party in the Filipino community. Photo by the author.

row focus on pregnancy and reproduction no longer made sense. The condition of migrant illegality was itself rapidly changing, and those changes and risks were what weighed heaviest on people's minds. To make sense of these developments, I followed a core group of about fifteen women and men over an extended period, many but not all of whom I had known before the gerush began.

Volunteering at the three very different organizations—Mesila, the Open Clinic, and the Hotline for Migrant Workers—proved to be a valuable way to meet potential research participants, and it helped me become a familiar face to many members of the city's migrant communities. I hoped this familiarity might help neutralize concerns about my intentions. Concern about police informants ran high, and I wanted to make it clear that I didn't work for the police, and that I genuinely cared about the health and well-being of the people I hoped to meet. Often, I found myself volunteering at these organizations for fifteen hours per week or more. In an average week, I spent three evenings receiving patients at the clinic's reception desk and put in one afternoon shift as a volunteer at Mesila. With the Hotline I paid occasional visits to detention centers to help monitor detainee conditions; translated reports from Hebrew to English; and provided occasional accompaniment and language interpretation for migrants on challenging clinical, bureaucratic, and other errands. While conducting fieldwork, I approached these volunteer commitments as forms of "pragmatic solidarity"[69] with the people whose life projects and existential commitments I sought to understand and, eventually, represent in writing.[70]

Over time, and perhaps inevitably, these organizations became crucial research sites as well. During my primary period of fieldwork, I learned about the structure, objectives, and everyday workings of each group through ongoing volunteer involvement and regular participation in staff meetings, board meetings, and annual planning retreats and through dozens of semistructured interviews and hundreds of informal conversations with organizational staff and volunteers at these and their partner organizations. Early in my fieldwork I began archiving media coverage, government documents, and NGO reports, which made it possible to chronicle changing Israeli attitudes, both official and unofficial, toward the country's changing population of "other" Others over a twenty-year period, beginning with Fishbain's pioneering coverage in the late 1990s.

Groping for an Ethnographic Voice

This book is an ethnography: an empirically grounded study anchored in over eighteen years of research, analysis, and critical reflection—including a good deal of reflection on my own motives, values, and presumptions. Twenty-first-century anthropology makes no claim to pure objectivity; as anthropologists, we recognize that any account we produce will bear the imprint of our own particular lifeworlds, including who we are, what we care about, and how we embark upon and conduct our research. At the same time, our accounts are shaped in profound ways by the relationships we cultivate with those we most hope to understand.

Beyond the usual challenges that ethnographic research entails, others emerged in sharing my findings with students and colleagues, in written form and in talks for audiences in the United States and Canada, Europe and Israel. Opportunities to share my work have sparked both criticism and critique—for the two are not the same—that have sharpened my thinking, tempered my voice, and thickened my skin. For better or for worse, an American Jewish researcher who subjects any facet of Israel to scholarly scrutiny will, perhaps inevitably, pay a price—no matter how rigorous one's research, how deep one's community ties, how strong one's familiarity with Israel, how fluent one's Hebrew, or how intimate one's bonds with Israeli friends and family. In their book *Anthropology's Politics: Disciplining the Middle East,* Lara Deeb and Jessica Winegar examine the personal and professional risks involved in questioning what they call "compulsory Zionism" in the American academy.[71] Although Deeb and Winegar concern themselves with only a particular set of critical voices and positions, their broader point is an important one: Producing scholarship that runs counter to popular framings of Israelis and Palestinians, Israel and Palestine, is risky business.

Given the volatility of the region and the issues at stake, it only seems reasonable that readers might want to know more about their narrator and guide through these pages. I have spent nearly five years of my life in the region that comprises Israel and Palestine, including the two years I lived in West Jerusalem before beginning this research. English is my native tongue, but I speak, read, write, and occasionally publish in Hebrew. Although born and raised in the United States to American-born parents and (with one exception) American-born grandparents, my life is peopled with close Israeli family members and intimate friends. My own lifeworld is enriched not only by bilingualism but also by the joys and possibilities of code switching in and out of languages and cultural realities. I have studied Arabic, albeit not enough; spent time in East Jerusalem and the West Bank; and traveled in Egypt, Jordan, and Turkey. These glimpses into other parts of the Middle East, along with years of classroom experience teaching American undergraduates about the complexity of the region, have also helped calibrate my ethnographic lens. So, too, did my year in Jerusalem as part of the motley crew of Wallenberg Fellows described earlier.

For most of my life, I have been acutely aware that my American citizenship and nationality are products of history, politics, and chance. Although we barely spoke of it when I was a child, much of my father's extended family perished in the Shoah (Holocaust). On my mother's side, my grandfather,

Kalman Pesach (later "Carl") Kleiner, was born around 1912 in a region that flipped between Polish and Russian control in the first decade of his life. Kalman was the youngest living child of his parents' seven; his mother, Leah, died giving birth to twins, neither of whom survived. According to family lore, his eldest brother served, and died, as a Polish soldier in World War I. Two of his siblings emigrated to Palestine in the late 1920s. When my grandfather was small, his own father, Shmuel, left for America seeking a better life, emigrating first to New York and then to Cleveland, Ohio. After his father's departure and his mother's untimely death, my grandfather and an older brother remained in Poland—for a time with relatives, and for a while in an orphanage. In 1929, on the eve of the Great Depression, these two teenagers crossed the Atlantic Ocean on a ship whose name, in my grandfather's heavy accent, always sounded to us like "Hilda France" (*Île de France*) seeking what proved to be an uneasy reunification with their long-lost father in Cleveland, the city in which my other grandparents, my mother, and eventually my siblings and I were born, and where both sides of my family now have deep roots.

More than any other factor, it was my grandfather's strand in this family history, which I came to know only through hazy filters of generation, memory, and time, that led me to make two interlinked commitments as a young adult. First, after several visits as a teenager, I decided to deepen my understanding of Israel, a country I had been raised—by my suburban American Jewish community as much as, if not more than, my immediate family—to support without question. Through these visits I grew close to my grandfather's extended family in northern and central Israel. Among them was his nephew, then in his 60s, who shared a childhood memory of my grandfather: the Yiddish-speaking American soldier who paid their family a visit, in full military uniform, at the end of World War II (on his way back to the United States, after concluding his service in the Asian theater). The more I learned of these familial ties, and of the precariousness of Jewish realities in the early twentieth century, the more I began fantasizing about the country as an alternative home. Enthralled by these counterfactual possibilities, I made a second commitment as well: to become fluent in Hebrew.

After completing my university studies, this passionate investment ripened into the cascade of burning questions that accompanied me to Jerusalem in 1996. What was the "real" Israel behind the postcards, summer trip photos, bus window views, and packaged tours catering to Jewish visitors from abroad? For much of my twenties, I pursued these questions with zeal, digging beneath surfaces and peering around corners to observe—and respond. Entirely new worlds revealed themselves to me, first in Jerusalem and later in Tel Aviv, the city that is, in many respects, Jerusalem's cultural foil. Over time, Tel Aviv became home. I came to feel more comfortable in that city than anywhere I had lived or visited in my country of birth. As my language skills approached fluency and my accent faded, I became at least as acclimated to Israeli life—or, at least, to a certain slice of Israeli life—as childhood friends who took on Israeli citizenship by "making aliyá." To all who asked those ubiquitous questions about aliyá, I offer this book, with its menu of cautious optimism and serial disappointment, indignity and indignation—occasionally my own, but more often others'—as a partial response.

By invoking my grandfather's story, I do not mean to reinforce hollow myths of the United States as an idyll for migrants seeking a better life, although I certainly grew up hearing such tales. When Kalman Kleiner arrived at Ellis Island in 1929, the new quota system, just instituted in 1924, took no pains to conceal the country's enthusiasm for certain immigrants and antipathy toward others. Yet this particular teenage boy carried good fortune in otherwise empty pockets. Although clearly not of "premium" immigrant stock, my grandfather was just white enough, as an Eastern European Jew, to count as assimilable.[72] Had he been African, or Asian, his fate would likely have been very different. And had he hailed from nearby Mexico, he may well have been among the 15,000 Mexicans deported in the very year of his arrival.[73] Even more important than his ability to squeak by as "legally white" was another advantage that set him apart from thousands of other European Jews who would gladly have followed in his footsteps. However distant and unfamiliar their father had become after a decade-long separation, the laws of the day allowed my grandfather and his brother to immigrate to the United States with his sponsorship as their first-degree relative.

The differences between my grandfather's migration story—a story of family fragmentation, hardship, risk taking, and no small measure of good luck—and the stories of Elijah and Comfort, Philip and Olivia, and other migrants I came to know in Tel Aviv are either vast or negligible depending on one's angle of vision. Today, the majority of Israeli citizens are either Jewish immigrants (olím) or their descendants. The people I describe as global migrants—people arriving with no bureaucratically legible Jewish ties—have been barred from most avenues of inclusion in Israeli society. Unlike my grandfather, they found little chance of securing a stable job with benefits and a pension, becoming union leaders, marrying citizens, or having citizen children who might leap across social and class boundaries. No matter how hard they work or how much they contribute to their community or society, most have been racialized and abjected—or deported, through coercion or violence, to their countries of origin. What is it like to be seen as a kind of detritus of globalization, a reservoir of people whose disposable, replaceable "working hands" have value only at the price of their humanity, their dignity, or their capacity to flourish? How might those who hide in Israel's shadows find ways to break through these constraints and pursue existential imperatives they hold dear, including the imperatives to "convert givenness into choice" and live decisively, on their own terms?

By engaging these intimate questions through an existential and phenomenological lens, this book is a call to sharpen our sensitivity to the powerful impact of historical, political, and economic context on the fabric of human lives. As we turn to the lifeworlds of global migrants and the Israelis concerned about them, we cannot lose sight of some potent influences of enormous scale and magnitude: how the rise of nationalisms in nineteenth-century Europe fomented pogroms—and sparked dreams of safety and security for the continent's Jews. How a new state took shape in the shadows of Nazi destruction, at once breathing life into an old-new nationalist dream and, in the same instant, causing a *naqba*, a catastrophe or "founding trauma"[74] whose reverberations are no weaker and no less devastating today. How a bloody century of war, imperial collapse, and neoliberal development managed to exacerbate, if not catalyze, the global inequalities that grew, rather than shrank, as we rounded the corner into a new millennium. A single ethnography could not possibly do justice to all of these threads. Yet we should not be surprised when they appear, at times in surprising ways, in the intimate lifeworlds at the heart of this book.

Arc of the Book

These intimate lifeworlds frame the following two chapters, which survey the experiential damage wrought by the gerush, Israel's first major campaign to deport global migrants en masse. For migrants who came to Israel seeking a better life for themselves and their families, this campaign of illegalization and criminalization lay plain the incontrovertible fact of their abjection from the Israeli social body and body politic. Chapter 1 ("Illegalized") probes the pivotal moment in which the Israeli state set this campaign in motion. How did the meaning of "illegal" status change once the gerush began? How did the texture and contours of migrants' everyday lives—their experiences of time and space, of embodiment, of home—change as a result? Fuller answers to these questions emerge in Chapter 2 ("Indignities and Indignation"), which catalogues many of the humiliations that result from migrants' illegalization, criminalization, and abjection in Israel and harm their sense of dignity. From this inventory of indignities, we turn to the community of Israeli advocates and activists, a varied bunch who nonetheless have two things in common: a profound sense of indignation about their government's abjection of migrants and their families, and a refusal to be complicit. These divergent voices— migrants' and their supporters'—help us consider how, and why, we might approach dignity anthropologically.

Chapter 3 shifts gears to consider how ideology, collective memory, and national anxieties can restrict migrants' opportunities for membership and in- corporation into contemporary states and nations. This chapter ("'Real' Others and 'Other' Others") maps Israel's local moral economy, paying particular attention to how Israel's ongoing occupation of Palestinian people and lands has influenced contemporary attitudes toward global migrants. I show how entrenched representations of Palestinians as the country's real Others were mobilized to advance new templates of Otherness involving a new array of other Others: global migrants who, despite their varied countries of origin, migration pathways, and migration motives, have been lumped sloppily to- gether in Israeli public and political discourse as "foreign workers" or, more recently, "labor infiltrators." With the initiation of the gerush these forms of Otherness began to converge in striking ways.

And yet, as Chapter 4 reminds us ("After the Bombing"), crucial differ- ences persist in how Israel's real Others and other Others are imagined and portrayed, with profound effects. In January 2003, at the height of the gerush, a double suicide bombing rocked South Tel Aviv, killing twenty-three people. The perpetrators were Palestinian, and nearly a third of the victims were global migrants. In this chapter, I juxtapose three very different memorial events held in the wake of that bombing. Taken together, these moments of mourn- ing foreground a pair of tough questions: Whose lives are grievable, and whose are not? And for those beaten down both by sociopolitical abjection and by deadly political violence, how might life once again become bearable after devastating tragedy? I point to one avenue of possibility: migrants' efforts to find, or create, inhabitable spaces of welcome, or small zones of familiarity, comfort, meaning, and safety in the shadow of laws, policies, and practices explicitly designed to make them feel unwelcome.

Still, a bearable life is very different from a *livable* life. Chapter 5 ("Perhaps, to Flourish") explores how people facing sociopolitical abjection endeavor not simply to survive but to flourish and thrive. I turn to two African couples in Tel Aviv—Solomon and Rachel, and Olivia and Peter—who exemplify what Michael Jackson identifies as "a recurring theme of existential thought—this stubborn human refusal to take life lying down."[75] Their stubborn refusal to relinquish control over the shape and direction of their lives is neither private nor internal. Rather, as their stories reveal, the pursuit of a meaningful, dignified, flourishing life is fundamentally about the people we care about most, and about our sense of obligation to one another as well as ourselves.

I conclude by reflecting on the broader implications of these local configurations and experiences of Otherness as patterns of global migration grow ever more complex and their stakes ever higher for more and more migrants—and, arguably, for all of us—in today's tumultuous world. What might we learn by approaching global migrants not as ciphers, symbols, or mere drops in what one *New York Times* writer indecorously described as a "sloshing tide of humanity,"[76] but as people struggling "to realize lives they consider morally worthy, even in the most blighted and uncompromising circumstances"?[77] What happens if we honor the particularity of individual lives and "give issues of existential power the same value as issues of political power"?

*   *   *

Some may find these pages difficult to read. They certainly were not easy to write. Regardless of readers' particular inclinations, I hope all will find in them a sincere effort to reflect on a complex set of human predicaments without falling into the trap of feeling obligated to choose between what Hannah Arendt described as "reckless optimism and reckless despair."[78] In lieu of these bleak options, let us instead choose ethnography, which brings us closer to the vital if turbulent lifeworlds forged in between.

CHAPTER 1

Illegalized

When I see an Israeli smiling on the street I think, eh?
Why are you smiling? Why am I not one of them? I am
not smiling. I have to be looking around like this and this
and that. . . . Anxiety all day at every time, I tell you.
> —Peter, South African man living in Tel Aviv

People are always peering out from around corners.
When the bus comes, one person runs out from his
corner, then someone else from another corner, and
someone else from another. It's like a war here. It's like
the Partisans.
> —Tanya, Ukrainian woman living in Tel Aviv

In the book of Jeremiah, the God of the Hebrew Bible announces a new regime of law, a regime designed not only to regulate the external, social world
of human affairs but also to penetrate the innermost dimensions of human
activity and experience. "I will put my law in their inward parts," the divine
voice declares.[1] For its rabbinic interpreters, this law is the secret to sustaining a community in exile, a community forbidden access to its most hallowed
ground—the sacred Temple in Jerusalem, destroyed by the Babylonians in
586 BCE. Christian interpreters, on the other hand, read this passage differently: as a covenant of renewal, a covenant that births a new religion.

Biblical scripture, divine promises, and Christian worship figure centrally
in the lives of many global migrants in Israel, but my interest in this passage
is not theological. Rather, I hear in these ancient words an imperfect analogy to the here-and-now—the kind of analogy flagged in modern Hebrew

with a handy rabbinic loan word, *l'hávdil*, that links two things as meaning-fully related and, at the same time, "vastly different, a thousand times differ-ent."[2] Might this scriptural mapping of law onto life have something useful to tell us about the palpable effects of modern-day state power? Might the pen-etrating intentions of these words, ostensibly of divine origin, resonate, *l'hávdil*, with those of a contemporary state that claims biblical roots? In this chapter, I argue the answer is, yes. I invoke this passage of scripture meta-phorically, to launch an exploration of how abjecting certain groups of un-wanted residents can allow a state to creep under the skin and reconfigure embodied experiences of time and space, life and self.

When global migrants began coming to Israel in the 1990s, there was no public hue and cry. In most of the country and to most of its inhabitants, their arrival was barely palpable. When their presence was discernible—for instance at elder-care facilities, urban construction sites, or commercial farms—Israelis tended to view these new migrants as relatively benign if patently unassimi-lable Others. A new era began in 2002 with the initiation of the gerush, which recast migrants as criminal interlopers and clarified their status as a new kind of "national abject,"[3] a term I borrow from Imogen Tyler's analysis of social abjection in Britain, introduced earlier. If Britain's "national abjects" include stigmatized and excluded figures of "the underclass," "the Gypsy," "the bogus asylum seeker," and "the illegal immigrant," Israel's most clearly defined "national abjects"—Palestinians, or simply "Arabs" (in Hebrew: *aravím*)—were now joined by a heterogeneous new group: "foreign workers" (*ovdím zarím*). A decade later, they would be joined by a third group: asylum seekers, cast accusingly as "infiltrators" (*mistanením*).

Once the gerush had begun, global migrants in Israel were bound together by the newly created, media-savvy Immigration Administration as "foreign workers" who ostensibly threatened the state and the nation's collective future. Migrants without authorization were the campaign's primary target, but nearly all faced risk of arrest, detention, even deportation regardless of whether they had arrived with a work permit or a tourist visa, as an asylum seeker or a victim of sex trafficking. Any advantages or freedoms that illegality may pre-viously have entailed—for instance, the ability to switch employers, compete for wages, or move freely through public space—quickly vanished. With a new cloud of deportability[4] looming overhead, the effects of illegalization hardened, intensified, and crept inward. And as the Immigration Adminis-tration grew more robust and efficient, national leaders amped up their de-portation agenda, and the consequences of migrants' exclusion intensified in turn. Patterns of illegalization, racialization, and criminalization became ever more tightly entwined, and people caught in the campaign's crosshairs faced a growing array of indignities and humiliations. By no means were these effects accidental; as politicians sometimes declared openly to the press, the government's intent was precisely to intimidate migrants into leaving on what leaders described, however euphemistically, as a "voluntary" basis.

Later I explore how core elements of Israel's local moral economy were interpreted to cast Israel's global migrants as a new kind of national abject. But first, this chapter asks a more intimate question: How did the gerush affect the texture and rhythms of everyday life for unauthorized migrants in Israel—their experience of "abjection as lived"? Using the lens of critical phenomenology, I view migrants' illegality in three dimensions—as a form of juridical status, a sociopolitical condition, and a way of being-in-the-world—and explore three questions. First, how did the everyday dynamics of illegalization change as a result of the gerush? Second, what can these changes tell us about the nature of unauthorized migrants' sociopolitical abjection in Israel? Finally, and most importantly, how did this radical reconfiguration of illegality become palpable in migrants' everyday lives? How did it affect their embodied experiences of time and space, sociality and self?

"Illegality" as Mode of Being-in-the-World

As the scope and impact of human migration have intensified in recent decades, migration researchers have struggled to keep up. One especially important body of work has analyzed the "peculiarly powerful but amorphous legal concept" of migrant "illegality"[5] that concerns me here. No longer can we rely on a "facile binary of documented versus undocumented."[6] We now understand that so-called illegal statuses are social creations that change over time, vary across space, and differ in gradation and impact for different groups, or even for different members of the same group in a single place over time. We know that illegalization is not simply about one's official status; it is also a sociopolitical condition—indeed, a sociopolitical process—with powerful, if variable, effects. Yet a stubborn blind spot persists. We still have much to learn about the deep impress of illegalization on migrants' individual and group lifeworlds. By delving deeply into one localized tangle of configurations and experiences, we begin to understand how illegality can become a mode of being-in-the-world for those who carry this stigmatizing status.

How can we capture the intimacies of sociopolitical abjection, or the impact of illegalization on the warp and woof of human lives? Instead of an approach that pulls *away* from the messy complexities of lived experience, I propose we draw nearer to the texture and contours of everyday life. We need to reflect, together with our migrant interlocutors, on the felt immediacies of this ideologically charged, and contextually variable, form of exclusion. These are the hallmarks of the book's critical phenomenological approach—an approach that challenges us to explore how history, ideology, and political economy shape local modes of sociopolitical abjection, while employing a gaze wide enough to apprehend its accompanying sensory, embodied, and existential effects.

Deportation Regime

To grasp these intimacies and immediacies, we need to understand not only the mechanics of the gerush but also the context in which this new deportation regime was set in motion. Equally significant were government efforts to retool public discourse surrounding global migrants in ways that cast migrants as inescapably "foreign" and confirmed their abjection from the body of the nation.

"Like a Military Campaign"

To implement this campaign of mass arrest and deportation, the architects of the gerush hired close to five hundred dedicated officers, established monthly arrest quotas, and created four new detention centers, including one located in what previously had been the Renaissance Hotel in the northern city of Nazareth. Constructed in anticipation of a "Year 2000" influx of Christian pilgrims that never materialized,[7] the facility stood empty for several years. With the initiation of the deportation campaign, the Immigration Administration, short on detention cells, proposed a deal. The usual amenities were shut down, metal bars were installed on the windows, and, with the wave of an ironic bureaucratic pen, a section of the Renaissance Hotel in Nazareth became the "Renaissance Detention Facility." The original hotel sign, only slightly amended, was left hanging in the entryway. In rough translation, it reads: "Welcome to the heart of the Renaissance, hotel with a commitment to excellence and attention to service" (Figure 7).

Figure 7. Hebrew sign (in rough translation) reads: "Welcome to the heart of the Renaissance, hotel with a commitment to excellence and attention to service." This photo appeared in *Haaretz* with the caption: "A mocking sign hanging in the facility's lobby." Photo: Yaron Kaminsky.

How might a migrant from, say, Nigeria or the Philippines end up in the "Renaissance Detention Facility"? To answer this question, we need to understand the form and design of the deportation apparatus. Designed explicitly to operate "like a military campaign,"[8] it involved not only the police and the prison system but also the Ministry of the Interior (which appointed judges to preside over fast-track deportation hearings), the Ministry of Labor and Social Welfare (which installed representatives in detention centers), the border authorities, and commercial airlines (which reserved places for deportees on regular flights).

A brief overview of the Immigration Administration's strategy is helpful. In addition to carrying out surveillance in migrant neighborhoods, it employed techniques of racial profiling to cast a wide net, at times catching people whose presence in the country was fully legitimate. Among those who faced unwarranted arrest were a handful of recognized asylum seekers, a number of "legitimate" tourists, and, in an incident to which I will return, a Filipina neurosurgery resident at a major Tel Aviv hospital. The Immigration Administration created an "information hotline" that doubled as a channel for reporting unauthorized residents to the authorities, often leading to their arrest and deportation. At times, migrants used the hotline to settle scores with fellow community members or even, in the case of conjugal disagreements, with members of their own families. Other police tactics were designed to undermine community solidarity and dismantle leadership structures—for instance, by cultivating informers and targeting community leaders for arrest. And we cannot overlook the Immigration Administration's "Voluntary Departure" campaign, which encouraged unauthorized migrants to "self-deport."

Arrest, detention, and deportation quickly became a messy business. According to many migrant advocates, the initial cohort of Immigration Police officers appeared to follow orders mechanically, at times unthinkingly. Numerous individual complaints and comprehensive reports by human rights organizations described officers as unwilling to listen and quick to criminalize and arrest, often with humiliation and physical violence. Even as evidence of police brutality accumulated, Immigration Police supervisors generally failed to investigate, let alone mete out punishment; instead, such practices continued with impunity. In one especially well-documented instance, a whistleblower inside the agency dared bring these abuses to light—and suffered grave consequences, both professional and personal, as a result.[9]

Xenophobia—from Above

When the gerush began, the government could not reliably assume the Israeli public would blame unauthorized workers for the country's high unemployment or look favorably on their criminalization and deportation. A handful of high-profile politicians had become well known for their anti-immigrant remarks, but press coverage of migrant workers before the gerush tended to be as sympathetic as it was sporadic. To bolster its case to the public, the newly created Immigration Administration, with support from elected leaders and prominent demographers,[10] embarked on a wide-ranging campaign that tapped core currents in Israel's local moral economy—for instance by portraying migrants as a demographic and security threat. Like their counterparts elsewhere, these new "national abjects" were strategically deployed as "ideological conductors mobilized to do the dirty work of neoliberal governmentality,"[11] even as many of them were doing the dirty work, both literal and figurative, of facilitating the continued occupation of Palestinian people and lands.

One core tactic involved a series of inflammatory announcements circulated widely via national print and broadcast media. At the peak of the gerush, radio announcements were broadcast frequently enough—just before the hourly news, several times each day—that an attentive ethnographer could easily record them off the air. All narrated in an authoritative, low-pitched male voice over a background of haunting music, these "public service announcements" cast the euphemistically labeled "foreign worker problem" as a grave social issue requiring a nationwide—indeed, a personal—response. The following, typical announcement played fast and loose with statistics in framing unauthorized migrants' presence as an economic concern: "One in 14 workers in the state of Israel is an illegal worker. In other words, there are 160,000 illegal foreign workers. No taxes are paid on their earnings, but their residence here is very costly to the state. This doesn't make economic sense. It's an impossible situation for the Israeli economy. We created it; it's our obligation to fix it. So with all due respect to whoever comes to work for you, this doesn't work." Among other specious assertions, this announcement claimed that microeconomic arguments supporting migrants' continued employment were trumped by macroeconomic arguments favoring their expulsion. Others went further: "Right now, a national campaign is being conducted to end the phenomenon that is causing the state tremendous economic and social damage. Every day, hundreds of businesses and private homes are being investigated. Violators are subject to fines as high as 80,000 shekels [about US$18,000], criminal convictions, and/or two years' imprisonment. Employing a worker without a permit is illegal, and it doesn't work." For Israeli listeners, the implications of such ads were clear: non-Jewish migrant workers are not Israeli, they cannot become Israeli, and they simply should not be here.

Other messages were less subtle, including a print advertisement showing a photograph of migrant workers in jail beneath the tagline, "Soon they'll be going home." Local human rights organizations quickly brought their opposition to this particular ad to the country's High Court. The court deemed early campaign messages such as this one "hateful and inciting"—and forbade their dissemination.[12] Yet even after the High Court's admonishment led the Immigration Administration to tone down its language, the Administration continued to foment anti-immigrant attitudes across a range of media platforms. By actively promoting xenophobic sentiment in a familiar idiom, this newly created government body advanced the government's agenda of criminalization, detention, abjection—and mass expulsion.

Many Israelis were inclined to accept this narrative, but others, including Ma'ayan, one of the founders of the Hotline for Migrant Workers, didn't buy it. Ma'ayan had a firsthand view of how announcements like these could influence employers' treatment of their migrant employees. She hadn't given the country's migrant workers much thought until reading Einat Fishbain's newspaper articles. She then attended a demonstration in support of migrants' rights—simply because it was on a holiday, "and it was near my house." After the demonstration, she felt compelled to join the newly created, still volunteer-run hotline. She began fielding calls a few hours a week, later ramped up her volunteer involvement, and eventually took on a leadership position within the organization. In one of our long interviews, Ma'ayan told me how her earliest interactions with migrant employees and disgruntled employers alike left her "exploding from the inside." She was incensed, for instance, by "the contemptibleness of how . . . [you have this] poor person, on one hand, who worked, and [on the other an] employer [who's] refusing to pay him, and he hangs up the phone on him, or says to me on the phone, 'What, I owe him? *He* owes *me* money! Do you know how much damage he did to me by getting arrested?'" For Ma'ayan, conversations like these shook her faith in the machinery of justice: "I wanted to take a hammer and break this wall. It upset me, the matter of injustice. . . . There's no law, there's no order, and there's no justice. Where are all the things we thought existed . . . a just legal system, and that the state treats people fairly, that it gives them a fair chance to succeed? These people have no chance; they've been deceived from the moment they arrived, they had no chance to begin with. . . . That's the madness here."

Marked Doors

Several months into the deportation campaign, I began hearing stories—rumors, I initially assumed—that undercover police were trekking around South Tel Aviv in the daylight hours, marking doorframes in preparation for late-night arrests. When I began looking closely, I saw the small marks I had heard about, sometimes in black permanent marker, sometimes in red. Soon afterward, the Tel Aviv weekly newspaper *Ha'Ir* called attention to this police technique in an article titled "Marked Doors,"[13] accompanied by images of marked doorframes, with addresses (Figure 8). The subheadline read, in part, "The Immigration Administration puts Xs on the doors of foreign workers they intend to arrest. The workers understand the sign and generally flee to another apartment." Of course, not everyone with a marked door could pick up and move right away. Recall Elijah's alternative: sleeping in a public park to avoid being home should the police come banging on the door in the dark of night.

The marking of doors may be an efficient tactic for deporting migrants—and, moreover, for sowing fear and affirming their abjection. But it can also be viewed otherwise—as an unsettling, if unintended, inversion of a hallmark moment in the Hebrew Bible: the Israelites' Exodus from Egypt, retold each spring by Jews worldwide, including a majority of Israeli Jews, on the annual

Figure 8. "Marked Doors." Source: Rona Kuperboim, *Ha'Ir*.

Passover holiday. According to the Haggadah, or Passover narration, the Egyptian people were struck with ten horrific plagues culminating in the smiting of all Egyptian firstborn, which finally compelled the fearful and angry Pharaoh to expel the Israelites—themselves foreigners in the land of Egypt—before changing his mind and chasing his newly released slaves into the sea. In the biblical text, however, it is the Israelites who mark their own doorframes—with the fresh blood of sacrificial lambs, at divine instruction—in a coded message to the Angel of Death to "pass over" their homes and spare their firstborn. The inversions here are striking. In modern-day Tel Aviv, it is not foreigners but natives who placed the secret signs. And these markings are not self-inscribed tokens of protective blessing, but a secret code used by those in power to identify, humiliate, and expel foreigners residing peacefully in the land.

Here, a key irony of the Jewish national project bears mention. Despite most Israeli leaders' fervent commitment to preserving the "Jewishness" of the state, government officials responsible for dealing with "illegal" migrants rarely, if ever, conceive of their professional duties in direct relation to Jewish history, either modern or mythic. Neither has the Israeli government portrayed global migrants as anything other than a temporary solution, albeit a problematic one, to local labor demand. Even so, this biblical heritage figures in Israel's local moral economy and trickles into contemporary public discourse, however obliquely. We need look no further than the term "foreign workers" (*ovdím zarím*). Used as a vernacular catch-all term for nearly anyone who has arrived in Israel outside the bounds of the Law of Return, the phrase *ovdím zarím* carries another distant echo: of the biblically forbidden ancient practice of *avodá zará*—idol worship.

"When Israel Was Israel . . ."

Before the gerush, my migrant friends and acquaintances often told me, things were different. One afternoon nine months into the deportation campaign, my Nigerian friend Ruby stopped over at my apartment, a newly renovated, high-ceilinged flat in the still gritty, but quickly gentrifying South Tel Aviv neighborhood of Florentin, to catch up on the latest news and gossip. As we sat with sodas and snacks on futon sofas I had inherited from a friend, Ruby brought me up to date on the past week's events. The previous day, the Immigration Police had chased her Nigerian husband, Franklin, after he dropped off their son Jesse at the babysitter's—but, after a heart-pounding dash and some fancy footwork, he managed to elude them. A few days earlier, a couple we both knew had returned to Nigeria after deciding they'd had enough. Recently, the police had begun marking doors with permanent marker—and people were scrubbing the marks off with bleach. One man she knew found his door marked, and friends warned him not to sleep there. That night, there was a raid on the apartment. Things were never like this just a few years earlier, Ruby lamented— back "when Israel was Israel."

My Nigerian friend's wistful observations highlight the dramatic changes that took place with the initiation of the gerush. Africans who had arrived in Israel in the 1980s and 1990s, when global migrants had been fewer in number, remembered an even easier time. "In 1983–84 they were pampering us," I once heard a veteran Ghanaian resident lament. "As you walked down the street, people would come up and say, 'Do you want work? Do you need work?'"

Things changed in the late 1990s as Tel Aviv's migrant communities expanded rapidly, both numerically and institutionally. More and more migrants were arriving via the tourist loophole, settling in without legal status, and supporting themselves with hourly jobs—cleaning homes and offices. Meanwhile, more and more workers who had arrived *with* authorization, many of them Filipinos who had arrived as caregivers, were slipping out of legal status and competing for the same jobs. By 2000, the municipality of Tel Aviv-Jaffa estimated that 60,000–80,000 global migrants lived within the city limits. In a back-of-the-envelope tally the clinic director and I produced one slow afternoon at the Open Clinic, we realized the city's population of global migrants, as reflected in the clinic's patient files, hailed from more than sixty different countries.

Despite the constant low-grade risk of arrest, unauthorized migrants tended to move in, around, and through public space with relative freedom in the years before the gerush. Most were busy with the exigencies of everyday life as a migrant and transnational breadwinner: working and shopping, socializing and going to church, saving and sending money homeward. They were not walking on eggshells, or scoping out their surroundings for any sign of danger. A friend once described the pre-gerush era nostalgically as "the time of unlimited freedom."

Back then, seasoned migrants explained to me, petty theft was a much greater worry than arrest and deportation. Different theories circulated regarding the perpetrators of these minor crimes: other migrants—or Israelis? Thieving roommates—or landlords? I heard many tales of break-ins, mostly when no one was home. Monica, from India, lived in a ground-floor apartment in HaTikvah with her husband and their Israeli-born child. All of the gold jewelry she had received for her wedding was stolen during a burglary. Claire, Ruby and Olivia's hotheaded friend, received little sympathy when her apartment, located not far from Monica's, was broken into for the third time. By then (her friends chided her in the mellifluous creole I loved to hear), she should have wised up and started carrying her valuables on her person. In Jaffa, Gloria and her husband William, both from Ghana, lost money, electronics, and other valuables during a break-in. They suspected a friend of their roommate, who was in detention at the time of the robbery awaiting deportation.

There was little migrants could do to protect televisions or video cameras while at work or in church, but cash is a different story. "People carry money on their persons for fear of break-ins," Peter explained to me in a lengthy discussion of the topic with his wife, Olivia, and several of her relatives. "People used to hide money in their apartments. Then some Africans got with the thieves and revealed the hiding places: under mattresses, in the TV." Punning on the name of Israel's long-lived Bank HaPoalím—the "Workers' Bank"—Peter described those who carry cash as "mobile HaPoalím." Yet unlike Israeli workers, who can open up a bank account wherever they wish, most migrant workers had only their bodies as repositories for their savings.[14] Two of Peter's relatives, who were among the first African migrants to arrive in Israel in the late 1980s, saved over US$20,000—all of which they wore in money belts beneath their clothes every day. Someone else recalled a cousin of Olivia's who had shown up at a wedding "looking really fat. Under his clothes he had shorts with multiple pockets stuffed with wads of dollars." Of course, wearing one's earnings was no fail-safe solution. Although I never heard reports of violent muggings in this time period, I did hear of lost money belts and snatched bags. One Nigerian woman I interviewed told me about her brother's especially devastating loss: US$27,000 gone—just like that.

Once the gerush was in full swing, money was still on everyone's mind, but migrants had other reasons to be anxious and vigilant. Now, they were quickly coming to realize, the precarious lifeworlds they had cobbled together on Israel's margins could come crashing down in one fell swoop.

Illegalization: Intimacies and Immediacies

Once the deportation campaign kicked into gear, a deeply embodied sense of anxiety permeated unauthorized migrants' everyday lives. Hunted down on the streets, at work, and even in their homes late at night, migrants found that not only their presence but even their very persons were now criminalized. The Immigration Administration had developed an arsenal of techniques that both portrayed and treated them as wanted criminals, and the palpable threat of arrest and deportation began reverberating in every corner of their already complicated lives.

This patterned embodiment of anxiety and indeterminacy exacerbated the structural vulnerability that all unauthorized migrants in Israel endured. Yet it bore down with particular force in the lifeworlds of those least likely to "pass" as Israeli Jews (of European, Middle Eastern, or Ethiopian descent)—or, alternatively, as authorized migrant workers.[15] Migrants from Africa and Asia were among the most convenient targets of the gerush since their Otherness, at least from the Immigration Administration's presumptive standpoint, was written on their very bodies. These groups, including the Nigerians, Ghanaians, and Filipinos I knew best, faced heightened risk of arrest, humiliation, and even physical brutality at the hands of the Immigration Police. Racialized migrants were torn between the experience of body as subject and body as object: between their own lively experiences of embodied selfhood, on one hand, and the reductive labels imposed on them by the authorities, and by many individual Israelis, on the other. All this held true well before the deportations began, but the state's Othering gaze bore down with much greater intensity once the Immigration Administration had begun ramping up its efforts. As a result, migrants in Israel increasingly faced the fate described by psychiatrist and philosopher Frantz Fanon as the experience of being "sealed into . . . crushing objecthood."[16] On an experiential level, these brute facts of Otherness and exclusion were inescapable; on a physiological level, the resulting stress harmed their health and well-being and, for migrant parents, the health and well-being of their children.[17]

In response to these incursions, many developed new ways of inhabiting and moving about in their bodies: distinct "somatic modes of attention," as anthropologist Thomas Csordas puts it, or "culturally elaborated ways of attending *to* and *with* one's body in surroundings that include the embodied presence of others."[18] Below I consider two somatic modes of attention: bodily vigilance and troubled sleep.

Bodily Vigilance

The other day, I was waiting behind a bus stop with a friend. There were two Israelis sitting there. The bus had just passed, and an African woman from my building had gotten on—the one with the cute daughter. We used to say, "Hello" even though she doesn't know Hebrew and I don't know English, but still we'd always say, "*shalóm, shalóm.*" So I'm talking to my friend, who's also illegal, and over her shoulder I can see cops in gray uniforms. I'm waving my hand as I talk, but as soon as I see them I stop what I'm saying and keep waving my hand. I can't stop waving my hand. So I say to my friend, "My hand is moving by itself." Otherwise I stayed completely frozen until the cops left.

                                —Tanya, Ukrainian woman living in Tel Aviv

During the occasional, small-scale waves of arrest and deportation in the 1990s, men were the primary targets. Now, both men and women were targeted, although the risks were not identical. No formal policy was issued, but many women with children assumed that motherhood would grant them immunity. For a time, the authorities held to this "tacit understanding."[19] The massive influx of state funds behind the gerush yielded about 1,000 new beds for detainees, but only two facilities were set up to accommodate female detainees, and none was equipped to detain parents with their children.[20] Men, on the other hand, faced a different landscape of risk.

For migrants I knew, men and women alike, brushes with the police were increasingly a topic of everyday conversation. Some of these encounters involved wild-goose chases through the narrow streets and alleyways of South Tel Aviv. Franklin, who lived a few blocks from the site of the building collapse on Natan Street, had more than a few such stories to share. He had trained as a teacher in Nigeria, but now both he and his wife, Ruby, worked as housecleaners to support themselves and their family, eventually including both Israeli-born Jesse and Junior, their older son, who remained in Nigeria in his maternal grandmother's care. One afternoon, at their flat in HaTikvah, Franklin explained how he was "always hiding, looking around you everywhere you go, to the right, left, front, behind. You get home at the end of the day and thank God you've made it through another day—and then you stay there unless you really need to go out." Franklin's somatic mode of attention was forged from multiple elements: others' stories of arrest and near arrest, his own brushes with the police, and the sedimentation of physical sensations associated with, and evoked by, his daily departures from the private spaces of home and work into the more perilous, exposed spaces of public streets, markets, and buses.

I heard similar stories from South African-born Peter, who spoke often and at length about the anxiety he felt every day, an anxiety that would kick in even before he left for work each morning. He was always on guard, he said, always looking around, always keeping eyes and ears open for the distinctive light blue shirts of uniformed police, or for officers in civilian clothing. While walking down the street, especially in areas known to be "hot," Peter said, he would stay alert, ever ready to duck down an alleyway or side street. While waiting for the bus, his only option for travel to and from work, he would stand some distance from the bus stop, then race on at the last minute, heart pounding, in case the police were lurking. He would quickly scan the bus as he stepped on, then search for a seat—preferably as close to the door as possible. "I plan out escape routes," he told me. He was perpetually ready to jump off the bus if a police officer stepped on to ask passengers for identifying documents. Despite his embodied attentiveness, Peter ultimately was arrested on three separate occasions, the third of which resulted in his deportation. But I am getting ahead of myself.

Less than two weeks after his first arrest and temporary release, Peter was nearly arrested again, this time on his way to work in Modi'in, a city about halfway between Tel Aviv and Jerusalem. Later that otherwise typical afternoon, Peter, Olivia, and I hung out in the small room they rented in a shared apartment just meters from HaTikvah's main thoroughfare, chatting and drinking soda while Ethan, their pudgy infant son, explored their tight quarters. With characteristic precision and zeal, Peter explained what had happened just a few hours earlier: "This morning I went to take the 6:15 bus to work in Modi'in. The bus leaves the Central Bus Station at 6:15, and usually gets to the [local] stop at 6:18. This morning I had a strange feeling, so instead of waiting at the stop, I hid near the stop in the thicket. Before the bus came, a police van came and was there, waiting. They were there a few minutes. I was nervous but I was relieved that I was hiding, squatting in the thicket. Then they left, the bus came, and I went to work." As Peter knew well, risk was written on his body, encoded in his skin. Unlike most migrants from South America or Eastern Europe—my Ukrainian friend Tanya, for instance—the chance that Immigration Police officers might assume Peter was Israeli and leave him alone were virtually nil. Although the papers in his pocket would theoretically demonstrate he had been released on bail and was thus temporarily immune to a repeat arrest, he could not abide the possibility of another ordeal. Constantly exposed to a barrage of foreboding signs and sensory cues, including the Immigration Police's occasional entry into his perceptual fields (white vans, blue uniforms, confrontations on the street), Peter's sense of being-in-the-world was fundamentally shaped by anxiety about the possibility of his arrest and deportation to South Africa as a penniless, failed traveler.

The prospect of failing as a global migrant weighed heavily on him and many others. Peter once showed me an old photograph of himself in front of a large house in his village. Its owner, he said, had earned his fortune in New York. Nearby was another house built by someone who had traveled to Holland—and who was later discovered to have earned his fortune dealing drugs.

"People don't care how you made your money," Peter told me. "It just matters that you've earned it. People don't care if you kill for it. This is what people want to see." If you are deported back home to Africa, he and Olivia often told me, "you are nothing." You are ridiculed in public, in the market— "even the major, central market," according to Olivia. Even by people you don't know. For Peter, the worst shame and ridicule would bubble up in pubs, where men gather to drink palm wine and gossip. "People will get tipsy and say, 'This man was deported from Israel,'" he said. "You won't be able to show your face in public. You will lose your dignity."

Although adamant that he was no criminal, Peter could not shake the weight of this stigmatizing label. "We know we are illegals," he told me time and again, "but we are not criminals. Yet this is how they treat us!" The palpable effects of criminalization followed his every move through public space, and the difference between his own somatic modes of attention and those of average Israelis could not have been starker: "When I see an Israeli smiling on the street I think, eh? Why are you smiling? Why am I not one of them? I am not smiling."

As the Immigration Police grew in size and skill, the stakes of migrants' visibility and exposure were ratcheted up in ways that reinforced these patterns of embodied vigilance. Peter, Franklin, and others struggled to negotiate the tension between body as object and body as subject: between their own embodied experience in social contexts and the deeply racialized symbolic code that Israeli citizens and police officers used to "read" their appearance. In Chapter 3 we will return to this ideologically charged aesthetics of Otherness, which is tightly bound up in the biopolitics that undergird Israel's local moral economy.

Troubled Sleep

Fears of arrest, deportation, and the potential collapse of one's lifeworld began to plague migrants not only in the daytime but also at night. Some, like Elijah, felt safer spending nights away from home altogether—even if it meant sleeping outside, in a public park. Others were plagued by nightmares that left them sleepless and weary in the daytime hours.

Priscilla, a Ghanaian mother of a newborn baby boy, recounted one such nightmare when we met for an interview in the apartment that she, her husband, Mark, and their son shared with several other migrants in the Tel Aviv suburb of Ramat Gan. In Priscilla's dream, Mark was arrested, and her pleas for mercy were rebuffed as the arresting officers prepared to take him away. In the dream "I saw police catch my husband, and they put the handcuffs on [him]. I say, 'It's my husband, I have a small baby!' They say [to him], 'We don't care about your baby . . . you are going. You are going to your home.' I say, 'No! No no no!'" Priscilla must have cried aloud in her sleep, because her husband woke up, alarmed. "Listen," she told him, "I had a bad dream that the police caught you." Mark tried to calm her down. "No," she remembers him reassuring her. "God [is] protecting us. . . . No police catch me." The couple then got up and knelt together by the side of their bed to pray. For Priscilla, as for many other migrants I came to know, prayer was a precious salve. "I pray," she told me. "I pray in the night, at one o'clock. I pray a lot. Because you know, we are here, and we don't have anyone to help us. Only God. . . . And God is a good Father. When you talk to him, he hears you and answers you." For many migrants and migrant communities, prayer and faith were invaluable resources for making life bearable—for creating inhabitable spaces of welcome, however small and ephemeral—in the long shadow of the gerush.

A year later, once the campaign was well under way, dreams like Priscilla's had become more common—as had the realities they darkly anticipated. In a phone conversation with Olivia, then eight months pregnant with her second son, she described the deep worry that had begun infecting her sleep.

"If you are sleeping you are worrying," she told me. "Maybe they'll come to break down your door today. It's a thing of everyday. I wake up in the morning with my heart beating. Yesterday by 5 A.M. they took Linda's husband and beat him."

"But how are *you*?" I wondered, listening even as I tried to assimilate this news.

"We are fine," she replied. "Only we are afraid, that is the only thing. We are hiding, but we are still here. Maybe the situation will change today, maybe tomorrow. For now we can do nothing." She wrapped up our call with just the right Hebrew idiom: "*Ma la'asót*?" What can we do?

Bodies in Space

The intensification of the gerush also reshaped embodied experiences of time and space. Before this portentous policy shift, migrants realized that most of the Israelis they daily encountered—employers, landlords, bus drivers, shopkeepers—saw them as foreign, Other. Most understood that these patterns of perception were tightly bound up in a local biopolitics of inclusion and exclusion involving a firm distinction between "us" and "them," "brothers" and "others."[21] Few seemed aware of the extent to which these binaries can shift depending on speaker and circumstance: Jews and Arabs, Israelis and Palestinians, Ashkenazi and Mizraḥi Jews, veteran Israelis and immigrants, religious and secular, rich and poor. For most migrants I met, the history and complexity of these distinctions were hazy at best. From a pragmatic standpoint, the details mattered little. All that mattered were the incontrovertible fact of their Otherness, the increasingly palpable nature of their exclusion, and their urgent desire to avoid being "caught." Through those efforts, many found their everyday experiences of time and space transformed.

The exigencies of routine travel, especially to and from work, created inescapable daily challenges. A lucky few could arrange to be picked up and dropped off by their employers, which immunized them against the risks of public transportation during the particularly perilous morning and evening rush hours. Others, like Franklin, gambled with their household finances by traveling to work by taxi despite the exorbitant cost. Round-trip taxi fare to work cost Franklin 80 shekels—a full 40 percent of the 200 shekels (about US$44) he could reliably earn in a night's work. But by his reckoning, the reduction in earnings was negligible in comparison to the reduction in risk for himself and his family.

Yet Franklin's taxi rides were a luxury few migrants could afford. Most could do little more than limit their movements through public space, reduce their reliance on public transportation, or pray. "What can we do?" Olivia lamented. "We are praying every day. Peter is going to work, only now he does not stay too long because of the situation, or he will go and come early. We need money—what can we do?"

Given the paucity of available alternatives, most migrants I knew simply resigned themselves to using public transportation. Yet a handful elected for self-propulsion—by bicycle. One cycling devotee was Naana, a longtime Ghanaian resident of Tel Aviv and prominent community leader. Riding the bus made him intensely anxious, Naana once told me as we discussed the gerush in the living room of his shared South Tel Aviv apartment. You were constantly exposed: while walking from home to the bus stop, waiting for the bus, riding through multiple neighborhoods for long stretches of time, exiting the bus and walking to one's place of employment, then repeating the process several times over before heading homeward at the end of the day.

At the same time, Jewish Israelis feared public buses too—or avoided them, or forbade their children from riding them—but for a very different reason: fear that a Palestinian suicide bomber might choose their bus as a target. Of course, migrants were equally vulnerable to this risk. In a survey I conducted in early 2003 with a sample of patients at the Open Clinic, respondents were asked what they feared more: suicide bombings or arrest. Of 150 respondents, 57 percent ($n=86$) expressed equal fear of both bombings and arrest, 29 percent ($n=43$) were more afraid of bombings, 8 percent ($n=12$) were more afraid of arrest, and 6 percent ($n=9$) said they feared neither.[22]

I never posed this particular question directly to Naana, but he made it clear that bicycling was always preferable, even for relatively long distances. Not only could he travel the quiet side streets instead of busy central thoroughfares, but he also had the flexibility to duck behind a building or into an alleyway should he detect, or even suspect, a nearby police presence.

Given my own newfound enthusiasm for urban cycling, Naana's comments struck a chord. I could understand the sense of freedom and control he felt while careening around corners, and his puzzle-like pleasure in bypassing traffic snarls by maximizing a keen working knowledge of side streets and shortcuts. Of course, he faced a risk I never did. Locking up and unlocking one's bike takes time, and for Naana, those few moments were always nerve-wracking. When the wind whistled past, cycling felt safer than passively riding on, or waiting for, a public bus. But in those brief moments of stationary exposure, the risk of deportation became intensely palpable.

Military Metaphors

By the time the campaign reached its peak in 2005, some migrants, including my Ukrainian friend Tanya, occasionally described Tel Aviv as a kind of war zone. A university-educated chemist who left the chaos of post-Soviet Ukraine to clean apartments and offices in Tel Aviv, Tanya was tough, savvy, and always optimistic. She proudly wore a cross around her neck, and she had long felt shielded by her ability to blend in with the large population of Russian-speaking olím who live in South Tel Aviv, many of whom who had Jewish relatives, and thus access to Israeli citizenship, even though they themselves were not Jewish. When Tanya, too, started feeling imperiled, I knew the intensity of the deportation campaign had ratcheted up once again.

I first met Tanya and her husband, Sergei, after they had struggled with a long and demoralizing series of failed pregnancies. We met at the Open Clinic, and I had the privilege of getting to know Tanya as she celebrated the first tentative weeks of her one successful pregnancy, which resulted in the birth of a much-beloved daughter, Larissa. During the tentative months before Larissa's arrival, we forged a close friendship in Hebrew, the lingua franca we continue to employ with divergent degrees of competence—and, on occasion, much hilarity. (For her, in Hebrew, the world unfolds in the first person feminine.) I had often heard Tanya speak kindly of the Africans in her neighborhood, especially mothers like herself.

Eighteen months into the campaign, many of the authorities' "easy targets" had either been arrested or had fled to other neighborhoods. Tanya and Sergei's apartment building, once inhabited by Filipino and African families with whom Tanya was on a *"shalóm, shalóm"* basis, had emptied out—except the tiny, one-room rooftop structure they had expanded, through Sergei's construction efforts and Tanya's resourcefulness, into a drafty but serviceable multiroom dwelling just steps from HaTikvah's central thoroughfare. A few blocks away, Olivia and her family, and Ruby and hers, continued struggling along. By that point, when even migrants from Eastern Europe and the former Soviet Union had become targets, Tanya's nerves were fraying. "You know I'm strong," she told me, "but this is too much."

Tanya was not the only one who used military metaphors to describe the electrified atmosphere of the gerush. Just a few months earlier, Peter had compared the Immigration Police to the elite Golani unit of the Israeli army: "I call them the HaTikvah Golani Brigade because they run, they kick, and they fight. When they encounter you it's like they're going to war." Without missing a beat, he recalled a friend's recent arrest—while traveling by bicycle—that put the officers' newfound readiness to use force on clear display. Before his friend could realize what was happening, "they had made a U-turn in their vehicle and cut him off. It was a near miss, and he would have tripped over. Four men came out of the van and confronted him, [asking] 'Where are your papers? Where are your papers?' He said, 'We are preparing to go, we have [plane] tickets.' The way the four came, it was like they were at war. . . . One just dove—on the pavement—and grabbed his legs so he couldn't get away. My friend struggled, and the man held tighter. It was a confrontation, and it turned to be like a fight. He was trying to free himself and it turned into a fight." What surprised Peter most was an apparent change in what he had assumed were the implicit rules governing physical contact between arresting officers and detained migrants. Now, it seemed, arresting officers showed little reluctance to use physical restraint, or physical aggression, in full public view.

Peter's story might tempt us to conclude that Naana was just kidding himself about cycling being a safer bet than riding the bus. Yet this hasty conclusion would miss an important point. Naana may not have been able to change his life circumstances—although, as a community activist, he was among the handful of migrants willing to take the risk of actively trying. What he could do, however, was change his experience of this frightening reality. Instead of allowing state policies of criminalization to overtake his experience of the world, Naana's insistence on self-propulsion enabled him, in a small but meaningful way, to respond to one of life's fundamental existential imperatives: to turn "givenness into choice" and live decisively, at least partially on his terms.[23]

Like Naana, Franklin too drew confidence from his athleticism and physical strength. On one occasion, speed and agility did help him evade the police. One lazy Saturday afternoon, as we relaxed in their apartment after a long morning in church, Franklin described the incident that led him to stop taking public transportation. He had been at a bus stop on Etzel Street, the main artery in HaTikvah, when it happened. At first, he didn't even notice the van next to him, but once he did, he raced off into the neighborhood's narrow streets and alleys, sped through the *shuk* (open-air market), and slid into a taxi to make his escape. The van doubled back toward the end of the shuk, apparently expecting to catch him there, but he knew the area too well to fall into their trap. That was the moment he stopped taking buses to work. Although the taxi rides burned a hole in his daily earnings, he felt it was worth it.

Earlier, Peter, too, had been confident in his ability to outrun the police, but stories like these eroded his confidence well before he himself faced arrest: "In the past, everyone said if they try to catch you, make an attempt to run and they will not follow you. Now, you can run for many miles and they will follow you. If you go crawl in a hole they will wait for ten hours for you to come out. I can't continue like this forever. I can't continue like this forever. I can't continue like this forever. I can't continue like this forever." Unlike most of the migrants and human rights activists I knew, Peter accepted the Israeli government's efforts to arrest and deport unauthorized migrants as legitimate. What he opposed, and feared, were its militaristic tactics: "Okay, we have overstayed and we are illegal, so you have to arrest us. But is that the way to do it, like war?"

Home

By the time the gerush neared its peak, nowhere felt safe—not even home. Rented rooms or flats in Tel Aviv—usually small, and almost always shared— could never be the kind of brick-and-mortar houses many migrants were working to build back home in the Philippines, Nigeria, Ghana, or elsewhere. Still, these provisional homes had become important spaces of welcome, and their habitability was a deeply embodied concern. These were spaces in which people could, for at least a few moments each day, unseal the experience of "crushing objecthood." They offered an "alternative sensorium"[24] in which migrants could make aesthetic choices. Modulate sound—of voice, music, television—in ways that might feel risky at work, or in public. Arrange, and rearrange, space to maximize comfort, pleasure, and sense of safety. In many apartments I visited, photographs of family, friends, or familiar places in

Israel or back home were on proud display. Often images of Jesus or the Virgin Mary hung on the wall. The preparation and consumption of food also played crucial roles in these alternative sensoria. At small import shops around the city and the open-air pedestrian market in Nevé She'anán, the neighborhood adjacent to the Central Bus Station, migrants could find cooking staples uncommon in Israeli stores: palm oil and semolina, yams and shrimp-flavored bouillon cubes, fish pastes and familiar greens. At the same venues, a robust local market in imported music and DVDs—religious programs, television shows, and popular feature films from migrants' countries of origin, many sold in bootleg versions—offered temporary escape.

Still, shared flats in Tel Aviv could offer only limited freedoms. I never met a single migrant who lived, as I did for part of my fieldwork, in a flat entirely on his or her own. Instead, homes were inherently social spaces. Although the privacy I craved may not have been my friends' and research participants' ideal, many families I knew would have been thrilled to have a space of their own, uninterrupted by the burden of sometimes unfamiliar, and occasionally untrustworthy, flatmates.

The condition of migrants' housing varied considerably, but nearly every apartment I had occasion to visit was crowded and cramped. For most, including Olivia and Priscilla, "home" was a single room, shared with immediate family members or a roommate, in a multibedroom apartment with a common kitchen and bathroom. Some apartments had telephone landlines, while many others did not. Most had access to cable television service. Although some migrants rented shared flats with a common living area, more frequently every potentially habitable area was walled off, and often padlocked, to maximize the number of inhabitants. From migrants' perspective, cramming in multiple residents may have seemed like a good way to distribute the cost of rent, but often it had the opposite effect. Landlords, realizing that higher residential density per flat meant they could extract even higher rents than otherwise possible, divided up their own properties in clear violation of housing codes. Only a handful of families I knew lived in private spaces of their own, among them Tanya and Sergei, who converted their single room with basic plumbing into an amazing rooftop compound that could accommodate their desires to cook, dine, entertain, and even sleep outside (and host the occasional overnight guest, like me) on sweltering summer nights.

Sometimes residents in a shared apartment knew each other through familial, social, or community ties, but often flatmates were linked simply by chance, need, or convenience. Sharing space with strangers is always risky, even when one's belongings can be protected under lock and key, and for many living in tight quarters, getting along with neighbors proved challenging. Within apartments, tensions and conflicts could arise over just about anything. Common gripes involved shared expenses like utility bills, deposits, and goods for communal use (like toilet paper and cleaning supplies); disputes about cleanliness and hygiene; sensory impositions like strong-smelling food—and, of course, rumors and gossip.

Filipinos' places of residence tended to differ in one crucial way from those of most West Africans. Before the gerush, most West Africans in Tel Aviv worked on a live-out basis, cycling each week among multiple jobs cleaning homes and offices. For them, home was a full-time place of residence. For many Filipinos, the situation was different. The vast majority of Filipinos living in Israel on an authorized basis worked as caregivers and stayed six days each week, twenty-four hours a day, in their employers' homes, and some Filipinos who had already slipped into illegality maintained this rhythm. During live-in workers' weekly days off—usually Saturday evening to Sunday evening—tens of thousands of Filipinos travelled to Tel Aviv from all over the country to meet up with friends, attend church and social events, and relax in their tiny, often tightly packed homes-away-from-home.[25]

The most crowded flat I visited was for a birthday party I attended with Christina, a Filipina woman I had met at the Open Clinic when she came seeking care for termination of an unwanted pregnancy. Christina and I spent a good deal of time together before, during, and after the day of her procedure. Not long afterward, she invited me to join her at a Saturday night party in a small apartment near the Central Bus Station. Several dozen women and a handful of men crowded into the small flat, located a few flights up from Har Tzion Boulevard, the noisy main street that brought a high volume of bus traffic in and out of the city's central depot. At one point during the evening's festivities, we were offered a quick tour—including a peek at the sleeping room shared by the flat's weekend residents. In the bedroom I saw four sets of bunk beds, all jammed up against each other for maximum, and maximally affordable, part-time occupancy.

Late-Night Raids

Once the deportation campaign began, these shared living arrangements posed new risks. When one resident became a target of the Immigration

Administration—for instance, if a neighbor complained, or if someone with a grudge called to complain about another community member—all residents were at risk. Whatever sense of protection and stability migrants' modest homes may previously have afforded, the persistent threat of a raid meant they could feel safe no more. As stories of late-night raids spread like wildfire through migrant communities, some accurate and others embellished, migrants realized the rules of the game had changed. Burglars and thieves were still a concern, but now, homes had become spaces of far more acute vulnerability, penetrability, and danger. If the state sought to put its law in migrants' inward parts, by then it had certainly succeeded.

Kwejo's late-night arrest was typical. An aging father of four, Kwejo and his wife, Patricia, had come to Israel from Ghana nearly fifteen years earlier, in the mid-1980s. Unlike their later-arriving compatriots, they arrived under the auspices of an agricultural exchange program between the governments of Israel and Ghana. Once the program ended, they stayed on and cleaned homes to support themselves, their three older children in Ghana, and their youngest son, Moshe, who was born and raised in Israel. Friendly, funny, and fluent in Hebrew, Moshe had lots of close Israeli friends from school.

Over the years, Patricia and Kwejo struggled with the everyday realities of labor migration and illegalization, including the challenges of long-distance parenting. They also struggled with their own chronic health problems and frequently visited the Open Clinic, where I saw them often. Early in the deportation campaign, a devastating fire tore through their South Tel Aviv flat. The volunteer coordinator at Mesila asked if I could pay them a visit and help assess the damage, and their needs.

However harrowing the fire and its aftermath had been, Patricia told me several months later, Kwejo's arrest was worse. "The country is shaking," she said when we sat down at Mesila to talk about what had happened, her anguish visible in her comportment and audible in her tremulous voice. "Things have never been like this." On the night of Kwejo's arrest, "The police came in at 5 A.M., banging on the door. I opened it, and they slammed the door into me. It cut my hand and I bled all over. Moshe was in the house, and he tried to speak with the police. I didn't understand what he was saying. He was born here! They shouldn't deport the father. . . . Now I'm afraid to go everywhere—to the *Taḥaná* [bus station], the shuk, everywhere. I think all the time about the police." After a decade and a half in Israel, Patricia experienced both the fact and the manner of Kwejo's arrest as a basic attack on her sense of dignity. "Why are they treating us like animals? This is not how you treat human beings but how you treat animals. We are human beings, we are not animals. They should not treat us like animals. . . . Israel was never like this. We are not criminals, we are human beings!" At the time of his father's arrest and deportation, Moshe was thirteen. Soon afterward, he and his mother moved in temporarily with the family of a friend from school.

Violence and Its Shadows

Some late-night arrests involved considerably more violence than this. Arresting officers were reputed to break down doors with crowbars and axes. Sometimes they hit, pushed, and kicked migrants, occasionally causing long-lasting physical injury. On some occasions, children bore witness to their parents' arrest.

After a raid in a particular apartment or building—often precipitated by a report from a police informant and a telltale mark on the doorframe—other residents would scramble for alternative housing. Frequently this involved a hasty move from South Tel Aviv to a more distant area where the Immigration Police presence was assumed to be lighter.

Many arrests did not involve physical brutality, but physical violence, compounded by more familiar forms of structural and symbolic violence, had become an imminent possibility. This shift in police practice signaled an ideological shift: a deepening logic of abjection that cancelled out any earlier characterization of unauthorized migrants' presence as benign. Now, with the gerush, the country's new, "other" Others had been recast in ways that paralleled the country's ostensible "real" Others—Palestinians. Key hallmarks of this shift, as I explore more fully in Chapter 3, included the authorities' readiness both to presume guilt and to deploy violence with relative impunity. As a result of the state's military-like deportation campaign, itself bolstered by discursive moves like the public service announcements described earlier, unauthorized migrants were now racialized, illegalized, arrested, and expelled. They had become "illegal foreign workers" (ovdím zarím lo ḥukiím), a new kind of national abject.

These changes spurred migrants to develop new tactics in an attempt to protect themselves, their families, and their flatmates. Some were little more than cognitive tricks. In Olivia and Peter's apartment, for instance, the heavy shutters were always closed, even in the sweltering heat of Tel Aviv summers.

Along the opposite wall, the windows were covered over with cardboard, leaving the apartment dark and stifling. A small Israeli flag, the kind that attaches to a car window, dangled from the light fixture. One afternoon, as I held Ethan in my arms and he batted it around playfully, I asked Olivia about it.

"What's the deal with the flag?"

"Peter thinks it will fool the police into thinking Israelis live here," Olivia replied, her tone intimating illogic in her husband's thinking.

"But . . . it's on the inside of the house," I tentatively observed, "and the windows are all covered."

"I don't know," she said, "he just thinks it's a good idea." We shared a cynical laugh.

Even with the door locked and the flag hanging from the light fixture, home no longer felt safe. Loud noises at night would wake them in a panic wondering if the police were pounding on a neighbor's door—or their own. Too many of their friends, fellow church members, and acquaintances had been arrested for them to sleep easily. Peter himself never took to sleeping outside, but after his first arrest and subsequent release, the family took other measures: they found someone who could borrow a car—me—and quickly "packed out" to a new apartment a twenty-minute walk from the center of HaTikvah and, they hoped, far from the authorities' penetrating gaze.

Other tactics involved countersurveillance and collaboration among flatmates. Some took turns sitting up at night in pairs watching for suspicious vehicles.[26] At any sign of danger, the flatmate on guard could awaken the others so all could crawl out a window to a designated hiding place on an adjacent roof. Others slept in their clothing—and not just everyday work clothes, but the finer clothes one would wear to church, or on special occasions—to avoid being deported in the garb of a pauper. I also heard second- and thirdhand stories from both Ruby and Naana of women responding to late-night police raids by stripping off their clothing and answering the door partly or fully naked in an attempt to shame police officers into leaving them and their families alone. Naana suspected these tales were apocryphal, but Ruby helped me see that such tactics tapped into an established West African cultural logic of "naked protest": a last-ditch attempt at "*doing* politics" from a position of sociopolitical abjection.[27] Whether Naana or Ruby was correct, the circulation of these stories emphasized the depth of migrants', and especially migrant mothers', growing desperation.

As these haphazard tactics reveal, any sense that the private space of home might serve as a haven from the outside world largely dissipated as the gerush intensified. Instead of offering spaces of privacy and respite, homes sometimes felt even more dangerous than markets, bus stops, and public streets.

The Rhythm of Days and Weeks

This reconfiguration of "illegality" also transformed many migrants' experiences of time, including both the quotidian rhythm of days and weeks and the ability to plan for the future. Not long after the campaign had begun, I heard descriptions of a palpable difference in risk between weekdays and weekends. Early in the week, Immigration Police officers, some in uniform and others in civilian dress, were on the prowl. On Fridays and Saturdays (the Israeli weekend), arrests felt less likely since, as Peter put it, "on the weekend, the police are home with their families." Since Saturday had long been considered a "safe" day, many Christian migrants continued attending Saturday services at either the parish Catholic church in nearby Jaffa or one of the city's smaller and less institutionalized Protestant or African independent churches.[28]

As the Immigration Police ramped up their efforts, the temporality of everyday risk shifted. Nine months into the campaign, I asked Olivia, Peter, and Claire about these changes. The previous Thursday, a raid had taken place in a nearby apartment building.

"They took a building full of people," Olivia said. "Maybe twenty."

"Now you can't go out at night," Claire added.

"At night?!" Olivia retorted. "You can't go out at any time. No hour is safe."

Peter parsed the danger over the week's course. "Thursday is a dangerous day. We were saying Sunday, Monday, Tuesday are bad days; Thursday, Friday, Saturday safer." Now, he added, taking the recent raid into account, "Thursday is a bad day, too."

"Every day is a bad day now," Olivia interrupted.

About a year and a half into the campaign, Ruby and I considered the impact of these changes. For most of their four years in Israel, she and Franklin felt they had lived well. During the week they worked hard, and on Saturday mornings they went to church, always dressed to the nines. Warm and gregarious, they cultivated a multicultural web of friendships, not just with fellow Nigerians but also with South Africans, Filipinos, and others, even taking the occasional American ethnographer under their wing. Young Nigerian men, including a few in their twenties who aspired to soccer careers on Israeli teams, looked to Ruby and Franklin as surrogate parents. More often than not, their flat was full of people and music.

They loved going to parties and social gatherings—and hosting them. I'll never forget the bash they organized for their son Jesse's first birthday: a day-long excursion to the desert and the Dead Sea by tour bus, led by a Nigerian friend who moonlighted as a tour guide. Ruby and Franklin managed to fill half the bus with friends and relatives, who paid their own way. On the long drive, we swapped opinions about Israeli politics, American music star Whitney Houston's recent trip to Israel, and the perplexing status of the Black Hebrew community[29] established in the southern desert city of Dimona over three decades earlier. Our guides took us to visit the desert home of founding Israeli prime minister David Ben Gurion in Sde Boker, and then Franklin and Ruby hosted a fabulous beach dance party, complete with booming sound system and a (miraculously still-firm) ice cream cake, on the salty shore of the Dead Sea. But that was then, and now things were different: "Franklin is barely going out now. He's afraid. He's just working at a pub on Friday [nights] for fifteen hours and on Saturday for eight. He's cleaning on Wednesday, every other Thursday, and some Fridays. He had another job but he gave it to Olivia. Any time he's out of the house I'm nervous, even when he's called after he's arrived. The whole time he's out of the house I'm nervous. When he's leaving work I always tell him to come home direct, not to stop anywhere." I later heard Peter compare his situation to Franklin's, again invoking a military metaphor: "The wife told him to stay in the house, so he doesn't go out. He just works Friday and Saturday, on the safe days. He's not in the line of fire like I am."

Phone Calls in Church

Another interruption in the established rhythm of days and weeks occurred at a particularly inopportune time for Pastor James Opoku, spiritual leader of the evangelical church that Ruby and Franklin, Olivia, and Claire attended, often with me tagging along. On several weekday evenings and each Saturday morning, the congregation gathered in a former industrial building located near the Central Bus Station, just a stone's throw from the Open Clinic, Mesila's office, and the homes of several other migrant families I had come to know.

Theirs was by no means the only church on the block, or even in the building. All shared the same aesthetic: white walls, indoor-outdoor carpet, a raised altar at the front with a large mural on the wall—at Pastor Opoku's church, a tranquil nature scene—with the congregation's name announced above the altar in prominent lettering. In the front left corner stood the congregation's full set of musical gear: microphones, guitars, a keyboard, a shiny drum kit. Some Saturdays Pastor Opoku and his fellow ministers wore suits, and sometimes they wore clerical robes. Like many evangelical congregations in and around Tel Aviv, the congregation spanned cultural and linguistic boundaries and worshipped primarily in English, with occasional singing and praise in other tongues. On a typical Saturday, my friends and I would stroll in midservice, usually at around 11 A.M.

The newfound danger of Saturdays hit Pastor Opoku's church especially hard precisely on the morning he and his congregation were gearing up to celebrate the dedication of his newborn daughter. That morning, pastors from various churches were in attendance, along with other honored guests, so the pastor, his family, and his congregation were in the spotlight.

I arrived with Ruby, Franklin, and little Jesse, whose own dedication we had celebrated in the church not long earlier. As usual, Ruby and Franklin's arrival made a splash. Ruby had accented her brightly colored, form-fitting clothes with deep red lipstick and a new pair of translucent high heels, and Franklin kept his sunglasses on throughout the day's worship and celebration. When we arrived and took our seats, fashionably late even by usual standards, Ruby immediately realized her friends Mary and Irene and their husbands were missing. Franklin whispered down the row with a request to borrow my cellphone, which I passed down without a word. A quick call and a few whispered conversations later, we knew rumors were circulating that the Immigration Police were on the prowl. Suddenly Saturday was a bad day too, much to Pastor Opoku's dismay. Not only was the congregation's low attendance a blow to his prestige, but it had financial repercussions as well: fewer guests meant fewer gifts honoring the arrival of his child.

Pregnancy, Parenthood, and Protection

As anthropologist Liisa Malkki notes, children often are invoked as "embodiments of a basic human goodness," or as "seers of [universal] truth" that adults fail to perceive, or that they cynically ignore. At other times, children are regarded as quite literal "embodiments of the future." In short, a good deal of "ritual and affective work [is] done by the figure of the child." Yet for children born to unauthorized migrant parents in countries such as Israel, the notion that "Children are our future"—itself an "utter cliché," as Malkki puts it[30]—simply falls flat. Not only are these children excised from the state's prospective self-image, but the very notion that *these* particular children might be the face of Israel's future frightens those who cleave most tightly to the biopolitical logic that frames them as a "demographic time bomb."[31]

Whether or not they are attuned to these tropes and fears, global migrants in Tel Aviv reproduce, like people the world over—sometimes with forethought and intention, and sometimes without. In the months preceding the gerush, I spent much of my time talking and cooking, shopping, and trekking around the city with pregnant women and new mothers. My original research questions, formulated several years before the gerush, revolved around migrant women's experiences of fertility decision making and childbearing in a country in which pregnant migrants had been cast as a demographic threat by several national politicians. Foremost among them was Eli Yishai of the Shas Party, who as minister of labor and social welfare had repeatedly told the Knesset that "they have to be deported before they become pregnant."[32] Several years later, Yishai accused migrants of cynically using their children as "insurance cards" and, invoking the language of military occupation, as "human shields."[33]

At the time, few regarded Yishai's early comments as much more than bombast. In fact, savvy NGO advocates launched a countervailing effort that effectively leveraged the pronatalist sentiments embedded deeply in the country's local moral economy to help secure key reproductive and child health benefits, including subsidized prenatal care and delivery coverage, childhood immunizations, and well-child checkups regardless of parents' migration status.[34] Although these NGO efforts did prove successful, they had no impact on the *sociopolitical* status of children born to unauthorized migrant mothers. Israel has no provision for birthright citizenship, so children born in the country to migrant parents have no automatic right to citizenship—or even to residency status. As a result, allegations that migrants to Israel were bearing children in a strategic effort to secure their own status (i.e., as "anchor babies")[35] make little sense.

Politicians like Yishai sought to portray migrants' choices and actions as canny and manipulative, but their own voices tell a different story.[36] From their standpoint, the idea of having a baby solely to guard against deportation was absurd. For those who did have children, however, carrying them through public space could help control one's subjective sense, if not one's objective risk, of arrest. People assumed, often rightly, that Immigration Police officers—whether motivated by pragmatism or empathy—were less likely to arrest a migrant with a child than a migrant traveling alone. My Filipina friend Marina, for instance, often dragged along her toddler, Eden, whenever she moved about town: on shopping trips to the shuk for groceries, to her evangelical church near the old Central Bus Station, on social calls. Marina could have left Eden home with the girl's father, who was usually responsible for her care but, following an ordeal described in the coming chapter, he rarely left their apartment for fear of being arrested—again. Instead, Marina often struggled through city streets and buses with a boisterous toddler *and* multiple bags laden with fruits, vegetables, and other groceries. Yishai's accusation sounds different in her voice: "*She* is my visa!" Marina would explain, gesturing toward her rambunctious little girl with the spiky ponytail. In dragging Eden around town, Marina had no sinister political intent or military strategy in mind. She was trying, however modestly, to achieve a bit of peace of mind, and ultimately to protect her family and their chance for a future together.

As the gerush gathered steam, more and more migrant parents made similar choices. Mothers were vigilant about carrying documentary evidence of their children's birth, sometimes in a neat file and sometimes in a plastic bag bursting with hospital release papers and medical records. On evenings and weekends, men would move around town with children too: Franklin took his son Jesse; Peter took Ethan; Tanya's husband, Sergei, took Larissa. At times, adults with no children of their own, like Olivia and Ruby's friend Claire, would stop by and ask to "borrow" another's to run an errand. Olivia was sometimes annoyed by Claire's requests but understood her friend's reasoning. "A woman without a child is like a man now," she once told me.

For adults like Claire, occasional efforts to perform parenthood may have proven helpful in a pinch, but in a broader sense they worked against communal interests by fueling the authorities' suspicions that migrants regularly engaged in tactical deceit. About nine months into the campaign, I discussed this deepening hermeneutic of suspicion with Meirav, a social worker at Mesila. Now, Meirav said, the police had lost sympathy for mothers with small babies and husbands in jail: "Every day a woman with a day-old baby comes, and they refuse to release the husband." Two thoughts lodged in my mind as I heard Meirav describe this shift in bureaucratic disposition. First, as a Mesila employee, she, too, was a public servant—albeit at the municipal, not national, level. Meirav's attitude, which I knew was shared widely among her coworkers and Mesila's volunteers, points to a wide gap between municipal and national dispositions toward global migrants, a theme to which I return in Chapter 4.

Second, I knew Meirav as not only a sensitive and committed social worker but also a new mother herself. "The situation for mothers with babies now is terrible," she told me. "In principle they don't release husbands of new mothers, and if they do it's only on bail. They're leaving people literally without food, without food for their children. Mesila is organizing food for people. We've become a real food cooperative here. The other day a woman came, and she had no food to give her little girl. I saw her giving the baby water and asked why she wasn't giving her food. She said, 'Because I don't have any.'" I asked whether Mesila had publicized cases like this or shared them with the police as a way of demonstrating the consequences of their tactics. "We do," she replied, "we met with the police. They say, 'These people need to get out of here.' They think African women get pregnant in order to stay. As for Africans, the police hate them the most. They say they're the most manipulative. When they go to their homes, they throw themselves at [the police], throw their children at them. . . . The situation is terrible." By this point in the gerush, the authorities no longer saw claims of motherhood as an automatic cause for empathy or assistance. From their standpoint, it seemed, there was no motherhood for the sake of motherhood. Instead, migrants' claims of pregnancy and parenthood were presumed to be manipulation or performance, in either case orchestrated to excuse migrants' illegitimate presence and extend their stay in the country. Whatever occasional grain of truth may have undergirded these assumptions, the resulting hermeneutic of suspicion harmed not just migrant parents but often their children as well.

"Pirate Day Cares"

As Meirav and other Mesila social workers witnessed on a daily basis, parents' sociopolitical abjection can impinge in profound, even irreversible ways on their children's lives. In Israel, these damaging effects begin to accumulate in the informal day-care arrangements—often dubbed "babysitters" (*babysitterim*), "pirate day cares" (*ganím pirátiyim*), or even "child warehouses" (*maḥsanéi yeladím*)—where most children born to unauthorized migrant parents spend their earliest years.

Since the late 1990s, these informal day cares, which vary in form and quality but are uniformly unregulated, have been the only viable day-care options for most children under age three who were born to migrant parents. In Israel, no public day-care option is available for any children at this age, but many Israeli citizen children attend private (often nonprofit) day cares that face greater scrutiny both from the authorities and, as importantly, from parents who risk little in voicing their concerns. Nearly every migrant parent I interviewed had put their Israeli-born children in a "pirate day care," and nearly every prospective parent expected to do the same, save the handful—including my Ghanaian friends Gloria and William—who sent one or more children "home" to be raised by a relative or close friend.

In these improvised settings, many of which still existed as of 2018, one or two adults may supervise as many as ten, twenty, or even thirty children. With ratios like these, even caregivers with experience and the very best intentions struggle to manage the basics of feeding, diapering, and comforting all of the children in their care. Infants and toddlers often spend long days—up to twelve hours or even more—isolated in a crib. Most of these settings are private apartments located in aging residential buildings, and caregivers often reside in an adjacent room. Many day cares lack fire escapes and adequate ventilation, and some have unauthorized electrical connections, unsecured doors or gates, unsafe balconies, and other physical hazards. Mesila staff and volunteers discussed these risks frequently and documented them in the agency's annual reports.

Over the years, I saw some of these risks firsthand. In the day cares I had occasion to visit, almost always in the company of Mesila social workers, days tended to unfold with little daily routine, and many children received limited attention, physical contact, or opportunity for direct interaction with other children or adults. Neither did children tend to receive much stimulation in the form of stories, toys, music, art activities, or outdoor playtime. Without a formal curriculum in place, a television often served as children's primary companion. Meirav herself offered a visual narration of these conditions in a PowerPoint presentation she prepared when Mesila hosted a tour of South Tel Aviv for a group of Knesset members. Slide by slide, she offered a photographic time-lapse comparison of her own infant daughter's daily routine and that of a child born to African parents who spent over twelve hours a day in a "pirate kindergarten."

7 A.M.   Daniel is already in the crib—and Tal is just waking up.

8 A.M.   Tal arrives in her family day care—and Daniel is in the crib.

10 A.M.   Tal is playing with friends—and Daniel is in the crib. . . .

7 P.M.   Tal is at home getting ready for dinner—and Daniel is still
in the crib. . . .

And there are hundreds of children in a situation like Daniel's.

Most of these day cares were opened by migrant women, who saw them as an alternative to the more physically demanding, and less lucrative, work of cleaning homes and offices.

My Ghanaian friend Gloria, for example, set up a day care in her South Tel Aviv apartment after struggling with health challenges that limited her mobility, followed by a difficult pregnancy. She traded their living room furniture for two rows of white plastic cribs, bought a few child-sized chairs and tables, and took eleven toddlers into her care, all born in Israel to parents from West Africa or the Philippines. When I visited at about 5:30 one evening in December 2006, eight children were still there, including several who had been dropped off as early as 6:30 A.M. Some sat or lay listlessly in cribs watching a children's program on a large television, but others ran around and played. As in other "pirate kindergartens" I had visited, the children were excited to see a new face, hungry for attention, and quick to climb all over me. The comparison to Meirav's slideshow was right there in my field notes: *Mostly the job of babysitter seems to involve being there to make sure kids eat, have clean diapers, and nothing bad happens to them. Not about stimulation or education or enrichment. In other words, the exact situation represented in the slide show Meirav shows when she makes presentations about Mesila.* As close as Gloria and I had become, I found it difficult to keep my mouth shut about her new professional path.

I was deeply disturbed, even overwhelmed at times, by the patterns I saw in pirate day cares—many of them a good deal bleaker than Gloria's—but most migrants and activists I knew were less focused on these risks to children than on adults' more acute risk of arrest and deportation. I took some solace in knowing that from one year to the next, Mesila was investing more and more of its energies in monitoring and, where possible, working to improve these day-care settings. Just a few days before my visit to Gloria, I interviewed Limor, a Mesila social worker, who said the agency was now taking a stronger position on day cares like these, in part because its recently appointed director was prepared to hold politicians' feet to the fire. After observing the problem for years but holding back criticism, Mesila's new stance, as Limor put it, was that "allowing this [these day cares] to exist is to be complicit with crime."[37] For some time, the agency had organized caregiver training courses for migrant "babysitters," arranged volunteer placements matching Israeli university students with day cares, collected donations of material resources, and occasionally coordinated specialized opportunities like music classes taught by volunteer teachers. Now, Mesila was more actively reporting to city leaders, national legislators, and state bureaucrats; testifying in Knesset committees; and participating in a Knesset subcommittee focusing specifically on children of migrant workers.

At the same time, I knew these efforts faced resistance at every turn. Limor, for instance, described a recent workshop that Mesila had held for social workers at the university where she herself had trained. She described it as a shocking and deeply painful experience—as "one of the most difficult moments I've faced"—because of the strong and vocal opposition some workshop participants expressed to Mesila's aims and efforts. "I felt they were beating me up" (Heb.: "*she'hetzlifu li*"), she said about the social work colleagues she encountered that day. "They were saying that what I do is a crime!"

Other obstacles involved caregivers themselves. During my first visit to Gloria's day care, I asked whether any volunteers from Mesila had paid her a visit, and her response was telling: "No. What do I need them for?" By her account, Mesila's meddling had forced a woman she knew either to close her own day care or to move it somewhere else—and now Mesila runs it, and the woman makes less money. "I don't need them," Gloria insisted. "I'm not interested in having them involved." At the same time, I couldn't help but notice a stack of flyers announcing an upcoming meeting at the Central Bus Station about the rights of women "foreign workers" in Israel, sponsored by none other than Mesila in partnership with the Kav La'Oved Workers Hotline. When I asked, she said she planned to attend.

In 2005, Mesila took a different step toward intervening in pirate day cares: They established a day-care center, and later a small network, called "Unitaf." Although they did not yet exist when the gerush began, I had the opportunity to visit on several occasions during return trips to Tel Aviv. The Unitaf day cares, which mirror the teacher expectations, curriculum, and safety standards of day cares serving Israeli citizen children, offer an enriched environment to a small number of children. Although they are subsidized through major fund-raising efforts, they remain more expensive than their informal alternatives and offer fewer hours of day-care coverage. Despite these barriers of added cost and limited hours, the Unitaf day cares' limited capacity meant they were unable to keep up with local demand.

As a result, most children born in Israel to irregular migrant parents have continued to end up in pirate day-care settings, whose potential long-term impact on children's health and development has long been well documented. "By the time they enter formal educational settings," Mesila reported as early as 2007, "every one of these children suffers at least one if not more forms of developmental delay." The municipal agency's report continues: "We are not exaggerating when we say we are convinced that the overwhelming majority of infants and young children in these frameworks meet the criteria for children at risk as a result of spending most hours of the day in an atmosphere of physical and emotional deprivation that severely delays their development."[38] Eventually these conclusions were echoed in the State Comptroller's annual report, albeit with little subsequent impact on state policy.[39]

When I look back, Gloria's home day care was relatively safe, clean, and well run in comparison to many others Mesila documented over the years, including those I visited over a decade later with Danna, a Mesila community social worker. On a sweltering summer morning in 2014, Danna and I met up at the entrance to HaTikvah's open-air market. She had three site visits lined up, and in each day care we visited, children of Eritrean asylum seekers comprised the majority those enrolled. The first day care was much like the one Gloria had opened in her apartment a decade earlier, albeit smaller and with less space for children to move around or play in. In the second, just a few blocks away, we found a single, harried Eritrean woman alone in a ground floor apartment with nearly forty rambunctious children. The owner of the day care, a West African woman, was nowhere to be found, nor did she respond to Danna's repeated phone calls. Despite the day's escalating heat index, the children had no ready access to water. Only an unlocked screen door stood between them and the street. As we waited for the woman in charge to return, Danna and I scrambled to put a water cup into each child's hands, and Danna wondered aloud about whether she should call the police. Should she call, because these infants and toddlers were clearly at risk? Or refrain from calling, because any act that raised concerns about Mesila's relationship to the police would erode whatever measure of trust the city's migrant communities might reluctantly place in their small social welfare organization?[40]

As Danna deliberated, she started gathering the kids who were big enough to walk into the open courtyard behind the apartment—an empty, partly

shaded rectangle of concrete—and tried to engage them in an activity. Together we beckoned them into a circle, encouraged them to hold hands, and
launched into a children's song with simple hand motions. Few responded.
Two or three children joined in, but most just gathered in a crowd, staring at
us blankly.

Their stares reminded me of an interview I had conducted years earlier
with Uri, an Israeli music teacher who, under Mesila's auspices, had offered
music classes in a day care similar to this one. At first, Uri explained when
we met in a Tel Aviv café, he couldn't figure out why he was unable to connect with the children. But then

> I figured out that when I'd hand them the [musical] instrument, they
> wouldn't see it. I mean, for example, let's say this is a stick [he took
> my pen]. I'd hand them the stick, sometimes I'd offer it to them in front
> of their eyes and I'd see that often—this would blow me away—they
> wouldn't see the stick. . . . I'd hand them the stick, and . . . they wouldn't
> respond. Not out of some kind of apathy or disinterest, they just
> wouldn't notice that I'm gesturing, that there's a kind of gesture.
> That . . . I want to give them something. . . .
>
> These are things that blew me away. As soon as I realized this,
> I said okay, let's turn this into a game. Instead of just [handing the in-
> struments out one by one] it became a kind of [game]. . . . It was a really
> a skill, a really basic skill involving hand-eye coordination, that they
> just didn't have. . . . I'm talking to you about things that [most] 3–4
> year old kids do without any problem. Without any kind of problem
> at all! But children at this age, and even children a little bit older, didn't
> really understand what exactly I was looking for. Now this, you know,
> is about bodily discipline, you know, sitting up straight, sitting
> down. . . . You open your ears, and you're there. . . . [But] They were
> totally all over the place.

That morning, in the courtyard with Danna, I could see exactly what Uri
meant. In the years since my visits to Gloria's day care and my interview with
Uri, I had become a parent myself; in fact, I had kissed my own almost two-
year-old daughter goodbye that morning just before hopping a minibus to Ha-
Tikvah to meet Danna. The differences between these day-care centers and the
carefully regulated, learning-rich environment where my partner and I had
grown accustomed to dropping off our own child each morning could not have

been starker or more palpable. Yet there we were in the heart of Tel Aviv, a dozen years later and just a few blocks over from Natan Street, where our story began. "People always say, 'If you call for the same standards [in migrants' day cares as in Israeli day cares], everyone will laugh at you,'" Danna told me, but "if there were a day care like this near my house, I would be deeply disturbed."

Question Marks

From a developmental standpoint, the long-term impact of spending one's early childhood in settings like these is predictably devastating. These effects became eminently clear in an interview I conducted with Eli Nechama,[41] principal of Bialik-Rogozin, the Tel Aviv school with the highest proportion of children from global migrant backgrounds, the same week I accompanied Danna on her rounds. Fifty-one national backgrounds were represented among the school's student population, Nechama said when we met in his office, school bells and hall noise echoing in the background. Many were born in Israel to global migrant parents, but others had arrived with their families, including many who had fled Eritrea and Sudan and, after harrowing journeys through the Sinai desert, sought asylum in Israel. He spoke proudly of the school's successes, and frankly about its challenges. "Everything you would normally assume in a regular school needs a question mark," Nechama said. The majority of students arrive wholly unprepared for the formal educational system, and most exhibit multiple forms of delays—"developmentally, physiologically, motorically, emotionally." The impact of these challenges permeates nearly every aspect of the school, Nechama continued. "We treat them all as post-traumatic children."

For students born in Israel, Nechama traced many of these developmental delays to the "babysitters" (as he called them, borrowing the English word). "To the best of our knowledge, the children are there just so there's [some kind of] adult supervision, so their development is elementary at best." As an educator and state employee, however, he had no ready alternative to propose. "As for the babysitters, we tend to say they're a response developed by the community for itself. . . . So however bad we may say it is, what's the alternative? For a child to stay at home alone? We've seen that, too. Social welfare has identified children who were left home alone—babies, older children. So despite all the criticism, at least there's an adult there." Despite these extraordinary challenges, Bialik-Rogozin School achieved some notable successes in the years preceding our interview, including a 91 percent success rate at the state matriculation exams (*bagrút*), compared to a national average of 55 percent.

The school also garnered international attention after it was featured in a provocatively titled 2010 documentary film that received an Academy Award: *Strangers No More* (Figure 9). As the film skyrocketed toward Oscar recognition, Israelis across the political spectrum leaped to celebrate its message, however truncated a national portrait it might present. Former prime minister Ehud Olmert described the school as "miraculous," "unprecedented in Israel," and a model of how Israel can treat those who are different and those who come to the country seeking refuge. Former ambassador to the United Nations Danny Gillerman said he "always wanted to show the real face of Israel, the one that wasn't just bloodshed and warfare. . . . There can be no better *hasbara* [public diplomacy] than this movie, to show what type of country we are and what type of country we can be."[42]

Even as *Strangers No More* was being touted as evidence of Israel's compassion and humanity, a more complicated—and grimmer—tale unfolded simultaneously and in parallel. In photos and video footage, the national media began publicizing a new stage in Israel's efforts to deport global migrants: a new, "child-friendly" detention facility at Ben Gurion International Airport featuring a colorful jungle gym, carefully arranged toys, and wall paintings of cartoon characters Winnie the Pooh and SpongeBob Square Pants.[43] Eli Yishai, now serving as interior minister, returned to the headlines with a familiar refrain. Allowing children of unauthorized parents to remain in the country, he argued, would "damage the state's Jewish identity, constitute a demographic threat and increase the danger of assimilation."[44]

At Wit's End

Fifteen months into the gerush, I returned to Israel after a five-month absence and paid Olivia and her family a visit. My heart sank when she opened the door to their apartment that December day. Olivia looked exhausted, haggard, bordering on tears. When I had left for the United States in August, she had been just a few months pregnant. Now, their second child, Jonathan, was two weeks old. Their older son, Ethan, was nineteen months old and well into toddlerhood—one moment all hugs and toothy grins, the next moment deep in a temper tantrum, crying and throwing himself on the floor in an effort to capture his mother's attention. In addition to nursing tiny Jonathan, Olivia was unable to

SIMON & GOODMAN
PICTURE COMPANY
presents

STRANGERS NO MORE

*For most children, going to school is as simple as going around the block.
For others, it's the end of a long and dangerous journey.*

produced and directed by
KAREN GOODMAN and KIRK SIMON
executive producer LIN ARISON
co-producer & editor NANCY BAKER
cinematography BUDDY SQUIRES
original music score WENDY BLACKSTONE
a production of SIMON & GOODMAN PICTURE COMPANY

Figure 9. Publicity poster for *Strangers No More*. Source: Simon & Goodman Picture Company.

resist Ethan's tearful pleas and allowed him to nurse as well. Her struggles in this fragile postpartum period were straining her patience, and her body.

When it was my turn to hold newborn Jonathan, memories of Ethan's birth, just before the gerush had begun, flooded back. I remembered how lovingly Olivia had tied him to her back with a length of brightly printed cloth, eventually teaching me to do the same. How she had described the comfort and protection she felt with Ethan's tiny body wrapped tightly to her own. Now, new motherhood offered no such security. Just last week, the husband of her friend Mercy had been arrested despite Mercy's rapidly approaching due date. His pleas, and multiple phone calls to the Immigration Administration from both the hospital and Mesila, had failed to achieve his release, and he was taken to "Nazareth"—now a frightening metonym for the fast-moving deportation apparatus. When Mercy "put to bed" three days later, Olivia said, the prison authorities refused to release him. He stayed in jail, and she delivered their baby alone.

For Olivia, stories like Mercy's were no longer new, just terrifying. By now, she had shed any lingering hope that new parenthood might offer meaningful protection. Instead, a cloud of anxiety loomed over the isolated apartment into which I'd helped them move less than a year earlier. Peter, petrified by the possibility of arrest, was now loath to leave the house. The previous week he had skipped five full days of work. With so much on his mind, he showed little interest in the children, which exacerbated Olivia's burdens and deepened the strain on their already fragile marriage.

Conclusion: Illegality Embodied

"There is nothing matter-of-fact about the 'illegality' of undocumented migrants," anthropologist Nicholas De Genova reminds us.[45] Moves to illegalize and criminalize certain migrants and immigrants (but not others) always reflect an alignment of commitments spanning multiple spheres: politics and economics, law and ideology, local moral economy and public discourse. The gerush reflects precisely such an alignment, and it became a key turning point in Israel's, and many Israelis', disposition toward global migrants. The deportation campaign's rapid reconfiguration of migrant illegality radically transformed what it meant to be "Other" in Israel—specifically, to be viewed as an "Other" who is neither Jewish nor Arab, Israeli nor Palestinian. Not only did this aggressive campaign of Othering and expulsion confirm unauthorized migrants' status as a new kind of national abject, but it also fueled a growing sense of indignation among Israeli citizens who felt compelled to reject their government's language and logic, its policies and its actions. Only by tracing the historical and sociopolitical roots of this critical event can we begin to understand its cascading effects, which continue to reverberate both for global migrants who managed to avoid deportation and for those who arrived well after the gerush under very different circumstances, and their children.

For far too long, migration scholars attended to the juridical and sociopolitical aspects of migrant illegality while neglecting a third key dimension: the ways in which illegality generates new modes of being-in-the-world. Legal anthropologists such as De Genova observed nearly two decades ago that "migrant 'illegality' is lived through a palpable sense of deportability,"[46] but offered little insight into how deportability might become palpable. Similarly, Susan Coutin's influential ethnography of Salvadoran migrants to the United States gestured toward key experiential consequences of illegalization, but staked a claim that is perplexing from a critical phenomenological standpoint: the claim that those facing juridical exclusion are consigned to "spaces of nonexistence." Clearly Coutin is referring to a kind of *legal* nonexistence, where "nonexistence" is understood as an effect of the law—or, more precisely, of the "erasure of legal personhood." Even so, people branded with the stigma of "illegality" are not just "beings . . . created and delegitimized through law."[47] They are human beings whose experiences of legitimation and delegitimation unfold in concrete social situations, at specific junctures on longer trajectories, both personal and historical, and with profound consequences, both moral and existential. Although migration scholarship has become more sensitive to these considerations, it stands to benefit from richer engagement with some of the most vital questions of all: How do states put their laws in migrants' "inward parts"? Why? And with what effects? Simply tracing the changing dynamics and configurations of migrants' sociopolitical abjection is not enough. Rather, we need a lens broad enough to capture how these changing configurations catalyze, and are imbricated in, a wide range of embodied consequences and experiential transformations.

In this chapter, we have seen clearly how changing configurations of illegality can invade one's inward parts. We have seen how techniques of racialization and criminalization led Olivia and Peter, Ruby and Franklin, Naana and Claire to experience their bodies as newly and perilously visible. How the nagging risk of arrest and deportation catalyzed new somatic modes of attention, like heightened bodily vigilance and troubled sleep.

How movement and rest, daytime and night, solitary moments and times of communal celebration, public streets and the private space of home all became sites of anxiety and trepidation.

In giving ethnographic primacy to these intimacies and felt immediacies, it is crucial to remember that these consequences are not experienced in solitude. During the gerush, migrants were constantly attuned not only to their own risk of arrest and deportation but also to that of their loved ones, flatmates, community leaders, fellow church congregants, and casual acquaintances. These effects were neither incidental nor coincidental; they were the intended result of state policies designed to sow enough insecurity and fear that individuals, families, even entire communities might make a "voluntary" choice to leave the country.

Importantly, these embodied sensations do not just register phenomenologically, in the domains of subjective and intersubjective experience. They can also have far-reaching physiological and health effects. Early anthropological work on embodiment took the revolutionary step of showing how the body, as Csordas put it, is "the existential ground of culture and self."[48] Yet a parallel and separate body of health research theorizes embodiment very differently: in clinical and epidemiological terms. These parallel approaches to embodiment—the experiential and the epidemiological—become intimately entwined, especially for people who migrate and their families.[49] Perhaps our clearest view of how sociopolitical abjection can become embodied involves children in Tel Aviv's pirate day cares, whose earliest years transpire within what Coutin calls the "force fields" of illegality that envelop their parents' lives. Pediatricians and developmental psychologists concur that the first three to five years of life are the most critical to children's long-term physical, social, emotional, and cognitive development. In those sensitive years, the force fields that pervade migrant parents' lifeworlds engulf their children as well, which can pose grave danger to their developing minds, bodies, and selves. As we have seen, these harms accrue over time and across developmental stages, from infancy and toddlerhood into adolescence and adulthood.[50]

There is no doubt that sociopolitical abjection can penetrate one's inward parts. Damage the human form. Curtail the human capacity to flourish.

CHAPTER 2

Indignities and Indignation

"We are shit. We are *shit*." Marina repeated herself for emphasis. "Like ants who hide and run away and crawl into the ground to avoid being seen."

It was a Friday afternoon in January, and the one-room apartment that had become a hideaway for this family of four—Marina and Raymond, both migrant workers from the Philippines, and their two small children—was freezing cold. They had a small electric heater, Marina said, but didn't run it often. Electricity cost too much. A cold place to spend long days, I thought. We sat side by side on the edge of the family bed, and their daughter, Eden, now twenty months old and clearly tired of being cooped up inside, scampered around trying to catch some attention. Meanwhile, Raymond attended to five-week-old Joey, who was bundled up in layers, socks on his tiny hands to keep them warm. The day Joey was born, at a Palestinian hospital in Bethlehem, Raymond had been locked up in an Israeli jail, slated for deportation.

Life in Israel hadn't always been like this. Both Marina and Raymond had arrived with legal authorization to work as live-in caregivers for elderly Israelis. Marina, who arrived after a three-year stint in Singapore as a domestic worker, came from the northern part of the Philippines and Raymond from the south, but they were recruited by the same employment agency to work in Israel. They met while caring full-time for elderly residents in the same building in a central Israeli town. Both found the intimate labors of full-time caregiving physically and emotionally taxing, but they appreciated the security of stable jobs and the opportunity to send a steady stream of money homeward—in Marina's case, to help educate two younger brothers, and in Raymond's, to his wife and their young daughter.

However binding those long-distance ties, the here and now has a power all its own. The two grew closer, and before long, Marina was pregnant with

Eden. With Eden's birth, Marina lost her job—and, following Israeli labor policy, her visa.[1] Before the gerush, illegality had its benefits. Marina moved into a shared apartment with several other Filipinos in Holon, just south of Tel Aviv. She found a full-time, live-out position as a nanny earning twice what she had earned as a live-in caregiver with a visa and put Eden in a day care where other community members brought their babies as well. Raymond continued at his live-in job and joined them in the shared flat on his days off. On Saturday evenings, Marina worshipped in a mostly Filipino evangelical church that met in a basement near Tel Aviv's old Central Bus Station, where I joined her on several occasions. Raymond's visa expired when Eden was seven months old. "It's very difficult for him to find a job because he's a man," she explained. "Even old men want a lady to take care of them." Unable to find permanent work, Raymond took care of Eden at home, which relieved them of the need to pay for day care. For a time, they were able to manage. Then she learned she was pregnant for a second time. She kept the news from her employer for fear of losing her job.

The night the Immigration Police came looking for Raymond, everything changed. Now they lived like fugitives. They felt pursued like "ants" and treated like "dogs," like "shit," like "criminals." Marina fought back tears as she described their careening descent from legality into illegality and respectability to humiliation, apologizing along the way for losing her composure.

Late at night, she recounted, during the ninth month of her second pregnancy, the police came looking for Raymond. They banged on the door of their crowded flat, frightening the entire building in the process. Ignoring Marina's bulging belly and repeated cries of protest, the officers hit Raymond, handcuffed him, and took him away in the winter night wearing only a light T-shirt. As the police carted him off, Marina remembered standing at the top of the staircase sobbing, pleading for mercy, and, in desperation, even threatening suicide. "They hit him. They punched him. They kicked him. They took him without nothing. With slippers. Didn't even ask him to take a jacket over the pajamas. They didn't care. They treat us like a dog. Not like a human. . . . Maybe *they* are dogs because they treat us like this." When Marina asked the police officers why they were there,

> They said I'm making trouble because I was crying. I was crying, I'm begging them please not to catch him. The man . . . said, "When are you giving birth?" "This month. November." I said, "This month I'm giving birth. Please. . . . I have a baby." They saw that I have a baby,

that I have the first one. They saw my baby that she was still sleeping.
"I'm begging, I'm begging you please!" I was crying and shouting. . . .
The police was holding me because I'm really trying to kill myself that
day. . . . Because I was thinking, Sarah, if they catch him they send him
back. I'm pregnant. And then, where can I go? Who is going to help
me? . . . This is how criminals are treated. In our country it's horrible
to be a criminal. Criminals murder, things like this. Is he a criminal?
How is he a criminal? He just doesn't have a visa.

The next morning, their flatmates also moved out, leaving Marina alone with
a frightened toddler and a rapidly approaching due date.

By the time I heard Marina's account of that night—and of what happened
next—I had already heard the events of Joey's birth recounted twice, each time
by an Israeli human rights advocate appalled by what struck them as a crazy
urban legend. Here's the first version, as recounted at a weekly staff meeting
of the NGO that runs the Open Clinic, with a few details filled in.

Generosity—or Suspicion?

The other day, a Filipina woman traveled from her home in central Israel to
Bethlehem (across the Green Line in the Palestinian West Bank) to give
birth. Although she was obviously in labor, the soldiers at the military
checkpoint between (Israeli-controlled) Jerusalem and (the Palestinian city
of) Bethlehem refused to let her pass. Eventually they relented—but on the
condition that she cross on foot. The woman reached the hospital in Bethlehem, where she delivered a healthy baby boy not long after being admitted. *Her husband?* He's in jail, slated for deportation. Usually the (Israeli)
Ministry of Interior, if pressed, will release an unauthorized migrant from
detention if his wife has delivered—but this time it refused. *Why?* other
NGO staffers asked. The ministry official who received her petition—a
woman who once publicly compared herself to the little Dutch boy who
saved his country by plugging a crumbling dike with only his finger—
didn't believe the woman had just given birth. Only a gynecological examination would yield definitive proof, the official declared—hence the visit to
the Open Clinic arranged by Yael Friedman, an increasingly well-known
migrants' rights advocate who accompanied her to the clinic. *Unbelievable,*
the NGO staff members concurred.

Four days after this staff meeting, I encountered the superhuman figure of the laboring Filipina border-crosser once again, this time during an activist gathering at Yael's apartment. She and several other Israelis had recently established the Hotline for Migrant Workers (later the Hotline for Migrants and Refugees), a grassroots organization created to monitor the treatment of migrants who had been arrested, detained, and placed in deportation proceedings. Within a few years, the Hotline would become the country's most prominent migrant rights NGOs. At that early meeting in Yael's living room, however, their ranks were just beginning to swell.

As we sat in a large circle, Yael gave her own account of Marina's recent saga. She added a detail: Marina's delivery in Bethlehem was premature— several weeks before her due date. On the day prior to her delivery, Yael had appealed on Marina's behalf to the Ministry of Interior. By the time Yael and Marina appeared at the ministry, just hours after Marina had given birth, the (female) official in charge was incredulous. To her, Marina clearly had fabricated the story of her pregnancy by shoving pillows under her shirt, then borrowing a neighbor's baby in a crass effort to tug at Israeli heartstrings. Viewed through the ministry official's hermeneutic of suspicion, Marina was deceitful until proven otherwise—a savvy manipulator exploiting Israeli generosity to achieve her partner's release. Only one thing, the official decreed, could prove otherwise: a medicolegal examination of her body's most intimate parts.

Yael and other human rights activists took a different view altogether. From their standpoint, Marina's was clearly a victim's tale. Through their hermeneutic of generosity, Marina was not just vulnerable but also truthful, and deserving, and her decision to conceal her pregnancy from her employer was frankly immaterial. In their view, the ministry official's demand for an invasive examination simply redoubled the violence of an exclusionary government regime. As Yael described their meeting at the Ministry of Interior, the assembled activists grew incensed. Later I caught a ride back to central Tel Aviv with several of the most vocal critics, and the conversation continued on our drive homeward. "That woman is crazy," one insisted loudly as we squished tightly together in our driver's small car. "Completely nuts! And she has this horrible handwriting that she uses to determine issues of life and death—unbelievable!"

And what about Marina? In her account, this is above all a tale of embodied abjection: of being made to feel like ants, like dogs, like shit. In this chapter I explore how experiences of abjection can violate individuals' *sense of dignity* in ways that are purposeful and systematic—and existentially damaging. I return to her account later in the chapter—and to another important matter as well: the sense of indignation that catalyzed a small but vocal community of Israeli migrant advocates and activists and fueled their refusal to be complicit in their government's policies and actions.

But first, we must ask: What would it mean to explore dignity anthropologically? To engage this question, a genealogy is useful.

Genealogies of Dignity

Although it may have ancient roots, the notion of dignity, in this contemporary moment, has become a lively topic of both popular debate and scholarly concern. Dieter Grimm, a former justice of Germany's Federal Constitutional Court, describes dignity as "a rather old philosophical and a quite new legal concept of rapidly increasing interest."[2] Intellectual historian Samuel Moyn makes the similar observation that "'dignity' is suddenly everywhere in law and philosophy, even though it has long been in decline in general usage."[3] In the tight span of a recent decade, at least a dozen books appeared on the topic.[4]

Genealogies of dignity vary, but most converge around five distinct uses that follow a rough chronological sequence. First is the ancient Roman idea of *dignitas*, understood as worthiness, or rank. A second understanding, grounded in the Hebrew Bible, describes human beings as being created "in the image of God" (Hebrew: *b'tsélem elohím*; Latin: *imago Dei*). A third formulation, proposed by philosopher Immanuel Kant, anchors dignity in the human capacity for rational autonomy and moral action. A fourth claims dignity, black-boxed, as the definitive bedrock of human rights theory and practice. This fourth usage, which emerged in the twentieth century and undergirds a long list of human rights conventions and national constitutions, has been aptly described by one political scientist as "whatever it is about human beings that entitles them to basic human rights and freedoms."[5] A fifth, theologically informed set of usages stands in tension with the human rights interpretation: In some streams of Catholic thought, the notion of dignity has "long bolstered the vision of a highly hierarchical society."[6]

In a slim overview of the topic, philosopher Michael Rosen offers one final usage that leans helpfully, if coincidentally, in an anthropological direction. For Rosen, the concept of dignity may be "a mere receptacle" that holds "no coherent meaning of its own but is given content by a range of extraneous

political, social, and religious convictions."[7] As an ethnographer, I welcome
Rosen's recognition of the concept's malleability and polyvalence, even if
his broader philosophical aim—"to untangle the idea of dignity" by exploring the "*systematic* reasons behind the different (and often opposed) uses of
the term"[8]—diverges sharply from my aim here.

Beyond matters of definition and genealogy, scholars in philosophy,
political theory, law, bioethics, and public health have grappled with a wide
range of fundamental questions: How does the notion of dignity figure in
divergent domains of scholarship and practice? How is it related to other core
concepts like inequality, justice, recognition, capabilities, or human rights?
From an anthropological standpoint, something is palpably missing from
most of these accounts and analyses. In nearly every instance, dignity remains an idea: an abstraction untethered to everyday realities or existential
predicaments and constraints.

Anthropological Reticence

Despite the burgeoning interest in dignity in these other fields, anthropologists have had relatively little to say on the topic. One reason for this anthropological reticence is clear. Dignity is often engaged in normative terms, and
most sociocultural anthropologists strongly resist any blanket assertion of
universal human features or normative human values. We find a clear example, and an apt analogy, in anthropological work on human rights. As Mark
Goodale and others have explored at length, anthropology's relationship to
human rights has been rocky, ambivalent, and fraught with tension at least
since 1947, when the American Anthropological Association refused to throw
its weight behind the draft proposal that became the 1948 Universal Declaration of Human Rights.[9] A tremendous amount of ink has been spilled since
1947 over anthropology's relationship to human rights theory and practice.
And what, according to the Universal Declaration, is the bedrock of those
rights? Nothing less than dignity itself, as the declaration's first article makes
clear: "All human beings are born free and equal in dignity and rights."[10]
Against the backdrop of heated anthropological debate about human rights
themselves, the lack of anthropological engagement with their presumed
grounding becomes all the more interesting.

Another cluster of reservations would resonate with nineteenth-century
German thinkers like Karl Marx and Friedrich Nietzsche as well as Arthur

Schopenhauer, who, writing at a time when "various strands of 'human dignity' had . . . become fused into a cliché of pious humanitarianism," described
it as "the shibboleth of all perplexed and empty-headed moralists."[11] Can anthropologists engage dignity—either invoked by name or in a more expansive,
even metaphorical sense—and avoid these traps? Although anthropological
voices in current discussions of dignity have been relatively few and far between, this appears to be changing as a handful of anthropologists engage
the varied dimensions of this slippery concept: legal and moral, subjective
and intersubjective, aesthetic and sensorial, material and existential, emic
and etic.

In *Gangs, Politics and Dignity in Cape Town,* for instance, Steffen Jensen
invokes dignity as a central framing concept.[12] Dignity, he contends, is what's
left when all else is gone: "everybody supposedly has dignity, while at the
same time it is what nobody wants." In this sense, Jensen essentially swaps
out the central term in well-worn arguments about human rights[13] and puts
"dignity" in its stead. Although this move holds provocative potential, Jensen's
text offers it largely as summation rather than as point of departure for a
fuller analysis.

The relationship between dignity and human rights figures differently in
another South African study: Antina von Schnitzler's work on sanitation, citizenship, and legal claims making in Soweto. For von Schnitzler, dignity is
not a "presocial and prepolitical value that universally grounds claims to
human rights," but a mutable concept whose "precise meaning . . . is ultimately
often produced in court." She analyzes a legal case in which a South African
court faces a "paradoxical task": "to establish *how much* water would be required to sustain a 'dignified existence.'" Its task, "in other words . . . [is] to
measure a value commonly defined by its immeasurability and singularity."
Here dignity emerges as a potential vehicle for "transformative jurispru-
dence."[14] What's at stake in this neoliberal, postapartheid setting is the degree to which dignity can be successfully *performed* by those claiming harm
or, alternatively, *measured* by experts.

In addition to attorneys and judges, other "technicians of human dignity"
may include theologians, bioethicists, and political actors, as Gaymon Bennett explores in a book that conjoins bioethics, political theology, and a Fou-
cauldian strand of sociocultural anthropology. Bennett contends that growing
interest in human dignity stems from its transformation during the mid-
twentieth century from something that must be cultivated into something
that must be protected. Tracing key moments in Catholic theology (Vatican

II), human rights (the crafting of the Universal Declaration of Human Rights), and bioethics (the U.S. President's Council on Bioethics under George W. Bush), Bennett argues that "the figure of human dignity has, since the late 1940s, become a commonplace of political, ethical, and religious discourse and practice."[15] The resulting conceptions of dignity, he asserts, have transformed understandings of intrinsic human worth and precipitated new modes of governance and care.

Dignity also figures in medical anthropology, especially in studies of mental illness or, alternatively, of the proper treatment of human bodies and their constituent parts, especially at life's beginnings and endings.[16] Links among dignity, personhood, and the proper disposition of bodies and their parts figure in studies of reproduction and reproductive technologies, brain death, and the extraction and transplantation of human organs. Sherine Hamdy's ethnography of Islam and the bioethics of organ transplantation in Egypt offers one example. Interestingly, however, it is only in the final dotting of i's and crossing of t's that Hamdy comes to recognize the centrality of dignity to her analysis. As she explains in an epilogue, it is only in retrospect that she realizes her project hinges on two distinct but related concepts: *karama* (Arabic: the dignity of the living) as well as *hurma* (the dignity accorded the body after death).[17]

Others view dignity through a socioeconomic lens, for instance by probing links among dignity, debt, and social interconnectedness. Clara Han's ethnography of crushing debt, political violence, and social connectedness in Chile offers one example. Under the Pinochet dictatorship, ample state-provided credit "gave the poor access to material resources for a 'dignified life'": homes, appliances, furnishings, televisions, computers. In the postdictatorship period, however, the liberalization of the Chilean economy plunged poor families into debt, and the new key to *"vivir con dignidad"* (living with dignity) was to save face: to maintain an image of solvency and material success.[18] For many Chileans, what sustained these performances were quiet, even silent acts of care from neighbors, friends, and kin, many of whom were struggling themselves.

Rahul Chandrashekhar Oka's study of Somali refugees in a Kenyan refugee camp engages similar themes. As refugees, his research participants pursue what economists would call "irrational" consumer practices in an effort to achieve some measure of *sharaf* (in Somali) or *heshima* (KiSwahili), both of which Oka renders in English as "dignity."[19] The ability to buy small luxuries—tea or coffee, soft drinks, meals with meat or fish—provides a fleeting sense of normalcy and, as a result, of dignity regained. Oka suggests that "the act of purchasing and sharing favored foods that seem to temporarily minimize [the] realities of refugee life plays far more important a role than merely satisfying hunger."[20] What matters here is not just the luxury itself but often the very possibility of engaging in everyday forms of social reciprocity: sharing, and the welcoming gesture of hospitality.

My own approach builds on, while departing appreciatively from, these and related anthropological engagements—including anthropologist Jarrett Zigon's important caution against taking people's use of terms like dignity at face value.[21] Below, I ask: What happens if we reframe anthropological inquiry to put existential concerns front and center, then approach dignity through that prism?

Dignity: Lodestar, Vector, Striving

Earlier I suggested it is not the ethnographer's task to hammer out a precise definition of dignity or to seek conceptual correlates across languages and cultural settings. Reified or abstract conceptions of dignity, whatever their genealogy, would seem to hold little anthropological value, especially those ripped from the intersubjective matrix of human being-in-the-world. From an existential standpoint, as elaborated below, the notion of dignity is most visible, palpable, and useful when *in motion*: as dignity harmed, denied, violated, or stripped away—or, conversely, as dignity pursued, safeguarded, recuperated, reclaimed.

From this vantage point—which relinquishes any desire to define, schematize, or quantify—dignity emerges as a rich and lively metaphor. As more vector—a force with magnitude and direction—than thing. As a lodestar that guides the striving of individuals and groups, especially those whose social worlds are gridded by constraint and fraught with indeterminacy. Nussbaum puts it this way: "The notion of dignity is closely related to the idea of active striving."[22] Like physicists' particles and waves, metaphors like these—vector, lodestar, striving—can help us engage meaningfully with this otherwise abstract philosophical concept. As tools for making sense of ethnographic realities, such metaphors can help us "understand"[23] and "untangle"[24] the struggles that animate complex human lifeworlds.

This approach to dignity traces a wide semantic arc and points toward an array of imperatives that are widely shared—not in any normative sense, but in an experiential sense, as integral dimensions of what it means to be human. It casts dignity as one of those "existential values on which humans set greatest store" even if it does manage to "defy definition."[25] As one of those "vital sources of life"[26]—alongside freedom, respect, honor, recognition, trust, and agency. As a "scarce and elusive *existential* good . . . *whose value is incalculable.*"[27] Above all, it pushes back against any "dominant meaning of the concept" and encourages us to proceed, instead, by exploring "what the familiar concept of 'dignity' points to rather than taking it as the aim or end of moral activity."[28]

Understood in this way—as a *sense*—dignity gestures toward a powerful cluster of desires that are fundamental to most people's experience of being human: to be "recognized as a person in [one's] own right," as opposed to being "reduced to an object of other people's wills, a slave to their desires."[29] To feel meaningfully connected to others, rather than forcibly excluded or alienated from communal life. To feel grounded and secure in a world that can be disordered, unstable, and frightening. To exert some measure of control over our lives. To feel that the life circumstances into which we are thrown, whatever they may be, do not deny us the chance to shape the world we inhabit. To feel recognized as a person of worth, and value—as a person who matters, who counts. Human lives, values, and priorities differ in innumerable ways. Yet these values and priorities seem to converge in a certain existential imperative: the imperative to pursue what we might call a meaningful, dignified existence, a life in which we, and those for whom we care most deeply, can flourish.

How might we glimpse this sense of dignity? For ethnographers, our challenge is to understand how dignity is lived—both in positive terms, as dignity pursued, and in the breach. In this chapter, I build on the critical phenomenological framework developed earlier to consider how top-down policies, as well as individuals' words and actions, do not simply violate migrants' sense of dignity but also interfere with their capacity to pursue those ground projects that are so fundamental to who we are, as Mattingly puts it, that we might not recognize ourselves without them. Later in this chapter, I consider the ground projects of Israeli citizens who feel compelled to advocate on migrants' behalf—and in Chapter 5, I flip things around to explore how people facing sociopolitical abjection cleave to these existential imperatives despite the humiliations and harms they face below. Both in its violation and in its pursuit, individuals' sense of dignity is inherently social, relational, and intersubjective. As a result, it is always unstable—ever a precarious attainment, if it can be attained at all.

Dignity's Moving Parts

Not only is migrant illegality in Israel "lived through a palpable sense of deportability,"[30] as we saw in the previous chapter, but it often involves recurring threats to dignity and patterned forms of dignity violation. One way to approach these patterns is to consider what Nora Jacobson, inspired by public health pioneer Jonathan Mann, calls "all of dignity's moving parts."[31] Jacobson distinguishes between "two distinct (though related) phenomena . . . *Human dignity* is . . . the value that belongs to every human being simply by virtue of being human. *Social dignity* is generated in the interactions between and among individuals, collectives, and societies."[32] Put differently, human dignity is largely the bailiwick of theologians and philosophers, while social dignity—ever "extrinsic, subjective, contingent, and dynamic"[33]—opens up empirical questions of ethnographic significance.

To explore social dignity and its moving parts, Jacobson interviewed a diverse group of Canadians, many of them facing poverty, homelessness, and serious health vulnerability. Her findings yield two catalogs that are useful in parsing microprocesses of dignity violation as they unfold intersubjectively, in real time. First is a catalog of resources needed to live a "dignified life," among them physical necessities (air, water, food), conditions (hygiene, security), services (education, healing), instrumental supports (work, transportation, information), and social assets (personal relationships, recreation). Second is a catalog of offenses and affronts that she describes as "dangerous to dignity." Many items on this wide-ranging list—rudeness, condescension, diminishment, indifference, disregard, suspicion, objectification, discrimination, contempt, vilification, exploitation, assault—are familiar to my migrant interlocutors. These findings convey a sense of social dignity as "a quality of individuals and collectives . . . constituted through interaction and interpretation and structured by conditions pertaining to actors, relationships, settings, and the broader social order."[34]

Importantly, dignity violations are not just interpersonal; often they bear collective dimensions as well. Two political theorists—Hannah Arendt and

Avishai Margalit—are especially helpful in making sense of these broader reverberations. For Arendt, a "meaningful, dignified existence"[35] is contingent
on being a recognized participant in the political community. Exclusion from
the political community, in Arendt's view, means being denied the chance
to "live within a framework where you are judged according to *who*, and not
what, you are," or the opportunity to "be treated as a person based on your
words and deeds, and not merely on your membership in a category."[36] This,
in short, is the meaning of Arendt's famous observations regarding "the right
to have rights" and its abrogation. As philosopher Serena Parekh explains,
Arendt is keenly attuned to the "existential side of human rights" and "gives
a deeper dimension to the term 'human dignity' that is so often used in human
rights discourse."[37]

Arendt's view resonates with that of Margalit, who decries "the rejection of a person or a group of people from the human commonwealth"[38]
resulting, among other consequences, in humiliation. Humiliation, Margalit writes, involves "the rejection of human beings as human, that is,
treating people as if they were not human beings but merely things, tools,
animals, subhumans, or inferior humans."[39] Above all, it involves "blindness
to the human aspect"[40] of persons, individually or as a collective: seeing
them only in one dimension—or not seeing them at all. His central claim is
straightforward: a decent society is a society that does not humiliate.

Two clarifications sharpen Margalit's thesis. First, a decent society is a society whose institutions do not humiliate. Second, a decent society does not
humiliate "*anyone* under its jurisdiction"—whether or not they are citizens.[41]
Margalit notes explicitly that his philosophical argument is influenced by his
own experience—he is both an Israeli philosopher and a leading antioccupation activist—including his exposure to the systematic ways in which the
Israeli occupation humiliates Palestinians. Elsewhere he draws empirical support for his argument from the case of migrant workers in the United States,
those "illegal Mexican immigrants whose lack of a work license turns them
into serfs, if not degraded slaves, of the employers who keep them and hide
them" as well as other "foreign workers (*Gastarbeiter*), who do the dirty work
in developed countries without being citizens there."[42] Margalit's inattention
to the analogous population in his own country is simply an artifact of time;
his book appeared in 1996, just as migrant workers were beginning to reach
Israel in large numbers.

Already we have beheld the humiliating impact of the gerush and its various techniques and strategies. Recall Patricia's impassioned account of the

late night arrest of her husband, Kwejo: "This is not how you treat human beings but how you treat animals." Similarly, Marina's recounting of Raymond's arrest invoked metaphors both bestial and fecal. For these women and their partners, Margalit's words ring painfully true: "Humiliation involves an existential threat."[43]

Arendt and Margalit are iconoclastic thinkers, and certainly neither is an empirical researcher. Yet their insights support the ethnographic project advanced here: the project of exploring what a *sense of dignity*, broadly and existentially construed, might mean in human lives.

A Catalog of Violations

If a meaningful, dignified existence is contingent on living "within a framework where you are judged according to *who*, and not *what*, you are"—if it depends on being "treated as a person based on your words and deeds, and not merely on your membership in a category"—then the sociopolitical abjection faced by illegalized migrants in Israel forecloses precisely this possibility. Well before the gerush, Israeli state efforts to criminalize unauthorized migrants had pushed most of them into zones of anxious clandestinity. Once the mass deportations were under way, migrants' vigilance about avoiding unwanted attention only intensified. Most took pains to avoid arguing with employers or appealing to the police for protection. Few were willing to speak to the media (as I learned on the one occasion I tried, and failed, to help a journalist find someone willing to talk about obstacles to obtaining reproductive health care). And, as we will soon see, most were unwilling to organize politically. Although the quest for invisibility proved challenging for most, it verged on the impossible for migrants from Africa and Asia, whose bodily features were especially likely to be read as evidence of their Otherness and the consequent impossibility of their assimilation into the Jewish-Israeli collective.[44]

Chapter 3 examines these local biopolitics and their roots in Israel's local moral economy of inclusion and exclusion, deservingness and undeservingness. Here, I take up a different question: How might illegalization, criminalization, and sociopolitical abjection violate migrants' sense of dignity, or confound their efforts to pursue the ground projects that anchor them in the world? How might these incursions interrupt people's strivings for a flourishing future? Ethnographic investigation of these questions yields its own catalog of violations, a catalog rife with accounts of being "nobodied," accused, humiliated, animalized, silenced, and expelled.

"Nobodied"

To minimize their risk of unwanted exposure to the Immigration Police, some people I knew massaged their life stories into innocuous personae that would fit their employers' stereotypes, or the stereotypes they imagined their employers held. Yvonne, whom I met two years before the gerush, was among my first instructors in these games of tactical self-representation. A university-educated single mother from Nigeria, Yvonne shared an apartment in Florentin with her three-year-old Israeli-born son, Junior; an older Nigerian couple; and another single tenant. Before we settled down in the apartment's common room to talk, Yvonne showed me the small room she and Junior shared: narrow, tidy, modestly furnished. She showed me the book she was reading on bus rides to, from, and between housecleaning jobs: a thick paperback, probably seven hundred pages long, about three generations of Chinese women during the Communist Revolution. When we met in 2000, well before the gerush, she felt comfortable reading on public buses without focusing obsessively on the doors. Once at work, however, she never mentioned her university education, or even her reading habits. "Of course I can't realize my potential," she said. "At work, you know, I'm a different person, a nobody. You *try* to be a nobody. At work, I don't have an identity. . . . We learn this from other people's experience. You're not intelligent, you don't like anything cultural or artistic, you can't conduct an intelligent conversation. Do you understand me? Among us are doctors and nurses, do you understand? Lawyers, architects, engineers, you understand? Teachers, people with master's degrees, MBAs, MScs. Do you understand?" To secure her livelihood and stabilize her lifeworld and that of her young son, Yvonne felt compelled to downplay her intelligence, her education, and her worldliness. Instead, she pursued what philosopher Lewis Gordon, elaborating on Fanon, describes as a kind of "perverse anonymity."[45] Fanon writes in *Black Skin, White Masks*, "I am overdetermined from the outside. . . . I slip into corners; I keep silent; all I want is to be anonymous, to be forgotten. Look, I'll agree to everything, on condition I go unnoticed!" Our conversation, it seemed, offered temporary reprieve from this crushing sense of racialized erasure, a chance to step back from its absurdity and respond to my curiosity with her own moral demands: a demand to bear witness. To understand.

Yvonne's tactics of self-effacement certainly were not unique. I heard similar accounts from others, especially Africans with professional backgrounds, including an architect, a midwife, a teacher, and a bank official. Their remarks bring to mind Liliana Suárez-Navaz's ethnography of irregular migration to Spain. There, Suárez-Navaz suggests, immigrants "always have to prove they are *not* what people think of them."[46] While this may hold true for some, Yvonne and other migrants I met in Israel felt burdened by the opposite: to them, it felt safer to perform a dumbed-down version of what one imagined people think of them.

Fanon's searing reflections on racialization and racism pulse through Yvonne's account of her efforts to disappear into "nobodiness." For unauthorized migrants who are judged habitually for *what* they are—"illegal" migrants, Africans, Asians, non-Jews—rather than *who* they are, the self-denigrating pursuit of "nobodiness" takes a deep existential toll. Yvonne's words also reveal a telling similarity between Israel's various "national abjects"—specifically, between her status as an other Other, and that of the country's designated real Others, Palestinians. Citing the terse poetry of Dennis Silk, Margalit notes that the labor regime that developed between 1967 and the first intifada hinged on a bargain similar to the one Yvonne describes. Margalit writes of "'vanishing powder' that is sprinkled, so to speak, on Arabs from the occupied territories who work in Israel, a powder that makes them invisible: 'A good Arab must work, not be seen.'"[47]

When we spoke in her living room, Yvonne insisted her tactics were all performance, yet representation and experience are entwined in complex ways. This complex interrelationship between racism, nobodiness, performance, and dignity is precisely what animates Martin Luther King, Jr.'s revolutionary "Letter from a Birmingham Jail."[48] Addressed to the group of white religious leaders who publicly opposed his direct strategies for advancing civil rights as "unwise and untimely," King admonished them in soaring prose. He described his as a struggle of utmost urgency for those who "are forever fighting a degenerating sense of 'nobodiness.'" What his fellow ministers failed to grasp, King argued, was the gravity of what was being denied, from an existential standpoint: the chance, in Arendt's terms, to be judged according to *who*, and not *what*, one is.

Accused

The risk of being nobodied is especially high for live-in caregivers, for whom boundaries between "work" and "home" can become uncomfortably blurred as two distinct forms of care—the professional labors of caregiving and the personalized, affective investment of caring concern—become uncomfortably entwined. This blurring of boundaries only deepens the vulnerability of migrant caregivers to "dignity assaults," as anthropologist Cati Coe observes in her ethnography of Ghanaian home health workers in the United States.[49] The assaults Coe enumerates—enduring classist and racist attitudes, needing to accommodate employers' sleep schedules and eating customs, feeling stuck or even imprisoned—are especially acute for migrant workers who lack legal authorization. Lorena, a Filipina woman whose life was turned upside down by a false accusation of theft, helped me see how such conjugations of vulnerability[50] can threaten not just one's livelihood but also one's sense of dignity.

Lorena is tall and thin, shy and soft-spoken. Her delicate smile melded a deep sense of humility with quiet resignation to the circumstances of a life far from home, and far from her own eight children. Before coming to Israel, she lived with her husband and their family in a rural community in the Philippines, where she sold vegetables at the local market. When we met she was in her mid-forties, and she knew exactly how long she had worked for the Sterns, a Jewish Israeli family of five: "nine years and one month." Although formally hired as a caregiver—the only arrangement through which most Filipinos could work legally in Israel—she was actually employed as the Sterns' nanny and housekeeper. The family's two older boys had been in high school when she arrived, but their daughter had been just nine. "I essentially raised her," Lorena told me. "My own daughter I didn't care for like that." When Lorena's visa expired after four and a half years, she simply continued working. No one made a fuss.

During her nine-plus years in their home, Lorena felt gratified to have earned the Sterns' respect and affection. They treated her as an integral part of the family, she said. When she faced an occasional bout of sadness or loneliness, she reminded herself that her wages were advancing her children, one by one, through high school, then college. And she thought of her grandchildren, now two years old and eight months in age, although she had never met them in person.

In fact, Lorena had seen her own children just once since arriving in Israel, on a difficult visit three years after her initial departure from home. On that visit, she was devastated to learn that her youngest, who had been five months old when she left, now called her eldest daughter "Mommy." Lorena told her husband she would prefer to stay in the Philippines with them, but he insisted she return: "You must stay in Israel to educate the children." And so, feelings bruised but aware that her earnings were vital to her children's future, she returned to Israel, and to the Sterns.

Years later, a valuable diamond necklace suddenly disappeared—and Lorena's life was upended in an instant. To her shock, Mrs. Stern jumped to accuse Lorena of theft, spitting out her words with a harshness she had never before seen. "Of course I didn't take the necklace!" Lorena told me. "The wife is irresponsible with her jewelry, and her daughter likes to take jewelry and wear it." Lorena insisted she was innocent, but the accusation stood. The Sterns demanded she repay them the cost of the necklace (US$2,000) and threatened to call the police. Terrified, Lorena packed her overnight bag and left. She never returned to retrieve the rest of her belongings. This cascade of violations—unwarranted suspicion, vilification, humiliation, contempt—left her shaken and fearful.

Lorena felt fortunate that she could quickly find full-time "live-out" work with some friends of the Sterns, whose home she had cleaned on her days off for the previous seven years. Their continued trust provided some solace, and she was thankful to find full-time accommodations in a shared flat with several other Filipinos. Yet her everyday life was now darkened by perpetual anxiety and fear. She was afraid to open the door to the apartment. Of the spinning blue lights on the police car down the street. Of getting on a bus to go to work. "What should I do if I'm arrested?" Lorena often asked me, aware of my involvement with Mesila, where we first met when she brought her young niece seeking care for an unwanted pregnancy. "How long do they keep you in jail?" I had few answers, but each time she asked I scribbled down the relevant phone numbers and addresses I knew. Beyond that, I could offer little reassurance. "This is the worst thing that has happened to me in my life," Lorena told me through tears as we sat in a hospital waiting room while her niece met with an obstetrician. "If my children were done studying, I'd be happy to go home. But they're still studying, and if they can't complete their undergraduate degrees then all my hard work and sacrifice will be lost. It's not like we [Filipinos] want to stay here forever. I miss my family. I just need three or four more years."

Humiliated despite her innocence, Lorena eventually told her children what had happened but extracted their promise not to tell their father. She feared his reaction, and she was determined to see their educations through. She had weathered the pain of distance as her children had grown and matured, the waning of their affection, even her displacement as mother. All of these blows had been bearable as long as she felt confident that her absence had a purpose.

By continuing to work for the Sterns long past the expiration of her visa, Lorena had been lulled into a false sense of security. Her national origin and outward appearance—as a (now-undocumented) Filipina woman in an anonymizing sea of tens of thousands of *documented* Filipina workers—had buffered her from unwanted police attention. Now the precariousness of her status and her risk of deportability were constantly palpable, and nearly paralyzing. When I asked, she found it difficult to say what was worse: the indignity of having lost her long-time employers' trust or the shame and humiliation of suddenly being criminalized for doing what she had long felt, as a long-distance mother, was best for her family.

Humiliated

For pregnant women and new mothers, the risks and challenges were different. Before the gerush, many women had insisted that pregnancy and new motherhood conferred a feeling of protection and a meaningful measure of immunity to arrest. Once the deportation campaign was under way, however, whatever flimsy protections may have existed largely disappeared. Now the authorities were suspicious of women's claims to be pregnant or the mother of a small child. This new hermeneutic of suspicion had profound consequences for Marina, whose partner was arrested late in her second pregnancy, and for Olivia, who struggled to care for a toddler, a newborn, and a husband who was too terrified to leave the apartment for work. Whether the impact was immediate and direct, as for Marina, or indirect, as for Olivia, this shift in governmental disposition left many women both fearful and humiliated.

Supi, a single mother from Ghana, had much to say on the topic. About 18 months into the gerush, she and I sat side by side in a South Tel Aviv meeting hall catching up while waiting for a gathering of West African religious and community leaders to begin. The forum met weekly to address issues of common concern, and this week, arrest and police violence were on the docket.

Today, the group would host a guest speaker: Yael Friedman of the Hotline for Migrant Workers (as I discuss later in the chapter).

As we waited for others to arrive, Supi offered her own perspective on the electrified atmosphere. "People are being treated like animals," she said. "They didn't used to arrest women, but now they're arresting women—even pregnant women." I realized as she spoke that the two of us were among the only women in the hall, and she may have been the only mother. She told me of a pregnant Nigerian woman she knew who had been deported, and another pregnant woman who had been arrested a day or so earlier and was still detained.

New mothers were vulnerable as well, including Felicia, a thirty-five-year-old Ghanaian woman and mother of a six-month-old baby girl, who was arrested outside of her apartment building in a Tel Aviv suburb.[51] The authorities still seemed hesitant to arrest mothers of small children—especially single mothers like Felicia, whose husband had been deported to Ghana just a month earlier—but such unwritten protections hinged on the arresting officers' willingness to believe a mother's claims. In Felicia's case, they were skeptical.

When she was arrested, Felicia pulled out her daughter's photograph and health card from the municipal Mother-Child Clinic, but the officers paid them no heed. "'It's not true, she's lying,'" she recalled one of them saying. "He ordered me to get into the police car and pushed me in." At the police station, "They asked me: 'Where's the baby?' and I said: 'In my friend's house.' They said: 'Let's go there,' and I agreed. On the way, the policeman who was driving asked me . . . 'What kind of diaper does she have?' and I said: 'Huggies.' 'And what is she wearing on top?' . . . [so] I told him. He asked me again who was taking care of her and I told him my friend was." The officers drove her to the address provided. When they found no one home, "The officer driving the car started pushing and beating me. Then he kicked me hard. I fell down, and he stomped on my stomach and kept kicking me with his shoes [on]. He had a flashlight in his hand, and he hit me on the head with it until everything went black." Later, at police headquarters, an officer interviewed Felicia and called her "a big liar."

When an immigration official eventually did agree to review the documents in her possession—including her daughter's birth certificate and hospital release papers—he conceded that Felicia was, in fact, telling the truth. Even after her friend arrived with the baby, however, the arresting officers remained doubtful. They asked if she was breast-feeding. When she said yes, "They said they would bring a woman to check and see if I'm really nursing.

I agreed, and I was taken to the toilets. The woman started squeezing milk out of my breasts as if I were her cow. After a few minutes they agreed to give me my baby and told me to go."

Felicia's encounter lends empirical strength to both Arendt's and Margalit's arguments. The arresting officers' vision, forged in an atmosphere of racialized biopolitics, top-down xenophobia, and institutional suspicion, afforded them little more than a cipher-like view. Regarding Felicia as less than fully human, they found it acceptable to treat her in the manner she describes: like an animal. Untroubled by the sloppiness of their heuristics, the officers acted on a presumption of *what* Felicia was, paying little heed to *who* she might be. They were quick to silence and accuse; to demean her and violate the intimate boundaries of her body. With relative ease, she was denied political belonging (as Arendt put it), cast outside the human commonwealth (in Margalit's terms), and excluded from the moral community (following Didier Fassin). Eventually she was released. But first, she was humiliated.

Animalized

This chapter began with Marina's downward spiral from legality to illegality, and from respectability to humiliation. A key point in this downward spiral involved her late-night odyssey from her flat in central Israel toward Jerusalem by minibus, and across the Green Line to deliver her second baby, Joey, in a Palestinian hospital in Bethlehem. At the time, Marina's toddler, Eden, was in a neighbor's care, and her partner, Raymond, was jailed pending deportation on grounds of unauthorized residence.

As we heard earlier, human rights activists were indignant, if unsurprised, to hear how Marina and her partner had been treated by representatives of the state—including the Ministry of Interior official who demanded she undergo a gynecological exam to prove she had just delivered. But this was not the worst of her humiliations. The simple and devastating fact is that this time around, Marina hadn't wanted to be pregnant at all. For her, as for many other poor women who are denied access to contraception and reproductive health care, sociopolitical abjection manifested itself as a form of biological tyranny: as the inability to terminate an unwanted pregnancy.

At first, she didn't even know she was pregnant. During our first long conversation in her family's one-room flat, Marina told me her periods were always irregular, and she had felt none of the sensations she recalled from her first pregnancy with Eden: sensitivity to smells, dizziness, vomiting. This time, "I didn't feel anything. It was normal." She had recently begun a new job as a nanny in the upscale suburb of Ramat Aviv, and as her family's sole breadwinner she was loath to lose it. When Marina finally realized what was happening, she felt unmoored.

As she described her frantic and ultimately failed effort to obtain an abortion, my mind was racing. I thought through the various options I could have presented to her had we met across the reception desk at the Open Clinic, or during one of my afternoon shifts at Mesila. And I recalled the time, not too long ago, when I had faced a similar predicament myself, but with more luck, more social support, and more money. As I listened to Marina's story, I found it hard to contain my frustration that she had failed to benefit from the small but sturdy network of reproductive health care resources that a cluster of Israeli activists had cobbled together.

Lacking medically supervised options, Marina had tried, unsuccessfully, to terminate the pregnancy by taking various drugs recommended by friends. She described one of them as an ulcer medication that can cause miscarriage as a side effect; most likely it was misoprostol, which was available for pregnancy termination in Israel, but only by prescription. Despite these regulatory controls, I knew other migrant women who also had obtained and self-administered the drug, with similarly disappointing results. Following these failed attempts, some would wait out the rest of their pregnancies wracked with anxiety, terrified about the potential harm they might have caused the fetus.

When the ulcer drug failed Marina, she turned in desperation to a hospital in Tel Aviv, where her suspicions that a surgical abortion would be too expensive were quickly confirmed. "How much?" I asked. "Four thousand shekels," she laughed cynically—about US$1,000. "Where can I get the 4,000 shekels?"

Her next option was a Palestinian hospital in the West Bank. "I heard in Bethlehem they do abortions," she explained, so "I went to Bethlehem. I was alone." When she arrived, the doctor refused to terminate the pregnancy, "because it's a very big baby inside." What they suggested next she found appalling. They said, "If I cannot afford to have a baby, they are willing to help me to have a baby, and after I give birth they will take the baby." "What did you think of that?" I asked. "I was thinking, I carry it nine months, and after that I am giving them? . . . It is not normal. It is not [something] a human being [should do]. I think it's like a dog because it's giving the child [up]. So I was thinking, if I am carrying the child this nine months, then afterwards I am giving them—no. I cannot do that." Although innumerable adoptive parents and adopted children would take umbrage at this characterization, Marina experienced this proposal as an affront to her humanity. Could her best option really be to gestate a child, then relinquish it—in her words, "like a dog"?

Unsettled by her experience in Bethlehem, Marina turned back to Israeli hospitals, where she received confirmation, once again, that a pregnancy at that stage could technologically and legally be terminated, but the cost was simply insurmountable. Then, like many other women whose lives are constrained by interlocking systems of structural vulnerability, she resigned herself to biology: she would carry the unwanted pregnancy to term—the pregnancy, ironically, that she was too poor to avoid. And like many other women in her position, she sought divine help: "I decided that okay, maybe God can help me with everything, maybe I can continue this. I've got nothing [else] to do."

This was the backdrop to Marina's late-night race to Bethlehem one November night, contractions well under way and her partner in jail, to deliver her second child. She had been exhausted all evening and begged her daughter to sleep. "I'm so tired. So 8:00, 9:00, until 11:00, again at 1:00 I still feel so bad." As the night wore on, she started "talking to my baby, saying, 'Maybe tomorrow you can come out.'" When she realized the contractions were only growing stronger and closer together, she asked her friend Jeannie to take her to Ichilov, a public hospital in Tel Aviv, to deliver. A mutual friend had undergone surgery there and been charged 3,000 shekels per day—and when the friend was unable to pay, Jeannie warned her, the hospital had been reluctant to remove her stitches. She tried to convince Marina to avoid a similar fate by traveling to Bethlehem, where Jeannie had delivered her own child. "'Why Ichilov?'" she asked. "'You don't have much money. . . . If you have the time to go to Bethlehem, I will help you to go there.' I said, 'It's the middle of the night.'" Short on options, Marina conceded, and together they embarked on their late-night journey.

When they arrived at the checkpoint between Israeli-controlled Jerusalem and the Palestinian city of Bethlehem, the Israeli soldiers on patrol were confused. "They kept asking us 'Why Bethlehem? There's no hospital in Israel? No—go back to Israel!" She recalled threats: "You cannot go there because otherwise we will shoot you!" It was dark—the middle of the night—and Jeannie was afraid. Marina remembered crying, and being unable to walk. Eventually "one of the soldiers saw I'm not pretending." He pitied her and let them through.

On the Palestinian side of the border, the taxi drivers were "very nice"; they carried her into a taxi and took her straight to the hospital. There was no doctor on duty when she arrived—"only the nurse, but I cannot wait already. I just lay down and pushed, and after a few minutes my baby came. When I lay down there it's 4:30." Joey was born at 5:15 A.M.

After lunch, Marina signed herself and her newborn out of the hospital against medical advice. "They said it's not normal. I am begging them. I told them, explained that I have a first baby in Tel Aviv, no one will take care of her. But I'm normal, I'm okay, I'm strong."

"And the baby was healthy?" I asked, stealing a glance at him from across the chilly room.

"All thanks [to] God, he's okay. He's healthy. I thank God for that." The doctor on duty had strongly disapproved of her discharge request. "He said, 'I'm going to sign, but you have to sign this that if something happens to you, it's not our responsibility. Because you are forcing us to sign.'" It sounded like the physician was concerned primarily with the hospital's liability, but other hospital staff were less charitable. "They said, 'You are an animal.' I said, 'I don't care what you are saying, I just want to go home.'"

Later, she heard similar things from members of her own community. "All my people, they say that, 'Oh, you are like a pig that you give birth and then you run already."

"Who said this?" I asked. "Filipino people?"

"Yeah, because they are wondering, 'Why [did] you just give birth and then [you're] home already?" In a later conversation, I heard Marina describe her experience in these very terms: "I just lay down and gave birth. Just like a pig that gave birth and went home."

After returning home with newborn Joey and picking up Eden from her neighbors, the first thing Marina did was travel to Yael Friedman's office at the Hotline to seek help achieving Raymond's release from jail: "Because I really need to go. I really need him to come out. I really need the help." When she and Yael reached the Ministry of Interior, as we've heard, the official they encountered accused her of fabrication and deceit.

Channeling Indignation

Yael and her fellow activists and advocates couldn't prevent ordeals like Marina's, but they could offer some measure of support or even, on occasion, resolution or redress. Who are these activists and advocates, what sparked their interest in people like Marina—and what fueled their indignation?

Early in my fieldwork, I sought out volunteer opportunities at the Open Clinic, the Hotline for Migrant Workers, and Mesila—not just to meet migrants and launch my project but also as an act of solidarity, and in the hope of offering something to the city's migrant communities in return. What I initially failed to realize was that my organizational promiscuity was raising eyebrows, and suspicions.

This suspiciousness underpins the distinction I draw in this book between politically engaged *activist* groups, like the Hotline and the Open Clinic, and *advocacy* groups like Mesila which, in keeping with its municipal mandate, works hard to steer clear of overt political statements. Israeli activists and advocates have much in common, and relationships among them, and their organizations, are dynamic and evolving in response to internal leadership changes as well as shifts in municipal and national policy. Still, significant differences in ideology and political outlook sustain palpable tensions that, on occasion, erupt in overt expressions of mistrust or even outright hostility.

Given my own organizational involvements, I was curious about the many volunteers and professionals I came to know. Three things were clear: most were Ashkenazi, many were women, and hardly any lived in South Tel Aviv. At Mesila, most staff members were professional social workers, including Ayelet (who sent me to Comfort's side after the building collapse on Natan Street), Meirav (who was troubled by the Immigration Administration's hardened stance toward mothers and children), and Danna (who took me on her rounds of South Tel Aviv daycares a decade after the gerush). We've met Uri, the music teacher who offered music classes in a pirate day care as a Mesila volunteer. At the Hotline, I met activists like Ma'ayan (whose experience fielding calls from migrant workers and employers left her "exploding from the inside") and her friend and compatriot, Yael.

The Open Clinic also drew a varied bunch: Ilanit, an artist and South Tel Aviv resident who preferred her new African neighbors to the injection drug users who hung out on her street. Yaniv, a hipster high school graduate who opted for National Service (*Sherút Leumí*) in lieu of compulsory military service, then was disappointed to find himself working with migrant workers instead of Palestinians. Marcela, an elegant bookstore owner and, decades earlier, *oláh* (Jewish immigrant) from South America, who kept tabs on Spanish-speaking patients long after her volunteer shifts. And I'll never forget elderly Leah, a tiny woman with failing vision, a severe limp, and the formal Hebrew of a television broadcaster. Although she strained to read computer screens, Leah's voice never faltered when she enumerated the wrongs committed against migrant workers, which she saw as evidence that the nation's moral fiber was fraying and her own Zionist dreams eroding.

Increasingly intrigued by the diversity within this motley crew, I felt compelled to learn more. Over the years, I interviewed more than forty migrant advocates and activists, sometimes on multiple occasions, among them men and women, young adults and retirees, occasional volunteers and pioneering civil society leaders. A few were intimate friends, many were acquaintances, and some I was meeting for the first time. While I cannot dive deeply into their stories here,[52] two common features bear particular mention. Although their motives and politics ranged widely, these advocates and activists had two things in common: a strong sense of indignation at their government's treatment of global migrants and migrant families, and a refusal to be complicit in migrants' abjection from the nation's moral community. Instead, most sought concrete opportunities to connect with their newly arrived neighbors face to face.

Advocates and activists invoked different idioms of social justice mobilization in explaining their motives and goals. Some pointed to human rights; others to a sense of humanitarian compassion. Some felt compelled by their own professional code of ethics (for instance as a social worker or health professional, journalist, or attorney), while others drew moral lessons from Jewish historical experience or collective memory. Hardly any articulated their motives in religious terms, although a few, especially at Mesila, spoke of "Judaism as culture and not religion," or cited well-known biblical phrases like "love your neighbor as yourself," while insisting the value of such statements was primarily humanistic, not religious.

Whatever their motives, most advocates and activists hoped to achieve more than simply help a handful of people. What most sought, and many found, were opportunities to enact a set of values that ran counter to those driving government policies they found objectionable. Often this involved an explicit effort to "transform their identities and radically re-envision their place in relation to other members of the community."[53] Importantly, these motives and values did not necessarily align strictly with those of the organizations individuals joined. For many, the pathway to migrant advocacy or activism was less the result of comparative deliberation and selection among discrete options than a function of social networks, or happenstance. As a result, interviews occasionally revealed surprises—like the volunteer physicians at the Physicians for Human Rights–Israel Open Clinic who were more humanitarians than human rights activists, or the Mesila volunteer who described herself as an anarchist and an antioccupation activist.

For those who felt compelled to join the migrant aid and activist community in the years of the gerush, what options were available? In addition to Mesila, with its municipal roots and commitments, the first major efforts on global migrants' behalf arose in the late 1990s by established human rights organizations. The Open Clinic, for instance, was established in 1998 by Physicians for Human Rights-Israel, which had been founded a decade earlier to protest Israeli violations of Palestinians' health and human rights in the OPT. Although the clinic's rapid growth bespoke urgent need among the city's migrants, some staff and board members saw it as a distraction from the organization's original aim of fighting to end the occupation. Other key players included the Association for Civil Rights in Israel, the oldest and most broad ranging human rights organization in the country (established in 1972), and the Kav La'Oved Workers' Hotline. Established in 1991, Kav La'Oved was created to protect the labor rights of Israeli citizens and Palestinians living in the OPT, but readily expanded to include both authorized and unauthorized migrant workers. Other NGOs were grassroots products, including the Hotline for Migrant Workers. Established in 1998 to monitor the conditions of migrants who had been arrested, in time the Hotline grew to become the country's leading migrant rights NGO.

At the time of the gerush, Israel's landscape of advocacy and activism differed from its analogs in Western Europe and North America. Rather than lobbying for citizenship rights or even regularization of migrants' status, local goals were more modest, like the enforcement of existing labor laws, health care access for vulnerable groups, and protection from deportation on humanitarian grounds. Notably, these Israeli groups tended not to link migrants' needs or rights to other political causes or movements. Although this avoidance of coalition building was often strategic, some advocates (but not activists) were committed to observing a bright line between their support for migrants and other campaigns linked to the political left, especially efforts framed as antioccupation or pro-Palestinian.

Yet the most striking feature of this landscape in the era before the gerush was something else altogether: the relative absence of political activism by migrants themselves. Unlike countries in which migrants enacted what anthropologist Peter Nyers calls "abject cosmopolitanism" in order to resist their "targeted exclusion,"[54] in this era Israelis almost always took the lead. Migrants who tried to join them—including Naana Holdbrook, to whom we'll soon return—often paid a steep price.

Refusing Complicity

> It is better to be in disagreement with the whole world
> than, being one, to be in disagreement with myself.
> —Plato

For Marina, Raymond, and other migrants facing sociopolitical abjection, the pursuit of dignity is an existential imperative. For Israelis involved with migrant advocacy and activist organizations, most of whom have not experienced sociopolitical abjection in their own flesh, this pursuit takes different shape and form. For these Israelis, it is not the lived experience of violation or exclusion that compels them to respond but an awareness that *others* are being violated and excluded *in their name*. For many, the pursuit of dignity is thus principally a moral, as opposed to an existential, striving. We might describe it as a defense of human, as distinguished from social, dignity. In practice, this pursuit involves a refusal to be implicated in the abjection of others or in their exclusion from the moral community. In a sense, their refusal is an enactment of what critical theorist Ariella Azoulay calls the "fundamental and inalienable right . . . not to be perpetrators."[55]

The distinction I draw tentatively here—between the pursuit of social dignity as existential imperative and the pursuit of human dignity as moral imperative—was evident at the Friday evening leaders' meeting where I caught up with Supi, and where Yael was guest speaker.

"The situation is very bad," Yael told the group once everyone had settled in, "and I don't think it will improve." She described the Immigration Police's changing tactics, introduced some of the Hotline's efforts to promote legal and policy change, and instructed her audience to be cautious if the police did show up at their door. "You can demand to see a warrant," she said, but took care to mention the potential risk in trying to realize this right. "There is a chance that if you demand a warrant in an assertive way, they might still break down the door and beat you—maybe even more because you asked." A no-nonsense pragmatist, she strongly cautioned against any actions or comments that might be interpreted as either manipulation or insubordination. "If they manage to break down the door and you say your passport is in the embassy, or with friends, [this] makes them angry, and makes them beat you even harder."

Yael said that a recent Hotline report documented a pattern of violence and humiliation during arrests: breaking down doors during late-night raids, arrest of parents in front of their young children, physical abuse, serious injury.[56] When Hotline activists presented their findings at a special Knesset session, she continued, the head of the Immigration Police minimized their scope and gravity, insisting that "only" twenty-three apartment doors had been broken, and that officers had a warrant in each case. In her presentation to the gathered African community leaders, Yael flatly rejected his claim: "I saw more than 23 just during Passover"—a holiday, it bears mention, that lasts just seven days.[57]

Her recommendations offered little hope of bringing the gerush to a halt; at best, following Yael's advice might cushion the impact of arrest and deportation on a few individuals or families. Still, this leaders' meeting offered Supi and her compatriots a rare opportunity for face-to-face conversation—on their terms, and their turf—with an Israeli who shared their outrage over the indignities and fears engendered by the gerush. It also created a unique space of dialogue by giving the leaders an equally rare opportunity to voice their fears, frustrations, and anger to an attentive Israeli audience—even if it was an audience of one, and even if they were lobbing their complaints at the wrong target, as the forum's leader pointed out with some concern.

Nearly all of the leaders' protestations involved violations of dignity and fierce desires to see it reclaimed. "If you are illegal, you are not a criminal," one leader insisted." "They should not treat us as if we are animals," declared another. Eventual departure from Israel was inevitable, most seemed to agree. What mattered were the terms and circumstances: "We would not like to go home as prisoners. . . . We shall go, but not by arrest."

Some of the leaders' pleas for mercy invoked potent historical analogies. "Okay, I overstayed," one said, "but we shouldn't be sent home in chains. They are reminding us of something: the slave trade. They are reminding us of Poland, Germany, taking someone in front of his wife, children." Others were blunter still: "We the foreigners know we are illegal, [but] this is a minor picture of the Holocaust." Rather than contesting such analogies or calling for greater precision or nuance, Yael described a conversation with a police officer about a smaller-scale deportation campaign eight years earlier during which migrants had been arrested on the streets, in full public view. She remembered the officer telling her that "many old people complained" that it stirred up images of the Holocaust. Instead of stopping the deportations, Yael continued, the police had changed their tactics to "go to houses because no one sees."

Although she reiterated several times that she was a human rights activist and neither a political leader nor a police functionary, many of Yael's interlocutors appealed to her as a potential guarantor of their dignity and a stand-in for other Israelis—those before whom they most wanted to supplicate, negotiate, historicize, self-humanize. For them, the struggle for dignity was a matter of both practical and existential concern.

Yael Friedman's choice to put herself in uncomfortable situations like this one over and over, day after day, and year after year reflects the moral imperative she and I discussed at length on several occasions. For reasons both personal and political, her refusal to be complicit—and, moreover, her well-publicized efforts to combat state strategies of abjection—were fundamental to her sense of self and her understanding of citizenship and its obligations.

Yael's level of commitment to migrant aid and activism is unusual, as is her capacity to persist without burning out. Some might describe her dedication in terms of selflessness or altruism, but these frames fall short—and they miss a crucial point. Although I never asked directly, I am confident that Yael and many other migrant advocates and activists would agree with philosopher Michael Rosen that the "duty to respect the dignity of humanity" is—at least on some level—"fundamentally a duty toward ourselves."[58] In this respect, they stand not only with Plato and Socrates but also with their interpreter Hannah Arendt. For Arendt, these conceptions of moral duty have no theological basis. Rather, they are about the capacity to live with oneself: "Since even when you are alone you are not altogether alone . . . The reason why you should not kill, even under conditions where nobody will see you, is that you cannot possibly want to be together with a murderer. By committing murder you would deliver yourself to the company of a murderer as long as you live."[59] For Yael and many (but not all) of her compatriots, the active refusal to be complicit in migrants' sociopolitical abjection ranked among those commitments that are, as Rosen puts it, "so deep a part of us that we could not be the people that we are without having them. In failing to respect the humanity of others," he continues, "we actually undermine the humanity in ourselves."[60] For these activists, the pursuit of human dignity was a clear imperative.

Political Agency and the Right to Have Rights

In the final section of this chapter, I want to return to the existential stakes of sociopolitical abjection—especially the stakes of being denied recognition as a legitimate political actor. I learned most about these existential consequences from a community leader we've already met, and whom Yael came to know well: Naana Holdbrook,[61] the inimitable chairman of the African Workers Union (AWU), one of the only migrant-initiated *political* organizations to emerge in Tel Aviv in the late 1990s and early years of this century. His experience bolsters Arendt's famous claim that the capacity for political speech and action is the most fundamental human right. For Arendt, being recognized as a political actor is "not only necessary because it brings with it a legal identity and a body to protect your rights, but also because without the capacity to speak and act, we are deprived of a fundamental dimension of our existence."[62]

Dozens of migrant organizations sprang up in and around Tel Aviv in AWU's heydey, among them churches, sports leagues, drama clubs, lending clubs, and even an afternoon Spanish school for children of South American parents. Most were organized along lines of language, religion, ethnicity, gender, national or local origin, or some combination of these features. These groups did not aim to regularize their community members' status, or even to improve their living or working conditions; virtually none had overtly political aims or ambitions. On this apolitical landscape, AWU was a rare exception.

A chemist and high school science teacher by training, Naana came to Israel from Ghana's Cape Coast in the mid-1980s and stayed for seventeen years, earning a living cleaning houses to support his son and extended family back home. As he knew well, the gerush was not Israel's first campaign to deport unauthorized migrants. When a much smaller campaign had been launched half a decade earlier, he and a handful of other men from Ghana, Sierra Leone, and Congo had taken a bold and unprecedented step in creating the AWU. Naana and his colleagues wrote letters, gave speeches, published op-eds, and coordinated public gatherings. They drafted policy proposals, secured meetings with members of Knesset, and gave interviews to the local and international media. For many reasons, including the authorities' tendency to target migrant leaders for arrest and deportation, these were risky steps. "Nobody volunteers entirely of his own free will to be a leader," Naana once commented. "It always involves great personal risk."[63]

A charismatic man with a sharp intellect, an infectious laugh, and a savvy understanding of Israel's local moral economy, Naana honed his leadership skills as president of an African football (soccer) club in Tel Aviv before taking up the post of AWU chairman. Although neither the precise source of AWU's mandate nor the precise contours of its constituency was ever entirely clear, Naana's political voice gained unusual reach and prominence. A polished public speaker, he was among the most confident and well-connected leaders to emerge in Israel's migrant community in that period.

AWU's early allies included several left-leaning members of Knesset. Some were instrumental in helping the AWU establish itself as a state-recognized nonprofit, including Avraham Poraz, who later served as minister of interior and oversaw the (first) one-time arrangement granting permanent resident status to a limited group of migrants' children. In the late 1990s, AWU leaders also pursued the support of the member of Knesset Naomi Chazan, for whom I then worked as an intern. In fact, I remember preparing Knesset entry passes for AWU leaders in Naomi's office in anticipation of their first scheduled meeting. At the time I was still living in Jerusalem, and I remember being surprised to learn that a community of African migrants had settled in Tel Aviv. Half a decade later, over glasses of soda and a tin of Pringles potato chips in Naana's South Tel Aviv apartment, these memories streamed back as he pulled out a prized possession: the black binder documenting years of interaction with politicians and academics, NGO activists, and high-ranking police officials. Among the documents were several Knesset entry passes, each a rectangular sticker printed with the bearer's name, identification number, and date of visit. Perhaps I had prepared one of them myself?

When the mass deportation campaign was announced, most African migrants in Israel retreated into the shadows and struggled to decode the tactics and strategies of the newly created deportation apparatus. As the campaign intensified, a new, heavier cloud of deportability loomed overhead. Techniques of illegalization, racialization, and criminalization became ever more tightly entwined, and everyone caught in the campaign's crosshairs faced new forms of indignity and humiliation. By no means were these effects incidental, or accidental; the campaign's explicit intent was to frighten and intimidate those not yet caught in its dragnet to "self-deport."

Under these circumstances, the last thing most migrants thought to do was stake any kind of political claim. Just a handful of grassroots leaders, including Naana, chose otherwise. Although his Hebrew was limited, Naana avidly followed both Israeli domestic and international news. He carefully cultivated a network of Israeli supporters, associates, and colleagues—and an uncanny ability to navigate his adopted country's ever-turbulent political waters. To strengthen his arguments, he regularly read both of the country's English-language newspapers, preferring the right-leaning *Jerusalem Post* to the left-leaning *Haaretz* because the *Post's* right-wing analyses and columns on the Hebrew Bible, Jewish history, and the modern Jewish experience offered what he called "better ammunition."

Naana was not opposed, however, to publishing his own views in the more left-leaning of the two publications. In mid-September 2002, soon after the gerush was announced, he published an op-ed in *Haaretz* titled "We, Your Housecleaners." "For us Africans," he wrote, "poverty is not a concept. It is real and we live in this tragic situation. Poverty has many faces and shapes. Poverty is hunger. Poverty is lack of shelter. Poverty is being sick and unable to see a doctor. Poverty is dying of a curable disease. Poverty is not being able to go to school and not knowing how to read and write. Poverty is living one day at a time. Poverty is not having a job. Poverty is losing a child to illness brought about by unclean water. Poverty is being poor and knowing your chances of ever climbing out of the hole are not good. This is our situation and we need the help of Israelis to make a difference in our lives." In the deftly argued piece, Naana stakes various claims ranging from the historical (drawing parallels between the suffering of Jews and black Africans) to the demographic (highlighting the proportionally small number of Africans now living in Israel), to the religious (citing the "core Jewish traditions of hospitality and kindness as enshrined in the Torah: 'And if a stranger sojourn with thee in your land, ye shall not vex him. But the stranger that dwelleth with you shall be unto you as one born among you, and you shall love him as thyself; for ye were strangers in the land of Egypt' (Leviticus 19, 33–34)").[64]

Several days later I saw Peter and Olivia and asked if they had read Naana's piece. Although surprised to learn that an Israeli paper had given Naana a platform, Olivia suspected it would make little difference: "Israelis won't care." Peter took a different view. He found Naana's public exposure unwise and his published plea for compassion and mercy misplaced. "We know first of all that we are breaking the law," Peter repeated on this occasion, as he had on many others. As "illegals," he explained, their best bet was to avoid making waves, and to avoid asking for anything at all. He could tolerate the risk of arrest on public streets, but not the late-night raids that were becoming more frequent. "Just not that. Because if they come to your home and break down your door, where can you go?"

Naana's leadership efforts may not have garnered universal support, but he was well known in Tel Aviv's African community, respected, admired. To walk South Tel Aviv's streets with him, I learned, was to trail along with a local dignitary. One of Naana's typical public appearances took place several months after this op-ed appeared, at the annual International Migrants' Day event held at Tel Aviv's Cinemathèque. Unlike his companions on the dais—including a Hotline representative who expressed vigorous opposition to the gerush and a City Council representative who linked the systematic violations of migrants' rights to Israel's occupation of the West Bank and Gaza—Naana steered clear of overt political critique. After thanking the assembled crowd for their efforts to "uplift the welfare of the foreign workers in Israel," he described the corruption, civil wars, poverty, and social inequality that compelled Africans to "leave our homelands and our loved ones." By working as housecleaners in Israel, he and his compatriots could "provide a safety net for our loved ones in Africa who solidly depend on us." He framed his appeal in biblical terms, citing the passage from Exodus that had become a mantra for Israel's migrant advocates and activists alike. In closing, he interwove his targeted plea with another with more universal appeal. "The time has come to help us forget poverty and overcome despair," he told the audience with characteristic flair. "We want to conquer poverty, and we need your help."

Naana's pleas for empathy and compassion were conspicuously conservative in both style and content. Nowhere in his speeches, op-eds, or media interviews do we find the transformative political demands articulated in the same time period by *sans papiers* activists in France or, a decade later, by DREAMers in the United States. Of course, this conservatism was a tactic—and it was among the only tactics available to him. Other leaders were being

deported one by one as their presumptive constituents scrambled for clandestinity. Although speeches like this one invoked a discretionary politics of
humanitarian sentiment rather than staking any rights-based claims, they
allowed Naana to achieve something remarkable, if tenuous: to defy the state's
best efforts to deny him political agency.

Still, Naana knew his public persona offered no protection from the ba-
nality of arrest. To Immigration Police scoping out the Tel Aviv streets, he
was just another "illegal" migrant, another out-of-place African man who
could be chased down, humiliated, and beaten with impunity. An arrest in
broad daylight, he once told me, would be a terrible slap in the face. If his
number came up, he wanted to be arrested in his home, *because of* his
leadership—to be recognized for his actions instead of being anonymized as
just another conspicuous interloper in racialized public space. Naana's desire for political recognition recalls similar demands in other times and
places, like IRA prisoners in Northern Ireland, women and men, who insisted their British captors acknowledge the political reasons for their incarceration.[65]

This desire to be seen and heard as a political being brings us back to a
theoretical tangle noted earlier in passing—the tangled relationship among
anthropology, dignity, and human rights. Once again, Arendt is helpful. As
Serena Parekh notes, Arendt's work is distinguished by the recognition of "an
existential side of human rights" that "gives a deeper dimension to the term
'human dignity' that is so often used in human rights discourse." Parekh adds,
"This is the existential dimension of human rights unique to Arendt's analysis: they are not just about legal entitlements from the state, but a matter of
how we understand ourselves and are recognized by others. If we cannot act . . .
we are left with a life of alienation, a loss of meaning, and a loss of being at
home in the world and with others. Understood in this context, the right to
have rights guarantees that one has access to that part of existence."[66] We might
call that part one's sense of dignity.

About eighteen months into the gerush, Naana's number did come up,
and the police showed up at his doorstep, deportation order in hand—but
with no handcuffs and no crowbar to the door. In that sense, his wish was
granted. Instead of breaking down his door late at night or arresting him with
the brutality Naana knew had grown increasingly common, they did not cart
him off to jail to await deportation, and he was even granted more than a
month to organize his affairs. Treating him otherwise, the authorities likely
suspected, could have sparked public outcry.[67]

A year after his deportation to Ghana, Naana published a column in another Israeli publication, the *Jerusalem Report*, narrating the pain of his forced return. He described a welter of feelings: the euphoria, and culture shock, of landing in one's homeland after nearly two decades away; the embarrassment of returning hastily and unprepared; the bewilderment of seeing his seventeen-year-old son, now "a young man of my height," in the flesh for the very first time. His words disclose a complex moral economy in which the usual currencies of migrant life—money, sentiment, risk—prove less fungible than earlier presumed. It is an economy of variable risks, and deeply uncertain returns. As I read Naana's words now, I hear his voice in my head, knowing that his essay, crafted months after his expulsion from a country he knew so well, was meant to speak for many. "I told myself that the sacrifices I had made to help my little boy and others around me were worthwhile," Naana writes.

> But they were relying on me to continue the financial support—for their education, medical expenses and other things—to alleviate the dehumanizing effects of poverty. And since I was bundled out of Israel in a hurry, these grand gestures of support to the extended family had to be curtailed. Deporting me has led to the suffering of 15 people. With this came the waning of respect for me as a savior of the family. To see people suffer because I cannot help any longer is unbearable. Depression, desperation and other forms of anxiety set in. Finding work in my field at my age is virtually impossible in Ghana. My day-to-day activities are centered on going to old friends in high places to see if there is any chance of getting employed. But despite their promises, they give me little comfort. So here I am, an unemployed chemist and former house-cleaner to well-off Israelis, courtesy of the Immigration Police, and Israel's policy of deporting migrant workers. . . . This policy has even led to the suicides of some Ghanaians on their return home, something that has gone unnoted by the Israeli media. The humiliation of being deported, of having lost the ability to educate one's children, of being an outcast in a family . . . can prove too much to bear.[68]

Part elegy, part lament, Naana's words remind us that migrants' experiences of sociopolitical abjection and, sometimes, expulsion, are deeply embodied, and that they bear both universal and particular dimensions. His own experience is informed not only by culturally based values and expectations and by the shock of his own plummet in status but also by the global political economy itself—a rigged game in which an educated (black) Ghanaian's best shot at supporting his family may entail a risky journey over land and sea to live precariously as a voiceless nobody in cramped quarters cleaning the comfortable homes of better-off (white) people.

In his piece, Naana acknowledges that the terms of his own expulsion could have been worse. He writes of compatriots "with permanent scars" from beatings they received who will "never forget the humiliation, the violation of the human spirit and the blatant intimidation they suffered at the hands of the police, or those Israelis who capitalized on the deportations to deny the employees their basic rights and compensation." Still, to appear on his family's doorstep now, much older and empty-handed, signaled a crushing defeat. A powerful and venerated family asset turned humiliated (and humiliating) liability, Naana describes his suffering, and that of his fellow deportees, in terms both existential and psychological: "To see people suffer because I cannot help any longer is unbearable," he writes, giving explicit voice to deportees' mental anguish and to suicides that go without public mention. Despite this "terrible, depressing situation," Naana concludes his missive with a message of praise and hope: praise for the "many Israelis—employers, friends, members of human-rights groups, journalists—whose names will be etched in my memory for a very long time."

Conclusion: Dignity in Motion

> The pathetic fact is that the only enemies of dignity are
> human beings.
>
> —George Kateb

Dignity, as Grimm puts it, is indeed both "a rather old philosophical and a quite new legal concept of rapidly increasing interest." Given its complicated genealogy, it is a confusing one as well, and in contemporary parlance it comes freighted with heavy legal, theological, and other forms of normative baggage. But to those who would write off dignity as "a useless concept,"[69] I disagree. From an ethnographic standpoint, as this chapter has sought to show, what matters more than untangling genealogical threads or hammering out precise definitions is the challenge of exploring how this term is often "the only concept historically available" to capture a powerful cluster of desires and existential imperatives that most of us share. An ethnographic lens helps us break free from abstract *notions* of dignity and directs us to explore, instead, individual actors' experiential *sense of dignity*, whether in positive terms or in moments of violation. An ethnographic approach also brings new questions to light. It invites us to explore how dignity becomes most visible, palpable, and meaningful in motion. How it figures—often in the distance but always with powerful pull—as a kind of vector or lodestar in human lives.

Marina and Yvonne, Lorena, Supi, and Naana have much to teach us about dignity's pull, and about its moving parts: the social processes of dignity violation, the circumstances under which violations occur, their impact on the texture and contours, intimacies and immediacies of migrants' lifeworlds. These Filipino, Nigerian, and Ghanaian residents of Tel Aviv show us how sociopolitical abjection can imperil one's sense of dignity at home, at work, or while moving through public space. When cultivating—or muting—one's capacity for speech and action. When arrested, or through forcible deportation. Abjected migrants may find themselves nobodied or accused, humiliated or animalized, silenced or expelled. During the gerush, these violations of social dignity—defined by Jacobson as that sense of dignity that emerges "in the interactions between and among individuals, collectives, and societies"—were neither random nor accidental. These exclusions, misrecognitions, and occasional bodily incursions were part of a strategic, top-down effort to complicate migrants' lives and impel them to leave Israel, ideally but by no means necessarily of their own accord.

Yet individual lifeworlds cannot be reduced to existential harms and humiliations. For my migrant interlocutors, violations like these did not dim the lodestar of a dignified, flourishing life—a life in which one can follow through on one's fundamental orienting commitments. We have seen how some migrants cleaved to these ground projects despite the humiliations they would daily confront. Recall, for instance, Yvonne's explanation that she tries "to be a nobody"—not because she is willing to be banished to a "zone of nonbeing," but as a calculated tactic of psychic and social self-defense, to protect herself and her young son. We can recall Lorena's desire to keep working in order to secure a viable future for her children even after the waning of their affection, and after the unexpected and painful implosion of her close bond with the Stern family. And then there is Naana's postdeportation dispatch to the society that abjected him—and to the advocates and activists who gave him continued reason for hope. These acts reflect that cluster of desires most of us share: the desire to feel meaningfully connected to others. To be recognized as a person in one's own right—a person who matters—and not just an object of others' designs, fears, or desires. To exert some measure of control over the unruly circumstances into which we have been thrown. To live without risk, or fear, of humiliation.

For the small, indignant, and heterogeneous group of Israelis described here, the gerush violated migrants' social dignity—and their human dignity. These advocates and activists rejected their government's portrayal of global migrants as a kind of "detritus humanity"[70] who could be abjected without compunction. Instead, they saw these government efforts as grave violations of migrants' *social* dignity—and they refused to be complicit. They made the uncommon move of seeking opportunities for face-to-face encounter with people their government was telling them to devalue and fear. We must be careful not to romanticize these efforts, which often were multiply motivated—for instance, by politics, ethics, and on occasion even by exoticizing curiosity or orientalist fantasies that shored up migrants' Otherness but assigned it a positive, rather than negative, moral valence. Still, by pursuing—or, in some cases, creating—unusual spaces of encounter, these Israeli citizens took the unusual step of seeking to repair violations of social dignity enacted by their government, ostensibly in their name.

For many, the desire to help restore migrants' (social) dignity stemmed from their view of the gerush as an affront to *human* dignity as well: a violation of "the value that belongs to every human being simply by virtue of being human." Here, social dignity and human dignity signal two very different courses of ethical action. One involves bearing witness to another person's experience of violation but rejecting its premise, and then engaging in focused and purposeful efforts—face-to-face, in spaces of intersubjective encounter—to help repair and restore the other person's sense of wholeness or integrity. Another involves a different imperative altogether: an imperative to refuse the poison of complicity. Recall Arendt: one who commits murder is destined to spend the rest of one's life in the company of a murderer.

Advocates and activists did not necessarily agree about the greatest potential harms of the gerush, and they certainly disagreed about the appropriate response. As we have seen, these differences stemmed partly from dimensions of personal biography, but also from the divergent idioms of social justice mobilization they invoked in considering these questions. Some were motivated by a desire to show migrants another face of Israeli society—to show that "not all Israelis are like that." Other critiques involved more abstract commitments, for instance to universal values, international human rights law, or powerful memories of collective persecution over the *longue durée* of Jewish history.

In all, Israeli migrant advocates and activists did align—and, as I write these words, continue to align—as a meaningful counterweight to state-level policies and practices that cast global migrants as Others and seek to exclude, abject, and deport them (often, paradoxically, by casting migrants' presence in Israel as an affront to the nation's integrity, if not its dignity). I see their diverse volunteer efforts and professional labors as attempts—small-scale, sometimes slow, and often clumsy—to forge Israeli society anew. To create a more decent society. A society that does not humiliate. A society, in short, they could comfortably inhabit. According to this vision, which ran counter to that of the Immigration Administration and its supporters, migrant men, women, and their Israeli-born children are not ciphers or bogeymen. They are real people who already are part of the country's changing cultural fabric: legitimate members of the country's moral community whose lives already are woven into Israel's story, and will remain so, even if they are forcibly expelled.

For these advocates and activists, as for ethnographers, global migrants, whatever their legal status, are people worth listening to, worth getting to know. They are people who matter.

INTERLUDE

Sweet Mother

Sweet mother, I no go forget you
For this suffer wey you suffer for me yeah . . .
—Prince Nico Mbarga, "Sweet Mother"

At Ruby and Franklin's place, whenever football wasn't on TV, there was music. Franklin was an avid music lover and a talented DJ with wide-ranging tastes: Congolese soukous and Ivorian zouglou, Nigerian highlife, Jamaican reggae, American rap. And Ruby? She would dance to pretty much anything—even the Dixie Chicks, the American country band I played one afternoon for Reggie and Pete, two of Franklin's admiring young teammates from their weekend football team, after I heard them daydreaming aloud about Texas. To the first twangs of the band's classic "Long Time Gone," Ruby abandoned her cooking and grabbed my hand. "You have to dance like this," she laughed, as we do-si-do'd around the furniture, nearly kicking Franklin and "the boys," as she called them, with our flying heels.

Ruby rarely missed a chance to dance—at home, in church, at the parties she loved so much—but there's one song she loved above all: "Sweet Mother," the 1976 megahit that continues to pluck at millions of African heartstrings. If you don't know the song, look it up. Play it. Try not to get up and dance—I dare you.

The song's lyrics are catchy, redolent with the love of a grown child who now waxes nostalgic, singing in retrospective appreciation of unflagging maternal devotion and sacrifice. Although Ruby never put it quite this way, the song struck me as her soul's melody, a musical accounting of her dream to bring lightness and joy to her family and be known, lovingly, as always having put her children first.

On the morning their son Jesse was born, the love that anchored her world and knit their family together expanded to fill their small hospital room. Franklin had called me at 7:15 A.M. to say that Ruby was in labor, and at their invitation I joined them an hour later. She endured painful contractions in proud silence, a handkerchief from the church held tightly in her hand to dab the occasional tear from her eye. Franklin sat close to his wife in a vinyl-upholstered hospital chair, deeply attuned to the rhythm of her distress. "Sorry, sorry," he repeated over and over, pained by his inability to bring her comfort.

For those eagerly awaiting the experience, few things may be more miraculous than the birth of one's child. For Franklin, Jesse's arrival was doubly miraculous since he was not their first but, in fact, their second-born son. When Franklin left Nigeria for Israel, Ruby had been pregnant with their first, Junior, who was now nine. Although he knew his elder son by face, and by voice, Franklin had never seen Junior in person, never touched his skin, never held him in a paternal embrace. For Franklin, tiny Jesse gave him his first chance to father face-to-face.

Some months later, right after our Dixie Chicks debut, Ruby and I sat on the couch looking at photos of that unforgettable day. The visual snippets captured by my little camera only strengthened the footballers' admiration for their elder "Uncle." We had agreed that some of the day's photos were for female eyes only, but these photos Ruby wanted the boys to see. The image they loved most showed Franklin just moments after Jesse's arrival, eyes closed and hands aloft in praise as he stood at her bedside. "You need to blow that one up and hang it on the wall!" Reggie declared.

As I knew well before Jesse's arrival, theirs was a love story through and through. Ruby was good at retelling the tale of their courtship, which began when she was just 18 and still in school. One school vacation day, she had accompanied her mother to the market to help sell jewelry and clothing. Franklin, a young teacher several years her senior, had noticed her. He wanted to introduce himself but held back, instead sending a friend to speak on his behalf. Although taken by Franklin's good looks and charm, Ruby was shy, and she feared her mother's firm hand. She told his friend she would come back and speak with him the following week—which she did. They both delighted in those first stolen conversations, but as her affections ripened, Ruby grew anxious, afraid her mother might punish her for having a boyfriend. Eventually she turned to an aunt, who spoke with her mother, who then sat down with Franklin himself.

"She asked if he wants to marry me or just go out with me and then dump me," Ruby remembered. She recalled the exchange between Franklin and her mother in detail. "He said 'I love her, I want to go out with her and see if we like each other.' 'And then dump her?' 'No!'" After receiving her mother's blessing, they dated for a while before approaching Ruby's father, who had long since separated from her mother and ultimately offered his blessing as well.

Ruby loved her husband deeply, and she wore Franklin's initial on a gold chain around her neck. She was young when he left for Israel, and pregnant. Although she felt safe and supported in her mother's house, Ruby was timid when the time came to deliver her first child. When she began feeling occasional labor pains, she didn't tell anyone. A strong woman could bear the pain in quiet, she had told herself. Two days after that, when the pain had become excruciating, she finally told her mother, who scolded her for not speaking up sooner. Her mother wanted to go right to the hospital, but Ruby refused. "I'm going to have this baby right here in this kitchen," she remembered telling her mother, who then called a nurse who lived down the street. The nurse came quickly and confirmed that the baby was on his way. Soon after, Junior was born.

During Junior's earliest years, both Ruby and her baby were loved and cared for in her mother's house, but Ruby missed her husband. Although she could hardly bear the thought of leaving Junior, she was determined to join Franklin in Israel and round out their family—and leaving Junior with her mother was the only way. If he had stayed in Nigeria, she told me midway through her pregnancy with Jesse, "I'd probably be done having my children by now—three or four total."

It took two years and US$3,000 to secure a spot on a pilgrimage trip to Israel, but they did it. When Franklin finally picked her up at her hotel in Nazareth and brought her to the southern resort city of Eilat, where he had been working as a cleaner, she was thrilled that the sparks between them hadn't dimmed. Now, finally, they had settled into a new life in Tel Aviv. They were respected members of their church, work opportunities were plentiful, and Junior was thriving in Ruby's mother's care. They spoke regularly with their relatives in Nigeria by phone, sent remittances, and swapped glossy photographs taken in church and at celebrations. And now, with Jesse's safe arrival, they had finally managed to expand their family.

Franklin was over the moon to meet his son, and he prepared for milestones in the baby's life with gusto. The small kola nut ceremony in their apartment, when the infant received his name. His dedication ceremony several months later, celebrated on a Saturday afternoon after church, in a large hall bursting with guests and gifts, food and drink. The church pastors bestowed rich blessings upon these beloved pillars of the community and their new-born son. During breaks in the afternoon's lively music and dancing, friends young and old took turns picking up the microphone and offering their own blessings for the child and his parents. A friend seated near the door kept a log of monetary gifts. Whenever Jesse wasn't snuggled in my arms, I was in the middle of the floor, dancing up a storm in the heavy brocade outfit Ruby had dressed me in, trying my best to keep my head wrap from toppling and matching wraparound skirt from sliding off my narrow hips.

This was in the spring of 2002. By the time we celebrated Jesse's birthday a year later, much had changed. Some things, however, remained constant. For the most part, their church community was still an inhabitable space of welcome. So, too, were the weekend parties they managed to attend and, on occasion, host, including Jesse's first birthday bash at the Dead Sea, which they wisely held far from South Tel Aviv and the regular beat of the Immigration Police. And for friends with less stable home lives and a tougher shot at motherhood's blessings, like Olivia and Claire, their door remained open.

CHAPTER 3

"Real" Others and "Other" Others

> I'm not for the [suicide] bombings. I think they're wrong.
> But if this is what the Israelis do in the center, where
> everyone can see, just think of what they must be doing
> to the Palestinians in the bush, where no one can see.
> —Supi, Ghanaian migrant and single mother living in
> Tel Aviv

"We are not terrorists!" boomed Emeka, a tall, mustached Nigerian man in African garb who stood near the back of the improvised church. Once a manufacturing space, the cavernous hall was now spruced up with a bit of thin carpeting, a simple altar with microphones, and row upon row of white plastic lawn chairs serving as pews.

The arrival of thousands of unauthorized migrants in South Tel Aviv over the past decade had breathed new life into many of the area's industrial buildings turned churches, including this one and those adjacent to it on busy Levanda Street. But today's meeting, on a sweaty summer afternoon, was no worship service. Instead, Emeka and seventy-odd other migrants, mostly West African men, along with a few Filipinos and others, had convened at the invitation—however improbable—of the Immigration Administration, whose year-old mass deportation campaign was about to enter a new phase. I sat near the back with my Nigerian friend Uche and two of his friends, one Nigerian and the other Filipino, and we saw many familiar faces.

The event's organizers, Naana Holdbrook among them, had promoted the gathering as a chance for dialogue, perhaps even negotiation. But the police had come with another goal in mind: to announce their new "Voluntary Departure" operation. In exchange for a pledge to leave the country within a

Dear families,

About a month and a half ago, a new person took on the position of Head of the Immigration Administration. When he began his post, the Head of the Administration met with dozens of foreign workers in their workplaces, homes and entertainment spots. The Head of the Administration witnessed the conditions and severe hardship in which you live, studied the trials and tribulations and as a result, decided to launch a project aiming to minimize the harm inflicted on the families who have been staying in Israel illegally – in other words to encourage you to leave Israel with dignity, after fully exhausting your rights.

The project will be implemented in several key stages:

The first stage will begin on August 1ˢᵗ, 2003 and will continue until the end of August. The Immigration Administration plans to enable the families staying in Israel illegally to register at any of the immigration stations located throughout Israel and to settle their departure date.

Families who register at any of the immigration units during the month of August and settle the date of their flight will be able to stay in Israel until October 1ˢᵗ, 2003, with the promise that the Immigration Administration will not implement any law enforcement activities or make any arrests against these families.

During these two months, we ask each family to make all the necessary arrangements in Israel, including buying plane tickets, settling any salaries as yet unpaid by their employers, terminating leases, as well as all matters pertaining to getting organized for leaving.

The second stage will begin on September 1ˢᵗ, 2003 – the Immigration Administration will launch law enforcement activities and arrests against families who did not register at one of the Immigration units during the month of August and did not settle the matter of their flight date.

The Head of the Immigration Administration is appealing to each family in person with the following requests:

Do not let us arrest you.

You deserve to leave Israel with dignity.

Please go to the Immigration Administration station closest to your home and arrange the date of your flight without delay.

Figure 10. Section of flyer announcing the first "Voluntary Departure" operation.
Source: Israeli Immigration Administration.

month, undocumented families could now register to leave Israel, and in exchange gain a brief period of temporary immunity to the indignities of arrest, detention, and forcible deportation. The Immigration Administration enumerated the proposal in a fluorescent yellow flyer prepared, in English, for wide distribution (Figure 10). "Do not let us arrest you," read the flyer. "You deserve to leave Israel with dignity."

Emeka, for one, was unmoved. "We are not Palestinians!" he exclaimed once the floor had opened for questions, his gaze arcing over the crowd toward the officers clustered at the front of the hall. He stood tall, microphone in hand, his voice brimming with anger and frustration. "We are not against you. We came here for a purpose, just like [migrant workers] do all over the world. . . . Work with your conscience. If it were to be you, how would you feel? . . . Do not treat us with stony hearts. We did not fall from hell. We came from some- where. . . . We are not criminals even if we are illegal. . . . We are human ir- respective of the fact that we are black." Emeka's plea bore little chance of derailing the gerush or mitigating the humiliation and violence that trailed in its wake, and after the meeting I heard various people complain that he had become too emotional.

A top-ranking police official known by his first name in some of the city's migrant communities—I'll call him Rafi—tendered a hasty response. "We think you are good people," he insisted, his English staccato and rough. "We don't think you are criminals. If we thought you were criminals, we wouldn't face you like this."

Emeka and the others gathered would undoubtedly have disputed these claims, but both sides did agree on one point. Unauthorized migrants in Israel were Others—but not *that* kind of Others. For most of the anxious crowd, this was cold comfort.

*　　*　　*

In many respects, the gerush described in this book was typical of early twenty- first-century deportation regimes: A state deems unauthorized migrants' pres- ence a problem, then draws on a familiar arsenal of tactics and techniques to criminalize, arrest, and expel them en masse. From migrants' standpoint, the heightened risk of deportation becomes the backdrop to everyday life. Fear of arrest grips the mind, and the imagination. One never knows what an en- counter with the authorities might entail. Broken-down doors and a late-night beating? Arrest and humiliation in view of one's children? Expulsion, with empty pockets, to a life of shame? When migrant communities are targeted by an aggressive deportation regime, accounts like these are no longer shock- ing or exceptional. As they circulate and repeat, each time with a new cast of characters, such stories become familiar, even banal—until they strike close to home.

As the unusual exchange between Emeka and Officer Rafi makes clear, deportation regimes are also deeply localized, their logic and expression deeply particular. The tone, tenor, and dynamics of the gerush simultaneously reflect and shed light on what I have described as Israel's local moral economy, that shared matrix of historically and culturally particular memories and emotions, values and expectations that sets up the parameters of everyday discourse and collective moral reflection. As I described in the Introduction, residents of the region are all slotted into one of three distinct groups within the country's local moral economy: ratified citizens (Jewish Israelis), "real" Others (Palestinians), and "other" Others (global migrants). This chapter asks: What moral values and ideological commitments underpin this classificatory logic? What are its historical and cultural roots, and what are its effects—especially for those designated as Others? Finally, how did local notions of Otherness change with the gerush?

I begin by tracing the contours of Israel's local moral economy, whose imprint on Israeli political and public discourse is deep and perduring. I then turn to the smoldering analogy that lurks beneath the surface of the gerush—the very analogy that Supi invokes, and Emeka so emphatically rejects—and consider how Palestinians, including both citizens of Israel and Palestinians in the Occupied Palestinian Territories, are imagined and treated by the Israeli state. As we will see, two techniques of state power that have long shaped Israel's treatment of Palestinians—racialized profiling and a readiness to use violence—both figured in the state's campaign to cast global migrants as a new kind of national abject and expel them from the country by the tens of thousands. One result of this shift in governmental disposition was a narrowing of the gap between the country's "real" and "other" Others, with consequences that continued to reverberate nearly two decades later.

Local Moral Economies

The notion of local moral economies melds and recasts two influential approaches in contemporary anthropology, each calibrated to a different level of analysis: moral economy (at the collective level) and local moral worlds (at the level of subjective experience and intersubjective engagement).

The concept of the moral economy, or moral economies, has become increasingly prevalent, especially among anthropologists seeking alternatives to either the field's originary—and, in some respects, depleted—concept of culture or its more recent, if now waning, intrigue with human suffering and pathos.[1] Initially put forth by E. P. Thompson (1963) and further developed by James Scott (1976), the concept has undergone a good deal of revision and reinterpretation—in addition, some say, to hijacking and misinterpretation, overuse and "banalization."[2] A deep dive into its genealogy is beyond this chapter's scope. Yet the term's increasing prevalence reveals its usefulness in showing how complex human predicaments involve a tangle of political processes, material pressures, moral commitments, and emotional dynamics.

One especially useful formulation, offered by the Moral Economies research group at the Max Planck Institute in Berlin, is grounded in three key insights. First, human collectivities are based "on values and morals" that are deeply entwined with "emotions, whether positive or negative, [that] are crucial for the way in which citizens lead their private and public lives." Second, moral economies are not "static and harmonious"; rather, they are inherently "dynamic and contested." Finally, moral economies are not simply about exchange, finance, or even money—"what today is called 'economy'"—but cast a wider net that "encompasses broader societal spheres and systems." According to this definition, moral economies "govern and integrate different spheres—the political as much as the social, cultural and economic—and imbue them with special moral concerns and emotional demands."[3]

Anthropologist Arthur Kleinman's notion of local moral worlds captures a parallel constellation of concerns at the level of subjective experience and intersubjective engagement. In these intimate domains, we all struggle with fundamental questions of "what really matters," whether in a single moment of turbulence or crisis, or more generally, as we proceed through life's scenes and stages. "What is at stake," Kleinman writes, "undergoes great, even extravagant, elaboration through the cultural apparatuses of language and aesthetics and across divergent social positions of gender, age cohort, political faction, class, and ethnicity. Yet the fact that some things really do matter, matter desperately, is what provides local worlds with their immense power to absorb attention, orient interest, and direct action."[4] In linking a sociological conception of moral economies with Kleinman's experientially attuned notion of local moral worlds, my claim is a simple one. We cannot fully understand human predicaments, individual or collective—or, for that matter, the sides, stakes, or consequences of localized debates about such predicaments—without considering the lively traffic between *public* assertions of value, on one hand, and personal, even *intimate* questions of what matters most to individual people or communities, on the other.

The notion of local moral economies bears several distinct features. First is its ability to capture ethnographic complexity and historical depth without becoming entangled in what many anthropologists consider stale or essentializing notions of culture. Another is a clear-eyed recognition that "the moral" is never the flat equivalent of "the good." Moral commitments may be deep-seated, emotionally charged, powerful, and defining; indeed, they may anchor the very ground projects that orient us in the world. Yet depth of feeling does not stamp any moral commitment, individual or collective, as inherently *good*; however deeply felt, personal commitments may nonetheless be mired in injustice. Kleinman puts it this way: "What is at stake in a local world may involve a moral economy of systematic injustice, bad faith, and even horror. Yes; from an ethnographic perspective what is at stake, what morally defines a local world, may be, when viewed in comparative perspective, corrupt, grotesque, even down-right inhuman. That is to say, the moral may be unethical, just as the ethical may be irrelevant to moral experience."[5]

Human beings speak and act from radically different positions within local moral worlds—sometimes in good faith, sometimes in bad. Localized debates about controversial issues emerge precisely at points of contact, and friction, between divergent or contradictory views. An ethnographic approach to local moral economies can help map out such landscapes of dispute. So, too, can it reveal how the very values and commitments that anchor one person's, or one community's, sense of dignity may in fact violate those of another. After all, as Mattingly points out, "taking morality seriously does not presume that people are good but rather that they are evaluative in moral terms about their own actions and those of others."[6]

Israel's Local Moral Economy

To make sense of Israel's complex and fractious local moral economy, we need to home in on a cluster of themes that frame everyday reality in Israel, but pull different people in very different directions. One is the three-pronged biopolitical logic noted above (citizens/"real" Others/"other" Others). Other themes include a deep, if unsettled, sense of historical memory; omnipresent concerns about security; a profound degree of demographic anxiety; and a tenacious, religiously derived—but not necessarily religious—ideology of "fruitful multiplication" that resonates with the Hebrew Bible's commandment to "be fruitful and multiply" (*prú u'rvú*). There are others as well, including Israel's foundational self-description as a "Jewish and democratic state." Another is a deep preoccupation with how Israel appears, and presents itself, to the world—concerns that find expression in the work of *hasbará*, a term for "public diplomacy" that carries overtones of "propaganda" in the service of the country's public image.[7]

Like the frame of a building, these themes are always present, if not always perceptible—yet their structuring influence cannot be avoided. Within a building, one cannot move without maneuvering around its framing beams and supports, walls and orifices. Similarly, to navigate Israeli sociopolitical reality, one must reckon with these themes and collective concerns.

Of course, the durability and ubiquity of these concerns does not mean that all Israelis approach them in the same way; to the contrary. As Israel's migrant advocacy and activist community reminds us, a single local moral economy can give rise to radically different, even contradictory frames for understanding weighty issues of collective concern. These divergent frames engage common sources of emotion, memory, and moral value, but invoke and admix them in substantially different ways. Competition among perspectives on controversial issues can be stark and fierce even though—indeed, precisely because—they are cobbled together using contradictory interpretations of the same potent raw materials. As an Israeli anthropologist pointed out after reading the penultimate version of this book, it is in some ways absurd to even gesture toward the proposition that there is one Israel, or something homogeneous enough to be called "Israeli society."[8] I agree. My claim is a different one. Regardless of one's ethnic identity, socioeconomic status, place of residence, level of religiosity—or even one's religion or nationality—speech and action in Israeli sociocultural space always unfold in some degree of tension with, or at the very least in relation to, the core themes identified here as undergirding the country's local moral economy.

In sum, wherever one is positioned in Israeli society, these core themes are pivot points, and their varied interpretations influence public, political, and even private discourse in resounding ways. This holds true whether one's ancestors immigrated from Yemen, survived the Shoah (Holocaust), or fled their Palestinian village in 1948 in the heat of war. Whether one has a single child, or ten, or none. Whether one lies awake at night worrying about the country's demographic makeup, or has harsh words for those who lose sleep over such concerns. Whatever one's background, all are attuned to these core concerns, each of which runs, electrified, through Israeli political and socio-cultural space. Below I consider each in turn.

Historical Memory

Regardless of ethnicity or political orientation, all Israelis—Jewish and Arab; Ashkenazi, Mizraḥi, Russian or Ethiopian; native-born or *oléh ḥadásh* ("new immigrant")—live in history's long shadow, and in conversation with powerful currents of historical memory. For Israeli Jews, a thick and variegated tapestry of collective memory weaves centuries of cultural and religious flourishing across vast expanses of the globe—from North Africa and Europe to Central Asia and the Indian subcontinent—together with legacies of antisemitism and persecution and, for some, deep liturgical longings. Beginning in the late nineteenth century, as many empires were on the wane and nationalisms on the rise, some of these yearnings found expression in the modern Zionist movement, which generated a wide range of literary, theological, and political visions, including the rough blueprint for a modern-day Jewish homeland in the biblical Land of Israel.[9]

Although the Zionist project was forged in the crucible of nineteenth-century European nationalist fervor, its political incarnation on the global stage cannot be disentangled from long legacies of antisemitism, especially the Nazis' genocidal machinations during World War II. For the Israeli state and most Jewish Israelis, the annihilation of six million Jews during the Shoah constitutes what Dominick LaCapra calls a "founding trauma": a potent collective memory of mass trauma that can become reactivated when a group feels threatened.[10] As historian Idith Zertal explains,

> The Holocaust and its millions of dead have been ever-present in Israel from the day of its establishment and the link between the two events remains indissoluble. The Holocaust has always been present in Israel's speech and silences; in the lives and nightmares of hundreds of thousands of survivors who have settled in Israel, and in the

crying absence of the victims; in legislation, orations, ceremonies, courtrooms, schools, in the press, poetry, gravestone inscriptions, monuments, memorial books. Through a dialectical process of appropriation and exclusion, remembering and forgetting, Israeli society has defined itself in relation to the Holocaust: it regarded itself as both the heir to the victims and their accuser, atoning for their sins and redeeming their death.[11]

Individual perspectives on the Shoah vary widely depending on family history, ethnic background, and, increasingly, degree of generational distance from World War II. Yet state efforts to institutionalize Holocaust memory continue to advance a collective narrative that presumes more or less equal relevance to all (Jewish) citizens. Eight days before the annual Yom HaAtzmaút (Independence Day) celebrations, public life pauses for Yom HaShoáh (Holocaust Remembrance Day, officially Yom HaZikarón LaShoáh u-laGvuráh—Holocaust and Heroism Remembrance Day). On this annual holiday, established by law in 1959, ceremonies are held at military bases, in schools, and by communities and public organizations. A national memorial service at Yad VaShem, the national Holocaust memorial in Jerusalem, is broadcast live, and television stations focus the day's programming on the atrocities of the Shoah and its aftermath. Radio stations pause their usual broadcast schedules for a full day of mournful music. And in late morning, sirens wail throughout the country for two minutes and everyone, wherever one may be, is expected to stand still in a shared national moment of remembrance. One year, I found myself driving with friends on the main highway from Tel Aviv to Jerusalem as the siren began to sound. Like everyone else on that windy ribbon of uphill road, we stopped, got out of the car, and stood silently on the hot asphalt until the siren ended, its echo fading into the wind sweeping over the hills.

In recent years, the centrality of the Shoah to Israeli national self-understanding has become a matter of critical reflection and vigorous debate, especially among Israeli writers and filmmakers, journalists and political leaders. Still, its imprint remains far-reaching and profound—and, crucially, polysemous. As my conversations with migrant advocates and activists made clear, the reactivation of a "founding trauma" can catalyze a powerful sense of obligation to help others fleeing persecution, even at a distance of several generations. Yet it can also have the inverse effect—by sowing seeds of aggression, violence, and destruction. We can look to these legacies of traumatization for insight into the tone and tenor of Israel's ongoing occupation of Palestinian people and lands.

The Trope of Security

A second core element of Israel's local moral economy is a ubiquitous concern about security, which the Immigration Administration leveraged successfully in launching its deportation agenda. The success of the gerush hinged, to no small extent, on the government's ability to recast global migrants, who previously had been portrayed in more benign ways (i.e., as a curiosity, a convenient solution to labor market woes, or, at worst, a nuisance) as a growing threat to the state's security and the nation's integrity. To understand this discursive makeover, we need to step back and consider how notions of security are conceptualized, articulated, and leveraged in contemporary Israel.

According to Michel Foucault, contemporary society "has become, preeminently, a 'society of security'" in which the work of governing "involves a distinctive circuit of interdependence between *political security* and *social security*."[12] This observation could have been written to describe Israel, where an official state of emergency has been in effect since the state's establishment in 1948, and where questions of state security are a pivot point in political, policy, and public discourse. For the majority of Jewish Israeli leaders and citizens, these concerns involve not only the country's political, physical, and economic security but also its "ethnonational"—that is, demographic—security.[13] Across the political spectrum, as anthropologist Juliana Ochs argues, Israelis tend to "see their fear and their desires for security as beyond politics, and thus become ignorant of the structural logics of exclusion that discourses of fear and security serve to reproduce."[14]

Jewish Israelis often articulate these concerns in frankly existential terms: as a question of the state's capacity to provide a safe haven for Jews worldwide in accordance with the Zionist movement's founding vision. Yet a small minority of Israelis, including many migrant advocates and activists, invert the question. For this handful of citizens, concern about the state's capacity to offer safe haven to the world's Jews cannot override other concerns and values like respect for human rights or international law. Meanwhile, for Israelis on the political right, the idea of valuing the international human rights regime over Jewish national interests is seen as foolish at best and treasonous at worst.[15]

Both in Israel and on the global stage, the aims of the Zionist movement and the Israeli state became objects of considerable critical scrutiny and debate in the first decades of the twenty-first century. Yet broadening debate *about* the region seems not to have radically changed political views *within* it, at least not within Israel, except to the extent that public opinion has shifted heavily to the right. A majority of Jewish Israeli citizens, and many newly ascendant politicians, cleave ever more tightly to arguments for protecting the country's "Jewish character" (*tzivyón yehudí*). For most, this means leaving the door open to all potential Jewish immigrants via the Law of Return and preserving the public symbols and ceremonies that mark the country as socioculturally Jewish: the state flag, the national anthem, and the schedule of the workweek (with Saturday as the national day of rest) and the calendar year (in which Jewish holidays are observed). Popular arguments about safeguarding the country's "Jewish character" extend well beyond these largely symbolic gestures to include support for laws, policies, and practices—including, most prominently, the controversial "Nation-State Law" passed in 2018—that test even the most flexible interpretations of the state's self-characterization as both "Jewish and democratic."[16]

Against the backdrop of this sharp rightward shift, virtually any state measure taken in the name of security—physical, economic, or demographic/ethnonational—has tended to garner a strong and reflexive measure of support from the Jewish Israeli public. Indeed, Jewish Israelis' anxiety about security consistently remains so strong that "the Israeli public will accept in the name of security afflictions that had they been applied in other domains . . . would cause a revolt to erupt."[17] Many a right-leaning politician has launched, sustained, or reinvigorated a career by leveraging these long-standing fears.

Biopolitical Logic

The relatively rigid biopolitical logic described earlier draws support from multiple sources, including these historical memories and security concerns as well as a distinction between "us" and "them," or between "brothers and sisters" (Jews, Israelis)[18] and "others" (non-Jews, non-Israelis) that is generally accepted by most Jewish Israelis as a simple matter of common sense. One result is a racialized sociopolitical hierarchy in which nearly everyone present in Israeli sociopolitical space can be classified as a ratified citizen, "real" Other, or "other" Other. A fuller discussion of this biopolitical logic and sociopolitical hierarchy would probe the internal tensions *within* Jewish Israeli society, including divisions between religious and secular and among Ashkenazi, Mizraḥi, Russian, and Ethiopian Jews.

Later in this chapter, I compare the circumstances of Palestinians on either side of the Green Line: Palestinian citizens of Israel (described by the state as "Israeli Arabs") on the western side, and Palestinians living under Israeli occupation on the eastern side. As we will see, both groups are imagined—albeit in different ways—as Israel's "real" Others, and both groups of Palestinians are distinguished in public and popular discourse from recently arrived global migrants who came seeking economic opportunity, or freedom from persecution, or both.

The state's view of its presumed real Others has borne weighty consequences for new Others now living on its margins. The gerush illustrates these effects. After nearly a decade of turning a blind eye toward global migrants' growing presence, the deportation campaign was its first major effort to infuse this protean category of other Others with politicized content. In so doing, the Immigration Administration drew on discursive tropes and governmental practices that had long been deployed against Palestinian citizens and, even more so, against Palestinians in the Occupied Territories.

Put bluntly, before global migrants' arrival, Palestinians already inhabited a "zone of indistinction":[19] a space in which the sovereign power of the state perpetuated itself by distinguishing explicitly among different kinds of people. By applying existing templates of Otherness to a new category of other Others, the gerush categorically denied global migrants the possibility of joining the collective "us" and clarified that they form another kind of national abject—a new form of unwanted, "detritus humanity." In overlaying existing templates of Otherness onto a new, heterogeneous group of Others, the gerush thus set a decidedly exclusionary course that only intensified in subsequent years.[20]

Demographic Anxiety

Earlier I intimated that Jewish Israelis' concerns about physical security are linked to another, related sentiment: a sense of "ethnonational security" that finds clearest expression in the powerful undercurrent of demographic anxiety that courses through Israeli public and political life. Demography is a major topic of national concern in many immigrant-destination countries, if not always for the same reason,[21] but its ubiquity in Israel is particularly worthy of note. Leading demographers are frequently quoted and interviewed in the mainstream media, and demographic issues are a perpetual topic of public discussion, debate, and policymaking. As the "public service announcements" described earlier make clear, the architects of the gerush tapped into this anxiety by characterizing global migrants as purveyors of not just economic but also social and demographic harm.

A provocative argument by political scientist Ian Lustick introduces the possibility that the conversation might have unfolded otherwise.[22] In the 1990s, following the Soviet Union's collapse, approximately 900,000 people immigrated to Israel from the former Soviet Union as olím hadashím under the Law of Return. These immigrants received a formal welcome and full citizenship benefits, even though a substantial proportion of them neither claimed to be Jewish nor were recognized as such by the state. Israel's inclusionary disposition toward them was no foregone conclusion; their pathways to residence and citizenship hinged on a 1970 Supreme Court decision defining Israeli citizenship as open to anyone who could prove a direct, first-degree genealogical link to someone who *is* (or, were they still living, would have been) recognized by the state as a Jew. This decision, it bears mention, extended access to aliyá and Jewish citizenship to anyone who would have been defined as Jewish according to the Nazi definition codified in the 1935 Nuremberg Laws.

In Lustick's analysis, Israel's warm disposition toward its new arrivals from the former Soviet Union stood in clear tension with the country's declared goal of remaining a "Jewish state." The potential demographic "problem" of so many former Soviet immigrants' "non-Jewishness," he observes, has been consistently swept under the rug by statisticians, bureaucrats, and government officials, who have engaged in an ongoing game of classificatory and statistical smoke and mirrors in an effort to confirm the continued existence of a "Jewish" demographic majority. Lustick interprets these practices as evidence that the state's primary interest lies not in preserving the country's Jewish majority, but rather in keeping it "a non-Arab state" with a majority voting populace of non-Arabs.

Following Lustick's logic, unauthorized migrants' relegation to a new kind of Other slot in the brother/Other binary was not necessarily self-evident. In theory, at least, it might have been possible to fold a quarter-million global migrants, nearly all of them able-bodied workers capable of contributing meaningfully to the economy, into the Israeli national body precisely on the grounds of their "non-Arabness"—in short, to imagine them as a demographic asset rather than a demographic threat. Yet this argument never arose in political or public discourse as a thinkable option. Instead of embracing global migrants as a potential boon to the state, the government's preferred path of action hinged on their discursive transformation from a relatively innocuous if growing "nuisance" population into a metastasizing population of "criminal" interlopers: a new, threatening form of other Others.

Fruitful Multiplication

Beyond these flexible practices of counting and calculation, Israelis' deep-rooted sense of demographic anxiety has long found expression elsewhere: in an enduring pronatalist agenda, itself entwined with two additional elements of the local moral economy. The first: popularized religion. In public and political life, Jewish religious texts, customs, and values are strategically, and often didactically, invoked in public debates, frequently in dilute or secularized fashion. Among Israeli migrant rights advocates and activists, for instance, the most frequently invoked biblical passage draws a universalizing conclusion from a narrativized memory of particular (communal) suffering: "You shall not wrong a stranger or oppress him, for you were strangers in the land of Egypt."[23] Political opponents tend to cite a particularist Talmudic aphorism to counter this logic: "the poor of your city come first" (*aniyéi irḥá kodmím*).[24] Equally palpable is a tenacious and liturgically derived, but not necessarily religious, orientation toward what we can call "fruitful multiplication": a cultural celebration of the Hebrew Bible's divine commandment to "be fruitful and multiply" (*prú u'rvú*).[25]

On a collective level, demography and reproduction have long been central to "thinking, creating, and sustaining the Israeli nation-state,"[26] as anthropologist Rhoda Kanaaneh asserts, often in ways that reinforce the racialized biopolitical logic that pits interiorized notions of Jewish "us-ness" against threatening conceptions of Otherness. At the microlevel, cultural obligations to reproduce are deeply felt by most Jewish Israelis, especially women, regardless of their level of religious observance or commitment. For many, this cultural pronatalism is embodied in the simple, ubiquitous assertion that

yeladím zeh simchá—"children bring joy." At the same time, social expectations of parenthood are so strong that some sociologists describe Israel as a
"land of imperative motherhood"[27] in which motherhood is understood as a
"national mission."[28]

For Israeli Jews, "the imperative to reproduce has deep political and historical roots," including powerful religious and sociocultural motives.[29] Some
argue that Jewish Israeli pronatalism is about "replacing" the six million Jews
killed during the Shoah,[30] but other tropes are stronger, including a desire to
counterbalance the perceived demographic threat represented by Palestinian and Arab birthrates—and, especially in the state's early decades, a desire
to produce soldiers in its defense. As Kanaaneh and others make clear, however, institutionalized Israeli pronatalism is a "selective pronatalism" aimed
at ensuring a Jewish majority and protecting the state's "Jewish character."[31]
Palestinian citizens tend to feel precisely the same pressures, albeit in their
political inverse. In short, demography in Israel/Palestine is no dry academic
issue. As in many other regions, it is inextricably entwined with politics and
history, memory and affect, and framed in ideologically charged discourses
of nationalism and collective survival.

"Real" Others

> What the conceptual frame of abjection reveals is that
> neither the subject nor the nation-state is a solid or
> unitary entity, but rather an assemblage of practices.
> —Imogen Tyler

These elements of Israel's local moral economy—a deep sense of (traumatic)
historical memory, omnipresent concerns about security, a pervasive biopolitical logic, demographic anxiety, and a (selective) commitment to fruitful
multiplication—have influenced the treatment of Palestinians since the
earliest days of the Israeli state. This deep-rooted constellation of values,
anxieties, and concerns has consistently been channeled into templates of
Otherness rooted in a commonsense view of Palestinians as both categorically Other and, from a collective moral standpoint, as lesser in value than
Israeli Jews.

How might these templates of Otherness have influenced the state's dispositions toward global migrants? And how might those dispositions have

changed when the government started deporting migrants en masse? In the remainder of this chapter, I show how the tactics and techniques of the gerush tested Emeka's claim, voiced loudly at the community meeting with Officer Rafi and other Immigration Police officers, that a bright line distinguishes global migrants from Palestinians. Specifically, I argue that efforts to criminalize and expel global migrants during the gerush hinged on a growing willingness to treat migrants in ways that had long been deemed acceptable in relation to Palestinians. Two factors proved especially salient: high-stakes racial profiling and a willingness to respond to perceived threat or insult with violence. To evaluate this claim, we must first ask: How, in Israel, is real Otherness configured—and with what effects?

Palestinian Citizens

Approximately one-fifth of Israel's citizens are Palestinians who managed to stay in what became the state of Israel after 1948 or their descendants. For most of these unwilling citizens—"citizens of a state at war with their own people"[32]—staying in place after the war did not signal enthusiasm for the new state of affairs. Rather, as sociologist Nadim Rouhana writes, "As far as most of the Arab population in Israel is concerned, Israel was imposed on them by the force of the gun: a foreign ruling majority, an alien culture, an occupier, a dispossessor, and a state that in effect replaced the Palestinian existence with Jewish reality."[33] In a discursive effort to neutralize links to their Palestinian brethren under occupation and in diaspora, Israel describes these citizens as "Israeli Arabs." In Arabic, they are more likely to call themselves "Arabs of '48" or "Arabs of the inside" ('Arab al-Dakhil).[34]

Israel's 1948 Declaration of Independence promises "full and equal citizenship and due representation" for all, along with "complete equality of social and political rights to all its inhabitants irrespective of religion, race or sex" and a guarantee of "freedom of religion, conscience, language, education, and culture."[35] For the state's Palestinian citizens, however, these lofty commitments have never been fulfilled. Despite their formal inclusion, Palestinian citizens lived under martial law from 1948 until 1966, and till now they have faced interlocking forms of discrimination, both systemic and interpersonal.[36] According to political scientist Yoav Peled, this "citizenship deficit" stems from Israel's bifurcated citizenship regime, which provides republican citizenship for Jews (i.e., the possibility of active participation in the determination, protection, and promotion of the common good), and a more constrained form of liberal citizenship for Palestinians (based on passive possession of a bundle of rights).[37] Others use blunter terms, arguing that Palestinians in Israel hold second-class citizenship at best.[38]

Throughout the state's history, Palestinian citizens have endured mass expropriation of private land for the creation of Jewish Israeli towns, agricultural settlements, and industrial areas. They have faced restrictions on construction that impede the natural growth of towns and cities. Palestinian communities consistently receive fewer government resources to meet basic social needs like health and education than Jewish communities. Schools for Palestinian children (where instruction is in Arabic) and Jewish children (taught in Hebrew) are almost entirely separate, and curricula in Arab schools are defined by representatives of the Jewish majority. As Dan Rabinowitz and Khawla Abu-Baker observe,

> Economic stagnation, underdevelopment, unemployment, and poverty in the Palestinian community are inextricably linked to longstanding government policies of neglect and discrimination. All Israeli administrations, with the sole exception of Rabin's government in the early 1990s, left Palestinian towns and villages outside the loop when assigning subsidies and development incentives. Palestinians are excluded from a variety of welfare benefits and state-subsidized mortgages reserved for army veterans and new immigrants. The exclusion of Palestinians from essential economic spheres such as banking, import and export franchises, and advanced technology further contribute[s] to economic marginalization.

Overall, Rabinowitz and Abu-Baker continue, "Palestinian citizens remain unwanted guests in the Israeli economy, members of a community whose needs and claims are deemed irrelevant to what mainstream Israel defines as its worthy national goals."[39] This holds true even for Palestinian citizens who defy community expectations by serving in the Israeli military, generally for reasons more expedient than ideological. For these unusual soldiers, as Kanaaneh shows, military service generally fails to achieve either complete integration or immunity to discrimination and exclusion.[40] Although military service can yield material benefits, they generally fail to compensate for the community opprobrium accompanying the decision to serve.

Beyond the structural disadvantages and systematic discrimination that Palestinian citizens regularly confront, two additional expressions of governmental power reverberate in their everyday lives: routine mechanisms of racialized biosocial profiling and the latent but real risk of state-sponsored violence. Biosocial profiling "objectifies whole strata of people by assigning them into suspect categories" in an effort to predict behavior and, ostensibly, to control risk.[41] Profiling involves what Didier Fassin calls a "reduction of the social to the biological."[42] To profile is to seek out marks of origin, assign them different degrees of moral worth, and calibrate interactions accordingly. Profiling gives palpable social form and subjective content to prevailing paradigms of suspicion and hermeneutics of distrust. For those who are profiled, the constant repetition of negative or "injurious interpellations"[43] becomes sedimented and entrenched in ways that yield deep subjective harm. Through such techniques and practices, "subjects and states are reconstituted as longer histories of violence and struggle that converge within the bordering practices of the political present."[44]

In Israel, as in Britain, the United States, and other racialized societies, profiling is a taken-for-granted part of everyday life grounded in "amateur biology and common sense."[45] Public and private security personnel are formally responsible for everyday screening and surveillance, but members of the broader public are effectively deputized as well. Guards stationed at the entrance to schools, restaurants, malls, movie theaters, and other public spaces are trained to be suspicious of individuals with Arab bioprofiles, who often face additional surveillance measures and sometimes outright harassment. As a result, and "despite appearances as bustling, liberal, and open areas," Rabinowitz and Abu-Baker note, "Israeli cities remain, in essence, spaces designed for Israeli Jews."[46] At Ben Gurion International Airport, Palestinian and other Arab passengers trying to enter or leave the country—my Egyptian-American roommate, for instance—often are subjected to lengthy and humiliating security screenings.[47] Palestinian citizens also are treated differently from Jewish citizens by all levels of law enforcement including the police, state prosecutors, and the courts.[48]

Beyond these everyday modes of racialization and discrimination, Palestinian citizens also are more likely than Jewish Israelis to be targets of state violence, both in instances of suspected misconduct and while engaging

civically in political protest.[49] On March 30, 1976, for instance, six demonstrators were shot and killed by police at mass protests held in the Galilee to
protest the government expropriation of land for purposes of "security and
settlement." In subsequent decades, annual Yawm al-Ard (Arabic: Land Day)
events held to commemorate their deaths have played a pivotal role in po-
liticizing and mobilizing Palestinian citizens.

Palestinian citizens' sense of exclusion further deepened during the sec-
ond intifada, which began in September 2000 when then prime minister
Ariel Sharon provoked controversy by visiting the Temple Mount in Jerusalem's
Old City. The following month, Palestinian communities in northern Israel
held peaceful protests in solidarity with their brethren in the Occupied
Territories, and Israeli forces responded with violence. Thirteen Palestinians
were killed by police, among them twelve Israeli citizens. All but one of the
Palestinian citizens killed were under thirty. Two were teenagers.

Nearly a decade and a half later, in what one Israeli journalist described
as "tough, disgusting times in Israel/Palestine," another period of political
violence resulted in mass Palestinian casualties in the OPT and, within Israel, in the death of a Palestinian citizen under suspicious circumstances.[50]
In the spring of 2014, an escalation of vigilante violence that straddled the
Green Line both anticipated and helped precipitate the bloody war that soon
broke out in Gaza. After three Israeli teens were murdered by Palestinians
in the West Bank, the Israeli military responded by conducting an aggressive
sweep of the West Bank in search of those responsible. In an act of vigilante
retaliation, extremist Israelis kidnapped a young Palestinian teenager and
burned the boy alive in the Jerusalem Forest. Other radical Israelis responded
by mobbing and attacking Palestinian civilians on Jerusalem's streets. Meanwhile, Hamas began shooting thousands of rockets at Israeli targets, many at
civilian centers, from an elaborate network of tunnels in Gaza, and the Israeli
military responded with massive airpower and ground troops. By the end of
the fifty-day conflict, more than 2,100 people were dead, including nearly five
hundred children. Nearly all of the casualties were Palestinian, and much of
Gaza's already weak infrastructure was destroyed.

After the war, the atmosphere in the region remained tense. Following
several vehicular attacks on passengers at Jerusalem Light Rail stations, the
Israeli minister of internal security declared that "any terrorist who harms
citizens should be killed."[51] Less than a week later, his words were put to the
test. A twenty-two-year-old Palestinian citizen of Israel named Kheir Hamdan approached a police van in the Palestinian city of Kafr Kanna in north-

ern Israel, banged on the window with what officers described as a knife, and was killed by the Israeli police. Initially, the police "insisted the officers' lives were in danger" and that "the officers tried to stop the man by firing a shot in the air, but when he didn't stop, they feared for their lives and shot at him."[52] Closed-circuit footage told a different story: a story of police officers leaving their car as Hamdan ran away, then shooting him in violation of protocol. In a video that quickly circulated via social media, the officers can be seen "dragging the youth to the police car, instead of calling an ambulance and treating him on the scene."[53] Op-ed headlines following the incident highlighted the impact of both biosocial profiling and an entrenched disposition toward police brutality: "When it comes to Arab citizens, the police are quick on the trigger," read one headline.[54] "If you're an Arab, they shoot first," read another.[55]

In the wake of Hamdan's death, Israeli leaders expressed little regret; instead, they were quick to back the police. Right-wing finance minister Naftali Bennett, for instance, pivoted quickly from a cursory gesture of concern about police conduct to a full-throated expression of support for the use of violence as preventative measure. "A crazed Arab terrorist attacked a police car that our officers were in, in an attempt to murder them," he declared. "We can, and should, review our conduct, always" but "we surely mustn't abandon our security forces . . . If we don't give them our backing, we will see more and more Israelis being murdered with knifes [*sic*], [explosives] and car attacks."[56] For his part, Prime Minister Benjamin Netanyahu invoked the rule of law—but not to condemn police brutality. "Israel is a state of law," he said. "We won't tolerate disturbances and riots. We will take action against stone throwers, those who block traffic arteries, and those who call for establishing a Palestinian state in place of the State of Israel. Whoever doesn't respect Israeli law will be punished to the fullest extent. I will direct the interior minister to consider stripping the citizenship of those who call for the destruction of the State of Israel."[57] Six months later, the police department's office of internal affairs closed the case against the officers involved in Hamdan's death. All charges were dropped.[58]

Racial profiling may be an everyday occurrence in Israel, but acts of state-sponsored violence—the killing of Palestinian protesters on Land Day, in the first days of the second intifada, and in the wake of the 2014 Gaza War—become indelibly imprinted in Palestinian citizens' consciousness. Such moments linger as collective wounds—as painful reminders that despite the egalitarian language in Israel's Declaration of Independence, the rights and privileges of Israeli citizenship are not equally apportioned. Instead, some citizens' lives clearly matter more than others'.

Palestinians in the Occupied Territories

In many respects, the lives of Palestinian citizens are markedly different from those of Palestinians in the West Bank, Gaza, and East Jerusalem. Importantly, these distinctions—among Palestinian citizens, West Bank residents, Gazans, and residents of East Jerusalem—reflect no "natural" groupings; rather, they are consequences of the 1948 war remembered by Jewish Israelis as the War of Independence and by Palestinians as their own founding trauma: the *naqba*, or catastrophe.

Although many Palestinians in the OPT have relatives across the Green Line, their everyday lives are markedly different. Some inhabit ancestral lands, but many more are second-, third-, or fourth-generation residents of refugee camps established and maintained by the United Nations Relief and Works Administration. Nearly all Palestinians living under Israeli occupation were born, and have lived their entire lives, within a tight grid of policies and practices designed to address Jewish Israeli concerns about security, demography, and biopolitics. The lived impact of the occupation differs markedly from Gaza (led by the Hamas, an Islamist political party) to the West Bank (led by the secular Fatah Party, successor to Yasser Arafat's Palestinian Liberation Organization), to East Jerusalem (whose residents hold Israeli ID cards but are not Israeli citizens). Below I focus on the West Bank, where Jewish Israelis and Palestinian Arabs often live in close, and tense, proximity.

To grasp the realities of biosocial profiling and the immanent threat of violence for Palestinians in the West Bank, a deeper understanding of the occupation is needed.[59] But first, a note. To avoid getting tangled in arguments about either the legitimacy or strategic efficacy of Israeli military techniques, let me emphasize that the following discussion focuses on everyday people trying to navigate everyday life—women and men, adults and children who are probably much like you and me. A military spokesperson would call them "civilian noncombatants."

Since the 1967 war between Israel and neighboring Arab states, the Israeli military has governed the territories under its control through a sophisticated, high-tech, and constantly evolving regime of discipline and power.

This regime relies on a broad constellation of legal, administrative, and military measures that take concrete form: an intricate permit regime. Land expropriation and house demolition. Tight limits on water usage. A network of well-paved roads constructed for Jewish Israelis' exclusive use. Restrictions on freedom of movement, including a separation wall, military checkpoints, and other tangible structures and barriers. A logic of collective punishment.

While the impact of these measures on Israelis' physical security can be debated, their impact on the Palestinian economy and other institutions of Palestinian society is clear.[60] Between 1967 and the early 1990s, tens of thousands of Palestinians from the OPT earned their livelihoods working in Israel. The imposition of military closures on the territories in the wake of the first intifada quashed those job opportunities—and precipitated the first waves of government-authorized labor migration to the region. After the failure of the Oslo peace process and during the second intifada, Israel tightened the screws further, and Israeli military restrictions on Palestinian mobility effectively stilled major areas of Palestinian society and communal life. Neither goods nor workers can move about freely. Schools and universities cannot function effectively since the mobility of both students and instructors is greatly restricted (both within the region and to the rest of the world). And the already beleaguered Palestinian health care system cannot care for its deeply underserved, and often deeply traumatized, patient populations.[61]

In the West Bank, racialized biosocial profiling is a basic fact of everyday life. Military checkpoints—including the checkpoint Marina ultimately managed to cross in full-blown labor—divide the West Bank from Israel proper and are scattered throughout the West Bank itself. At these checkpoints, some of them permanent and others mobile, anyone who appears Jewish is granted broad freedom of movement. Those who look Palestinian, in contrast, are trapped in a tight, militarized gridlock. Signals of a Jewish Israeli profile include some combination of the following: a Hebrew accent untinged with Arabic, a Jewish name printed on a blue identity card (as opposed to the green identity cards West Bank Palestinians carry), yellow license plates (in contrast to green or white Palestinian plates), and possibly a *kipá* (skullcap) or women's head covering (distinguishing religious Jews). Regardless of their own ethnic background—Ashkenazi or Mizrahi, Russian or Ethiopian, Jewish or Palestinian Israeli—soldiers and Border Police are expected to read these clues and interpret them in accordance with the racialized regime they are charged with enforcing.

Most Israeli civilians who travel regularly around the West Bank are settlers. Many are not ideological radicals but citizens taking advantage of government subsidies and other policies that favor making a home across the
Green Line. Although the infrastructure of the occupation is meticulously
designed to minimize contact between settlers and Palestinians, a small minority of radical settlers deliberately seek out such encounters, at times engaging in provocations and even violent attacks in violation of Israeli law.
Often, such acts of provocation and violence unfold with the tacit support—
or even the explicit support and military protection—of the Israeli military.[62]

In contrast to Jewish Israelis' smooth bidirectional crossings at military
checkpoints, people with Palestinian IDs and profiles—young and old—must
queue up either in cars or on foot in an effort to pass through. At some pedestrian checkpoints, Palestinians wait for hours, sometimes in the beating
sun or driving rain, for an opportunity to plead their case. At the most crowded
checkpoints, men, women, and children wait shoulder to shoulder in narrow
passageways that look like animal pens. When they reach the front of the line,
they must convince the soldiers—often teenagers performing their compulsory military service, automatic weapons slung over their shoulders—that they
deserve to cross. Soldiers address Palestinian petitioners either in rudimentary Arabic or, alternatively, in Hebrew, which many Palestinians, especially
women from rural communities, neither speak nor understand. According
to Israeli, Palestinian, and international human rights groups, "The regime
practiced at the checkpoints is arbitrary and random. The rules change frequently, often to suit the whims of the soldier on duty at the moment. . . . The
policy of suppression and dehumanization that pervades the nature of control over another nation necessarily seeps into the awareness and behavioral
patterns of the soldiers who serve at the checkpoints and in the territories."[63]
While the practices of profiling and surveillance at checkpoints may have an
arbitrary cast, their consequences—including the indignities Palestinians regularly experience—are not arbitrary.[64] The checkpoints are part of a broader
ensemble of techniques, policies, and practices that tightly constrict and con-
strain Palestinians' everyday lives. Israeli leaders defend such practices and
restrictions in the name of security, but some critics liken them to the segre-
gationist logic of South African apartheid. For Palestinians in the West Bank
and East Jerusalem, this "soft knife"[65] of structural and systemic violence
cuts into the fabric of everyday life, and across generations.

Alongside this "soft knife" are other tools of occupation that cut quicker
and deeper, including many that involve physical violence:[66] the destruction

of built structures before confirming they are vacant. The beating and shooting of Palestinians who fail to follow instructions—even if that failure is because they cannot understand commands delivered in broken Arabic, or in Hebrew. The use of civilians as human shields during late night raids in search of suspects or weapons. The excessive use of force against crowds, including misleadingly named "rubber bullets" as well as live ammunition. According to the Israeli human rights group B'Tselem, over 4,800 Palestinian noncombatants were killed by Israeli security forces in the OPT, over a third of them under age eighteen, between the outbreak of the second intifada in 2000 and February 2017.[67] Once again, I have focused here on forms of violence against civilians who are not suspected of engaging in resistance. Those who are suspected of being combatants face far harsher forms of violence, often in contravention of Israeli and international law, including sleep deprivation, shackling, the use of stress positions and threats, and in some cases even extrajudicial killings.[68]

Even when it is substantively absent, the ever-present *threat* of physical violence is a cornerstone of the occupation. As Avram Bornstein notes in his ethnography of Palestinian life in the West Bank, "The lingering effects of violence continued to work even when it was not actually happening because it created permanent scars, both physical and psychological. It weighed in the air with imminence."[69] Violence is always potentially present in the West Bank, indexed by the armed soldiers, barbed wire, concrete barricades, towering wall, and occasional tanks and sounds of gunfire that form a persistent backdrop to everyday life. For Palestinians who have lived long years apart from imprisoned spouses, or who have lost loved ones to the conflict, these wounds scar intimate landscapes in ways that cannot be undone.[70]

Not all Jewish Israelis accept the violence of the occupation, or the occupation itself, as either inevitable or just. Some even share Azoulay's wish to claim their "right not to be a perpetrator" (albeit without necessarily invoking her term). Yet Israelis who try to spark public discussion about these topics tend to encounter powerful pushback.[71] Those who call for a national reckoning consistently face harsh, and sometimes ad hominem, attacks, especially from leaders and groups on Israel's political right. This applies even to former combatants who eschew violence and carry their battle scars into new struggles for reckoning and reconciliation, including activists from groups like Breaking the Silence and Combatants for Peace.[72] Given the structure of Israel's local moral economy, expressing certain political positions—especially those that foreground Palestinians' suffering, evoke (or invert) painful historical analogies, or question long-standing cultural beliefs about the military's moral purity—can involve a good deal of personal risk.

Templates of Otherness

How have Israeli policies toward Palestinians influenced the state's treatment of global migrants? Before the gerush, the government could not assume that mainstream Israel was primed to view global migrants as a threat. Unlike Palestinians, whose Otherness is, in effect, a "design principle" of Israeli citizenship, global migrants were unfamiliar to most Israelis. Although anti-immigrant sentiments from a few prominent national leaders had captured headlines, press coverage before the gerush had been sparse but generally sympathetic. If the state's campaign of criminalization and mass expulsion were to succeed, the public first needed to be convinced of its legitimacy.

Earlier we encountered some of the menacing announcements broadcast regularly by the Immigration Administration in an effort to bolster support for its new agenda. For Israeli listeners, the implications of these ads were clear and consistent with themes that echo in the broader local moral economy: non-Jewish migrants are not Israeli, they cannot become Israeli, and they should not be here. According to the ads, "foreign workers" were a new threat: a new kind of Other who imperiled the state's economic and demographic, if not physical, security. By drawing migrants into the public spotlight and imbuing their collective presence, and their very persons, with a laundry list of powerful negative associations, the state deliberately fomented anti-immigrant sentiment and clarified its view of migrants as categorically different from Jewish Israelis—and deserving of criminalization and expulsion.

Coordinating this discursive and conceptual shift was just a first step. In addition to vilifying global migrants in the mainstream media, the Immigration Administration deployed a range of other techniques meant to recast them as criminals, including racialized biosocial profiling and a new-found readiness to approach global migrants with batons raised. An aura of impunity accompanied the implementation of both tactics. In both respects, individuals *suspected* of being unauthorized migrants were presumed guilty until proven innocent. During the gerush, not just unauthorized migrants but also authorized migrant workers, recognized asylum seekers, visiting professionals, and even the occasional Israeli citizen got caught in their dragnet.

This logic of presumed guilt highlighted two of the Immigration Administration's underlying assumptions: first, that certain forms of phenotypic Otherness necessarily indexed criminality and deportability, and second, that these forms of Otherness—like Palestinians' purported "real" Otherness—legitimated verbal abuse, humiliation, and even physical violence. The arrest of Dr. Christine Santos clearly demonstrates these tendencies.

Guilty Until Proven Innocent: Dr. Christine Santos

Near the height of the deportation campaign, Dr. Christine Santos, a Filipina neurosurgery resident at one of Tel Aviv's major hospitals, was arrested on a central Tel Aviv thoroughfare, forcibly pushed into a police van under the serendipitous gaze of a filmmaker's camera, and taken to police headquarters.

The arresting officers refused to call her supervisor at the hospital to verify her professional identity. Instead, doubtful that a Filipina woman in Tel Aviv could truly be a physician, they joked to one another that "there's a doctor here if anyone isn't feeling well."[73] The video footage of her arrest was broadcast on the national television news along with an interview in which she appeared at work, dressed in hospital scrubs, displaying the purple bruises on her body.

Later I met Dr. Santos in a central Tel Aviv café for an interview, and she shared with me a letter she had sent to two Knesset members documenting the incident in detail. Her narrative of bioprofiling, criminalization, and assault is worth quoting at length.

> I was walking with a Filipina friend at 9:00 P.M. . . . outside the shopping mall when a man in uniform asked for our passports. We asked for his identification and my friend who can read Hebrew better than I do, confirmed that he is a policeman. . . . My friend gave him her Israeli identity card while I gave him my hospital ID—a plastic card which has my picture on it and which says that I am a doctor. He insisted that I give him my passport and I told him that the ID was enough.[74] When I asked why, he said that this is the law. At some point in the conversation, he raised his voice and said, "Why are you shouting at me?" in which I replied, "I am not shouting at you. This is just the way that I talk." From then on, the conversation started to become more unpleasant. . . . He grabbed my arm and motioned me to go to the police car. Then I told him that I am going to give him my passport.

I got it from my bag and handed it to him and he took it. Inspite [*sic*] of this, he held my arm very firmly and dragged me towards the vehicle. I fought against him and against the policemen who later on joined him in crushing my arms and legs and pushing me inside the van. I told them, "Why are you arresting me? I already gave you my ID and my passport. This is not fair. Give me a reason why you are arresting me." All I heard from them was, "Get inside!" At this point, several people gathered around us and I heard them yelling in Hebrew. . . . As the policemen were pushing me inside, passers-by were pulling me from the van. I was turned upside down with my head almost hitting the ground. It appeared like I was a rope in their game of tug-of-war. A filmmaker . . . caught some of it on tape when I was saying, "I'm Christine Santos. I'm a doctor from Ichilov [Hospital]. I gave them my ID and my passport and they are treating me like a criminal." I fought so hard to break free while repeating this question several times: "Why are you arresting me?" I never received an answer from any of the policemen. In my mind, something was not right there. It is a dictum that when a human being is arrested by a person in authority, this person in authority should say something like, "You are under arrest. You have the right to remain silent. Anything you say and do can or will be used against you in a court of law. You have the right to an attorney. If you don't have one, one will be provided for you . . . and so on." I never heard any of these words whether they be in English or something like this in Hebrew.

Given the rigid machinery of biosocial profiling in place, this expatriate physician could, in the arresting officers' minds and despite clear evidence to the contrary, plausibly be construed not only as an illegal resident but also as someone deserving to be apprehended with violence. According to this logic, the officers' response—to arrest her without clear explanation, verbally abuse her, "crush her arms and legs," and turn her "upside down with [her] head almost hitting the ground" as in a "game of tug-of-war"—was legitimate.

Flimsy Papers: Raphael Malonga

Raphael Malonga, an asylum seeker from Congo, also suffered injuries during an unwarranted arrest. I met Raphael, a mild-mannered, mustached man in his late twenties, when he came to the Open Clinic complaining of shoulder and arm pain after being arrested at a long-distance phone and Internet shop in South Tel Aviv. In the early years of the century, before the advent of free global communications platforms like Skype and WhatsApp, most global migrants had no home phones, and international cell phone calls were exorbitantly expensive. As a result, shops like these offered global migrants a vital lifeline to relatives and friends abroad—and they were an easy target for Immigration Police units trying to meet their arrest quotas.

When we met for our first formal interview, Raphael described in French-accented English how he had been arrested along with two other men: one from Ivory Coast and another from either Mongolia or China, he wasn't sure. Unlike most other Africans in Israel, Raphael was among a handful of people from the conflict-ridden countries of Congo, Sierra Leone, Liberia, and Ivory Coast who entered Israel in the late 1990s seeking asylum. (Just a few years later, about 60,000 Eritreans and Sudanese would seek asylum in Israel as well.) At the time, petitions for protection were not processed by the Israeli government, but by the local office of the United Nations High Commissioner for Refugees (UNHCR). Individuals with pending petitions received official letters that they were instructed to carry as proof of their temporary protected status. In principle, a valid document from UNHCR should have protected an asylum seeker from arrest.

Yet in Raphael's case, the arresting officers once again paid more attention to his biosocial profile than to the documents he tried to present. Instead of examining his papers, they ignored Raphael's pleas and took him and the other two men to the police station, where "they asked me many questions. They wanted me to sign a form, but I refused to sign because it was in Hebrew." If the officers were following standard protocol, the Hebrew document was likely a "Relinquishment of Property" statement, which detained migrants routinely were asked to sign upon arrest and in anticipation of their deportation. Raphael's refusal frustrated the arresting officers. "They said 'Why? Everyone else signs.' I said, 'If you bring it to me in French I'll read it and maybe I'll sign.' Then they started hitting me, beating me. I said, 'you can kill me but I won't sign. I was in prison in my own country, and I came this close to being killed.'" Tempered by his previous experiences of political repression and imprisonment in Congo, and aware of the fact that his arrest was unwarranted and unjust, Raphael refused to capitulate. Like Christine Santos, he rejected the criminal subject position into which the arresting officers were trying to force him.

Soon afterward, Raphael was transported from the police lockup to the migrants' wing at Ma'asiyahu Prison in the city of Ramleh. Eventually one of the prison officials did call UNHCR, the validity of his identifying documents was confirmed, and he was released. A volunteer from the Hotline for Migrant Workers picked him up from prison and took him back to his home in Tel Aviv. Hotline staff strongly encouraged him to file a lawsuit and testify against the officers who had assaulted him, but Raphael would not. Even after this ordeal—unwarranted arrest, verbal harassment, physical abuse, imprisonment—Raphael did not want to file a suit. Why? I asked, expecting him to suggest that a claim would go nowhere. His response was different: He harbored no ill will toward Israel or Israelis. His reasoning was theological: "You must love and bless the people of Israel because it says so in the Bible; bless and you'll be blessed, curse and you'll be cursed."

"Even after everything that happened with the police?" I asked.

"Yes," he insisted. I had difficulty believing him, especially after witnessing his repeated visits to the Open Clinic to receive medical care for his injured arm and shoulder. Over subsequent conversations and after a visit to his church, however, I came to see how this theological commitment was woven into his ground project—how it served as a guiding principle in his everyday life as a foreigner in Israel.

It is certainly within the scope of police authority to question the authenticity of documents presented to them. Yet the quick resort to verbal abuse and physical violence in the arrests of Christine Santos, the Filipina doctor, and Raphael Malonga, the Congolese asylum seeker, suggest how deeply this exclusionary biopolitical logic is embedded in the everyday practice of Israeli state power. In each case, phenotypic Otherness was interpreted as an incontrovertible marker of radical difference, as an indication of lesser value in comparison to Israelis, and ultimately as legitimate grounds for treating people with humiliation and violence. When biosocial profiles and legal realities turned out to be misaligned—as they were in these cases—law enforcement officials were slow to admit their error.

Conclusion

> "Border gaze," for those targeted by it, is more than an
> abstract theoretical concept; it is a highly tangible part
> of everyday life. It is forceful and sometimes formidable
> and deadly.
>
> —Shahram Khosravi

We began this chapter with Emeka, the Nigerian leader whose bold appeal to the Immigration Police reflected a keen understanding of Israel's local moral economy. "We are not Palestinians," Emeka declaimed, the microphone in his hand amplifying his words. "We are not against you." His plea, grounded in a bifurcated logic of Otherness, portended no change in police strategy or practice. Still, its rhetorical impact in that tense public moment was striking, and immediate. "We think you are good people," Officer Rafi, the police bigwig, quickly interjected. Although his response addressed just one of Emeka's claims ("If we thought you were criminals, we wouldn't face you like this"), his deeper meaning was clear. *No*, his words implied; *you are not Palestinians. On this point we agree.* Even as Rafi and his officers mobilized other elements of Israel's local moral economy to support unauthorized migrants' illegalization and forcible expulsion, the distinction between these two modes of Otherness remained self-evident. For migrants and their pursuers alike, it was a matter of common sense.

Whether we find this moment of evaluative convergence ironic, or paradoxical, or simply disturbing, one point remains clear. To make sense of it, we need to grasp the larger local moral economy in which it unfolded—that larger web of values, customs, and emotions that "govern and integrate different spheres—the political as much as the social, cultural and economic—and imbue them with special moral concerns and emotional demands." My examination of Israel's local moral economy has concentrated on two groups whose exclusion from the national body and body politic are commonly regarded as categorical and irremediable. Palestinians and global migrants initially were imagined and treated differently by different branches of the Israeli state, but the gap between them narrowed with the gerush, which involved the expanded application of a militarized "border gaze," to use Shahram Khosravi's term,[75] to migrants in addition to Palestinian civilians. As we have seen, this scrutinizing gaze and associated techniques and practices bolster both groups' exclusion from the moral community of people seen in Israel as deserving of political recognition, compassion, or even the benefit of the doubt.

Some might protest that this account is too quick to gloss over the nuances within local sociopolitical and racial-ethnic hierarchies, and I acknowledge there is some substance to this critique. Internal diversity and complex histories are masked when Muslims and Christians are grouped together simply as Palestinian, and when Ghanaians and Filipinos, Ukrainians, Congolese, and recently arrived Eritreans are grouped together as "global migrants." Yet the limitations of these classificatory labels do not diminish the thrust of my argument. Commonsense distinctions between ratified citizens, Palestinians (real Others), and global migrants (other Others) are palpable, and they persist even in the wake of major changes, including the arrival of around 60,000 Eritrean and Sudanese asylum seekers in the decade after the gerush.

Others might contend that this analysis is too quick to dismiss Jewish Israelis' concerns about physical security. It is frightening to realize that war is on the horizon. To be reminded regularly to make sure you have a working gas mask as protection against the realistic possibility of chemical warfare. To see suicide bombings happen, one after another, in the city you inhabit, on the bus lines you ride, and at places you know well from your daily routes and routines. To hear bombs explode a few blocks from where you're busy at work—an experience to which I return in the next chapter. To know people who are now paralyzed, or deaf, or dead as a result of political violence. And it is frightening to see beloved young relatives drafted for military service, one after another, in a period rife with conflict, rocket attacks, and wars—or to be drafted and serve oneself. During my years in Jerusalem, then Tel Aviv, these security concerns weighed heavily on my Israeli colleagues, friends, and family, and I came to know many of them intimately as well. This is not the place for an extended discussion of regional patterns of violence, or of relative levels of risk and responsibility. It is, however, an opportunity to note Jewish Israelis' tendency to depoliticize many of these fears and security concerns. As Ochs puts it, such depoliticization allows us "to become [or remain] ignorant of the structural logics of exclusion that discourses of fear and security serve to reproduce." In this chapter, I have sought to ensure that readers recognize those structural logics, if they did not already.

The broader lessons of the gerush extend well beyond this troubled region. To what extent do the preoccupations framing Israel's response to global migration—security and demography, collective memory and national "character"—find parallel elsewhere? In the years since the gerush, migration has become one of the most urgent and complicated issues of global, national, and local concern. In 2015 alone, more than 1.3 million people arrived in Europe by land or sea, and many then trekked slowly northward, on foot, to apply for asylum. En route, thousands of others fleeing violence, persecution, and poverty drowned at sea. From one country to the next, debates about migration reflect the dynamics and tensions within particular local moral economies. Many of the political emotions most salient in Israel hold similar sway, but other core concerns—influenced by countries' varied historical experiences, collective memories, colonial legacies, and military entanglements—are markedly different.

When we pay ethnographic attention to the commitments and dynamics shaping local moral economies—as well as the lightning rods within them—the far-reaching implications of global migration become clearer. Nearly all of us are affected, whether as migrants or relatives left behind, bureaucrats or elected officials, community leaders or activists, consumers or voters. And everyone in a given locale, regardless of social position, political outlook, or migration status, must navigate within the same ideologically charged discursive and sociopolitical field.

And what of dignity? During the gerush, an abstract notion of dignity itself became a kind of perverse bargaining chip. In both the first "Voluntary Departure" operation and the second, half a year later, the Immigration Administration held "illegal residents" responsible for ensuring their own dignity was protected and preserved. In light of the first operation's "success," flyers announcing the second explained the administration had "decided to give another chance to all the families staying in Israel who still did not take the opportunity to leave with dignity": they could "join a second family operation," or face arrest and deportation. In bold lettering at the center of a new flyer, the administration declared such punitive measures would be undertaken only if necessary, and then only with reluctance and regret: "*We hope that we will not be forced to take such action!*" the flyer read. If anyone refused to leave "voluntarily" and found their dignity violated at the hands of the Immigration Police, apparently they would have only themselves to blame.

CHAPTER 4

After the Bombing

The Politics of Mourning and the Pursuit
of a Bearable Life

On January 5, 2003, just after 6:30 P.M., two bombs exploded on a crowded pedestrian mall in Nevé She'anán, a South Tel Aviv neighborhood adjoining the city's massive Central Bus Station. We could hear the explosions at the Open Clinic, just a few blocks away. A few of the staff and volunteers behind the reception desk exchanged quick glances, but it took us a moment to realize the booms had, in fact, been bombs.

Twenty-three people were killed in the explosions, and over a hundred others suffered physical or psychological injuries. Among the dead were seven global migrants, some of them undocumented. The attack in Nevé She'anán, a neighborhood heavily populated by Ghanaians and Filipinos, Nigerians and Colombians, Romanians and Chinese, was similar to others carried out during the second intifada: two Palestinian men strapped bombs to their bodies and exploded themselves on a densely trafficked thoroughfare in a central Israeli city. Each bomb was packed with nuts and bolts to maximize damage. Afterward, several groups vied for credit; initially Islamic Jihad claimed responsibility, but soon afterward the al-Aqsa Martyrs' Brigade, the military wing of Fatah, contested the earlier claim.[1]

Although a few migrant workers had died in other bombings, this attack hit Tel Aviv's migrant communities and their Israeli friends and allies with particular force. The bombing also captured the attention of the media and national political leaders. Front-page headlines in the country's two tabloid

Figure 11. "One Destiny." Source: *Maariv*.

dailies emphasized the victims' shared fate: the headline in *Maariv* ascribed "One Destiny" to the dead (Figure 11), and *Yedioth Ahronoth* described them as "Blood Brothers" (Figure 12). On the cover of each, pictures of the deceased appeared in neat rows—a kind of snapshot democratization of the Israelis and migrants whose lives were lost. Internal headlines humanized the devastation

Figure 12. "Blood Brothers." Source: *Yedioth Ahronoth*.

in redundant cosmopolitan kitsch: "Crying in every language," read one. "Every injured person cried in a different language," echoed another.

Unlike bombings that preceded it, this particular attack momentarily blurred the boundaries between Israel's citizens and its other Others—at least in the realm of public conversation and debate. For a brief moment, as most of Jewish Israel lined up to condemn Palestinian terrorists as a kind of ultimate Other, the Otherness of injured and dead migrants was suddenly reined in to an astonishing degree—nearly, it seemed, to the point of full, if fleeting, symbolic inclusion in the national collective.

After the bombing, Israelis and migrant communities alike struggled to make sense of what had happened and groped for an appropriate language of mourning. Benjamin Netanyahu, then serving as foreign minister, made headlines during a visit to bomb victims at a Tel Aviv public hospital when he declared that in the wake of terror, migrant workers are *"basár me'bsaréinu"*[2]— flesh of our flesh. He added, "The terrorists came with the intention of hurting citizens of the world as well [as Israelis] . . . We are saving those same people with everything we've got, as flesh of our flesh. Every person has a right to life, and what is taking place here, in this hospital, is the answer to terror."[3] But were *all* migrant workers now flesh of Israeli flesh, or did this new possibility of inclusion bear an intolerable, indeed a mortal, price? How did this apparent wave of concern align with competing portrayals of "foreign workers" as abject figures who could be humiliated, beaten, and hauled off in the dead of night, before their children's eyes? And what of migrants themselves? After six months of an intensifying deportation campaign, how did the attack reverberate in their lives, and their moral worlds? How did they react to their community members' injury and loss? To their sudden characterization as members of Israel's moral community—or, at minimum, as people whose deaths were publicly grievable?

I pursue these questions by exploring how the Nevé She'anán bombing was mourned, and its aftermath endured, at multiple points in Israeli sociopolitical space. Framing this inquiry is a pair of concerns posed by Judith Butler.[4] First is the question of grievability: What makes a life grievable, or ungrievable? How might the local moral economy influence the politics of grievability in the wake of an attack like this one? The second question involves life's bearability. For people who have become inured to the realities of sociopolitical abjection and then survive a moment of devastating violence, how might the world be made bearable once again? Under such circumstances, what would a bearable life entail? We need to think these two questions together—the question of grievability and the question of life's bearability— while taking care, as Butler notes, "not to let them fully collapse into one another."[5]

First, though, we must look elsewhere: toward chaos, and terror, and death. I begin by recounting the events of that fateful evening, the "terror protocols" that quickly went into effect, and the modest ways in which migrant advocates and activists and I groped for some meaningful way to respond. I then consider how the bombing's migrant victims were mourned in three distinct moments. First is the official memorial service cosponsored by various national and municipal authorities and hosted by Mesila. A second, very different memorial event was the funeral, or "homegoing" ceremony, for a man I'll call John Efia Armstrong, a Ghanaian in his early forties and the first West African to lose his life in a suicide bombing in Israel. Finally, I return to Mesila to a previously scheduled community leaders' meeting held the day after the bombing, where the agenda was tossed aside to make space for the work of mourning.

The first of these events put Israeli authorities' ambivalence about the country's other Others on full display. The homegoing ceremony and leaders' forum, in contrast, both served as *inhabitable spaces of welcome*: small sanctuaries in time and space in which people—as a group, in a dyad, or even in solitude—can find some measure of familiarity, comfort, meaning, and safety in the shadow of laws, policies, and practices designed explicitly to make them feel unwelcome. However fragile and ephemeral they may be, such spaces are indispensable to people facing sociopolitical abjection. By exploring the power of such spaces precisely in the wake of terror and shock, destruction and death, we learn how those facing abjection struggle not only to survive, but also to follow another existential imperative with a longer time horizon: the quotidian, if vigorously uphill, pursuit of a dignified, livable, flourishing life.

In ethnographic terms, this trio of memorial events expands our view of Israel's local moral economy and the moral worlds of those who inhabit it. The moment of rupture created by the bombing immediately inspired a potent rhetoric of common humanity. At the end of the day, however, this lofty rhetoric yielded no real change in how global migrants were imagined, represented, or treated. Instead, the gerush marched obstinately onward while mourning migrant communities struggled to care for their wounded and bury their dead. As one television journalist put it, migrant residents of South Tel Aviv may have "earned a few days of compassion" in the wake of the attack, "but no more than that."[6]

Bombs

A few moments after we heard the explosions, the Open Clinic's codirector, Ariella, made some quick decisions. First: tell the patients—a task she assigned to me. At 6:40, I walked into the center of the waiting room, called for everyone's attention, and made my announcement in English and Hebrew: "There's just been a bombing in Nevé She'anán. You might want to contact your relatives and friends." I made sure my message was repeated in multiple translations until everyone present understood. Some patients pulled out cell phones to make calls or send text messages, but others remained still.

Back at the reception desk, the Israeli staff and volunteers were less tranquil. Someone switched on the radio to glean a few basic details, then turned it off as we tried to keep our focus on the constant stream of patients seeking care. Ariella decided not to close the clinic, instead leaving the emergency efforts to the first responders who, we surmised, had handled more than their share of chaos and bloodshed.

By the end of the shift, three staff members and a handful of clinicians were left, but none of us knew quite what to do. Ariella was panicking; she connected deeply with patients, but her tentative leadership style was ill suited to the evening's challenge. Her supervisor, who oversaw the clinic, was out sick and wasn't answering his phone. Neither the clinic nor its parent NGO had a relevant emergency protocol in place. We had no clear action priorities, and no mandate to contact other organizations to develop a coordinated response. In short, no one was prepared for a crisis like this one. Ultimately, the staff and volunteers took just a single concrete step: we made two posters listing emergency numbers, one for the clinic door and another to hang on the street at the site of the attack. In a move she later regretted, Ariella included her own cell phone number. The only calls she got that night were from journalists. When they rang, she later told me, she had no idea what to say.

Once the posters were ready, we trekked the few blocks to Nevé She'anán. By then, two hours had passed since the explosions. The scene had long since been cleared, and all of the usual suspects had taken up their posts: soldiers with weapons slung over olive-clad shoulders and police officers in blue. Hordes of local and international media with television cameras, audio recorders, notebooks, and mobile satellite vans. Municipal volunteers in fluorescent vests. Bearded men in white jumpsuits from the ultraorthodox Zaka organization,[7] which collects remaining fragments of human flesh at times like this in order to dispose of them in accordance with Jewish law. Crowds of gaping onlookers: elderly neighborhood residents. Well-dressed disaster tourists, probably from other parts of the city. Migrants from China, the Philippines, West Africa, Eastern Europe. A small group of right-wing protesters seized the opportunity to call for greater aggressiveness against Palestinians in response to attacks like this one. Used latex gloves littered the streets, and at the site of the explosions, small pools of blood glistened in the light of the streetlamps.

In the hours and days that followed, the Israeli authorities, media, and public largely followed their usual protocols. No longer fazed by a news flash announcing yet another suicide bombing, most Jewish Israelis filtered the news for any detail that might raise a red flag. Where was the attack? How many were injured, and how many killed? Do I know anyone in the area? Anyone who might have been passing through? After each attack, Israeli minds tend to follow well-worn neural circuits, and anxieties are usually quieted with a requisite three-sentence conversation: "Are you okay?" I heard several dozen times that night, sometimes in Hebrew and sometimes in English, from relatives and friends, including migrants I'd come to know. With each ring of the obligatory cell phone in my pocket, I offered the same rote answer: "I'm fine. Thanks for calling." Click. And the phone would ring again. Most Israelis are accustomed to these thought processes and communicative rituals—as were many migrant workers who had lived in Israel for any length of time (Figure 13). After confirming that tragedy has struck only others, shock recedes, and what returns is a sense of routinized, corporeal

Figure 13. "Mom, I'm fine." The text in the balloon (upper right) is "translated" into Hebrew (lower left). This cartoon was published two days after the bombing. Source: Ron Sussenbach, *Maariv*.

"fear of terror," as Ochs puts it, a fear "that hovers between the intimate and the discursive."[8]

For unauthorized migrants, things are not so simple. As we walked around Nevé She'anán that night, some struggled to remain invisible: those who hid in their homes traumatized, bleeding, or in pain rather than risk contact with the authorities for fear of arrest.[9] Some migrants brought injured friends and relatives to hospitals but left them there, unaccompanied, to avoid putting themselves at risk.[10] Others sought medical attention willingly, but offered false names or addresses. And among those who sought care, some were reluctant to trust the Israeli medical staff who treated them.

Injuries

Several days after the bombing, Ariella and I visited injured migrants at one of Tel Aviv's main hospitals, a thick multilingual sheaf of information sheets—in English, Hebrew, Mandarin, and Romanian—in hand. We knew none of the injured personally, but the hospital staff made no effort to block our visit; to the contrary. At this particular hospital, the Open Clinic and its parent NGO were relatively well known and well regarded, in part because a dozen or so clinicians, including several high-ranking unit heads, were clinic volunteers or even members of the executive board.

We began our three-hour visit on the neurosurgery ward, where a Chinese man in his late twenties was hospitalized after shrapnel from one of the bombs had burrowed its way into his skull. When we knocked, his room was already full of visitors—men from the company that employed him, we surmised—so we apologized for the interruption and left an information sheet. Later, on the trauma ward, we encountered the same group of men visiting another Chinese patient of about the same age. Despite the fresh flowers that brightened the room, he looked even more despondent than his compatriot. Once again, we left information sheets but ducked away to avoid imposition. We did, however, speak with the man's roommate, a man from Moldova who had been in Nevé She'anán with his pregnant daughter when the bombs went off. Both she and the fetus were fine, but the father had suffered a broken leg.

In plastic surgery, we met a Ukrainian woman who told us she sometimes made money selling cigarettes and other small items on the pedestrian mall. On the nightstand beside her bed was a small plastic vial containing a metal pellet the doctors had retrieved from inside her arm. In rough

Hebrew—learned from her Israeli husband, she explained—she rebuffed our offer to link her up with mental health support. "I prefer to deal on my own," she said. "If you didn't see it, you don't understand."

Then we found Paul, a Ghanaian man hospitalized with shrapnel in his leg. I knew of his injury and hospitalization from my Ghanaian friend Gloria, who had called to check in on me after the bombing. She mentioned Paul, whose wife had done some sewing for a close mutual friend of ours. Familiar with the Open Clinic and glad to discover this personal connection, Paul was happy to chat. As we sat beside his hospital bed in the brand-new, state-of-the-art hospital tower, he described what he was doing when he felt the explosions. A friend had recently been arrested, and he and a companion were en route to a meeting to brainstorm ways to help. After the first blast they scrambled to get out of the area, fearing another. When the second bomb exploded, Paul was hit in the leg by flying debris. He was lucky; another piece of shrapnel had grazed the left side of his neck but caused no harm.

"Were you afraid to go to the hospital?" I asked. Paul's answer was definitive: "No." In fact, he had dragged himself to the police, told them he'd been injured, and allowed them to put him in an ambulance. He recounted a story of a Ghanaian man injured in a terror attack four years earlier who had avoided seeking medical attention for fear of deportation and later died of untreated tetanus as a result of his injuries. Remembering this story, which Paul firmly believed to be true (but which we could not confirm), he told us he had entered the ambulance without hesitation.[11] Now, in the hospital, he was suspicious of his Israeli care providers. Would he receive second-class treatment, he wondered, because he is black? Paul was especially anxious about the doctors' plan to leave the shrapnel in his leg, a concern he mentioned twice during our conversation. Removing it would be expensive, he suspected, and the hospital probably just didn't want to spend the money on him. A phone conversation with one of his employers, speaking from the man's own military experience, failed to convince Paul of the physicians' reasoning: some shrapnel injuries, especially injuries to the bone, heal better without an invasive operation to extract what remains.

Our visit with Vadim, a bartender from Moldova who worked in a café on Nevé She'anán, was the most difficult of all. The bombing had struck on the eve of his 30th birthday, we were told, and it had injured his spinal cord and left him paralyzed from the waist down. Now on a respirator in the hospital's secluded intensive care unit, Vadim could barely speak. According to the nursing staff, not a single visitor had come to see him until the afternoon we arrived, when suddenly he had three: a cousin in her mid-forties, a friend in her twenties, and his employer, the woman who owned the café in which he worked. Barely able to speak a word, Vadim pleaded with them to spare his family the news. They had gone against his wishes and placed an international call to his sister nonetheless.

Dreams

Unlike Vadim, Paul, and others we visited in their hospital beds, some of those most devastated by the bombing were physically unscathed. Their wounds lay elsewhere, in the shards of life that could never be gathered or reassembled. Rebecca Armstrong, the widow of John Efia Armstrong, the bombing's sole Ghanaian victim, ranked among them.

Four days after the attack, Mesila's volunteer coordinator asked if I would meet Rebecca and accompany her on two errands: to the National Insurance Institute (NII) to arrange the transfer of her husband's body to Ghana for burial, then to a physician to evaluate her own health and well-being. With a pounding heart and a stomach full of knots, I agreed.

Mesila's director took me into her tiny office to brief me in advance. Rebecca wasn't sleeping in her own apartment, I learned; she was staying with one of her employers, a woman whose phone number I dutifully marked down. The employer would bring Rebecca to the NII office, and a man named Robert Yeboah, a senior member of Armstrong's family, would accompany her. I would meet them there.

As I later realized, Robert and I had met several years earlier. A kind-eyed man in his forties who spoke thoughtfully, with measured words, he ran a small business offering computer classes to migrants who hoped to advance their technological skills. In another room of the same apartment, he provided refuge to Norma, a Filipina woman who was left on her own with a newborn infant after the child's Ghanaian father had been deported. I remembered the day I met Robert. He had entered the apartment just as Norma and I were wrapping up a rambling interview—about the older children she had left in the Philippines when she came to Israel to work as a caregiver, losing her visa, her unreliable (and now deported) Ghanaian boyfriend, her current dire straits. On that day, Robert had been suspicious of my presence, and our interaction had been strained. What was I doing there, he wanted to know, and whom did I represent? Despite his suspicions, he responded gratefully when I later swung by to bring Norma a used baby stroller that had been donated to Mesila.

When we spoke by phone on this somber occasion several years later, Robert carried his heavy burden anxiously but with care. "My only concern is the transfer of the body to Ghana for burial," he said. "They"—the family in Ghana—"are waiting." Not long after we hung up, he called back. Given Rebecca's unauthorized status, he would bring her to NII only in the presence of an embassy representative, even if it meant delaying our scheduled meeting. His insistence raised my blood pressure; it would push our meeting close to the NII office's closing time (on a Thursday, no less—the final day of the Israeli work week). But Robert insisted, and I couldn't blame him.

When we finally convened in the NII offices, the room was crowded and the atmosphere tense. Rebecca and Robert filed into the small space accompanied by an embassy representative, a friend of Rebecca's, and me. Across the large desk were two NII clerks, both women. During the meeting, Robert was alternately distraught and angry at the two clerks, whom he accused of stinginess and racism. As the two Ghanaian men parried with the two Israeli women about passports, visas, plane tickets, and reimbursement procedures, Rebecca sat quietly, looking numb.

The clerks outlined the travel expenses NII would cover, which they characterized as generous: transport of Armstrong's remains, and accompanying one-way tickets for both Rebecca (whose visa was expired) and Robert (who lived in Israel with authorization by virtue of his marriage to an Israeli woman). Robert and his consular advocate pressed back. "We are asking for two-way travel and visas back to Israel," the consular official insisted. "They can't just leave without preparations."

"We can only offer Rebecca one way," one of the clerks replied. "If she wants to come back, she must apply for a visa to the Ministry of Interior." The Ghanaian representative reformulated his position. "If Rebecca decides not to go, you should be more considerate." I got up from my seat near the edge of the desk and slid over to stand behind Robert. I had been sitting too close to power, and I felt an urgent need to move.

"We are being more than considerate," the NII clerk sniffed. "If this had happened to me, I would receive the same."

"*Has v'halíla*," Robert replied in a perfectly pitched Israeli response, one of those flashes of secularized prayer that pepper everyday Hebrew speech. *God forbid.*

Only at our next destination, a small clinic run by a private insurance company, did Rebecca speak freely. "Are things you see in dreams true?" she asked me as we sat in the waiting room before her doctor's appointment. I fumbled for a reply, keenly aware of my designated role as a source of support and comfort.

Rebecca asked me join her in the exam room with the physician, a warm, kindly man I knew from his longtime role as a volunteer at the Open Clinic. "How are you feeling?" he asked Rebecca gently. He listened carefully as she recounted a tangle of symptoms that seemed to map poorly onto his diagnostic categories. She felt heat in her throat, she explained. Pains all over her body, in her veins, in her left hand. She had been sleeping okay—until this morning at 4:30 A.M., when she awoke in fear. And then, after she had gone back to sleep, her husband came to her in a dream: "He said, 'You know I am dead. Who are you sleeping with?' 'I am not sleeping with anyone.' He put his hand on me to comfort me. He was all white. He said, 'I have to go.' I escorted him, and we walked like we were boyfriend and girlfriend. Then he went, and I woke up."

Rebecca's dream brings to mind anthropologist Lisa Stevenson's reflections on the role images can play as repositories of ineffable truths. "We do not always want the truth in the form of facts or information," she writes; "often we want it in the form of an image. What we want, perhaps, is the opacity of an image that can match the density of our feelings. We want something to hold us."[12]

When the world is crumbling, even a wisp of a dream can have a powerful hold. The embrace of a dream can take a life on the verge of shattering and make it just a bit more bearable. Only then did Rebecca's earlier question about dreams, and truth, become clear to me. When grief and loss threaten to shatter us, a truth ensconced in something as fleeting as a dream-image can make all the difference in the world. At least for a moment.

Grievable Life?

Before turning to the question of life's bearability in the wake of devastation, we must first address the broader question of grievability in the wake of the bombing: Whose death counts? Who can—and cannot—be mourned? Under what circumstances, and by whom?

The question of grievability points not only toward death but also toward politics: toward hierarchies of human value and collective ways of reckoning who is deserving of compassion or concern and who is not. It reminds us that one way to ascertain the value of any individual life is ex post facto, through sociological autopsy. How is a particular individual, or group, imagined, represented, and treated in death?

In Chapter 3, I examined the architecture of Israel's local moral economy, including its ethnonational biopolitical logic, deep sense of demographic anxiety, and omnipresent concerns about security. These considerations profoundly influence both official and vernacular Israeli responses to the questions that concern us in this chapter: Whose lives matter, and what makes for a grievable life? Should dead migrants be grieved by the Israeli state, or the Israeli public—and if so, how?

Officially Remembered: The Israeli Memorial Ceremony

At the official ceremony memorializing the seven migrant victims of the Nevé She'anán bombing, these questions took on great urgency. Nearly every branch of Israeli state bureaucracy has deep experience mourning Israeli victims of war and violence. In moments of loss, violence, or tragedy, Israeli institutions tap into well-developed frameworks for public mourning grounded in the country's local moral economy and organized around familiar expressions of popularized religion: the Jewish custom of immediate burial. The rituals of sitting *shiva*.[13] The haunting melody of the *El Maléi Rahamím* prayer ("God of Compassion") and the life-affirming Kaddish (the customary prayer of mourning and remembrance, which actually makes no mention of death). Beyond these religious practices and borrowings, invoked even by many secular Israelis in moments of loss, are other tools of formal meaning making. Tropes of martyrdom rooted in historical memories of collective persecution and individual sacrifice. Steely assertions of the need to protect national security and maintain collective honor by avenging tragic deaths with a firm military hand. The task of remembering non-Jewish, noncitizen victims is less familiar—and far trickier. Just who can, and who must, be mourned? How should the state mourn victims of a Palestinian suicide bombing *who themselves had been abjected from the nation's moral community?*

At the official memorial service for the bombing's migrant victims, held nine days after the bombing, these questions demanded a response. Hastily arranged on short notice by state-level authorities, the early afternoon ceremony was hosted—but not planned—by Mesila, which the municipal director of social services described at the ceremony as "an open, warm, concerned home for the foreign community." Even as state-level policies aimed to illegalize, criminalize, and expel, the municipality chose a different tack—and Mesila's motto remained largely unchanged. I paraphrase this commitment, introduced earlier: *We will not interfere with government policies, and we assume most migrants' presence is temporary. But as long as they are here, they deserve a basic standard of respect and social welfare that it remains our duty to provide.* It is hard to imagine a state-level agency hosting a memorial of this sort.

The Politics of Performative Mourning

The official memorial ceremony was a largely perfunctory event that sought to balance three competing concerns: the pathos of the moment, the municipality's commitment to serving migrant workers' basic needs "as long as they are here," and the national government's interest in deporting a large number of unauthorized migrants as quickly and efficiently as possible. At the gathering, migrant victims were rendered visible primarily through Israeli eyes in a bureaucratic performance that ritualized grief with minimal affect. Speakers steered clear of the individual lives of the deceased, instead tacking a course between two contradictory official discourses: Jewish ethnonationalism on one hand, universalist humanism on the other.

About fifty people crowded into Mesila's cramped meeting area—a space that felt tight when half that number gathered—for the brief ceremony. Among those in attendance were representatives of the Foreign Ministry, the Ghanaian and Chinese ambassadors, municipal officials (some elected, others appointed), Mesila staff and volunteers, a few staff members from migrant rights NGOs, and several relatives and friends of the four Chinese nationals and one Ghanaian killed in the bombing. A pack of equipment-laden radio, television, and print journalists was present as well. We all stood; there was no room for chairs.

The ceremony began with a procession bringing three coffins through Mesila's narrow doorway and into the small room, where they were placed side by side on a raised platform draped in black. The coffins contained the remains of three of the Chinese victims. As I later learned from Einat, a Mesila staff member, no one had told Rebecca Armstrong that her husband's remains would not be present.

The speakers—representatives of the municipality and the Israeli Foreign Ministry, along with the Chinese and Ghanaian ambassadors—addressed the gathering from a microphone positioned just to the side of the coffins. A Chinese man I didn't know wept visibly. Rebecca, proud and beautiful even in mourning, stood tall, garbed in black from head to toe, heavy tears rolling slowly down her cheeks. At one point, Mesila's director shed a few quiet tears as well. Few others showed any emotion at all.

The brief ceremony was striking—"surreal" in some respects, as Einat later put it. First, the victims remained anonymous. Other than brief mention of their names, the deceased were memorialized as symbols, not as individuals. Second was the matter of language. More than half of those present probably spoke limited Hebrew at best, yet the ceremony was conducted almost entirely in that language. The municipal director of social services, who served as emcee, spontaneously translated occasional phrases into English, but the majority of his remarks and their flow and content were communicatively available only to fluent Hebrew speakers. In fact, even his translated remarks were accessible only to some. Since most Chinese migrants in Israel knew little English, their ambassador's remarks may have been the only words they understood. The Foreign Ministry representative spoke in English, as did the Ghanaian ambassador. In all, few if any of those present could follow the entire linguistic content of the event, which became eminently clear when two Chinese attendees chatted during a declared moment of silence.

The tensions among the event's sponsors were difficult to conceal. Although held at Mesila and emceed by the organization's supervising municipal official, the ceremony was planned and coordinated, Einat told me, at the national level. Thus the state, represented by the Foreign Ministry and the Interior Ministry, organized a memorial service that was possible only because Mesila—the sole organization capable of bringing generally opposing camps under the same roof and still broadcasting the desired message— was willing to cooperate and provide a venue. I was surprised that Mesila's director was not among the speakers.

When my next volunteer shift at Mesila rolled around a week later, I learned that no one seemed upset by the director's absence from the line-up. Speaking with pride, another staff member, Keren, drew a military analogy. In the days after the bombing, she said, Mesila was like a communications unit (*yeḥidát késher*) in the Israeli military. Her comparison bore twofold significance. Neither the Foreign Ministry nor the Ministry of Interior had any direct way of communicating with the city's various migrant communities (nor did the Open Clinic, as noted earlier). As a result, Mesila's role as a liaison at this sensitive moment was vital. Yet the army analogy evokes other powerful elements of Israel's local moral economy as well including, above all, the secular sanctity of allegiance to the state and its founding values. Although I didn't press for details, Keren's comment gestured both toward Mesila's Zionist commitments and, at the same time, toward the bright line distinguishing Mesila, as a branch of (local) government, from what some of its staff called "the organizations" (ha'irguním)—the network of activist NGOs whose explicit human rights idiom often pressed, sometimes aggressively, against the hegemony of the state.

At one point in the ceremony, this ideological chasm emerged in full force. When the Foreign Ministry representative began explaining why, in his analysis, suicide bombings occur, a well-known human rights activist erupted in protest. "Politics!" he shouted loudly. A few people chided him for interrupting. "You invited me here!" he retorted, angling for the door. "You bless them after they're dead," he continued. "The question is how you treat them when they're alive!" The now-unwelcome activist struggled to find a path through the dense crowd, and a Mesila staffer closed a window to drown out his voice. For the officials on hand, migrant workers were grievable, it seemed—but only in terms that aligned with their ethnonationalist narrative.

"Children of Light" Versus "Children of Darkness"?

What was the point of the memorial service, and to whom, if anyone, was it meant to bring comfort? The city's director of social services, a traditionally observant Jew, described it as an expression of the municipality's "commitment to solidarity between people," an obligation grounded in two components of Israel's local moral economy: "the collective memory of the Jewish nation" and a popularized understanding of the Jewish religion. At several points, he invoked the religious obligation—which, he reminded the assembled crowd several times, appears in the Hebrew Bible a total of thirty-six times—to care for "the stranger living among us." For him, collective memory and religious obligation converge at Mesila, which, he continued, "waves flags of social justice, brotherhood, solidarity, and human rights."

The remarks from Mesila's district-level supervisor were stiffer and more official. Speaking mostly in Hebrew, he steered clear of fraught idioms of moral

obligation grounded in either religion or collective memory. Instead, he foregrounded the municipality's cosmopolitan commitment to accepting migrants
as local residents who deserve attention, investment, and care. Yet his remarks
violated municipal protocol in one brief but notable way; he pointed to the
deep gulf between municipal and state-level dispositions toward global migrants. "The municipality does all it can—without help from the state—to
support the community of foreign workers, who constitute one-fifth of Tel
Aviv–Jaffa," he insisted. These migrants "want nothing more than to go to
work and return home in peace," and the municipality regards them as "residents with equal rights." With these words, Mesila's local supervisor foregrounded a major rift between the Tel Aviv municipality and the state—at a
public event, in the presence of journalists and foreign ambassadors. In so
doing, he mobilized the raw pain of the day's tragedy as evidence of the justness and humanity of municipal policies and the callousness of the state. Given
Mesila's perpetual efforts to avoid being perceived as a thorn in the side of
state-level authorities, his candidness was noteworthy.

Even more noteworthy, however, was the role of the national government.
As noted, two ministries were involved, at least in principle: the Foreign Ministry and the Ministry of Interior. Since this was an official memorial for deceased foreign nationals, the Foreign Ministry presence made sense. Although
the Ministry of Interior was mentioned as an official sponsor, no ministry
representative spoke, and none appeared to have been present. Toward the
end of the ceremony, after the attending dignitaries had laid wreaths on the
three coffins, the emcee announced that a representative from the Ministry
of Interior would come by later to lay a wreath although, to the best of my
knowledge, this promise never materialized.[14] Official remarks from the
ministry would have added an element of absurdity to an already peculiar
event. Recall, for instance, the Interior Minister's anti-immigrant views, and
the ministry official who insisted Marina undergo a gynecological exam.

The Foreign Ministry, however, did send a representative. Delivered in
English, his message largely echoed those of the two municipal officials. By
his account, this event was a chance "to pay tribute and say farewell to four
innocent men and women who came to Israel to make their living and to
send [money] to [their] families and instead have to be sent [home] in coffins." Going further than Foreign Minister Netanyahu's public statements, the
ministry representative expressed sympathy for the human plight of wounded
migrants. They should be remembered not merely as victims of terror, he insisted, but also as peace-loving, rational, and comprehensible: as honest,

honorable economic migrants whose primary objective was to improve their lot in life and that of their families. What distinguished his remarks was the fact that this position—wholeheartedly accepted at the municipal level but typically rejected by the national government—was articulated by a representative of the state. Now, several months into the gerush but while the blood was still drying on the streets, it was striking to hear a government representative humanize, rather than demonize, migrant workers.

As extraordinary as it was to hear state-level (and not just municipal) representatives publicly express sympathy for and solidarity with illegalized migrants, it came as no real surprise that some migrants—specifically, those who were bleeding, suffering, or dead—were folded under the national wing in this time of crisis. Like the municipal officials who spoke before him, the Foreign Ministry representative cast this particular bombing as a shared, collective tragedy in which Israeli citizens and their noncitizen, non-Israeli neighbors composed a single community of mourners. His logic was clear. Echoing the director of social services, he described Israelis and global migrants as common victims united against the unquestionable evil of Palestinian terrorism—as the director put it, as "children of light" united against the "children of darkness."

Grievable—Within Limits

In effect, this explicit marking of lines in the sand clarified the conditions under which dead migrants' lives were grievable in official circles. The government harbored clear assumptions about global migrants' political allegiances in relation to the Palestinian-Israeli conflict: Their allegiance, it was assumed, lay not with the perceived Palestinian "enemy" but instead with Israel. As we will soon see, such assumptions often proved true. Many Christian migrants living in Tel Aviv viewed their own destinies as intimately entwined with that of the Israeli nation, and many Christian migrant leaders allied themselves explicitly with Israel in a religious idiom that melded Christianity's Jewish antecedents with a biblical notion of Jewish chosenness.[15]

Ultimately, however, none of the speakers at the official memorial event broached the deeper questions lurking in the shadows: What had precipitated migrants' departure from their homes and drawn them to this troubled land? To what extent—and how—had Israel become dependent upon migrants' labor to build apartment buildings, harvest food, care for the elderly, clean homes and businesses? In what ways did government policies figure in so many migrants' quick slip from "legal" to "illegal" status? Questions like these figured nowhere in the day's proceedings.

Instead, the brief memorial conveyed an uncomfortable mix of messages. On one hand, the speakers insisted, terror doesn't discriminate. Yet this shared vulnerability became visible, and speakable, only in the wake of a very particular kind of violence. In the aftermath of a suicide bombing perpetrated by Palestinians, dead Israeli citizens and their noncitizen migrant neighbors could be described, briefly, as "Blood Brothers" sharing "One Destiny." But this common vulnerability could only become perceptible, and migrants' deaths only grievable, by tapping into the strongest and most resilient undercurrent of Israel's local moral economy: the biopolitical trope of innocent victims united against a demonized cast of real Others. "Children of light" pitted against "children of darkness."

Bearable Life?

When we shift from the political to the experiential realm, different questions emerge. How did migrants themselves respond to the devastating attack that struck their communities? In what ways, and for whom, did the bombing make life unbearable—and how might it be made bearable once again? "A bearable life," writes critical theorist Sara Ahmed, "is a life that can hold up, which can keep its shape or direction, in the face of what it is asked to endure. . . . The unbearable life is a life which cannot be tolerated or endured, [held] up, held onto. The unbearable life 'breaks' or 'shatters' under the 'too much' of what is being borne."[16] Unbearability may be occasioned by accidental tragedy or natural disaster, but it can also be the deliberate result of human action or inaction. As we've learned, various branches of the Israeli state have employed diverse tactics and strategies *whose very aim is to make certain lives unbearable.* Just how unbearable, in what ways, and to what ends can vary. But we cannot forget that this was a welcome effect, if not a deliberate aim, of the gerush[17]—just as it is a welcome effect, if not a precise aim, of many techniques of occupation.

In the wake of crisis, as the Nevé She'anán bombing makes clear, the matter of life's bearability takes on great urgency. As we learn from Rebecca, whose husband died in the explosion, these are individual struggles, and yet they are intersubjective as well. As Ahmed elaborates: "the struggle for a bearable life is the struggle for . . . space to breathe."[18] One can only breathe freely on the far side of crisis, in a space that feels inhabitable. A space where one feels welcome. At the funeral for Rebecca's husband, an entire community came together with just these needs in mind.

Homegoing: Funeral as Inhabitable Space of Welcome

At the "homegoing ceremony" for John Efia Armstrong, Ghanaians in Tel Aviv convened not only to insist on the grievability of their lost brother but also to pursue a renewed capacity to breathe and endure. Armstrong's funeral could not have been more different from the official memorial service at Mesila. Unlike that brief, largely perfunctory event, this deeply personalized tribute, held in a manufacturing space turned event hall near Tel Aviv's Central Bus Station and the site of the bombing, drew a crowd of at least one thousand people and stretched over more than six hours. Unlike the official ceremony, at which just a handful of Ghanaians were present,[19] Armstrong's funeral offered members of his Fante community, and the city's Ghanaian and West African communities more broadly, a rare opportunity to gather, mourn, and reflect on their fraught relationship to the Israeli state, nation, and society. And unlike the official memorial, the homegoing ceremony revealed how even in moments of terrible shock and devastating loss, people in precarious circumstances can find sparks of newness, or natality, and work together toward making life bearable once again.

Mourning

Held just under two weeks after the bombing, Armstrong's homegoing was organized by the Fante Club of Tel Aviv, an ethnic association of which he had been a member. Naana Holdbrook, another club member, described the event to me as the largest gathering of African migrants ever to take place in Israel. Most mourners were Ghanaians or other West Africans, along with a smattering of Israelis and a few members of other migrant communities. The ceremony was emceed, in English and Fante, by a well-known member of the Fante community. She introduced the day's speakers with her characteristic flair, among them the Ghanaian ambassador to Israel and a distinguished

Ghanaian theologian and religious leader representing the Anglican Church. About thirty-five of Armstrong's extended kin sat at the front of the hall wearing the traditional mourning colors of black and bright red. At the door, every arriving mourner received a long ribbon of red cloth to tie around his or her arm, forehead, or neck. Key elements of Christian communal worship—prayer and song; collective assembly and financial support for those in distress—were also integral to the homegoing ceremony, shoring up its role for mourners as an inhabitable space of welcome.

The ceremony was organized in two parts. The briefer first part, which lasted about an hour and a half, was a Christian memorial service replete with Bible readings, a religious sermon, and hymns and songs performed by the uniformed choir from the local Ghanaian Presbyterian church. The ambassador's remarks followed. In between the first and second portions of the ceremony, all those in attendance waited in a long, winding queue for a chance to shake hands with the chief mourners and honored guests. The trailing procession itself continued for over an hour.

During the second, much longer part of the ceremony, the tone shifted from the sobriety of Presbyterian formalities into a more animated Fante register. In between stylized moments of eulogy, the assembled mourners crowded at the center of the hall and celebrated Armstrong's life with long stretches of lively drumming and dancing (Figure 14). At one point, representatives of different social and religious organizations were called to the microphone, one by one, to present donations to the family of the deceased. Later Rebecca, surrounded by a tight huddle of women dressed in striking hues of red and black, made a slow tearful procession around the center of the hall in a mournful widow's dance. The entire ceremony was videotaped by several videographers, each carrying a heavy camera with blaring lights and a trailing power cord. One version of the video was later edited, reproduced, and sold for 90 shekels per VHS copy (about US$20). Overall, the afternoon's speeches, readings, and rituals evoked complementary emotions of sadness and joy: sadness at a life cut short, and joy at Armstrong's opportunity for life in the first place.

The Kinsman: "What Is Real Is You and Our Love for You"

Early in the ceremony, Robert Yeboah, Armstrong's kinsman and Rebecca's representative in negotiating with the authorities, was called up to speak.

Figure 14. Drumming and dancing at the homegoing ceremony. A portrait of the deceased rests on the wrapped chair in the foreground. Photo by the author.

Dressed in heavy, woven funerary clothes, a band of red cloth bound around his forehead, he took the microphone and, in a soft voice, offered a brief chronology of Armstrong's life before pulling out a folded piece of paper.

"We are all here," Robert said, glancing around the crowded hall, "joining hands together in love to give Efia a befitting burial. Efia, with your brothers and sisters around, we have these short words for you." He then read a poem, rendered here as best I can.[20]

> Efia, we say what we think we should do.
> You say die. We say our lamp oil has turned to water.
> You say die. We say we burn like a moth in the candle of your face.
> You say die. We say eyes. You say keep them open.
> We say liver. You say keep them working.
> We mention the heart-center. You ask, what is that? Much love for you.
>   Keep it for yourself.
> What is real is you and our love for you.

High in the air unnoticed the reality rises into a tomb.
You are the hero of peace.
Your death blow has taught us something.
Sometimes visible, sometimes not.
Sometimes devout Christians, sometimes staunchly Jewish.
Until our inner love feeds into everyone, all we can do is take these
      daily things in different shapes.

But as we beseech . . . the angels, the angels have this to say to you.
Walk in beauty. Live in trust. And know the benevolent Lord our God
      guides your way.

We all say again, you are a . . . hero.
You are a sacrifice of peace.
. . .
Efia, farewell.

Silence.

The Anglican Leader: "We Are All Taking Lessons from This"

Robert spoke in elegy, with great pathos, but the speakers who followed him
were practical, didactic. Each seized on this moment of gathering and solidarity to ponder lessons the community might learn from Armstrong's violent
demise. The first speaker, a charismatic Anglican scholar and leader, delivered
a half-hour homily replete with spiritual, political, and moral messages. Citing
one biblical passage after another, he encouraged mourners, but especially
Armstrong's widow, to remember that nothing can separate them from God's
love, not even the tragedy of a young life cut short. He noted the diversity within
the city's Ghanaian community and called for unity, love, and mutual support.

The prominent lay leader issued three appeals to those assembled in
mourning. First he addressed the Ghanaian Embassy representatives, applaud-
ing their efforts to assist the family of the deceased. Yet he also exhorted
Ghana's leaders to interpret the strife between Israelis and Palestinians as a
grim warning of what could happen should conflict erupt in Ghana. His
second message, directed toward the handful of Israelis present, was a plea:
to advocate on Ghanaians' behalf and petition the Israeli authorities to act

with compassion. "I am begging and praying [to] the people of Israel that they should look at our people mercifully. I am praying that each one of you will get your police chiefs to understand that our people came here to get something to go back. They don't want to live here. Because if the population makes their voice heard maybe the politicians will understand." His third and final message was directed to those in the Ghanaian community. In a few brief sentences, he managed to praise the community, encourage members to formally register their presence in Israel at the Ghanaian Embassy, exhort them to love one another—and scold those who had engaged in the dubious practice of informing on other community members to the police. In all, his message focused on community members' practical obligations toward themselves and each another. "When Efia died . . . somebody had to say he's a Ghanaian, and the embassy said it. And they were able to say [so] because Efia was one of those who went and registered. . . . If he hadn't gone, the embassy wouldn't have had the courage and authority to go and stand before the Israeli government to say this is a Ghanaian. You may say he looks like a Ghanaian, but on paper nothing. So let this occasion move each one [to go register] so there is somebody who can vouch for you. They can't vouch for somebody they don't know. . . . I beg you, we are all taking lessons from this." Although Armstrong's violent death had occasioned the large community gathering, the lay leader's speech placed less emphasis on his life or death than on collective lessons to be learned and steps to take going forward.

The Anglican leader's words were less personal than Robert Yeboah's, but they were no less valuable in establishing the homegoing ceremony, for migrant mourners, as an inhabitable space of welcome. At the same time, his sermon was an invitation to consider the contours, and the limits, of a bearable life.

The Ambassador: "Don't Feel Comfortable Here"

The second distinguished guest, the Ghanaian ambassador, also took a practical tack. The bombing was a great shock, he declared, and it brought the community together. So, too, did it reinforce the importance of registering one's presence at the embassy. He also saw the attack as evidence that the city's Ghanaian residents were not immune to local conflict: "from now on, we know we are part of this community. Anything that will happen here will touch us all."[21] But his final message was the strongest: "The most important thing—I don't think any of you strayed into this land. You came purposefully.

You knew what you were doing. Do what you want to do quickly and go home. Don't feel comfortable around here. . . . This is not your home. You are here for a purpose. Once you have achieved that purpose, please go." Whereas his predecessor melded theology, politics, and moral instruction in a message pitched to the Ghanaian community and their Israeli hosts, the ambassador's message was tighter in focus. For both, Armstrong's death raised questions that transcended the vicissitudes of everyday life on Israel's margins.

Armstrong's funeral was markedly different from the official memorial. Unlike the small ceremony held in the liminal space of Mesila, the homegoing was a well-publicized, traditionally structured gathering in a well-known community venue. The Israeli event neither humanized the victims nor raised any call for practical action. At the Ghanaian ceremony, in contrast, Armstrong was mourned as a distinct individual: as a man embedded in kin and social networks who died under circumstances both specific and noble. (He had already returned home on the evening of his death, the emcee explained, but went out once again because he had forgotten to make one small purchase and did not want to trouble his wife after a long day of work.) The funeral was as rich with culturally appropriate expressions of emotion as the earlier event was devoid of affect. And unlike the Israeli memorial, which was linguistically opaque to many, Armstrong's bilingual homecoming was designed precisely to perform the emotional work of collective mourning in a familiar linguistic and cultural idiom.

And what of the gerush? Although it played no part in the funeral's foreground, the looming threat was self-evident to all. "Don't feel comfortable around here," the ambassador advised. Similarly, the Anglican leader used his pulpit to appeal to the handful of Israelis in attendance: "I am begging and praying [that] the people of Israel . . . should look at our people mercifully. . . . Because if the population makes their voice heard maybe the politicians will understand." Even in mourning, desperation and pleas for mercy were on the tip of the community's collective tongue. Although attention focused momentarily on the bloody aftermath of one kind of terror, the specter of a second, entirely different variety hovered above.

Forbearance: The Community Leaders' Meeting

Well before the bombing and in its wake, Christian belief and practice offered many global migrants invaluable resources for bearing the indignities of their sociopolitical abjection. Although their religious commitments spanned a wide range of denominations (Presbyterian, Anglican, Catholic, evangelical, and African independent churches) and varied considerably in degree of commitment, many Christian migrants in Tel Aviv came to understand their own relationship to Israeli society, and to the Israeli state, in scriptural and religious terms. At the many migrant churches I visited—the Nigerian-Ghanaian evangelical church I often attended with Olivia, Ruby, and their families; Marina's mostly Filipino evangelical congregation; the Ghanaian Presbyterian church; and others—pastors and lay leaders tended to reinforce these interpretations. From their perspective, congregants ought to view their relationships with Jewish Israeli employers, neighbors, landlords, and others—members of God's "chosen people"—through the lens of their own religious obligations as Christian believers.

Importantly, these pastoral recommendations were generally theological and spiritual, not political, in nature. In other words, leaders' efforts to symbolically write themselves and their communities into the Israeli national story largely served *intracommunity* goals rather than advancing any externally oriented struggle for recognition, rights, or status. These symbolic goals, however apolitical, were neither shallow nor unimportant. They played a meaningful role in shaping migrants' lifeworlds, and they clarified the role of churches and worship communities as vital, and eminently inhabitable, spaces of welcome.

The Politics of Invisibility and the Stakes of Exposure

The strength and depth of these commitments shone brightly at the previously scheduled meeting of an ongoing leaders' forum organized and facilitated by Mesila on January 6, the day after the bombing. When the forum met that somber day, the prepared agenda was tossed aside so the leaders—a diverse group of nearly twenty West Africans and Filipinos, most of them Christian pastors from Nigeria, Ghana, and the Philippines, along with a handful of secular leaders, including leaders of the African Workers Union—could debrief and try to make sense of the previous day's tragedy.

When the community leaders gathered at Mesila, barely twenty-four hours had passed since the bombing. One by one, everyone expressed shock and horror at the attack and its quite literal closeness to home. Many lived in or near Nevé She'anán. Many had been within earshot of both explosions, as had one of the Mesila facilitators and I. And many were actively involved in the emergency response. Other leaders—as Patrice, an AWU leader, pointed out—would have liked to provide assistance but refrained, fearing arrest. As Patrice noted with regret, this fear prevented some leaders from helping their communities at precisely the moment their leadership was needed most.

Early in the meeting, participants described where they had been the previous evening. Jonathan, a secular Filipino leader, had spent the night in a local hospital with an injured friend who needed major surgery. Noel, a Filipino pastor, said that he had answered "tons of phone calls" from journalists whose goal, he said, was, "to convince Israelis that foreign workers are more scared of deportation than bombings, and that is true." The group responded to Pastor Noel's comment with a round of cynical laughter. The need to juggle these competing fears was disturbingly self-evident.

Fear of arrest and deportation also topped leaders' minds as they reflected on the bombing's broader significance and considered collective options for supporting their injured and mourning their dead. Several of the group's more optimistic members thought the flurry of attention to their communities, including public statements like Netanyahu's description of migrants as "flesh of our flesh," might offer an opportunity for increased acceptance of their presence in Israel. Others felt the ongoing gerush made any kind of public response too risky, even with Mesila's pledge of support. All were frustrated by the criminalization and illegalization they now faced, and many expressed sharp criticism of Israeli government policies. Still, nearly all of their criticisms were tempered by religious belief: by strong assertions that Israeli actions—individual and collective, personal and political—were part of a larger divine plan. For these community representatives, Israeli politicians as well as migrant housecleaners, Jews and Christians were part of a single, ongoing, biblically anchored tale of divine involvement in, and judgment of, human affairs.

Above all, the evening's discussion foregrounded the profound role of religious belief in helping participants frame and navigate their everyday experiences as individuals, as community leaders, and as Christian strangers in the Jewish-led Holy Land. The meeting revealed the centrality of Christian faith in most of their efforts to craft inhabitable spaces of welcome—both for themselves and, crucially, for their congregants and constituents—despite the turbulent circumstances engulfing their lives.

Leaders' Perspectives: Where Theology Meets Politics

For these leaders, everyday experiences of criminalization and sociopolitical abjection in Israel were framed by a shared model of theodicy and justice anchored in Christian doctrine. Throughout the meeting, nearly every issue that arose was refracted through this lens. "These people won't listen to us," Nathaniel, a Nigerian pastor, told the group. "Yet God has made a promise, and everything is part of God's plan." For Pastor Nathaniel, among others, belief in a divine plan that encompassed citizens and "foreigners," Jews, Christians, and Muslims, provided hope and strength both in normal times and in these anxious days of terrorist attacks, brewing war, and mass arrest and deportation.

Another element of this divine plan was protective blessing against harm, embodied in God's covenant with believing Christians. Noel, the Filipino pastor, invoked a biblical passage often cited in church sermons and personal testimonials (including Raphael Malonga's) as a scriptural heuristic for managing everyday interactions with Israelis: "I will bless them that bless you and I will curse them that curse you."[22] For Christian migrants whose livelihood and protection from arrest lay in the hands of their Jewish Israeli employers, landlords, and neighbors, this biblical aphorism provided a powerful incentive to acquiesce to Israeli wishes and avoid speaking out against Israeli actions, whether personal, institutional, or political.

For these leaders, a third dimension of the Bible's cosmic plan is divine retribution, which may be imperceptible in the immediate sense but inevitable in the broader span of divine observation and judgment. From this perspective, the cited passage foreshadows divine retribution against both Palestinian terrorists who harm God's Jewish chosen and Jewish Israelis who bring suffering to God's Christian chosen.

With these commitments as their guide, some leaders were prepared to contemplate a public, community-wide event to pray for the injured and mourn the dead. For them, the horror of the bombing and the depth of their communal pain rendered a step into the public eye worthy of consideration. After more deliberation, however, the group concurred that their feelings of mourning and loss would best find expression within a Christian religious framework: a prayer rally—"not a demonstration," as one of the confrontation-wary Mesila facilitators insisted, and as the group members agreed. In mulling over their plans, the leaders determined the rally should focus on two biblical verses suggested by one of the senior Ghanaian pastors and approved by the group with a rousing "Amen." His first suggestion, drawn from the New Testament, was 1 Timothy 2:2, which calls for "supplications, prayers, intercessions and giving of thanks [to] be made for all men, for kings and for all that are in authority, that we may lead a quiet and peaceable life in all godliness and honesty." The second verse, this one from the Hebrew Bible, was Psalm 122:6: "Pray for the peace of Jerusalem: they shall prosper that love thee."

In selecting these two verses, leaders reached consensus on several points. First, they agreed it might—though would not necessarily—be wise to coordinate a public response to the suicide bombing that had struck their communities. Second, they settled on a message. The verse from Psalms foregrounded the historical and theological dependence of Christianity on Judaism and, under the circumstances, of Christians on Jews. Praying for the peace of Jerusalem—a familiar metonym for both the people of Israel and the land (or in this case the state) of Israel—was understood as a way to incur favor both publicly, from Israeli leaders, and privately, from God. The verse from 1 Timothy, similarly double-voiced, conveyed a substantially different message: a plea for personal and collective deliverance from suffering and hardship. Pastor Noel explained the complementarity and double voicing of these passages in explicit terms: "We're trying to move the heart of God. That is the purpose of the prayer. But we can also try to move the heart of the government if we cannot move the heart of God." The leaders' scriptural choices highlighted an additional point of consensus as well: that any public event they organized would best be framed in religious terms. In short, they assumed their Israeli interlocutors—including political leaders and the broader Israeli public—would find a religiously framed message more compelling than an explicitly political one. In fact, they could not have been more wrong. Although theology has crept increasingly into Israeli politics, the politicians who put religion on the agenda, many of them ultraorthodox and religious nationalists, are but marginally committed to the principles of democratic governance—and few are part of the state's secular bureaucracy. In short, efforts to find common ground through biblical messaging were doomed to fail.

By the time of this conversation, I had gotten to know some of the leaders quite well and spent many hours attending African and Filipino church services in and around Tel Aviv, celebrating holidays and life cycle events with migrant friends and acquaintances, and discussing religious belief and practice with migrants who found strength and solace in their Christian faith. On the basis of those experiences, I am confident that the views these leaders expressed were not mere rhetorical tactics, but rather deeply held convictions about how Christian migrants, including those Israel classifies as "illegal," ought to be treated by the various branches of the state now governing the Holy Land. For these leaders, Christian belief and practice were absolutely pivotal to their own efforts, and those of their communities, to bear the indignities and anxieties of everyday life as an illegalized migrant in Israel.

In the end, the leaders were afraid to stage any public event without Mesila sponsorship, support, and protection—and yet, they concluded, even this would not suffice. Despite what they understood to be firm, good faith commitments from Mesila staff to protect participants from police harassment, they were ultimately reluctant to test the limits of this small municipal agency's power. Although leaders appreciated the *existence* of the leaders' forum as a rare space of collegiality, recognition, and respect, its potential to empower was severely undercut by Mesila's liminal position vis-à-vis the state as well as its need to walk a fine line between national-level compliance and municipal-level critique.

The leaders' forum thus stands in a border zone shaped by migrants' sociopolitical abjection, on one hand, and Mesila's structural liminality, on the other. In political terms, the leaders' ultimate voicelessness stemmed not only from these structural constraints but also from a fundamental disjuncture between their own and the Israeli government's understanding of the relationship between them. For the leaders, Christian religious belief offered more than just a potential framework for public articulation of fears and grievances. It also offered a set of everyday coping strategies, interactional heuristics, and, above all, a compelling historical and theological map of the relationship between themselves as Christians and their hosts as Jews.

Despite the depth and experiential power of this theological framing, Israeli officials—national and local, secular and religious—were patently unwilling to engage migrants' religiously framed claims. Instead, Israeli national policies were framed in discourses of state sovereignty, municipal policies relied on a fragile frame that wove together a pragmatic social work approach and an ideology of humanitarian compassion, and at both levels of

state authority, religion—absolutely central to migrant leaders' mode of in-
terpreting and being-in-the-world—was flatly rejected as a potential mediat-
ing framework. On this occasion, among others, I was struck by the jarring
disjuncture between Christian migrants' confident emplotment of contemporary Israel in religious scripts and narratives, on one hand, and Jewish Israelis' predominant secularism, on the other. Some migrants had been
primed to employ this theological lens well before their arrival, while others
were exposed to, or to varying extents persuaded by, such narratives at the
churches they now attended. The rhythm and public symbols of Israeli life—
Saturday as the weekly Sabbath, civic recognition of biblical and rabbinic
holidays, the use of Hebrew as everyday lingua franca—certainly reinforced
these messages, but in a confounding way. Rather than signaling widespread
acceptance of biblical narratives by Christians and Jews, such biblical traces
instead functioned for Christian migrants like linguistic *faux amis*—words
whose audible similarities mislead and deceive, like the English word "blessed"
and the French "blessé" (wounded).

Ultimately, the leaders decided not to organize any public memorial gathering, regardless of frame or message. Instead, they decided to protect themselves, and their communities, by choosing the path they expected would make
life most bearable: a retreat into the shadows. Although the leaders' Christian idiom may have failed to serve as a viable political resource, its role in
creating and supporting spaces of inhabitability and welcome cannot be un-
derestimated.

Conclusion: Toward a Livable Life

The Nevé She'anán bombing raises complicated questions of grievability and
bearability—questions about the politics of human value, on one hand, and
the existential consequences of sociopolitical abjection, on the other. I have
engaged these questions in tandem, taking care not to "let them fully collapse into one another."

Tackling the first of these questions, the political question of grievability, deepens our understanding of sociopolitical abjection by revealing how
Israel's biopolitics of Otherness is even more complicated than the previous
chapter might suggest. On the day after the bombing, it made perfect sense
to publish snapshots of dead migrants alongside images of Israeli victims on
the cover of a center-right-leaning Israeli newspaper. However heroic the sui-

cide bombers may be for some Palestinians,[23] *their* ungrievability from Jewish Israelis' perspective was equally self-evident. Their pictures would not, indeed could not, appear.

The Palestinian attackers' ungrievability stems primarily from their murderous intentions: from their desire to wreak havoc, destruction, and death in a busy civilian center. Yet there is more. For an overwhelming majority of Jewish Israelis, neither the perpetrators' culpability nor their ungrievability is an *individual* feature. Rather, their actions are collectively interpreted as evidence of something deeper and more elemental. More often than not, Palestinians figure in the Jewish Israeli public imaginary not as individuals—men or women; children or adults; citizens or noncitizens; supporters of the Joint List (of Arab political parties) or, far less commonly, Likud (the right-wing Zionist party); Fatah or Hamas—but as an undifferentiated bloc of enemies, or at least potential enemies. Culpability for violence is diffused; even Palestinians who never act violently on their own are presumed to support violent acts. The ubiquity of Israeli suspicion, which fuels security concerns and biosocial profiling and undergirds the apparatus of the occupation, has the effect of making life ever more unbearable. And so a grim cycle continues, spiraling ever downward.

Of course, a narrow focus on Palestinians as nothing but Others, enemies, and terrorists ignores crucial aspects of history and context, including various forms of *Israeli* culpability: for the *naqba*, for the state's harsh post-1948 military rule over Palestinian citizens, for the 50-year old occupation. Yet Israeli culpability for Palestinian suffering is overlooked, Palestinian culpability is collectivized, and resistance to occupation—especially in the form of either violence or support for violent acts—is seen as legitimating an ungrievable fate.

If the question of grievability helps clarify the complex dynamics of sociopolitical abjection, the question of bearability moves in another direction: toward the intimacies and immediacies of human experience. In becoming a survivor of Palestinian violence, a handful of unlucky migrants garnered the perverse privilege of being cast, if discursively and fleetingly, as *"basár me'bsaréinu"*—"flesh of our flesh." Yet this purported inclusion carried few benefits. The survivors Ariella and I visited in a Tel Aviv hospital were engaged most urgently with the residues of rupture and the question of what kinds of damage could and could not be borne: *Will I survive? If I do, what kind of body will I inhabit? Do I, with my broken body, still know this world? Can it still hold me? Do I still want to be part of it?* In the immediate aftermath of the bombing, life itself did not necessarily seem bearable.

At the communal level, Armstrong's funeral and the community leaders' meeting point elsewhere. Both memorial events show how people draw on available resources to find, craft, and cultivate inhabitable spaces of welcome, even in the face of abjection compounded by terrible devastation and loss. Such resources include mourning customs that help structure the emotional and social chaos that accompanies grief; religious beliefs and conceptions of theodicy; and story-telling strategies that lend meaning to loss by framing tragedy in the context of history, politics, and intimate relationships. Resources like these, and spaces like these, can play a vital role in making life bearable once again: in helping a life "hold up, . . . keep its shape or direction, in the face of what it is asked to endure."[24]

Yet these spaces illuminate more than just the pursuit of bearability. They are also windows onto the dynamics of creativity and constraint fundamental to the pursuit of something else, something more. Within such spaces, we see sparks of that uniquely human capacity that Arendt calls natality: the power to create something new, something that nurtures possibilities for a livable, dignified, flourishing life.

CHAPTER 5

Perhaps, to Flourish

Life is never simply bare survival, but rather a matter of
realizing one's humanity in relation to others.

—Michael Jackson

"I Would Die First"

One steamy late-summer evening, a tall, soft-spoken Ghanaian man we'll call Solomon appeared at the Open Clinic requesting the impossible. I was at my usual post behind the reception desk, where our small team was responsible for greeting patients, opening new patient files, and directing traffic in and out of the modest exam rooms where volunteer clinicians did their best to provide basic medical care, often using little more than a stethoscope, a pair of gloves, and their diagnostic skills. At the time, the clinic was the only health care facility in Tel Aviv—indeed, in Israel—that was consistently open and accessible to unauthorized migrants like Solomon.

From his furrowed brow and urgent tone, it was clear Solomon was verging on crisis. Fortunately, he hadn't come that day to see a doctor. By that point in the evening the queue was long, and it would have been nearly impossible to squeeze him in. Solomon asked for the clinic director, but she was out. Would you like to speak privately? I proposed, gesturing toward an empty consultation room. He followed me in, and we sat down on a pair of white plastic lawn chairs about a foot away from one other. Behind him was a padded black examination table; behind me, a messy desk. The instant I closed the door, I could feel his anxiety balloon outward and fill the cramped space.

"My request is simple," Solomon said. He and his fiancée, also from Ghana, planned to marry. They were already enrolled in a premarriage seminar at the nearby Catholic church. But before they could set a wedding date, they were expected to submit several documents to the church—including a doctor's letter attesting to their health. Attesting, he specified, that neither of them had HIV. At Solomon's request I pulled his patient file, and the problem was immediately apparent. Any such letter would be patently false.

As I began learning that day, Solomon was a college-educated man and respected member of the local West African community who had spent the past four years working as an unauthorized migrant on Israel's margins, mostly doing *shiputzím:* odd jobs and renovations. After establishing himself both financially and socially, he had "sent for" his bride: a beautiful woman named Rachel seven years his junior, whom he knew from his community back home. When he last laid eyes on her, he explained, Rachel had been desirably "fleshy" and voluptuous, but when she arrived in Israel, she was bony and thin. For some months, neither Solomon nor Rachel realized the gravity of her illness. Only when she showed him strange-looking sores on intimate parts of her body did he become worried. Soon afterward Solomon, who generally felt healthy, also began to feel ill. They turned to the Open Clinic for care and were immediately referred to the HIV clinic at a nearby public hospital. There, both learned they had tested positive for HIV.

The news, Solomon recalled, had left him despondent. He asked the doctor to give him something to drink "so it would all be over, to make it all end." But after the staff at the Open Clinic and the hospital's immunology clinic put them in touch with the Israeli AIDS Task Force, a local NGO capable of providing them access to antiretroviral medications (ARVs) on a consistent if ad hoc basis, his spirits lifted. Despite their unauthorized status and consequent exclusion from the national health care system, the task force was committed to ensuring access to care for anyone living in Israel with HIV.[1] Both Solomon and Rachel began ARV treatment, and both saw quick and dramatic improvement in their health. Now, Solomon explained, he felt much stronger. Life was once again bearable.

No longer yearning for death, he now wished to affirm life, and the future, by formalizing his marriage to Rachel—but without divulging their secret. Their marriage preparations were now well under way, but the stubborn obstacle of the doctor's letter remained. The church's premarriage course was nearing its end, and there was no turning back: "If we withdraw from the seminar, people will ask questions. It would be humiliating. We wouldn't be able to explain." Already "people are starting to ask why we haven't set a date."

As Solomon made clear during our conversation in that stuffy consultation room, he and Rachel were in a terrible bind. The seminar coordinator himself was African, and under no circumstances would they divulge their secret to him. "If people were to know, then I would die before the disease would take me," he insisted. "If people found out either my wife or I had HIV, we would be cut off from the community. *I would die first*"—at his own hand, if need be.[2]

This was their predicament, and with this conversation, part of it became mine as well. Each time we spoke, I grew more worried. I was certain Solomon's threats to end his life were no manipulation, no game. And much as I understood his request, I knew no clinic doctor would provide them with letters denying or obscuring their HIV status: not at this clinic or, I surmised, at any other. I knew because—despite my embarrassment, and in an effort to keep a promise to a desperate man—I asked one of the clinic's volunteer physicians. She looked at me like I was crazy, or at very least incompetent to receive patients at a medical clinic. I blushed with shame.

Solomon and I continued to brainstorm alternatives. What about a letter indicating, "There is no medical reason why this couple should not marry"? He refused. Marrying in another church? Out of the question. Even if civil marriage were available in Israel, which it is not,[3] their unauthorized migration status would likely have raised new obstacles. And so our conversations went. We had reached an impasse.

Then an idea struck. Now that Solomon had reattached himself to the world, to life, and to a future with Rachel, I realized, his greatest fears involved a possible tear in the delicate fabric of social relationships. Above all, he feared humiliation and disgrace in the eyes of his community. He was no crusader, no activist; he had no interest in "coming out" as HIV positive in an effort to fight the scourge of stigma. That would need to be someone else's battle. Neither was he preoccupied by concerns about arrest and deportation, at least not at the moment. His defining commitment was clear: to keep the pledge he had made to Rachel, and that he and Rachel had made to themselves, their families, and their community, by marrying, in timely and conventional fashion, in a Catholic wedding mass. This could only happen if their secret stayed safe.

I floated my proposal. What if we could bypass the Nigerian seminar co-ordinator, go straight to one of the parish priests—who himself was not African—and obtain *his* consent? Both Solomon and Rachel agreed; finally, we had a plan. At their request, and with the approval of the clinic staff and director, we agreed I would contact the priest, Father Joseph.

In our initial phone conversation, I was as vague as could be. Resisting the priest's assiduous fact-finding efforts, I spoke only of an anonymous couple without reference to name, nationality, or any other potentially identifying characteristic. Father Joseph struck me as friendly, and forthright. This was the first time he had encountered such a situation, he explained, and he didn't really understand the medical issues involved. In principle, he would sanction the marriage if three criteria could be met: Had they fully disclosed their medical conditions to one another? Did both want children? And, finally, could the marriage result in healthy offspring? After I affirmed all three,[4] he agreed to meet us at the clinic on a Saturday morning when no staff or patients would be around.

Terrified of potential leaks, Solomon was riddled with anxiety in the days before our scheduled meeting. When we convened that bright weekend morning, he came equipped with several messages for Father Joseph. Yes, they were being fully honest with one another about their health status, attending to their health, and taking their medications. And yes, they certainly wanted children. Solomon left it to me to explain that with appropriate medical treatment, healthy children were a realistic possibility.

But Solomon wanted Father Joseph to understand something more. "This is a social disease," he explained. "If people knew and ostracized [us] in the community, then that would kill me faster than the disease itself." His tone was somber, and for a moment I feared he would repeat the threats I'd heard him voice before—to take his own life rather than reveal to other Africans the condition that afflicted them both. I had strongly suggested he avoid any mention of suicide—a mortal sin, according to some versions of Catholic doctrine—during our meeting. "I know I'm well now," he affirmed. "*That's* what would kill me, if people knew, if people were talking." I breathed a deep sigh of relief when our meeting ended with an apparent resolution—and without reference to Solomon's earlier ultimatum.

Several months later, not long after the announcement of the gerush, a long-awaited invitation arrived. Solomon and Rachel were to be married, and I had the good fortune of being invited to a full slate of weekend events: the "groom's party" on the night before the wedding (where men and women gathered to celebrate the impending nuptials with music, food, and drink—and poke gentle fun at the groom), a formal mass in the Catholic church the following morning, and an extravagant party in a rented event hall later that evening. Rarely have I attended so jubilant a wedding reception. Throngs of elegantly attired African, Filipino, and even a few Israeli guests converged at the venue in South Tel Aviv, some seated at the head table and the rest of us in rows of facing plastic lawn chairs. Once the hall was bursting with music, color, and life, the guests of honor arrived, drumming and music heralding their entrance. With their bridal party clearing their path, Solomon and Rachel—having traded the morning's tailored suit and white gown for the flowing fabric and bright colors of matching African attire— danced into the hall to be honored and blessed. A towering pyramid of plastic champagne glasses overflowed in a fountain, and we all toasted their marriage, then ate, drank, danced, and playfully feted the bride and groom. Our quiet agreement with the priest, it seemed, had done the trick. Their secret was safe; their dignity preserved. Details of the new deportation regime were beginning to emerge, but for them, it seemed, a new chapter had begun.

To Survive, Then Flourish

When Solomon first learned of his HIV status and Rachel's, he was devastated. In that instant, all of his efforts—years of physically demanding, low-paid labor on the precarious margins of an unwelcoming and sometimes hostile society; deep investment, both emotional and financial, in the possibility of marriage and a family; steady engagement with his local communities, both religious and cultural; cultivation of the stalwart reputation so clearly on display at his groom's party, where he was playfully roasted by a phalanx of friends—all of these efforts and achievements withered before the disease that had begun ravaging not just his body and his fiancée's but also the future they hoped to co-construct. The risk of deportation now felt trivial; life itself had become unbearable. Death beckoned.

Then, fortuitously, therapeutic pharmaceuticals—HIV drugs— reinvigorated them with health, and hope. With support from Israeli health and human rights activists and, as important, HIV clinicians and clinical units, Solomon and Rachel were able to regain a stable foothold in the present; once again they could dwell in the world instead of feeling perched on a precipice. But as our first conversation in the clinic that hot August night made eminently clear, a bearable life was no longer Solomon's topmost aspiration. Newly reoriented to the world, he aimed further, higher. He wanted to renew his investment in the goals and commitments that had anchored his lifeworld before he and Rachel had learned they were ill. He glimpsed the power of natality: that open quality of action that allows us to set new things in motion, even create something entirely new. To live with dignity. Perhaps even to flourish.

From an existential standpoint, Solomon's yearning to create himself anew after facing his own mortality comes as no surprise. Aspirations to flourish have a clear temporal valence. They are fundamentally future-oriented and infused with possibility and hope about whatever measure of life remains. Such aspirations also have a social valence; they are not private or solitary, but profoundly relational. Although the desire to reground oneself may find expression in intimate spaces, it gains meaning through action—the action of knitting oneself back into the fabric of the world, creating newness along the way.

Livable Life?

What, then, is a livable life? A livable life is not bogged down by the pursuit of bearability, by the struggle simply to survive. It is a life open to strivings, both existential and ethical. A life in which we can stretch beyond ourselves and work toward making the world into which we have been thrown a world of our own. A life lived in dialogue with our own sense of the good, recognizing that our notions of virtue and goodness have both communal and intimate dimensions—and that they are ever evolving. It is a life anchored in the ground projects that define us and whose enactment gives life direction and meaning. A life open to desire, fantasy, and the open-ended possibilities of a "nonprojected future."[5] Literary theorist Sarah Chinn puts it this way: "Livability is constituted by not only access to love and sociability, but also the possibility of imagining one's own life."[6]

For people facing sociopolitical abjection, what might a livable life entail? In the previous chapter, we saw how groups and communities of illegalized migrants can craft inhabitable spaces of welcome. In such spaces, one does not merely exist, ever deferent to those committed to making life unlivable.

One finds opportunities to become otherwise. These spaces can thus become launching pads for existential pursuits: of groundedness, meaning, dignity. Once life is bearable, once we are certain we will survive, we can struggle for more: We can struggle to flourish.

What does this struggle look like? In pursuing this question, my aim in this chapter is to move beyond the landscapes of exclusion that have occupied us so far and delve more deeply into the choreography of dignity's pursuit. How do people facing sociopolitical abjection strive for livable lives—meaningful, dignified, flourishing lives—in worlds that are fundamentally uncertain, unpredictable, and threatening? What happens to these pursuits when abjection becomes conjugated with other forms of adversity and constraint?

Solomon and Rachel's path to marriage guides us toward these questions, and I now pursue them further by turning to Olivia and Peter, a Nigerian–South African couple we have met before,[7] and whom I have had the privilege of knowing for most of their nearly twenty-year partnership. Like Solomon and Rachel, Peter and Olivia have struggled to weave religious commitment and practice into lives already riddled with complex challenges and existential anxieties. Far from their closest kin and despite significant differences in nationality and culture, religious denomination and temperament, they have struggled to build a marriage that is sanctioned and supported by their respective families, church congregations, and local communities. During the tense years of the gerush and in the challenging years since, they have persisted—sometimes in parallel and sometimes in coordination, at some times successfully and at others less so—to craft lifeworlds that are, by their own standards, not just bearable but livable.

In the remainder of this chapter I want to listen carefully both to Olivia and to Peter—something they don't always manage to do themselves—and trace the moral arc of each of their lives and of the lifeworld they share with each another and their three children, all born in Tel Aviv. This exercise in longitudinal listening brings several insights to the fore. First, the pursuit of livability can vary dramatically among different people—including people facing the same kind of sociopolitical abjection, and even between people who share intimate quarters for an extended time. Second, Olivia and Peter's experiences highlight two conflicting dimensions of this existential pursuit. On one hand is the potentially transformative power of natality. On the other, we are reminded by Olivia and Peter, like Solomon and Rachel, that any such endeavor is inherently precarious, its outcome perpetually uncertain. And on all counts, gender plays a defining role.

Forging Friendships

Hey woman how are you and your family?
—Facebook message from Olivia (in Tel Aviv) as I sit at my desk
(in Connecticut) writing this chapter

Without Olivia, I'm not sure what form this book would have taken. As we became friends and confidantes, our worlds expanded in ways I am sure neither of us anticipated. The day before I returned to the United States after my longest and most intensive stretch of fieldwork, I paid Olivia and her family one last visit. We both teared up as she walked me to my bus stop on HaTikvah's main drag, slowed only a bit by her early pregnancy and the weight of pudgy fifteen-month-old Ethan, who was wrapped comfortably onto her back with the familiar length of Dutch print fabric I'd come to know so well. As we wove through narrow streets, we spoke of friendship. Of how much we had each learned, and grown, over the past few years. Of how rare it was to have a friendship, as she put it, "in which color didn't matter." She didn't know what she'd have done without me in the months leading up to Ethan's birth, she said. I couldn't find words to thank her for welcoming me into her life, I told her, and wished her a much easier time with her second pregnancy. I'll be back soon to meet the baby, I promised. Six months later, I was.

You've met Olivia before. She, Ruby, and Claire were the formidable trio of Nigerian women who, early in my fieldwork, welcomed me into their homes, their church, and their pursuits of both conjugal stability and medical care. When we first met, all three were pregnant, each under different circumstances: Ruby after years of waiting and very much by design, Olivia in what she eventually reframed as a fortuitous accident, and Claire in a desperate, and ultimately failed, attempt to anchor a doomed romantic liaison.

You've encountered Olivia elsewhere as well, including the shared South Tel Aviv flat where she lived in a single, stuffy room with Peter, the South African man who eventually, and reluctantly, became her husband. We've visited the evangelical church near the Central Bus Station I often attended with her, Ruby, Franklin, and many of their friends. We've witnessed Olivia and Peter's efforts to cope with the intensifying gerush: the changing temporality of risk ("now Thursday is dangerous too"), rising concerns about travel through public space, paralyzing anxiety that impeded sleep. We've heard how Peter, in particular, came to dread the possibility of being deported with empty pockets. And we witnessed Olivia's despondence as she struggled to support her still-nursing toddler and newborn son as well as Peter who, after narrowly escaping arrest for a second time, sequestered himself in their apartment while she shuttled among cleaning jobs to keep the family clothed and fed.

You might describe Olivia and Peter as an odd couple. She is tall, striking, elegant. Stunningly beautiful, even when casually dressed. With her winning smile and warm demeanor, she is easy to connect with, easy to befriend. It takes time to uncover her temper, which flares hot, but only when she's really upset. Socially, Olivia is a face-to-face person; direct connections with family and friends, neighbors and fellow churchgoers are more immediate to her than politics, history, or other, more distant modes of engaging the world.

Peter is different. He is bookish, reflective. Physically strong and wiry, he also tends to be stubborn, anxious, a little jumpy. Socially awkward, and occasionally indelicate. An eager albeit unschooled student of history and politics, he is also an avid follower of current events: in Africa, in Israel, in the world writ large. He is serious, intense, less likely than his wife to find relaxation or release in humor, or dance. They even worship differently. The large evangelical church I often attended with Olivia was always brimming with song and dancing, while worship at the smaller church Peter attended was a more solemn affair. What brought them together? Serendipity, followed by convenience, and then inertia—until the gerush caught up with them.

In the years we've known each other, Olivia and Peter have struggled with all measure of adversity. The gerush and its reverberations have taken a heavy toll. So too have the hardships they have inflicted, sometimes intentionally and sometimes unintentionally, on each other. Their predicaments, as individuals and as a couple, illuminate the key concerns in this chapter: divergent paths for pursuing a dignified, flourishing life. The power of natality—of changing one's experience of the world through the creation of something new. And, above all, the inevitable precariousness of these human efforts.

Their stories and struggles are illuminating for another reason as well. As most of us do, Olivia and Peter fall short of classical conceptions of a virtuous person. Yet even when they have disappointed one another, both have always embraced me in a spirit of friendship. According to Aristotle, friendship ranks among the building blocks of a flourishing life, in part because it offers myriad opportunities for self-critique, even self-transformation.[8] In the intimate domain of friendship, itself an inhabitable space of welcome, we reveal ourselves to others—and not just any others, but others to whom we accord moral standing in our lives. People with whom—and before whom—we are prepared to reflect critically on our words and deeds, contemplate our errors, and maybe even try to change.

All friendships involve differences that matter. Olivia and Peter know full well that unlike them, I have never felt anxious about moving through Israeli public space. That the color of my skin, inherited from my Eastern European ancestors, invites a hermeneutic of generosity when Israelis see me for the first time. That I have always been free to enter and leave the country more or less on my own terms, never felt a need to hide from the authorities. They know that as an American Jew, I can visit Israel without applying, waiting, or paying for a visa. That I am free to stay if I wish, become a citizen, even access financial benefits—tax breaks, housing subsidies, educational opportunities—to ease my way. We've never spoken at length about my choice not to follow that path, nor have we spoken much about my comings and goings over the years (nearly all supported by research grants or conference travel funds)—except to discuss what I might bring along on my next trip: blank VHS cassettes, boxes of hair relaxer and packets of hair extensions, books, T-shirts, or other gifts for their children. Unlike me, but like so many others, they came to Israel, then got stuck in a paradoxical state of immobility. In all these years, Olivia has never left. Her family in Nigeria has never met Peter, never met their children.

Other differences merit mention as well. Occasionally we have spoken of passports—specifically, their African passports versus my own American passport, a kind of magical talisman that garnered me more than a few spontaneous marriage proposals, including several from their friends and acquaintances. Another difference involves language. Both Peter and Olivia get by in Israel mixing the flowery, melodic forms of African English I quickly grew to love with a rudimentary, self-taught Hebrew adequate for shopping in the market, finding a restroom, or rebuffing insults from strangers on the street. Their view of Israeli society has been mediated through everyday interactions with employers and landlords, bus drivers and shopkeepers; the English-language media; and the grapevine. My own perspective as a fluent Hebrew speaker with Israeli mentors and colleagues, family and friends, is markedly different.

And, of course, there is the matter of money. Even as a graduate student on a tight budget, I had a savings account. A credit card. And, for a long while, a boyfriend with a car I could use. Meanwhile, I knew Peter and Olivia struggled to remit money to relatives back home, and that Peter's close relatives in Israel kept their savings in a money belt worn beneath their clothes. When we first met, I shared an apartment in trendy Central Tel Aviv, then moved to my own newly painted, freshly renovated apartment in Florentin, one of the city's gentrifying southern neighborhoods. They shared a cramped two-bedroom with two other adults across the Ayalon Highway in HaTikvah. When they finally did strike out on their own, their accommodations were never so comfortable, either in their distant apartment far from buses, shopping, church and friends or, in later years, in a tiny but better-situated flat with a bathroom ceiling that leaked in the rainy winter months. Rather than begrudging my circumstances or trying to exploit our friendship, however, Olivia and Peter have always reached out to me in a spirit of generosity and reciprocity. They have welcomed me in their home and accepted invitations to visit mine. Never have they asked me for a penny. And when they realized, not long after we'd met, that I had no television—something that didn't bother me, especially given my busy fieldwork schedule—they seized the opportunity to lend me their extra set. I'll never forget the evening Peter brought the TV over by taxi, then lugged it up four flights of stairs to make sure it was working properly. They had lost the remote control, so before making the trek, he spent 150 shekels (about $35) on a new one for me to use.

New Life: Blessing or Curse?

By the time Peter and I met, Olivia and I had already shared some difficult moments. Our first encounter was on a January evening in 2002, when she appeared at the Open Clinic, six months pregnant and petrified. I was volunteering at the reception desk that evening, and we started to talk.

Like Ruby, Gloria, and many other pregnant migrants in Tel Aviv, Olivia first sought prenatal care in East Jerusalem from a Palestinian physician known among global migrants in Tel Aviv for his affordable fees and Saturday hours. I'll call him Dr. Khalili. On Olivia's first visit she came seeking an abortion, but the results of Dr. Khalili's examination prompted a quick change of mind. An ultrasound to confirm the pregnancy revealed myomas—benign fibroid tumors—in her uterus. Given their size and placement, he said, it was a miracle she was even pregnant. If she terminated this pregnancy, he continued, she might not be able to have children in the future.

"If you want . . . I'll take it out," Olivia remembered him saying, "but you might not want to take the chance."

Dr. Khalili's news tapped a nerve. Peter did not want a baby, and Olivia was unprepared to make a choice that might leave her permanently infertile. Upon arriving in Israel, her near-term goals had been clear: to repay her travel debt, then send money home to her parents and siblings as often as possible while building some savings of her own. Yet her vision of a flourishing life involved far more than this. As a Nigerian woman in her early thirties, she was committed to grounding herself in the world by "having people":[9] a husband, children. Only by becoming a mother could she secure her identity both publicly, vis-à-vis her extended family and the various communities to which she belonged, and privately, in relation to herself. Certainly these goals reflect cultural expectations but, as I later learned, they also reflect the "individual pinch of destiny"[10] that shaped her particular experience of being-in-the-world—in this case, challenging family circumstances that had long caused her great pain. Although she was too ashamed to share those circumstances with Peter (and only later shared them with me), she knew immediately that abortion was no longer an option.

Peter would disapprove of her choice to continue the pregnancy—of this Olivia was certain. But Dr. Khalili's news was a breakthrough moment for her, a flash of insight and a spark of natality. In that instant, she made a momentous decision: to shift the anchor of her lifeworld from her family back home into the immediate, if unstable, here and now. Only by accepting this pregnancy, regardless of what the future might hold, could she expect to flourish—as a partner, if possible, but most importantly as a mother, ideally to a respectable brood of children. The risk of becoming a single mother was far preferable to the much graver risk of a childless life. "Lots of people are single mothers," she remembered telling herself in an effort to calm her anxieties.

When she returned from Jerusalem and revealed Dr. Khalili's diagnosis and her decision, Peter made no effort to hide his disapproval. But Olivia stood firm, even as her pregnancy progressed and the fibroids grew, causing her tremendous pain. "I had to stop working," she said during one of our afternoon visits. "Sometimes I can't walk, or prepare food, or take care of myself." As the pain grew increasingly intolerable from week to week, I could sense the rising tensions between them. Meanwhile, Peter was "moving around with friends from South Africa" whose influence had become increasingly corrosive. "I think he's taken a bad advisor," she told me.

For Olivia, the high stakes of this pregnancy only deepened her desire for a future revolving around marriage and family. Peter, on the other hand, was pulled precisely in the opposite direction. Like Olivia, he too had arrived in Israel with a mountain of travel debt and a slew of remittance obligations. Then, suddenly, his elderly father passed away. Although he couldn't travel home to join his family in mourning, they did expect him to fund the elaborate funeral ceremonies. Meanwhile, he was keenly aware that his close relatives, who had lived in Israel for a decade and financed his travel, soon planned to return to South Africa with the earnings they had saved over the years. Like them, he had no plans to live permanently in Israel. He saw Israel as a way station, a stepping-stone on a long-term path to a stable future as an established entrepreneur in South Africa, where he hoped to return proud and poised for a life of self-sufficiency. Anything that imperiled that dream—emotional entanglements, additional financial obligations, or, of course, the dreaded possibility of deportation with empty pockets—threatened his hopes for the future.

As I eventually learned, another transnational tie weighed heavy on him as well. Were Olivia to bear a child, this would not be his first; he was already father to a five-year-old daughter who lived in South Africa with her mother. Since he was Christian and the girl's mother Muslim, he was unwilling to marry. The families wouldn't accept it, he said. Yet he did send money to the girl's mother each month—the same amount he sent monthly to his own mother. Already burdened by this existing parental obligation, Peter was deeply reluctant to become newly encumbered with another relationship, and another child. The anchor of his lifeworld was not in Israel, nor did he want it to be.

In short, Olivia's diagnosis and uncertain reproductive future stunned them both. For Olivia, however, it offered a glowing spark: a flash of newness that spurred her to reorient in relation to herself, other people, and the world. For Peter, the same spark was explosive—a threat to his own vision of a flourishing life.

Pain, Risk, Screening

It was not fibroid pain that brought Olivia to the clinic on the evening we met. Instead it was a medical test result that led Dr. Khalili—in his office one hour, one language, and one nation away in East Jerusalem—to refer her to the Open Clinic just across the highway pass from the flat she shared with Peter in Tel Aviv. The screening test he recommended, a high-level ultrasound to assess fetal development, is the usual standard of care in Israel—but Olivia didn't know that, so she panicked. One of Peter's employers had undergone the same test, and a fetal abnormality had been detected. Starved for reassurance, she arrived at the clinic seeking an obstetrician's counsel. After her physical exam, I explained that the clinic could arrange for the screening at an area hospital, at a discounted rate. And then, as had become my custom, I explained the goals of my research and offered to accompany her. Without missing a beat, she agreed.

A few days later, as we rode together to the hospital by cab, a friendship was born. We had plenty of time to chat in the waiting room, and the sonogram, to Olivia's great relief, yielded the best verdict a neonatologist is likely to deliver. "Is the baby all right?" she asked anxiously. "I think so—according to what I can see on the ultrasound," the physician replied. Only when she had received the typed test results (which I did my best to translate from medical Hebrew into vernacular English), along with a stack of glossy ultrasound printouts, was Olivia willing to believe the news. At that point, envelope in hand, her mood lifted and her step lightened. "I feel much better," she trilled as we waited for the bus. We rode together, engrossed in conversation all the way, and parted with a hug.

Two weeks later, Olivia invited me over for an afternoon visit. The layout of their shared flat was typical for Tel Aviv: a small entryway, cramped kitchen, split bathroom (one room with a toilet, another with a shower and washing machine), and two adjacent bedrooms, edged by a narrow balcony. Like many migrants whose apartments I'd visited, the room they shared exploded with an accumulation of stuff: a television, VCR, and stereo; two landline phones, plus cell phones; and a desktop computer with a printer, which Peter used to keep up with current events—and which they had used to educate themselves about fibroid tumors. She showed me color images of fibroids they had printed out from an American medical website.

As we drank tea and ate the cookies I'd brought, Olivia described the debilitating pain that kept her from working. She was well into her second trimester now, and the attacks were so fierce they left her immobilized, sometimes for hours on end. They could strike anywhere, even at the bus stop on her way to work. On the day that happened, her employer, Aliza, had flatly refused to help. Although Olivia knew her as a kind and considerate woman, Aliza had heard the Immigration Administration's public service announcements and was afraid the police would figure out the connection between them and fine her 30,000 shekels (US$7,500) for employing an unauthorized worker. When Aliza declined to come and help, several strangers helped Olivia into a nearby post office, where she could do nothing but lie still for several hours until she was able to move once again. "People were looking at me funny, probably thinking 'this woman is crazy,'" she remembered, "but what could I do?" Her pregnancy had been riddled with pain, inconvenience, and embarrassment, but she had no regrets about keeping it.

In the months leading up to Olivia's due date, we saw each other often—on Saturday mornings at church, for afternoon or evening chats in their apartment or at Ruby and Franklin's, and, in her final week of pregnancy, as I accompanied her on multiple doctor's checkups and hospital visits. When she finally was admitted to the labor and delivery ward, she and Peter called, and I raced to the hospital to join them. After her long day and night of difficult labor, I had the honor of being at Olivia's side when, in the wee hours of an early spring morning, Ethan, their firstborn, entered the world: so tiny, and healthy, and beautiful. For much of that night, Peter sat stone-faced in a chair along the far wall of the labor and delivery room, or wandered the hospital's wide corridors.

Turbulent Beginnings

Several months after Ethan's birth, one of the clinic directors and I hosted a dinner party at my apartment for Ruby, Olivia, Gloria, and another friend from Ghana. Olivia came with Ethan, Ruby brought her newborn son Jesse, and even Gloria, who had warned us she might not make it because of her rapidly approaching due date, lumbered up four flights of stairs to my apartment. As we sat around a table laden with Israeli and American dishes we hoped our guests would enjoy, Olivia issued an announcement: at the end of the month, she and Peter would hold their wedding and dedication ceremony for Ethan. All of us—two Catholics, one Protestant, and two Jews—were on the guest list.

A few days later, on Saturday afternoon, Olivia called me up, her voice quivering, and asked if I could come over. I knew she and Peter had argued earlier in the week and guessed, correctly, that he wasn't home when she called. Worried, I hung up, put down my weekend paper, and biked over as quickly as I could.

Usually when I came to visit, Olivia welcomed me with a hug and an offer of something to drink: water, soda, malt beer. But today, I hadn't come as a guest; I had come as a friend. As she let me in I could tell she was fighting back tears, and she kept busy with her household chores as we spoke. Baby Ethan, wrapped in the brightly patterned length of fabric that always held him snugly on her back, slept soundly in the middle of their double bed. I found a place to sit and listened as a torrent of stories, and tears, began to flow.

As she stuffed laundry into the washing machine, Olivia said she'd asked me over to tell me her whole story, from the beginning. She wanted me to understand, and she wanted my advice. Me? I demurred, suddenly anxious about the myriad ways in which fieldwork and friendship can become entangled. But then I promised to listen and do my best.

Olivia then revealed the secret she'd long kept from Peter, that individual pinch of destiny that infused her thinking about partnership, and parenthood: She came from a "broken family," she explained—a family cleaved apart by divorce. Although she was the eldest of sixteen, only she and one sister shared both parents. Her greatest fear, she confessed with tears in her eyes, was to repeat the error of her parents' ways, that mistake that had caused her so much suffering growing up. It was the one misstep she had always hoped and prayed she could avoid.

Although I hadn't known of her parents' divorce or the emotional scars that remained, I did know how Olivia and Peter had met. She came to Israel to help support "my little ones"—her (half-)siblings. Italy and the United Kingdom had also seemed like good options, but visas were too hard to come by. When she landed at Ben Gurion Airport, she met a South African man who also had just arrived: Peter. They became friendly, and soon he invited her to share an apartment to minimize expenses. She declined: "I'd have to call my family"—to get their permission. "No you wouldn't," was his response. Turned off by the brazenness of his invitation, she instead found a live-in position as a domestic worker for a religiously observant Jewish Israeli family.

Olivia and Peter stayed in touch, but even as they began spending more time together she kept him at arm's length, in part because of their differences in temperament, which sparked frequent arguments. She told me she'll never forget the moment they decided to stop fighting and make a commitment to each other. They were sitting under a bridge near the apartment he shared with a flatmate, and she told him she wanted someone to marry. Someone serious. Someone to be "my brother, my friend, my husband." Someone who would understand her, love her, want to stay with her. Someone who understood that if she got pregnant, she wouldn't have an abortion. He told her he wanted the same.

Soon afterward, Olivia left her live-in job, moved into his flat on Tel Aviv's southern edge and, indeed, became pregnant. Then Peter changed his tune. From the moment he found out, she told me, he began pressuring her to end the pregnancy, saying he wasn't ready to start a family with her. "He's almost forty," she remembered thinking, initially unaware of his daughter in South Africa. "Why isn't he ready? We're not babies."

At first Olivia conceded, afraid to violate his wishes. She took massive amounts of medication, she told me—most likely the ulcer medication Marina had taken as well—in a deliberate attempt to miscarry. When her efforts failed, she traveled over an hour away to a Palestinian hospital in East Jerusalem, eventually finding her way to Dr. Khalili.

After she returned home with news of her diagnosis, and her decision, Olivia and Peter fought bitterly, often with raised voices. And then he started hitting her. On several occasions—once when she was four months pregnant with Ethan and again four months later—things got so bad she spent the night away from home. She could recall half a dozen occasions when he had struck her, including one time when she had appealed to his relatives to come to their flat and witness her bruises. After that incident, a pastor at her church became involved, and things quieted down for a while.

"What am I going to do," she wondered aloud, "have him deported?" By this point in her story Olivia had slid wearily to the floor, distraught by her predicament, and we now sat side by side in the apartment's small entryway. The washing machine churned rhythmically in the next room, and the sun peeked in through a high window, one that wasn't covered over with cardboard. "I can't raise this child by myself. . . . Plus I don't even know the father's address, only the name of his village." However determined she was to secure her status as a mother, the choice she'd made to bear Peter's child now left her feeling trapped: "I can't complain or allow anyone to know what's going on because Nigerians will laugh at me."

"But it's not your fault!" I protested.

"It doesn't matter," Olivia said. "They'll laugh at me saying I went with a nonnative, and now he beats me." From the final stage of her pregnancy through the first months of Ethan's life, tensions between them continued to simmer, at times boiling over. Now exhausted from the labors of parenting a newborn, maintaining a household, and working once again as a housecleaner, she was desperate for life to be not just bearable but livable once again.

Paternity Angst

In tracing the contours of her predicament that Saturday afternoon, Olivia helped me understand, from her perspective, what a dignified, flourishing life would entail. She wanted a child, and she wanted her child to have a father—and to know him. "Where I come from," I remembered her telling me the week before Ethan was born, "you have to know who your father is, and who your mother is, or you'll be humiliated and ridiculed." We had just finished watching a low-budget Ghanaian movie about a university student who lived in a villa with her wealthy mother, a business executive, while remaining tormented by the mystery of her father's identity. A few days later, when Olivia, Peter, and I spent many long hours together on the labor and delivery ward, the movie stuck in my mind—especially as Olivia repeated a single question to hospital staff over and over: What must I do to be sure Peter's name appears on the child's birth certificate as his father?

At the time, in my naïveté, her question had been opaque to me. Only later that night, after Peter and I had wheeled their newborn to the nursery so Olivia could get some rest, did he resolve my confusion, albeit inadvertently. They had never gone through any "traditional ceremonies," he mentioned. Contrary to what I'd believed during the early months of our acquaintance, they had never married. Slowly, the pieces were falling into place. Motherhood was foundational to Olivia's sense of dignity and her vision of a flourishing life, but ensuring her child's paternity, and his name, was no less crucial.

By the time of Olivia's frantic phone call and our Saturday afternoon conversation, Ethan was nearly five months old. Since his birth, she lamented, Peter "hasn't paid for anything for the baby. Not food, not diapers. Nothing. I say to him, 'this is your son, you won't support him?'"—but he dodged her questions. His refusal to take financial responsibility added another burden for her to bear.

Her most public burden, however, was the most painful. In their respective communities, new mothers generally are exempted from public obligations like work, church attendance, and social activities until several months following the arrival of a new baby. Only after a couple has sealed their union in a church wedding (if they aren't yet formally married) and dedicated their baby in a religious ceremony is a mother expected to return to routine. From a health standpoint (both physical and mental), this ceremonial logic is wise and protective of both mother and infant. And in ritual terms, such dedication and "outdooring" ceremonies are a vital step toward reconstituting the communal social fabric to incorporate not just a brand-new community member but also the new social roles that parenthood and family entail. Given the importance of weddings and dedications among churchgoing Africans in Tel Aviv, an extended delay in carrying out these rituals could easily provoke gossip, scandal, even social crisis.

For Olivia, Peter's foot-dragging was threatening along precisely these lines. She couldn't go to church or social events, and she wasn't supposed to work, although she had little choice given Peter's lack of financial support. Worse still, she had begun to feel the heat of communal chatter. "Nigerians are talking," she said. "If Peter were one of my people, I would just get up and leave and that's it." But he wasn't from her ethnic group—and he wasn't even Nigerian. Since her "people" already found her foolish "for going with a South African," she didn't feel she could risk leaving. Yet she was no longer sure she even wanted to be married to him.

Sober Wedding

Eventually Peter came around, and on a Saturday morning in winter, seven months after Ethan's birth, they were married in a modest ceremony during the weekly worship service at Olivia's church. The congregation's dynamic Ghanaian leader, Pastor Opoku, officiated.

Theirs was nothing like Solomon and Rachel's jubilant wedding weekend. Virtually everything about the event was sober, at times tense. The strain was apparent even in their wedding invitations, which we prepared using my digital camera and their desktop computer and printer. Beneath a multicolored header ("MARRIAGE BLESSING AND OUTDOORING"), a photograph of the three of them is centered in a stock image gilt frame. Olivia, well coiffed in a tailored ivory dress, looks straight at the camera. The modest red of her lipstick offers the photograph's only splash of warmth. In her arms is Ethan, pudgy cheeked and dressed in a sweatshirt, gazing sleepily off into the distance. Peter, in a black suit, stands behind Olivia looking toward her, tight-lipped. His hand rests on Ethan's shoulder. Beneath the frame, a single phrase is inked in bright pink: "TOAST—A wise and understanding wife is from the Lord." It is a perplexing photo, with nary a smile in sight.

On the evening before the wedding, a group of women from church, with Ruby in the lead, gathered at Olivia and Peter's apartment to cook. Ruby shared Olivia's apprehension about the marriage, but now that plans were in motion she was determined to make the party a success. As a friend, she explained, this was her obligation—even if she was tired after a long week of hard work, and she was. At some weddings and other celebrations, Ruby noted, only meat pies are served, referring to the mass-produced snacks of shredded chicken or ground meat wrapped and baked or fried in dough. "It would shame *me* if Olivia only served meat pies," she said. "You have to serve meat and fried rice."

Ruby was known in their church as a proud mother and a long-married lady who moved through the world with the full support of an affectionate husband—and as a lighthearted, hospitable woman who kept her word and extended a hand to those in need. As we all knew, Ruby's public demonstration of faith in Olivia and Peter's union would bring the newlyweds honor. Given the close and public nature of their friendship, her failure to do so could bring them shame.

With great gusto, Ruby rallied her troops that evening in the apartment's tiny kitchen. Unfamiliar with the recipes—and, frankly, anxious about the use of stand-alone, commercial gas burners indoors—I stayed in Olivia and Peter's room minding the cooks' babies while they worked. As the evening wore on, massive quantities of food appeared: industrial-sized buckets of salad, vats of boiled chicken, huge pots of rice flavored with imported shrimp bouillon cubes. Ruby took her duties seriously (Figure 15).

By morning, the trappings of a joyful celebration were in place. Olivia, hair carefully arranged, appeared in a flowing white dress (Figure 16)—but not the one she'd wanted; it hadn't arrived in time. In her father's absence, Olivia's cousin Samuel served as his stand-in. We bridesmaids wore long, shimmering blue dresses with matching three-quarter-sleeve jackets, at Peter's request, and the music was lively. Ruby, impeccably dressed from head to toe, took the microphone to bestow her own rich blessings and sing a song in the couple's honor. Several photographers and a videographer were on hand to document the proceedings.

At the ceremony, Pastor Opoku emphasized Olivia's obligations to "submit" to her new husband as part of the work of bridging their cultural differences. "When you become born again," he told the binational couple and his multinational congregation, "you leave your traditional culture and join the culture of God. In this marriage, Nigeria and South Africa are being united." He mentioned a Nigerian who had visited South Africa some years ago, where "he took a beautiful wife. Now Peter is penetrating the nation of Nigeria in taking this sweet bride." I cringed through much of the pastor's remarks, my arms heavy with seven-month-old Ethan, who was sharply dressed and compliant, if squirmy, for most of the morning. After the ceremony and worship service had concluded, Ruby and her cooking companions distributed plates of food and soft drinks to all in attendance. Soon afterward, everyone left.

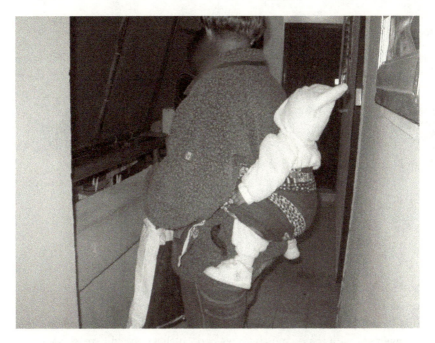

Figure 15. Ruby, with Jesse on her back, leaving Olivia and Frederick's apartment after completing food preparation for the wedding. Photo by the author.

Figure 16. Moments before the wedding ceremony. Photo: Mati Milstein.

A few weeks later, I mentioned that the wedding photographs taken by my Israeli photographer friend were ready, and that I would bring them along on my next visit. "The photos are beautiful," I told her. "You looked beautiful."

"I looked terrible," she replied. "I had many things on my mind that day, and I was frustrated during the whole thing. I was upset that my dress hadn't arrived, and that my parents weren't there."

"But are you happy now?" I asked. Her answer was quick, and definitive: "Yes."

"There Can't Be Two Captains"

So far I have focused on Olivia: on her conjugal deliberations, her complicated first pregnancy, her plunge into new motherhood. Her pursuit of dignity, and her sense of what it would mean to flourish. As we've seen, her engagement with these challenges was not solely about culture, or sociopolitical circumstances, or biography, but a potent amalgam of them all. But what about Peter?

Till now, I admit, I have presented him mostly through Olivia's eyes and mine. I have divulged choices and actions that cast him in a harsh light. Some of these moments infuriated me—even more, it sometimes seemed, than they upset Olivia. Although I never witnessed any acts of violence myself, I knew they had happened—and Peter knew I knew. Sometimes he even tried to reel me in as a witness in his defense. Occasionally he waxed ethnological, offering an apologia for the primacy of male authority in African marriages. "The values in Africa are different than Western values," he would insist. "In Africa the woman must be submissive to her husband. It's written in the New Testament." When the matter came up, I usually sat quietly on their couch biting my tongue.

I knew Peter's sense of masculinity, and male authority, were tightly entwined with his sense of dignity, but sometimes I couldn't help but push back: "Wait a minute, from what I've read, women in your place usually have quite a bit of power."

"Yes," he demurred, "our women are in charge—because they have money, and many of their husbands don't work."

"So look," I said, "you've just proven the Bible doesn't actually reflect reality." He tried another tack: "There can't be two captains running the ship."

Peter's views on marriage and male authority were by no means his alone; they were reinforced elsewhere, including Olivia's church. At Saturday morning worship services the very week before their wedding, Pastor Opoku had delivered a sermon that flooded back to me during their nuptials.

"A woman should always submit to her husband," the pastor had preached, "even if he's holding a blade to her neck." Shocked, I approached him after the service to ask for clarification, and to register my concern. Yes, he confirmed; I had heard him right. His advice troubled me very much, I explained, especially since I encountered women who had been abused by their husbands during my volunteer shifts at Mesila. Our exchange left me so uneasy I transcribed it as soon as I could. "A woman in this sort of situation should still submit?" I asked the pastor pointedly. "Yes," he insisted.

Sarah: Even if the woman has bruises on her body and is clearly suffering, she must still submit?

Pastor Opoku: Yes. She must submit and pray for God's intervention. If they live according to Christian beliefs, then God will intervene.

Sarah: What about when God doesn't intervene?

Pastor Opoku: God *will* intervene.

Sarah: But I've seen many examples to the contrary.

Pastor Opoku: The woman is a man's helpmate. He must love her, and she must follow his words. He is the head of the family. A ship cannot have two captains.

In my parents' household, I told the pastor, my mother and father had always shared authority and decision-making power. He disputed my recollections: "If you looked very carefully you would see the husband is the authority in certain areas, such as discipline." "No," I said, "my father has never disciplined me; my mother was always in charge of discipline." He insisted my recollections were wrong.

"My concern comes from the fact that I see women who are stuck with abusive husbands," I tried to explain. "Shouldn't they leave to save themselves?" Again, Pastor Opoku rejected my logic. "One cannot divorce, except in cases of infidelity. She should pray, she shouldn't leave." As Mesila's staff and other volunteers knew well, this model of male authority prevailed in a number of Tel Aviv's migrant communities—and at times it put women, and their children, at great risk.

I'd had no trouble confronting Pastor Opoku after a sermon that risked exacerbating a grave public health problem I knew to be present in his community. But arguing with Peter in his own home was more difficult. Each time he tried to box me in, I balked—then later, in private, made sure to remind Olivia that resources were available if ever she wanted to leave, and that the door to my home would remain open to her and Ethan. Each time, that is, until the day I confronted him head on. They had been married six months. Once again, Olivia was pregnant.

It all began with a morning phone call. I was preparing to leave town for a conference, and Olivia and Peter called with a request. Actually Olivia rang, then handed the phone to Peter, who asked if I would call one of Olivia's employers, apologize for her absence from work the previous week, and ask whether she could still come today. Last week, he explained, they had had a "physical confrontation," and Olivia hadn't made it to work. As I surmised and Olivia later confirmed, they had argued in the wee hours of the night—something about feeding Ethan—and he had hit her twice, on the head. In the morning she had had a headache and felt unwell, so she stayed home and, for nearly a week, ignored her employer's calls. Now it was her day to work for that employer again, and they needed Olivia's wages, hence Peter's effort to press me into duty.

Over the phone, it was hard to figure out what *she* wanted: Should I call? Not call? I couldn't tell. Unsure but determined to help them avoid additional lost wages, I told Peter I would ring Olivia's employer and explain, in Hebrew, that Olivia hadn't been well but hoped she could now return to work. The employer was perplexed by my call, but agreed. Meanwhile, the conference paper I was slated to present began with a vignette about none other than Peter. *I've opened the whole thing with a passage about his embodied experiences of criminalization*, I wrote in my field notes later that day. *How can I present this when I'm furious at him and worried for my friend, who's pregnant and already caring for a small baby?*

A week later I returned to Israel with a jumble of feelings. As soon as I could, I rushed over to see Olivia. After telling me more about that awful night, she asked me to confront him. "What should I say?" I asked. "Whatever you want," she said. "Just say you've been thinking about what he mentioned on the phone last week, and you want to say something about it." We both knew Peter was under a lot of stress. The machinery of the gerush was in full force, and he was terrified of being outside, of being around other Africans, of being arrested. And he was dead set on moving away from their current apartment to somewhere "where there aren't many blacks."

On my next visit, Olivia steered the conversation almost immediately to the confrontation between them: "Sarah has something to say about what happened the other day." Platitudes spilled forth from my mouth, which I later scribbled down in my field notes. "I understand something happened and it's really upsetting me, because Olivia is my friend and I care about her and love her, and when a friend of mine is hurting I'm hurting too," I had said. "I know people disagree, but anything can be discussed in words. Force and violence just create more problems." For most of the conversation, Olivia was flitting in and out of the room, keeping herself busy but remaining within earshot. I was avoiding eye contact, speaking in the third person, and steering clear of words like "hit" and "beat." I wanted Peter to listen, not feel attacked, so I tried to soften my message: "I'm speaking out of friendship and concern," I heard myself say. "I say all this with respect and admiration."

"Usually in a court of law they hear both sides of the story, listen to all the facts," Peter replied when I paused for a breath.

"I'm not a judge and not a lawyer," I said, "I'm speaking as a friend and as someone who cares deeply about Olivia and the whole family, and who doesn't want to see anyone I care about in pain or suffering."

"I know it sounds bad that someone would hit a woman," he replied, "that it sounds unimaginable that someone would hit a pregnant woman—but they'd have to consider the circumstances." He went on to offer his version of the night's events, including the "terrible things Olivia has said to him": Not being a good father. Threatening to call the police on him. He even suspected she was plotting his arrest through "spiritual means"—witchcraft.

I was afraid he would get angry with me, maybe kick me out. But he didn't. I don't know that I convinced him of anything, but he did listen, and when our conversation wound down, he even carried my bicycle down the stairs to spare me the trouble. As Olivia and I descended behind him, an African neighbor with a baby stroller alerted us that the police were out arresting people. I rushed down to grab my bike so Peter could come back in, to safety. *Such a screwed-up situation*, I later scribbled to myself. *On one hand I'm yelling at him for beating his wife, and on the other I'm trying to alleviate his fears and anxieties about the very threat that's raised the temperature in their household in the first place.*

By no means do I want to trivialize the impact of Peter's abuse in those early years. I hated how he treated my friend, and my strongest instinct was to protect her, her pregnancy, and eventually her—their—children. As I learned in the months after Ethan's birth and the subsequent decade and a half, Olivia had compelling reasons to cling tenaciously to their union, and hold on she has. Her commitment to their marriage, and to the preservation of their family, has compelled me to pause and think more deeply about the range of stakeholders and commitments animating Peter's lifeworld. Although I recognize the cultural pressures that bolstered his understanding of conjugal dynamics, I refuse to accept them as justification for violence. Yet this larger cultural context does help us see how Peter's values and actions are implicated in *his* ongoing struggle to preserve his dignity, to flourish, and to realize his humanity in relation to others.

In short, we cannot lose sight of the circumstances in which their tense marriage has unfolded. Neither can we ignore the other major threat to Peter's vision of a dignified, flourishing life—a vision that could only transpire, it seemed, back home in South Africa. For an African man living in Tel Aviv at the height of the gerush, the risk of arrest and deportation was ever present, ever palpable.

Arrest and Beyond

Nine months into the deportation campaign, and despite his vigilant efforts to stay under the radar, Peter was arrested—for the first time. A neighbor witnessed the event and called Olivia right away. At that point, being the father of an Israeli-born infant still offered meaningful leverage in achieving his temporary release. By the time of his second arrest about six months later, the hearts of the immigration authorities had hardened.

On the morning of his second arrest, Ethan was less than two, and baby Emmanuel was just a few weeks old. I happened to be in Tel Aviv visiting for the first time since returning to the United States the previous summer. At 8:15 A.M., Olivia called in a panic. Peter had left for work before six, but never confirmed that he had arrived. When his employer called to ask if he was on his way, Olivia knew immediately he had been arrested. She asked me to come, and I raced over as quickly as I could—but not before reaching out to Mesila, since I knew they had equipped her with a letter asking the police to avoid arresting either Olivia or Peter given her pregnancy, then the new baby. I spoke with Meirav, the community social worker, who faxed their letter to the Immigration Police. She told me an official had promised her Peter would be released within the hour, and that we should contact her if we ran into difficulty. Eventually we did, but no more help was forthcoming.

When I reached the apartment that morning, the lights were off, both children were asleep, and Olivia was a mess. She was so distressed she "hadn't even wanted to brush her teeth, or go to urinate." In between phone calls—to Mesila, to Peter's most powerful employer (a lawyer who nonetheless declined to help), to Talya (Olivia's Israeli cousin-in-law)—Olivia prayed. Eventually, she collapsed on the floor of weakness and exhaustion, overwhelmed by the prospect of raising two young children on her own. Ethan woke up and stumbled into the room, immediately attuned to his mother's worry and confusion. The image of him in that moment—his toddler eyes wide, anxious, searching—sticks in me. He absorbed the tension like a sponge.

Late in the morning, when none of our efforts were meeting with success, we decided to chance a direct appeal at the Immigration Police headquarters in Holon, just south of Tel Aviv. The four of us—Olivia, Ethan, the baby, and I—piled into a cab and traveled to the huge office complex where their headquarters were located. At the entrance, an electric gate and an entry hall housing a guard booth blocked our way. The guard was firm but friendly: "You can't go in there with children." Olivia and I exchanged worried glances.

"It's okay," I told her in English. "I'll stay here with the children. You go in." I looked to the guard and switched to Hebrew. "I'll stay here if you'll help me a bit." He was an employee of the office complex—not the police, he took pains to point out—and he received us with kindness. Olivia went in, I held the baby, and the guard let Ethan poke around and touch whatever captured his attention: a couple of broken buttons on his console, a newspaper supplement with photos of football players, a pair of cups and a plastic spoon.

As we waited, we saw people we knew come and go: a well-known leader of the Chinese migrant community. A Nigerian friend of Claire's. Another Nigerian man who recognized Ethan. "Has the father been arrested?" he asked. I hedged, aware of the velocity of rumors.

Eventually Olivia returned, frustrated. She had tried to speak with the officers in charge, but they had done their best to ignore her. She had called one of the officers "*mótek*" (sweetie) and "my friend," to which he had replied, "I'm not your friend, don't talk to me, talk to the wall." She didn't know what else to do but wait.

We spent hours in that entry booth. Olivia, completely worn down, nursed the baby. We had come without diapers or water, food or toys. The guard offered instant coffee to Olivia, then water to Ethan, who had refused to eat earlier in the day. Hungry and tired, he eventually started slamming his small body on the floor and crying. For a while, he was appeased by a game we played with my digital camera, flipping it back and forth to snap photos of him, then me, him, me. In between, I snapped photos of our surroundings, including the sign pointing toward the Immigration Police headquarters and the full-sized tour bus that transported detainees. ("Whatever happens, don't let him get on the bus," Meirav from Mesila had warned us that morning.)

Earlier Olivia's Israeli cousin-in-law Talya had promised to come, but hours ticked by with no sign of her arrival. Eventually she did appear, grumbling that she's now there every week: one time for a relative of Samuel's, then for a cousin, then for another friend. Once again, she would be late for work. With her confident, professional demeanor and—most important—being Israeli, it was obvious why everyone in their network was quick to pin their hope on her.

At first Talya's luck was no better than Olivia's, but eventually she found the Ministry of Interior representative Meirav had told us to find and pinned him down for a conversation. "We'll release him in fifteen minutes," was the man's response.

We waited back at the guard booth for the better part of an hour. Ethan was having temper tantrums, crying out "Daddy, daddy, daddy," and trying to run out into the street. Olivia was growing despondent. Talya had to get to work. We agreed that she would leave, Olivia would take the children home in a taxi, and I would take Olivia's phone (since my phone battery had died) and wait. As Olivia started preparing the children, the guard turned to us and asked in Hebrew, "Is that her husband?"

There was Peter, walking up the path, a free man coming out to greet his family. I couldn't read his emotions. Was he happy—or maybe sad? He certainly didn't seem nervous or emotional, as he'd been after his first arrest. On that occasion, he once told me, tears had streamed from his eyes when he first saw Ethan after his release. "I don't generally show emotion," he had said, and then immediately corrected himself: "I prefer to keep a strong appearance and not show such emotion." At the time, however, neither he nor Ethan had been able to contain themselves. Overjoyed to see his father, Ethan had kissed him, licked him—"like a dog whose master has been gone for a long time," Peter had put it. "I'd never seen anything like it."

On this day Peter's reaction was different. Had he wanted to be released? I wondered. Or had he perhaps concluded that deportation would afford him the opportunity to find a fresh start elsewhere without being accused of abandonment? I didn't dare to ask.

On the cab ride home, Olivia, Peter, and the children sat in the back seat, and I sat in front. I could hear Peter speaking to Ethan, seated on his lap, in his native tongue—which Olivia does not understand.

Back at their apartment, I didn't know what to do with myself. Stick around? Leave them in peace? When I asked, both insisted I stay. Whatever privacy I might have wanted had I been in their shoes was neither party's wish. Peter, in his usual way, immediately wanted to change the subject—in this case to the procedures for recruiting U.S. Marines. As gently as I could, I coaxed him back to the day's events. With some reluctance, he began to speak.

Conclusion: Precarious Attainments

Human flourishing, as philosophers John Kleinig and Nicholas Evans observe, is both process and achievement.[11] To flourish, we need food, shelter, and water. We need health, at least a minimum standard. And we need close relationships with other people. But we also need the wherewithal to live in dialogue with our defining ground projects—those synergistic products of others' expectations and our own views and values that become so integral to our sense of self we wouldn't recognize ourselves, and might not even want to go on living, without them. A livable life provides ample room for these pursuits.

For Solomon and Rachel, Olivia and Peter, livability cannot be taken for granted. Their struggles remind us that sociopolitical abjection rarely unfolds on its own. More often, it becomes conjugated with other forms of adversity and constraint: rigid gender roles and expectations. Regimes of religious authority. A sudden health crisis, or a terminal disease. The predicaments of these couples remind us that the lived experience of sociopolitical abjection is often, if not always and inevitably, entwined with other modes of being on the wrong side of power.

For Solomon and Rachel, a terrifying medical diagnosis suddenly made life unbearable. As long as death loomed overhead, their temporal horizons were foreshortened. Only when it became possible to reestablish a realistic vision of health were their chances of a livable life renewed. Various spaces of welcome proved vital to their pursuit of a dignified, flourishing life. The first of these spaces was crafted by Israeli advocates and activists, some at public medical centers and others at NGOs, who refused to exclude Solomon and Rachel from the moral community of people whose lives, bodies, and futures matter. From the perspective of these advocates and activists, the humanity of migrants living with HIV, their deservingness, and their value as human beings were never in question.

Other spaces proved equally important, including the Catholic church in which Solomon and Rachel hoped to formalize their union. They were desperate for the church to bless their marriage, but not solely as a matter of religious faith. Equally important, if not more so, was the chance to affirm their union before their community in a manner that would keep their secret safe. From the moment Solomon and I met, he made it clear that both facets of this commitment—formalizing their bond and keeping their secret—were absolutely essential to the preservation of their dignity. The alternative—shame, stigma, and humiliation—left him petrified, even prepared to precipitate his own death.

Under these circumstances, the Open Clinic offered a vital if fleeting space of welcome: a space where, in conversation with the priest, they could open up the black box of this holy sacrament in light of a deadly disease, the miraculous potential of biomedical advances, and the profound existential risks potentially posed by humans' tendency to judge in haste. At the unusual conversation I had the privilege of organizing, the priest and parishioners were able to agree, at least for a moment, on what a dignified, flourishing life entails. For both parties, one element was crucial: Solomon and Rachel's openness to the possibility of creating, sustaining, and taking responsibility for new life.

Olivia's pastor, an evangelical Protestant, posed no such question before agreeing to officiate at her wedding to Peter—although of course he had no need; they were already parents to a seven-month-old son. Both Ethan's birth and their eventual wedding were moments of vital importance to Olivia. As a Christian West African living in Tel Aviv, she knew that motherhood and marriage would secure her place in the world as a respectable woman. However tense the relationship between her and Peter, the birth of their children and the formalization of their union established her position in the community and, consequently, affirmed her sense of dignity and enabled her to plot a course for a flourishing life.

Peter's vision took markedly different shape and form. For a long time after his wedding to Olivia, the anchor of his lifeworld remained in South Africa and his overarching goal a life of stability, and financial security, back home. Although he was not proud that his livelihood depended on what he occasionally called "women's work"—housecleaning—he knew full well that he shared his employment prospects with most other African men in Tel Aviv. The greatest threat to his dignity would involve deportation, with empty pockets. For a long while, his relationship with Olivia and all it entailed—Ethan's birth, their wedding, the arrival of their second son, Emmanuel—were uninvited encumbrances.

Given these competing commitments, their ongoing tensions and fights come as no surprise—nor, I am sorry to say, does Peter's resort to physical violence. The techniques of the gerush, including the quotidian reality of profiling and the ever-present threat of violent arrest—only increased his anxiety about deportation and all that might entail. At the same time, his inclinations to lash out with violence found support in the local moral economy shared by many Christian, Anglophone Africans in Tel Aviv. According to Peter and Pastor Opoku alike, a ship cannot have two captains—and if the designated captain finds his authority challenged, he is justified in reestablishing it, even through violence. Anxiety spawns violence, which spawns anxiety, which spawns violence. A bitter, ugly cycle wears on. Under conditions like these, whose life is livable? Whose dignity is protected? Who has hope of flourishing?

For Solomon and Rachel, Olivia and Peter, and so many other illegalized migrants in Israel and around the world, one thing remains true. A meaningful, dignified, flourishing life "is never simply bare survival, but rather a matter of realizing one's humanity in relation to others."[12] And so, perhaps inevitably, it is always unstable—ever a precarious attainment.

Conclusion

In my view, the justification for ethnography is not
epistemological but existential.

—Michael Jackson

"Asylum seeker shot by mistake and beaten to death at the scene of the attack in Beersheva."[1] So read the headline on October 19, 2015, a decade after the gerush and three weeks into a wave of knife, gun, and vehicular attacks that some suspected might become a third intifada. In the southern city of Beersheva, a Bedouin man with a knife and a gun, himself an Israeli citizen, had just killed a nineteen-year-old Jewish Israeli soldier named Omri Levi in the city's Central Bus Station and wounded ten others in what was immediately described as a terror attack. Against the backdrop of nationwide panic, and in the heat of the moment, a security guard saw Habtom Zarhum, a twenty-nine-year-old asylum seeker from Eritrea who worked at a rural plant nursery and had come to town to renew his temporary status, and presumed him to be a second attacker. The guard shot the Eritrean man at close range.

As Zarhum lay defenseless in a pool of blood, an angry crowd gathered around, then attacked him in what was later described as a lynching. Some bystanders hurled insults while others spit on him and kicked him. Others in the crowd slammed a chair, then a long, heavy bench into his head. Another man held a tall stool over his flailing body: to protect him? To prevent him from fleeing? Several witnesses took videos with their cell phones. According to media reports, a crowd chanting "Death to Arabs" tried to prevent the emergency medical team from treating Zarhum. Hours later, Zarhum died in the nearby public hospital.

Almost immediately, Zarhum's ethnicity became evident and his shooting, beating, and death recast as a terrible "mistake." Just what was the mistake? Media commentators rushed to analyze the incident from every which angle:

heightened public fear of terror attacks, the dangers of vigilante justice, the new genre of cell phone snuff clips now going viral on social media.

Occasional, if unintentional, wisps of the Talmud, that centuries-old corpus of Jewish legal scholarship that enriches modern Hebrew with both precision and poetry, arose in public discussions of Zarhum's death—including the headline quoted above. The asylum seeker in question was not killed intentionally, but *b'shogég*: by mistake, inadvertently. Certainly his death was no accident; Zarhum was shot by security personnel, then brutalized by private citizens using enough violence to kill. In both Talmudic reasoning and everyday secular parlance, an act committed *b'shogég*—unaware that a basic principle is being violated—is less egregious than a purposeful violation. Killing Zarhum was wrong, the headline implied, but inadvertent in ways that mitigate culpability. This operative logic of inadvertence maps directly onto Israel's local moral economy as I have described it here. It was not quite Zarhum's killing that was the mistake. Rather, the mistake lay in assuming that the dark-skinned man targeted by the mob was one of the nation's real Others and not another, less threatening kind of Other.

On the day of Zarhum's death, a leading migrant activist publicly contested this logic of inadvertence, of murder "*b'shogég*," in a social media post. "Why mistaken identity?" she wrote. "They ID'd him as black, they ID'd him as foreign. They ID'd his blood as ownerless [*hefkér*], they ID'd that we'd been told it was okay. Considering the messages and the atmosphere these past weeks, the identification was perfect." The suggestion that Zarhum's blood was *hefkér*—ownerless, abandoned, bereft of anchoring social ties—reflects an explicit logic of abjection, of exclusion from the community, both sociopolitically and morally. A man whose blood is *hefkér* is precisely the kind of *homo sacer* that Agamben describes: He can be killed with impunity.

The following day, in a television news segment about Zarhum's death, the host's opening question reinforced precisely the tension between real and other Otherness explored in this book: "Is it possible the Eritrean subject paid this price because he didn't have a chance to say, 'stop, I'm on your side'?" ("*Atzrú, aní mishelahém?*").

*   *   *

What can we learn from the stories in these pages, some of them hopeful but others quite grim? The benefit of longitudinal insight lets us connect the dots between the gerush that began in 2002, the arrival of a new group of other

Others in the decade that followed (asylum seekers like Habtom Zarhum), and the plan proposed by the Israeli government early in 2018 to deport them, too. Before tracing the lines among these dots, let us revisit the book's core concerns and identify key challenges that remain.

First, we have seen how sociopolitical abjection operates, as Tyler aptly puts it, as a "design principle" of citizenship and statecraft. Of course neither Britain (the focus of Tyler's work) nor Israel has a monopoly on casting whole groups of people as "national abjects." From one national setting to the next, we find prominent figures who rally citizens, and often hustle votes, by trafficking in black-and-white ideas of "us" and "them." Although the motives for casting any particular group outside the fold reflect the tensions and dynamics within a country's local moral economy, the effects are similar. Those who denigrate certain groups as wholly and categorically other advance narrow interpretations of deservingness and undeservingness, obligation and exclusion, solidarity and collective identity. To recognize sociopolitical abjection as a design principle of governance is to focus not on singular events in historical, mythical, or biographical time, but instead on *processes* that unfold gradually, and concurrently, on multiple levels: political, economic, sociocultural, existential.

To make sense of these processes and their effects, we need to look carefully not only at how exclusionary categories are *configured* but also at how they are *experienced*. Earlier I proposed a critical phenomenological approach to the multiple, intersecting dimensions of migrant illegality: It is a juridical condition (that can take various forms), a sociopolitical status (that can change, and that affects different groups in different ways), and a way of being-in-the-world (that influences experiences of time and space, sociality and selfhood). Since proposing this three-dimensional framework over a decade ago, I have been humbled to see it gain some measure of traction. When we explore illegality alongside other templates of Otherness, as the Israeli case demands, we see the potential of this framework not only to enrich understanding of migrants' lives but also to help illuminate the roots, and consequences, of sociopolitical abjection in its many forms. Critical phenomenology invites us to grant "issues of existential power the same value as issues of political power."[2] A hallmark of this approach is its commitment to capturing multiple dimensions of Otherness in a single ethnographic gaze, while keeping existential questions at the fore.

Second, as a work of critical medical anthropology, this book has explored how sociopolitical distinctions become *embodied*: how they can penetrate the "inward parts" of people who have been cast out as Other, as abject. As I have suggested elsewhere,[3] the concept of embodiment frames two distinct areas of research that can, and should, be brought more closely into dialogue. Anthropologists of experience conceptualize embodiment as "the existential ground of culture and self"[4] and the anchor of individual and group lifeworlds. Key concerns include embodied experiences of time and space, patterns of sensory engagement, and somatic modes of attention. Yet a parallel and separate body of health research theorizes embodiment quite differently: in clinical and epidemiological terms. For social epidemiologists and other public health researchers, embodiment points to the complex ways in which human bodies quite literally incorporate aspects of our environments—social, political, ideological—in a manner that can be "read" on our biology, much like skeletal remains tell stories of people who lived long ago. Social-epidemiological work on embodiment has generated a wide range of powerful insights—for instance, into the biological impact of discriminatory processes like racism[5]—but overlooked the very experiential considerations that anthropologists see as the defining hallmark of this approach.

As I have argued, along with other critical medical anthropologists, these parallel approaches to embodiment—the experiential and the epidemiological—are inextricably entwined, especially in the lives of people who migrate.[6] Illegality and related forms of sociopolitical abjection can become embodied through chronic stress pathways that speed up processes of "weathering,"[7] or physiological wear and tear, that hasten sickness and death. Abjection becomes embodied when migrants are consigned to live in unhealthy environments, when they have little power to contest dangerous or unsafe work conditions, when they are blocked from obtaining needed medical care, and when they "choose" to self-medicate or pursue ineffective or dangerous alternative therapies. Migrants' abjection can become visibly embodied as improperly healed fractures, festering abscesses, advanced cases of treatable infectious disease, and belatedly diagnosed cancers. Importantly, it also becomes embodied when migrants internalize arguments that they are undeserving of care. These matters all require concerted attention, using mixed-methods research approaches—and the resulting insights demand prompt and effective translation into public and policy conversations.

I have focused at some length on how children of global migrants come to embody their parents' sociopolitical abjection: in pirate day cares and homes torn apart by deportation, in traumatized families and at public schools charged with preparing the same young people for life—if successful, for a dignified, flourishing life—despite these assaults. When it comes to children and young people whose bodies and futures are on the line, the stakes of asking the right questions, and putting meaningful insights in the right hands, are high indeed.

If the book's first two themes involve the impositions of abjection, the latter two point elsewhere: toward Arendt's notion of natality—the idea, however improbable it may sometimes seem, that "we are *free* to change the world and start something new in it."[8] I have explored how even under circumstances of profound exclusion and constraint, people nonetheless strive for a meaningful, dignified, flourishing life—a pursuit that resonates with Aristotle's notion of *eudaimonia*. Dignity has emerged as a prominent concern in a wide range of scholarly fields, but anthropologists have been slower to pick up the gauntlet, in part because of the term's polyvalence as well as its strong association with the Western philosophical tradition. I have argued in these pages that it is not the ethnographer's principal task to collect and compare conceptions of dignity across languages and cultural settings, to hammer down a precise definition, or to plunge into debates raging in other fields. Certainly we should probe those ethnographic moments in which dignity appears by name, especially when its appearance is unexpected or surprising. (Recall, for instance, the Immigration Administration's publicity flyers: "Do not let us arrest you," they read. "You deserve to leave Israel with dignity.") The ubiquity of the term on all sides of the Israeli-Palestinian conflict—in its Arabic, Hebrew, and English formulations—is equally worthy of exploration. Yet we should not limit our focus to such instances, nor should we make the mistake of simply taking people's invocations of dignity at face value.[9]

Rather than adopting any particular *idea* of dignity, this book has concentrated instead on something even messier and harder to describe: real-life people's keen—but also deeply variable—*sense* of dignity. From this angle, dignity appears as a rich and lively metaphor that is most perceptible *in motion*: as dignity harmed, denied, violated, or stripped away—or, conversely, as dignity pursued, safeguarded, recuperated, reclaimed. Understood in this way, a focus on dignity allows us to think ethnographically about what a "good life" might entail. It helps us make sense of that powerful cluster of desires that are fundamental to most people's experiences of being human. A sense of dignity as vector, lodestar, or striving—and the pursuit of dignity as an existential imperative—gathers together these widely held hopes and desires and invites us to consider their relationship to those ground projects, or orienting commitments, without which people would feel lost, unmoored, perhaps unrecognizable even to themselves. Dignity may remain elusive and unstable, but so does any aspiration that yokes us to an imagined future. Approached in this way, dignity figures most clearly as an imperative to make life bearable, or remake it as livable, or—if possible—to flourish.

And what of flourishing? This concept also brings baggage—philosophical, biblical, even botanical[10]—and carries various meanings. Here, too, anthropology has been reticent, with Mattingly's work as a vital exception. As she asserts, and as I have sought to illuminate further in this book, "Anthropology has a crucial contribution to make to this ancient philosophical portrayal of human flourishing."[11] For people living migrant lives on Israel's margins, struggles to flourish—to surpass "bearability" and hew to one's defining ground projects; to thrive—are varied, complex, and always relational.

For many, a flourishing life involved obligations to one's generations—to parents, living or dead; to siblings; to children. For others, it involved relationships to one's community, or to a divine power. Lorena could endure the pain of transnational motherhood as long as her remitted wages propelled her children through school, then university studies. Olivia's lodestar also involved kin: her siblings and parents in Nigeria, then motherhood and paternal recognition of her child, then the birth of another child sharing the same father. Solomon, returning from death's precipice, groped for a chance to reclaim a future: to marry joyfully, in a manner befitting his status and honoring his bride, rather than succumb to the shame and humiliation that disclosing their health status would entail. Under circumstances of less constraint, one's sense of flourishing might involve professional achievement, a political agenda, or a sense of serenity, but for unauthorized migrants in Israel, sights often were set lower. Under these circumstances, Naana stood as a clear exception. Hardwired for life in the public eye, he strove for recognition as a legitimate political actor against tall odds. Certainly all of these people had other defining goals as well—material, social, spiritual—but these were the orienting commitments they pursued both in everyday settings and in those fragile zones described here as inhabitable spaces of welcome. Their stories help us understand that feeling welcome, at least sometimes and in some places, is indispensable to a flourishing life.

The book's final theme, rooted in Israel's changing landscape of migrant advocacy and activism, involves the pursuit of what Margalit calls "a decent society"—a society that does not humiliate. The indignant citizens I met, interviewed, and volunteered alongside were stirred to action by a broad range of motives that Ma'ayan of the Hotline for Migrant Workers once cataloged for me as follows:

> There are motives related to identifying with the weak, with pain [ke'év], with the desire to help, with the desire to ease suffering . . . Look, there are Jewish ones, both because of the commandment regarding the stranger and also because of the feeling of Jewish Otherness . . . to prevent others from experiencing what we underwent. There are motives you could describe as ideological, of universal ideas, human rights, equality. There are motives related to pursuing justice—and I don't think it's the same motive; they don't lead to the same kinds of activity. . . . And one more: a perspective associated with being a better Israeli society. . . . Not only does it make us look bad in the world, or in other words it's bad for Israel and it has a negative influence on Israeli society, [but it also] destroys our values because it . . . corrupts us.

This full range of motives deserves fuller engagement than I have been able to offer here, as do the divergent idioms of social justice mobilization through which different Jewish Israeli advocates and activists have sought to channel their moral outrage.[12] By necessity I have glossed over the tremendous variation in their efforts, as well as the unruliness and evolution of the varied organizations themselves. So, too, have I glossed over the ways in which self-interest and other complex emotions can inform, and at times overwhelm, what are publicly presented as altruistic or broad-minded ethical pursuits.[13]

Even so, we have seen enough variation to recognize that most migrant advocates and activists in Israel had two things in common: a deep sense of indignation at their government's simplistic representation of global migrants as "the problem" and a refusal to sit in silent complicity with practices of sociopolitical abjection that violated their own moral values or, in some cases, their defining ground projects. I know some would distance themselves from the ideological freight of Azoulay's original formulation, but I am equally convinced that their actions stemmed, at least in part, from a desire "not to be a perpetrator."

In puzzling through what Jacobson calls "all of dignity's moving parts," I have distinguished between *social* dignity, that intersubjective quality of human interactions that can be explored empirically, and the abstract principle of *human* dignity that is often presumed to be inherent and universal. For advocates and activists, however, this distinction is not so clear-cut. People like Uri the volunteer music teacher, Mesila social workers like Ayelet, Meirav, and Danna, Ma'ayan and Yael at the Hotline, and the various directors of the Open Clinic actively pursued concrete, face-to-face opportunities to repair violations of social dignity imposed by their government, in their name. At times they succeeded, for instance when a physical space like an NGO office—or a personal relationship—provided a meaningful, if fleeting, inhabitable space of welcome.

Social actions have tethers, and for many, a key tether was precisely that abstraction labeled human dignity—in modern Hebrew, *kvod ha'adám*—or its companion concept: human rights (*zḥuyót ha'adám*).[14] In some respects the distinction between efforts to repair social dignity and attempts to advance human dignity followed a clear divide: between individual-level advocacy efforts (to facilitate or provide clinical services, or to mediate between a migrant and an employer or landlord, for instance) and efforts to achieve legal or policy change (through public demonstrations, lobbying, and legal suits). When I accompanied activists as they prepared to give tours of South Tel Aviv to national politicians, when they spoke before raucous Knesset committees in Jerusalem, and when they testified before the U.S. Congress in Washington, DC, late one evening from a borrowed office by video link, they were mobilizing their capacities for speech and action in an effort to build the society in which they wanted to live. They were responding to a moral imperative that was fundamental to their sense of self and their understanding of citizenship and its obligations. They were, in short, enacting the kind of commitments that are "so deep a part of us that we could not be the people that we are without having them"[15]—or, I would add, without acting on them. I offer these interpretations with confidence, in part because many of these activists became—and as I write these words nearly twenty years later, some remain—among my closest friends.

To understand how this imperative found expression—and where it met with resistance—we need to ask one final question: What changed in the wake of the gerush?

The Wake of the Gerush

The mass deportation campaign that began in 2002 was neither the first of its kind nor the last, but it was unprecedented in scope and scale, and it marked a pivot point in Israel's treatment of global migrants. We need to trace the changes that transpired in its wake, but first a side note is in order. Since the events of 2002–5 described here, in shorthand, as the gerush, the recruitment of authorized migrant workers in Israeli construction and agriculture, restaurant work and caregiving, has continued apace, as has the lucrative industry that facilitates it. Of those who arrive on a documented basis, many continue to slip into illegality and join new cohorts of what sociologists Adriana Kemp and Rebeca Raijman identified long ago as "illegal workers generated by the system."[16] In this manner, Israel has continued "to reap the benefits of employing foreign labor without experiencing the full social burden of incorporating them."[17] Although sociologists Moshe Semyonov and Noah Lewin-Epstein wrote these words—over three decades ago—about Palestinian workers who entered the Israeli labor market after 1967, they are just as applicable to migrant workers arriving in Israel today.

Community Collapse

Through its potent amalgam of intimidation and force, the gerush quickly hollowed out several of Tel Aviv's largest migrant communities, including the city's communities of West Africans, South Americans, and, to a lesser extent, Filipinos. As leaders were singled out for arrest, many churches and community institutions disbanded, and as the Immigration Police cultivated informers and carried out raids, trust weakened and social networks began to unravel.

Relatively few families chose to pack up and go home, but some did, either at their own expense or through the Immigration Administration's "Voluntary Departure" campaigns. Others, like Marina and Raymond, effectively went into hiding with their children. In some cases, women with small children—including Ruby and her son Jesse—boarded flights to Europe hoping to gain asylum and, one day, be reunited with their kin. Often such experiments ended badly, with migrants and close kin scattered among countries and continents. At times they ended tragically, with the untimely death of a beloved relative.

More frequently, however, families were torn asunder when fathers were deported from Israel, leaving their partners and children to fend for themselves. When parents hailed from different countries—South Africa and Nigeria, the Philippines and Ghana, Nigeria and Poland—the deportation of one partner was often especially devastating.

Of those who weathered the gerush, many—including Olivia—ended up as single mothers. Some could draw on reconstituted church groups or other social and community networks for support, but others struggled largely alone, and remittances rarely flowed in reverse. The disintegration of community resources and social networks also heightened the workload of Israeli organizations that supported migrants—activist groups, advocacy organizations, and relevant public services including mother-child clinics and public schools—while also complicating their efforts.

When Peter was deported following his third arrest, for instance, Olivia could barely keep her head above water. Her meager resources were stretched thin, and over a period of years our brief visits left me deeply worried about the development and well-being of her two young sons, and about her mental health. In that period, her life seemed bearable at best, and I knew my sporadic efforts to offer a bit of relief were barely a drop in the bucket.

"Israeli Children"

In due time, however, a pair of surprising "one-time" arrangements caught many by surprise, including Olivia. Although they effected no sweeping change in law or policy, these arrangements, one in 2006 and another in 2010, granted permanent resident status to a small number of children born in Israel to migrant parents, along with their families, and Olivia's was among them.[18] The first of these arrangements, which followed an intensive lobbying effort by activist groups, was ultimately made possible by a temporary reshuffling of parliamentary power.

Several years later, in 2009, a second activist campaign was sparked by the announcement that a new deportation campaign was around the bend—and that this time, children would be deported along with their parents. Outraged, a nimble, Facebook-savvy group sprang forth, meteoric, in response. This grassroots group, which provocatively called itself "Israeli Children," was founded by a handful of twenty-something Jewish Israelis who had been involved as staff or volunteers in Tel Aviv's migrant advocacy and activist communities. Despite this background, the new group took a very different tack. Relinquishing the rights-based claims and left-leaning politics typical of migrant activists, they adopted a more conservative strategy, arguing that children born to migrant parents and raised in Israel were in fact "Israeli in every way." To bolster their argument, they invoked a potent Zionist trope:

these children could not be deported because they "have no other country" ("*ein lahém éretz aḥéret*"). Leveraging their prodigious social media skills, Israeli Children organized large public rallies; consolidated a strong national media presence; and strategically cultivated high-profile supporters including well-known artists, journalists, government ministers, and other members of the political elite. With the announcement of a second "one-time arrangement" in 2010, the group scored an impressive, if provisional, win.

For Olivia and other families of eligible children, however, there was nothing provisional about this success. During the long process of applying, then waiting, then waiting some more, Olivia and her family relied on activists for both technical and moral support. In 2014, when we met up on HaTikvah's main drag for the first time in four years, we ran toward each other for nearly half a block, giddy like teenagers—and then, in the moment we caught our breath, Olivia showed it to me: the brand-new Israeli ID card she could hardly believe was hers. I held it between my fingers as we walked toward their apartment, my hands shaking in amazement.

Around eight hundred families received status through these two "one-time" arrangements, but thousands of others fell outside their narrow criteria. Among them were not only three hundred families who were deported, but also thousands of children born to Eritrean and Sudanese asylum seekers whom Israel refused to recognize, but could not deport given the international prohibition on "refoulement"—forced return to a place of political persecution or danger to life, liberty, or physical integrity.

A "Kinship of Genocide"?

When asylum seekers began arriving by the thousands in the years just after the gerush, some politicians and national leaders were quick to cast them as threats to the country's security and "demographic balance." Yet for a brief period in 2007, a countervailing view gathered broad support. As I observed that summer, their arrival catalyzed new forms of migrant advocacy and activism, largely in response to one specific group: men, women, and children fleeing what the international community had identified as genocide in Darfur. A new coalition of strange bedfellows quickly emerged involving veteran human rights NGOs, liberal religious leaders, and two very different celebrity members: a renowned senior Holocaust scholar and a slick young celebrity best known for his victory on an Israeli reality TV show similar to the American program *The Apprentice.*

For this wobbly coalition, the crisis in Darfur evoked collective memories of the Shoah—and it bound Israeli Jews and African refugees together in what one newspaper headline pithily described as a "kinship of genocide."[19] A surprisingly diverse cast of characters rallied to support this argument, including the chairman of Yad Vashem (the national Holocaust memorial in Jerusalem) and the chief rabbi of Tel Aviv–Jaffa. Within a few short months, a hodgepodge of spontaneous community initiatives, new NGOs, and smaller coalitions quickly sprang up, many of them led by an impassioned core of university students and other young people in their late teens and early twenties. Other key players included veteran human rights organizations; Zionist immigrant aid organizations; and religious groups of Jews, Muslims, Christians, and Messianic Jews ("Jews for Jesus"). Some collected food, clothing, and toiletries, while others organized housing, medical care, and Hebrew language lessons. Still others tried to help asylum seekers apply for asylum or refugee status, tasks that only grew more challenging over time given Israel's reluctance to fulfill its commitments under the 1951 UN Convention on the Status of Refugees that it helped draft.

After a few months, however, this powerful wave of fellow feeling dissipated, and asylum seekers were recast by Prime Minister Netanyahu, among others, as a new kind of "national abject": as "infiltrators"—in Netanyahu's words, "labor infiltrators" (*mistanenéi avodá*)—who threatened the security and "character" of the state. Even so, this brief episode sparked lasting changes in the advocacy and activist landscape, including the emergence of new frameworks for substantive partnership between Israeli and migrant activists. This development marked a notable shift from earlier efforts, in which Israelis had almost always taken the lead and spoken for, rather than with, their communities of concern. One additional development bears mention: Some of the young leaders who found their voices in 2007 later participated in the rise, and unprecedented success, of the "Israeli Children" campaign three years later.

Asylum Seekers and the New Dynamics of Abjection

Given these sociopolitical dynamics, it may come as a surprise that Israel did not see its first significant wave of grassroots xenophobia and anti-immigrant violence until 2012. By then, many of the 60,000 Eritrean and Sudanese asylum seekers who arrived after the gerush had taken up residence in the same South Tel Aviv neighborhoods where earlier groups of global migrants had lived. Yet their migration pathways and life circumstances were very different. Unlike the migrant workers who had come before the gerush seeking economic opportunity, asylum seekers had fled political repression and violence, and they tended to be considerably weaker, more traumatized, and ultimately less capable of finding their way. Moreover, they arrived in Tel Aviv not by choice, but through government policy: The authorities who picked them up at the border bussed many of them—in effect, dumped them—in a struggling urban area where residents were presumed least likely to protest.

Once in South Tel Aviv, many asylum seekers struggled to find accommodations. They also struggled to find work, which was officially forbidden for anyone with a pending asylum petition, although a tacit agreement blocked enforcement of this stipulation. On the streets of South Tel Aviv, homelessness and hunger among asylum seekers soon became major, and highly visible, concerns that sparked new forms of grassroots activism and a moderate, if insufficient, level of response from the municipality.

By 2012, however, some local residents were upset. Upwellings of public protest and social unrest rippled through South Tel Aviv as residents rallied to protest the high concentration of asylum seekers in their neighborhoods. Some of the protesters' grievances, including claims that asylum seekers spread diseases and raised crime rates, were easy to disprove. Yet the deeper catalysts of residents' anger—especially the long legacies of institutional racism and structural neglect that exposed South Tel Aviv's mostly low-income, largely Mizrahi neighborhoods to one wave of global migration after another in the first place—were indisputable. For many demonstrators, public expressions of empathy and concern for asylum seekers were another key irritant. They attributed these gestures to naïve, bleeding heart ("*yaféi néfesh*") Ashkenazim of greater means who lived in other parts of the city at a comfortable distance from HaTikvah, Neve She'anan, and other South Tel Aviv neighborhoods now home to large concentrations of asylum seekers. For some neighborhood residents, the perceived privileging of (non-Jewish) asylum seekers over (Jewish) Mizrahim was a form of elitist condescension that only added insult to injury.

Sentiments like these found sharp expression at local demonstrations, where community leaders and right-wing politicians used language that veered toward incitement. In particular, Likud Knesset member Miri Regev sparked a media firestorm at a May 2012 demonstration when she described African migrants as "a cancer in our body."[20] In apportioning blame for the community's suffering, Regev did not stop at blaming asylum seekers: "All the leftists who filed High Court appeals (against the deportation of African migrants) should be ashamed of themselves."[21] Immediately after Regev's incendiary comment (among other occasions), migrant residents were chased, threatened, and at times physically assaulted.

In the same year, the government instituted a range of new measures to block additional asylum seekers from arriving. These included a new "security fence" along the Egyptian border; efforts to amend the 1954 Prevention of Infiltration Law to permit the long-term administrative detention of asylum seekers (i.e., detention without trial); and a massive new detention center deep in the southern desert, called Ḥolot (Hebrew for "sands"). These measures met with quick and vigorous opposition from local and international human rights organizations as well as international bodies like UNHCR. A long cycle of legal challenges from human rights groups followed, with each High Court decision supporting the rights groups' claims and sparking revisions to these legislative efforts. Meanwhile, the Population and Immigration Authority (successor to the Immigration Administration) refused to accept or review asylum petitions. It also complicated asylum seekers' efforts to obtain and retain temporary protected status by granting only short-term protections requiring frequent renewal—the kind of renewal Habtom Zarhum sought when he met his death at the Central Bus Station in Beersheva. Drastic cuts to their office hours and locations created long lines, bottlenecks, and unintentional loss of status, resulting at times in detention in Ḥolot.

The state also pursued other means of pushing asylum seekers out of the country, including a revamped "Voluntary Departure" campaign involving secretive bilateral agreements with "third countries," eventually revealed in media reports to be Rwanda and Uganda. Asylum seekers were given a "choice" between long-term detention at Ḥolot or departure from the country with US$3,500 in hand and a flimsy assurance of protection. This arrangement continued for several years despite mounting evidence that asylum seekers whose departure for Rwanda or Uganda had ostensibly been voluntary faced grave risks to health, life, and limb.[22]

And then, in the first days of 2018, Israel's policies regarding global migrants appeared to have come full circle. According to the government's announcement, Ḥolot would be closed and asylum seekers would be granted one

Figure 17. Flyer announcing the 2018 "Voluntary Departure" arrangement for asylum seekers. Source: Israeli Population and Immigration Authority.

final opportunity to arrange their departure: a "Special Track for Voluntary Departure from Israel of Infiltrators" (Figures 17 and 18). If they refused, they would be deported to Rwanda—in explicit violation of Israel's obligations under international refugee law but, Israeli authorities claimed, with the consent of the Rwandan government. According to an agreement that was widely reported in the Israeli press but denied by Rwanda, the latter country stood to receive US$5,000 per deportee from the Israeli government.

On January 1, 2018, the Population and Immigration Authority launched an online application process and publicized the new arrangement in flyers

Figure 18. Satirical revision of the Hebrew "Voluntary Departure" flyer. This spoof changes "voluntary departure" to "deportation of refugees"; "calls on infiltrators" to "deports refugees"; and "depart voluntarily to their country or a third country" to "a journey of refugeehood, terror, torture, and danger to life." The diagonal banner reads, "The State of Israel violates the Refugee Convention, does not accept requests for asylum, and imprisons refugees." Source: Hotline for Refugees and Migrants.

that were easily accessible for download from their website in Hebrew, English, Arabic, and Tigrinya.[23] The public response was swift and forceful, and the ensuing political debate deeply contentious. Citizens and activists of all political stripes leveraged tools old and new in an effort to voice their opposition, including demonstrations, op-eds, open letters to the government, online petitions, and a flood of social media posts. Once again, migrant advocates and activists found themselves in new company—this time, much louder and more heterogeneous company than in 2007, when a broad coalition had spoken out to defend Sudanese asylum seekers fleeing Darfur. The coalition that arose in 2018 was far broader. Within a few short weeks, organized groups of influential Israelis—physicians and airline pilots, school principals and university academics, internationally known literary figures and high-ranking former diplomats, rabbis across the religious spectrum and elderly Holocaust survivors, among others—had issued collective statements registering their vigorous opposition. Groups of Jews from around the world—rabbis and cantors, community leaders, refugee law scholars, and Jewish members of the U.S. Congress, among others—voiced their opposition as well.

In South Tel Aviv, residents' reactions were equally swift—but far from unanimous. Sometimes the opposing sides faced off at demonstrations, each holding their own printed signs and banners. Posters on one side carried a striking message that I had never heard, let alone seen on a full-color printed poster, during the gerush of 2002–5: "South Tel Aviv Against the Deportation." Demonstrators on the other side used tame language to signal a much harsher, and more unabashedly racist and xenophobic, array of sentiments pulsing concurrently through social media, online comments on mainstream news sites, and political debates: "REHABILITATION of South Tel Aviv begins with DEPORTATION of the infiltrators."

In sum, the gerush that began in 2002 was not a singular event. It heralded the introduction of new kinds of "national abjects" and the adaptation of existing templates of Otherness to support the exclusion, criminalization, and expulsion of different groups of global migrants arriving via varied routes, from disparate locations, and under very different sets of circumstances. In subsequent years, the national political spectrum shifted further and further rightward, at times anticipating and at others falling into step with broader global trends toward heightened nationalist, populist, and authoritarian sentiments. As Israeli society and the political landscape took this sharp rightward turn, Jewish Israelis who acted in solidarity with those cast as national abjects—including Palestinians as well as migrant workers and asylum seekers—faced new forms of public vilification. New legal restrictions were designed to discredit, bankrupt, and shame activist groups, especially those that received support from philanthropic sources overseas. As increasingly far-right government leaders turned these screws ever tighter, various modes of opposition and resistance proliferated, some large and some small.

As Israelis across the socioeconomic and political spectrum struggled to make sense of government policies in light of their shared local moral economy, families of global migrants struggled to cope. In January 2018, a parents' meeting took place at Bialik-Rogozin, the South Tel Aviv school where a majority of pupils came from migrant backgrounds. Earlier we heard the Oscar-winning proclamation that students at Bialik-Rogozin are *Strangers No More?* as well as the more nuanced portrait painted by Principal Eli Nechama. At Bialik-Rogozin, he told me, "we treat them all as post-traumatic children."

Anxious about the impact of recent developments on his students and their families, Nechama convened a parents meeting, and now-veteran journalist Einat Fishbain wrote about it the next day.[24] "Our aim," Nechama said, "is to give children and parents tools for coping with the impossible situation they're experiencing right now. These are extreme situations that raise anxiety and worry and questions, and we need to respond to children's emotional needs above all else." One such tool: official certificates that he personally planned to issue to 1,600 parents in an effort to safeguard them from deportation.

Fishbain's article lay plain the difficulty Nechama faced in reconciling the school's mandate to inculcate core national values, as he understood them, with the escalating threats faced by students and their families: "We are supporting this just struggle and coming out against injustice, and we are not hiding this fact. . . . To the contrary, we've been doing this for twelve years— spreading the powerful light of what we do in this school, which is the pride of Israel all around the world. . . . We too are flying blind, with uncertainty about the future of many of our students, and at the same time we're still going on school trips and preparing for matriculation exams and planning for Adloyada [a playful celebration held on the annual Purim holiday] and in a month, in an almost absurd manner, a school group is traveling to Poland." In the shadow of a new gerush, Nechama was still sending his students to Poland, where Israeli pupils are sent annually by the thousands to internalize cautionary lessons now ricocheting wildly in Israeli sociopolitical space.

In April 2018, Netanyahu caught many by surprise when he announced that the mass deportation campaign announced on January 1 of that year had been cancelled, and that Israel had signed a deal with UNHCR whereby temporary residency status would be granted to one asylum seeker for every one resettled in a Western country. Human rights organizations immediately rejoiced, and left-wing Knesset members lauded the announcement as "the finest hour and an undisputable success of the community of asylum seekers and Israeli society."[25]

A mere five hours later, following an eruption of opposition on his own Facebook page and from parliamentary coalition partners as well as members of his own party, Netanyahu suspended, then cancelled the deal. He tendered his explanation on Facebook, where he insisted "I am attentive to you, and first and foremost to the residents of south Tel Aviv."[26]

Ethnography and Otherness

Ethnography is rooted in anthropology's peculiar affinity for Otherness, which takes many forms. One form of Otherness is central to this book: the purposeful Othering of certain people and groups, in particular times and places, for reasons grounded in particular local moral economies. This sort of Othering is never arbitrary, as we have seen; its roots are deep and far-reaching, and its consequences profound—often devastatingly so.

Yet Otherness has additional manifestations as well. Whenever a person sets foot on unknown terrain—as a tourist or a student, a journalist or an ethnographer, an economic migrant or an asylum seeker—Otherness trails along. At times, awareness of our own Otherness is thrust upon us—as invasive questioning, for example, or racist assaults. Others may delight in our Otherness—as something that invites curiosity, catalyzes new angles of insight, maybe sparks new bonds—whether we share in this delight, or feel exoticized, misunderstood, exploited. Or we may be blinded to our Otherness and its effects—blinded, perhaps, by social advantages that allow us to cruise through life without ever having to justify our presence, or fight to be recognized for *who*, rather than *what*, we are. Whether we are assaulted because of our Otherness, proud of it, oppressed by it, or oblivious to it, alterity is in every human interaction. In this sense, each of us is always an Other.

And then there is a third sense of Otherness, that anxious celebration of difference lodged deep in the heart of the anthropological endeavor. In summing up our field, anthropologists sometimes invoke a single, tight phrase: we aim to *make the strange familiar and the familiar strange*. To pursue this aim, inevitably, is to invite disorientation and discomfort. It is to invoke what anthropologist and psychoanalyst Ellen Corin describes approvingly as the "destabilizing power of Otherness."[27]

For Corin, one of anthropology's most powerful assets is its "perpetual principle of *inquiétude*, questioning, critiquing and contesting" that which appears settled or certain.[28] In her view, "an element of *inquiétude*"—of restlessness, worry, or anxiety—should always be part of anthropologists' "habitual ways of working." On one level, this inquiétude is a reminder that we must always think critically about the terms and categories that populate our speech, and about the stories that organize our worlds and anchor us within them. It is also a reminder of the importance of facing Otherness *on its own terms,* something far easier said than done. To conjure this "destabilizing power" is to make ourselves vulnerable. It is to risk discovering that any truths we take to be self-evident might demand further interrogation. To risk learning that they—rather, we—might be wrong. As Corin points out, we avoid these risks at great peril, both personal and collective.

Let me close with one more source of inquiétude, and a possible response. As Mattingly reminds us, "taking morality seriously does not presume that people are good but rather that they are *evaluative* in moral terms about their own actions and those of others."[29] Throughout this book, the slippery notion of dignity—despite its roving role as principle and quality, value and metaphor; its competing genealogies; and its etymological permutations (indignity, indignation)—has been assigned a singular moral valence. In short, I have generally presumed not only that the people we have encountered are pursuing what *they* understand to be "good" but also that their understandings of the good are themselves worthy of positive valuation.

I now want to complicate this picture in a way that opens up new questions of great urgency. Until now, I have mostly dodged an important question: What about those instances in which one's own pursuit of dignity and flourishing, or one's understanding of "the good life," causes harm, either intentionally or unintentionally, to others? I have broached this question briefly on several occasions. Both Peter's violence toward his wife and, more troublingly, his culturalist defense reflect a shared, patriarchal model of conjugality and dignity that left me angry, and fearful. The fact that Pastor Opoku shared Peter's view only ratcheted up my concern for the women in Israel's African community, some of whom I had come to know well and care about deeply. I have mentioned my strong urge to push back against these claims, and alluded to the difficulties in taking that step.

Another high-stakes clash involved the collateral damage that can ensue when migrants aim to secure their livelihood—and avoid the stresses and instabilities of housecleaning work—by taking the entrepreneurial step of opening a pirate day care. Visiting such spaces and realizing a good friend had opened up one of her own were among the most upsetting moments I faced in nearly twenty years of ethnographic engagement. I have spoken and written about how such spaces, sometimes characterized as "child warehouses," can severely curtail young children's capacity to grow, flourish, and even survive.[30] Yet I remain dissatisfied by the sometimes fumbling and ultimately meager nature of my own response.

In these turbulent times, it seems especially important to identify, and grapple with, such moments of ethnographic inquiétude. Ours is an era of gaping global inequalities, deadly wars, and technologically turboboosted patterns of human mobility, often at great risk and with profound consequences for all who are affected. Ours is also an era in which populist and nationalist sentiments have (re)introduced styles of political discourse, and modes of political leadership, that render the design principle of sociopolitical abjection both more explicit and more palatable to broad voting publics. These dynamics are exacerbated both by spurious allegations of "fake news" and by real-life "fake news" involving the active dissemination, through conventional and social media, of full-throated lies. Social media algorithms and search engine bots propel us ever deeper into echo chambers of like-minded people. Developments like these at the national level have catalyzed—and been catalyzed by—further disruptions in the diplomatic and geopolitical spheres.

For many of us, migration—or more specifically, migrants and the debates swirling around them—becomes our nearest window onto these roiling global dynamics. Whether one has been forced to leave unbearable conditions or watched others leave; whether one's community has been changed by migrants' arrival or fought to keep them away, migration—and the many dimensions of Otherness it entails—are inescapable dimensions of twenty-first-century life.

There is, of course, nothing predetermined about how such encounters with Otherness will unfold. Ethnography has taught us much about migrants' lives, and about the lives of citizens who see migrants' arrival as opportunity rather than threat. But what about those who witness contemporary patterns of human mobility and think—or feel—otherwise? Do we know enough about those who use their capacity for speech to proclaim anti-immigrant views, or their capacity for action to support political parties committed to ringing national borders with razor wire, bulldozing encampments, or pulling children from the arms of their detained parents?

Earlier I noted that some might find it foolish or naïve to place questions of existential power on par with questions of political power, as I have sought to do in this book. To those critics, I offer a simple response. Feeling curtailed in one's capacity to live a meaningful, dignified, flourishing life—whatever the reason—precipitates existential harm. This holds true not only for migrants and their allies but also for people who fear that social and demographic changes are unmaking their worlds and curtailing their own capacity to flourish. In short, violations of dignity are not only the *result* of dangerous politics; they can also be its cause.

Here, our task is clear. Whatever our politics, we need to cultivate the capacity to hear and recognize those whose experiences of indignity generate forms of indignation, and forms of political expression, that we may find perplexing, objectionable, even terrifying. For many, this task will pose extraordinary challenges—interpersonal, ethical, ethnographic. And yet, I submit, these are challenges we would be foolish to avoid.

Postscript

Planted in the house of the LORD,
They shall flourish in the courts of our God.
—Psalm 92:13

Allow me to jump forward in time and reintroduce you to Gloria, whom we last encountered when she lumbered up to my apartment for a dinner party in fall 2003, late in her first pregnancy. It was now the summer of 2017, and we had smartphones, and WhatsApp. In a flurry of text messages, Gloria and I arranged to meet on a Wednesday evening in the air-conditioned comfort of McDonald's, deep in the heart of Tel Aviv's massive and progressively dilapidating Central Bus Station. It had been years since we'd been able to sit down and really talk, just the two of us.

We had last seen each other three summers earlier, in 2014, when our families met at an ice cream shop at the city's northern port on a sweltering Saturday afternoon. That day we had busied ourselves making introductions, getting our children acquainted—three of theirs, one of ours—and settling everyone in at a trio of café tables beneath a wide awning, fast-melting treats in hand. I was playing presumptive host and wrangling my own energetic toddler while Gloria, serene and elegant in the day's church finery, put my husband, Sebastian, through his paces, managing somehow to keep her own children in check with little more than a quiet word here, a raised eyebrow there. We were just a month apart in age, but in motherhood years, Gloria was eons ahead.

When we first met at the Open Clinic in 2002, Gloria and William were still newly married—in a Catholic "white wedding," she often reminded me—and expecting their first child. It wasn't her pregnancy that occasioned our first encounter, but their support for Irene, a fellow church member, also from Ghana, who was struggling with major surgical needs that the clinic staff fought hard, and successfully, to resolve.

Since then, Gloria had always struck me as matronly and wise. I had watched her care patiently for Irene through the older woman's surgery and long recovery, and later attend lovingly to their firstborn infant son. During her first pregnancy, Gloria and William had encouraged my frequent visits, and at one point I accompanied them to Dr. Khalili's office in East Jerusalem for a prenatal visit. We made a half day of it, stopping for lunch in a Palestinian restaurant near the Old City's Damascus Gate and shopping in the open-air market before returning to Tel Aviv by minibus. They invited me to church events large and small: weekly mass, multinational parish-wide celebrations, meetings of their small worship group, whose members gathered regularly in a rented basement space, spoke in tongues, and sought healing through the laying on of hands. Gloria and William also included me in major milestones, including the birth of their son in a public hospital and his circumcision in their living room in Jaffa by an ultraorthodox Jewish *móhel*, or ritual circumciser. Following the child's baptism in the Catholic church, they held his dedication ceremony in the same hall where Ruby and Franklin had dedicated their son Jesse half a year earlier. Gloria invited both Ruby and Olivia to attend, and they did.

Gloria often prayed aloud that I would find a husband and have children of my own, and when she did I was usually quiet but grateful. Although my protracted studies and professional aims mucked up my chances for a long while, I had finally found a partner who passed muster. And there we were, on a bright Saturday afternoon, watching Gloria's youngest, then three, play big sister and spoon ice cream into my giggling one-and-a-half-year-old daughter's eager mouth. It was an encounter I had long dreamed about, but never dared to imagine.

It was hard to catch up properly that summer afternoon in 2014, but we did our best. Gloria and William were struggling on many fronts and yet, in their usual way, they focused on life's brightness. Unlike many others in the West African community, including their Nigerian flatmates and fellow church members Edwin and Uche, they had managed to stay in Israel. Years earlier, we had spent hours in their common living room debating theology and Zionism, European colonialism in Africa and American military might. Edwin, an avid sports fan and a great sparring partner in these debates, had been deported long ago. Uche, an architect and married father of two, had tried to join his wife and Israeli-born sons in Europe, but without success. But their worship group was still going strong, and Gloria and William were as deeply involved in church activities as ever. And their younger three children were joyful and thriving, although they pined for their eldest, the son they had sent to Ghana before his first birthday to be raised by a friend. "Sending him was the biggest mistake in my life," Gloria confessed. Without him near, she told me, their family couldn't feel complete.

That summer afternoon at the ice cream shop, Gloria had other news as well, which she shared with modest pride: She now held a leadership role at one of the Mesila-facilitated Unitaf day cares, the centers for children age three and under created with municipal support and private funding as an alternative to pirate day cares like those I had recently visited with Danna. She invited me to come by and see her at work, and a few days later I did.

In many day cares I visited over the years, including the one Gloria had started in her own apartment years earlier, children often looked bored, disengaged. When a new face appeared at the door, they would often make a beeline for their visitor and jump on him or her, vying anxiously for the newcomer's attention and affection. At the Unitaf day care, located within the Central Bus Station complex, the atmosphere could hardly have been more different. As Gloria walked me through its spacious rooms—each with its own designated nap area, toileting facilities, and age-appropriate, if well-used, toys—the children noticed when we appeared, but didn't lose focus. A few waved cheerily, but most returned quickly to their activities. It was late afternoon when I visited, and they looked rested, active, and well fed. Most of Gloria's colleagues were women of migrant backgrounds themselves, and most children in their care had been born in Israel to parents from parts of West Africa, the Philippines, Sudan, or most commonly Eritrea. At age three all children could be enrolled in a municipal kindergarten, but until then, this facility deep in the city's bus terminal was the best arrangement on offer, the gold standard for children born into Tel Aviv's migrant community and a far cry from the day cares Danna and I had visited the previous week. Yet costs at Unitaf were higher than in-home day cares, hours were shorter, and capacity was tightly limited, leaving thousands of other children, especially children of Eritrean asylum seekers, unable to benefit.

After showing me the kitchenette, where a printed menu of the children's daily meals and snacks (approved by the Ministry of Health, Gloria pointed out) was taped to the refrigerator, she guided me to the office she shared with one of the Israeli senior staff. As Gloria slid into the chair behind her large desk, the magnitude of her accomplishment began to sink in. *Here, she's the boss,* I thought to myself. Not only had she and most of her family managed, against the odds, to outlast the gerush and its aftermath, but she was among the only migrants I knew who had undergone professional training, then risen to a leadership role befitting her skills, her experience, and her character. During our visit I chatted with a few colleagues, one of whom shared a comment she had heard from a child: "Auntie Gloria must have been prime minister in the country she came from!"

We were pressured for time—Gloria had a church obligation, and my family and I were returning to the United States the following day—but we stole a few minutes to talk about the anti-immigrant sentiment that had risen sharply in the past year and a half in South Tel Aviv. We discussed the government's continued antipathy toward migrants, especially the asylum seekers from Eritrea and Sudan who had arrived in the past decade. I wondered aloud how she could stay so poised, so focused, despite the difficulties facing her family, her community, and the children she saw each day.

"It's because of God," Gloria explained in a tone I remembered well, a tone of calm piety that could conjure stirrings of faith in even the most religiously unmusical. She smiled, looking deep into my eyes: "God is great and will protect us. It's all in God's hands."

We marveled at the longevity of our friendship and the many moments we had shared over the years, and Gloria explained how she had learned long ago to retreat into quiet meditation in order to figure out whether someone was trustworthy: "I pray and pray." I was humbled by the implication of her words, and felt ashamed for having planned the week's meetings so poorly.

Before rushing off to our respective buses—hers heading south, mine heading north—we took a tightly framed selfie right outside the day care's main door, all hugs and beaming smiles. We had first crossed paths so many years earlier, so many life stages earlier. Now, as then, Gloria's feet were planted firmly on her path. She was secure in her inhabitable spaces of community, family, and faith. Many around her struggled, but hers was a life of meaning, dignity, flourishing.

Three years later, in 2017, my family returned to Tel Aviv for a visit, this time with not one but two small children in tow. On this visit, I was determined to do better than a quick afternoon meet-up and a hasty tour. At Gloria's suggestion, we arranged our meeting at the Central Bus Station—this time alone, without kids or spouses, at the neighborhood's standard meeting place: McDonald's.

Gloria and I had barely pulled apart from a long hug and settled into a vinyl booth when a nearby commotion distracted us both. A group of kids, high schoolers of West African descent, were hanging out at the next table.

Maybe they were a little rowdy, but they were teenagers, at McDonald's, on a
summer afternoon. From the corner of the restaurant, two older women with
faint Russian accents started yelling loudly, complaining about their noise.
The kids lobbed back a few retorts of their own in fluent teenage Hebrew, then
one of the women launched an angry tirade I hoped Gloria didn't understand,
although I knew she did. "You're all trash [zével]!" the woman shouted. "You
came here from the jungle, and now you're ruining the country! You all just
take and take, and what's left for us?" Eventually one of the kids switched to
colorful English, telling the older women to go fuck themselves.

Gloria stood up and turned toward the teenagers, her expression soft but
her voice serious. She chided them for losing their cool, then pivoted toward
the women in the corner with a compact apology on the kids' behalf: "Sliḥá"—
I'm sorry.

That was how our conversation began. Soon the teenagers got up and left,
as did the women in the corner. I struggled to digest what had just happened,
but Gloria was quick to glide back into our conversation, explaining how William's initial disapproval of her role at the day care had mellowed into respect
and pride. She told me how they recently had moved to a larger apartment a
solid fifteen minutes away by bus, in a neighborhood where they were probably "the only blacks." How her daughter was excelling in school and hoped
to go abroad after high school rather than "stay here, where she can only work
in a restaurant or something." And Gloria spoke of the painful loss, a year
earlier, of her beloved father back home in Ghana.

Several times as we spoke, we were interrupted by children and day care
parents who spotted Gloria through the restaurant's glass wall and came in
to offer their greetings. "I didn't realize it was you at first," one mother offered,
"but she said 'Auntie Gloria, Auntie Gloria.'" The woman's small daughter
had raced into the restaurant to collect a warm hug.

Before we parted ways, Gloria invited us to join her family for dinner that
Friday, and I was honored to accept. Two days later we arrived at their top-
floor apartment as the day was winding down, shortly before the buses stopped
running for Shabbat. Their children, all school age by now, were excited to
see our little ones, now four-and-a-half and two, and Gloria had prepared a
feast. Although their three-bedroom flat was a good distance from nearly
everyone they knew, it was larger and better designed for family life than their
previous apartments. Family photos adorned the walls, among them a large
poster celebrating the life of Gloria's father. The living room was organized
efficiently to accommodate a family's worth of furniture: a long dining table,

a pair of couches and coffee table, and, in the corner, a full-sized desk outfitted with a hefty computer.

As the adults spoke in the living room, Gloria and William's children entertained our daughter in the tiny bedroom two of them shared. With creativity and resourcefulness, they coordinated efforts to help conquer her shyness: colored pencils and paper, stories, a finger-puppet play. When I peeked in to check on her, I saw them skillfully crafting paper boats and airplanes, much to her delight. When dinner was served, the kids gathered around the coffee table and taught her to eat fufu, the traditional West African staple of pounded root vegetables served with spicy soup. I had just spoken a few days earlier with a Filipina friend, still in Israel, who complained that her elementary-age children were so lost in computer games and social media that technology was disrupting their sleep, impeding their studies, and interrupting their ability to make friends—like so many children around the world. When we'd met up, I could see what she meant. Not so with Gloria and William's children who, like their parents, received visitors with generosity, curiosity, and care. All challenges aside, and I knew from Gloria that each faced challenges, they were grounded. Flourishing.

As the children ate around the coffee table, the adults gathered at a dining room table heavy with large bowls of fufu and soup, potatoes and vegetables. My husband fed our two-year-old son on his lap as I walked Gloria and William through the main arguments of this book, focusing on ideas about dignity and the lasting impact of the gerush. Their reactions buoyed my confidence. What I described wasn't a matter of interpretation or opinion, William offered. "That *is* the story," he insisted. "It's a story too many Israelis don't know."

*   *   *

Rather than ending with William's words, I want to jump back in time to another, earlier moment. In June 2014, just weeks before the region erupted, once again, in terrible war, my family and I went to Tel Aviv. "How wonderful that you're traveling to Israel this summer," some of my American relatives chimed as we prepared for the trip. Whatever itinerary they may have imagined, and however beloved the denizens of my Israeli world, I was heading to the field—to the changing neighborhoods of South Tel Aviv—on a research trip that would leave me appalled and gratified in equal measure. In the following month, there would be war, and like so many others around the world, I would spend the remaining summer months agape, and aghast. By then, my only escape from the news—into this book— was no escape at all.

But before all that, in June, I left my family with my in-laws in rural Germany and embarked, alone once again, on a stint of fieldwork so overscheduled and intense that by nighttime my body was buzzing to a degree that occluded sleep. After a week, they joined me, and I had the rare, almost surreal opportunity to introduce my husband and our young daughter to some of the people whose confidence and friendship I had worked hard to earn years earlier, including Gloria and her family—and Olivia and hers.

Now, and against tall odds, Olivia and her family lived in Israel with legal authorization and residency status. Ethan, whose birth I had witnessed in a Tel Aviv public hospital, and whom I had held in my arms at his parents' wedding, was becoming a teenager. He had never left Israel. He was the same age as Junior, the son Gloria and William had sent home to Ghana before his first birthday, and who hadn't left that country since.

As for Olivia, she was newly ordained as a pastor—not in the church we attended together with Ruby and Claire, most of whose members had long since been deported, or left, or in a few cases died, but a new, smaller church she had joined more recently. Her new congregation met several times each week in a former industrial building in South Tel Aviv, nor far from the Open Clinic where we first met in 2002.

On that sweaty summer Saturday, dressed in the best church clothes we could muster after nearly three weeks on the road, my family and I attended the church's morning worship service. Before the full congregation—West Africans, for the most part, plus a few Sudanese and Filipinos—we were called up to the altar for a grandiloquent blessing, in Jesus' name, a blessing that made my German Jewish husband wince, but tapped something deep in me: that secret place where we hide our fears that ethnographic efforts, despite our best intentions, might be more exploitative than humane. With her public blessing that morning, in that inhabitable space where we were warmly welcomed, Olivia—now Pastor Olivia—reassured me that the bonds created between us were real and enduring, transcending time and so many layers of difference.

Introduction

Epigraph: Singer and Yehoshua 2003.

1. Shadmi 2003.

2. Sinai 2003.

3. The name and scope of this agency have evolved over the years. As of 2019, it is the Population and Immigration Administration.

4. Tyler 2013, 4.

5. Kemp 2007, 675, citing Israel Immigration Administration figures.

6. Bornstein 2002; Roy 2002; Buch Segal 2016.

7. Kemp 2004.

8. See, e.g., Willen 2011; Willen et al. 2017. My thinking is informed by the work of Miriam Ticktin (2011), Peter Redfield (2013), Didier Fassin (2012), and, in a different vein, Samuel Moyn (2010), among others.

9. Tyler 2013, 4. Subsequent quotations in this paragraph appear on 4, 21 (citing McClintock 1995, 72, on the notion of abjection hovering "on the threshold"), 13, 35, and 42 of Tyler's text. Emphasis added.

10. Willen 2007a, 2007b, 2014; cf. Gonzales and Chavez 2012.

11. Tyler 2013, 48.

12. *Fedayeen* were viewed as freedom fighters by Palestinians and terrorists by the Israeli state.

13. Tyler 2013, 9.

14. See, e.g., Holmes 2013; Horton 2016; Castañeda et al. 2015; Fleischman et al. 2015.

15. See, e.g., Csordas 1994; Desjarlais 1997; Kleinman 1998, 2006; M. Jackson 2005, 2013; Seeman 2009; Garcia 2010; Willen and Seeman 2012; Hollan 2012; Mattingly 2014; Pinto 2014; Zigon and Throop 2014.

16. M. Jackson 1996, 22, emphasis added.

17. M. Jackson 2005.

18. Willen 2007a; cf. Good 1994 and Desjarlais 1997.

19. Desjarlais 1997, 6, 223. Indented quote below appears on ibid. 25.

20. Mattingly 2014, 10.

21. Galtung 1971; see also Farmer 2004.

22. Mattingly 2014, 12, following Williams 1981.

23. See, e.g., Zigon 2007; Zigon and Throop 2014; Das 2010; Kleinman 2006; Fassin 2012; Robbins 2013; Fischer 2014; M. Jackson 2013; Mathews and Izquierdo 2009; Stoller 2014.

24. Mattingly 2014, emphasis added 9.

25. See, e.g., Keyes 2016 and Jones 2000.

26. Notable exceptions include Nussbaum (2000) and Kleinig and Evans (2013), who take broadly ecumenical approaches to human flourishing.

27. Mattingly 2014, 11; cf. Das 2010.

28. Zigon 2014, 757.

29. Biehl 2014, drawing on Hirschman 1971.

30. Kleinman 2006, 7.

31. Mattingly 2014, 10.

32. Mattingly 2013, 309.

33. Nussbaum 2011, 29–30.

34. Notable exceptions include Bourgois 1995; Jensen 2008; Han 2012; Hamdy 2012; Oka 2014; von Schnitzler 2014; Omidian and Panter-Brick 2015; Bennett 2016.

35. M. Jackson 2005, xxii; ibid. xii.

36. Ibid., 181.

37. Leder 1990.

38. Willen 2014.

39. Anthropologist Jarrett Zigon (2014) raises similar concerns in his work on "dwelling" as an ethical imperative.

40. M. Jackson 2009, 242; see also Lucht 2011.

41. See, e.g., Fassin 2009.

42. Kleinman 1998, 2006.

43. Peres 1993.

44. The "Green Line" refers to the armistice line established in 1948 to mark the boundary between the newly established State of Israel and the territories that remained under Jordanian control. Since the 1967 Six-Day War, in which Israel captured the West Bank and other territories, the Green Line divides what the international community recognizes as Israel proper from the Israeli-occupied West Bank.

45. See, e.g., Bornstein 2002; Roy 2002; Giacaman et al. 2007.

46. Semyonov and Lewin-Epstein 1987, 112.

47. Kemp 2004; Raijman and Kemp 2016.

48. Bartram 1998, 313; ibid. 307. These figures refer to noncitizen Palestinian workers from the OPT. In 1993. Palestinian workers composed 4.5 percent of the Israeli labor force, as Figure 2 shows with authorized migrant workers composing 1.6 percent. By 2000, these figures were reversed: Palestinians had dropped to 3.3 percent of the labor force, and migrant workers' representation had risen to 8.7 percent (Kemp and Raijman 2003, 8).

49. Raijman and Kemp 2007.

50. Brubaker 1992; Soysal 1994; Castles and Davidson 2000.

51. Kemp and Raijman 2003, 7.

52. Kemp 2004, citing October 2003 Israeli Central Bureau of Statistics data. Only authorized migrants are reflected in these official data.

53. Rosenhek 2000, 53.

54. These categories hold broad local salience, although the terms are mine.

55. Historically, a distinction has often been drawn between Ashkenazi Jews, originating in Northern and Eastern Europe, and Sephardi Jews from the Iberian Peninsula. In con-

temporary Israel, the term Sephardi has largely been retired in favor of Mizraḥi. The term Mizraḥi (literally, "Oriental") gained currency beginning in the 1970s as a new form of identity that celebrates the historical and religious legacies of, and links among, Jews of Iberian, North African, Middle Eastern, and sometimes Central Asian descent. The label "Mizraḥi" is claimed as an affirmative and politically unifying identity in the face of enduring Ashkenazi hegemony (Shohat 1999; Chetrit 2000).

56. Levenkron 2007.

57. UNHCR 2017; Birger et al. 2018.

58. Buchanan 2008; Kritzman-Amir 2009.

59. Kemp and Raijman 2003.

60. Kemp 2007.

61. See, e.g., McKee 2016.

62. Matabisi 1997.

63. In an earlier publication, I wrote about PHR-IL using the pseudonym BZA (Briut ve'Zḥuyot Adam, Hebrew for "Health and Human Rights"). See Willen 2011.

64. After attending staff meetings for over a year and doing my best to be a "fly on the wall," at one point I shared my thoughts, in the spirit of constructive criticism, on the format of weekly staff meetings. My critique was not well received by a prominent staff member who, incidentally, left the organization not long afterward.

65. See, e.g., Paz 2018; Kalir 2010.

66. Liebelt 2011.

67. ACRI, HRM, and PHR-IL 2016. Israel's binding arrangement had much in common with policies regulating labor migration in the Persian Gulf (Gardner 2010) and Southeast Asia.

68. In 2014, the Hotline for Migrant Workers changed its name to the Hotline for Refugees and Migrants.

69. Farmer 2004, 146.

70. My ethnographic focus on lifeworlds, life projects, and existential commitments reflects an enduring engagement with the anthropology of experience (Desjarlais 1997; Kleinman 1998, 2006; Throop 2002; Willen and Seeman 2012; Zigon and Throop 2014), sometimes described as phenomenological or existential anthropology (Csordas 1993; Good 1994; M. Jackson 1996, 2005); see also Garcia 2010; Pinto 2014; Stevenson 2014.

71. Deeb and Winegar 2016.

72. See Brodkin 1998 for an illuminating discussion of Jews, immigration, and whiteness in the twentieth-century United States.

73. Ngai 2004, 67.

74. LaCapra 2001, 23.

75. M. Jackson 2005, 182.

76. Bilefsky 2015.

77. Mattingly 2014, 10.

78. Arendt 1973, vii.

Chapter 1

1. The full phrase from Jeremiah 31:33 reads: "But this is the covenant that I will make with the house of Israel after those days, saith the LORD, I will put My law in their inward

parts, and in their heart will I write it; and I will be their God, and they shall be My people" (Jewish Publication Society 1917). Arthur and Joan Kleinman's (1994) essay "How Bodies Remember" first brought this passage to my attention.

2. Morfix 2018; see also Ben-Yehuda 1960.

3. Tyler 2013.

4. De Genova 2002.

5. Menjívar and Kanstroom 2014, 1; see also Chavez 1998; Coutin 2003; Menjívar 2006; Khosravi 2010; Lucht 2011; Gonzales and Chavez 2012; Sigona 2012; Boehm 2013; Holmes 2013; Bloch, Sigona, and Zetter 2014; Andersson 2014; Gonzales 2016; Ruszczyk and Yrizar Barbosa 2017; Castañeda 2019; Vogt 2018.

6. Suárez-Orozco et al. 2011, 439.

7. Expecting an "estimated four million pilgrims and visitors" in 2000, the Ministry of Foreign Affairs committed "millions of dollars and years of efforts . . . to make a Millennium pilgrimage to the Holy Land everything that it should be for each and every participant" (Israeli Ministry of Foreign Affairs 2000). Despite these investments, efforts to stage the Year 2000 as a "mega event" (Kliot and Collins-Kreiner 2010) failed for multiple reasons, ranging from administrative mismanagement to local political contention, religious disputes, and the outbreak of the second intifada in September 2000 (Cohen-Hattab and Shoval 2007).

8. National Police Chief Shlomo Aharonishky cited in Levy-Barzilai 2003.

9. *Haaretz*, Israel's newspaper of record, chronicled the case in an article titled "Instead of Looking for the Policemen Who Abused Foreign Workers, They're Looking for the Informer" (Sinai 2004).

10. See, e.g., Galili 2002; Leibovich-Dar 2003; Sinai 2002.

11. Tyler 2013, 9.

12. Izenberg 2003.

13. Kuperboim 2003.

14. Although migrants were permitted in principle to establish basic accounts at Israeli banks, bank staff members often were unaware of this possibility and refused to accommodate their requests.

15. Filipinos, for instance, could sometimes "pass"—not as Israelis, but as authorized workers, since so many of their conationals continued to hold legal authorization.

16. Fanon 1986[1967], 82; see also Tormey 2007.

17. Although a different set of research methods would have been needed to demonstrate these effects epidemiologically, growing bodies of medical and public health scholarship support the hypothesis that the kinds of embodied stress described in this chapter can yield adverse health effects, both short- and long-term (Krieger 2005; Gravlee 2009; Willen 2012b; Castañeda et al. 2015; Holmes 2013; Horton 2016.

18. Csordas 1993, 138.

19. Kemp and Kfir 2016, 385.

20. Kav La'Oved and Hotline for Migrant Workers 2003.

21. Rapoport and Lomsky-Feder 2001; cf. Dominguez 1989.

22. For more on these survey findings, see Willen 2012a. For more on Jewish Israelis' concerns about bus bombings, see, e.g., Ochs 2011.

23. M. Jackson 2005, xxii and xii.

24. Law 2005, 238.

25. See, e.g. Liebelt 2011.

26. See Wuhrgaft 2003a.

27. Tyler 2013, 117. See Diabate 2011, 321 for more on West African traditions involving women who "aggressively use their genital powers to rein in abusive patriarchal practices"; see also Stevens 2006.

28. Sabar 2008; Liebelt 2011.

29. Markowitz, Helman, and Shir-Vertesh 2003; J. L. Jackson 2013.

30. See Malkki 2010, 60, 58, 74.

31. Kemp 2007, 678.

32. Eli Yishai, meeting of the Knesset Special Committee on the Problem of Foreign Workers, May 16, 2000, cited in Kemp 2007, 679.

33. *Ynet* 2009.

34. Leading NGOs were the Kav La'Oved Workers' Hotline and Physicians for Human Rights–Israel. See, e.g., Willen 2005.

35. Chavez 2017.

36. A robust body of literature has explored the challenges involved in migrant motherhood. See, e.g., Colen 1995; Hirsch 2003; Sargent and Larchanché 2007; Luibhéid 2013; Feldman-Savelsberg 2016.

37. In Hebrew: "latét l'zeh l'hitkayém, ze latét yad la'pésha."

38. Schwartz 2007.

39. Office of the State Comptroller 2013.

40. Mesila staff were well aware of this risk. See, for example, Mesila 2007, 42.

41. Since I interviewed Nechama in his official capacity, I use his real name here.

42. Olmert and Gillerman quoted in Hartman 2011. Parenthetical note appears in original. For more on *hasbará*, see p. 264, note 7.

43. Several years after these developments, a joint report by three NGOs documented the impact of detention and imprisonment on children (Physicians for Human Rights–Israel, Israeli Children, and Hotline for Migrant Workers 2013).

44. Ettinger 2011.

45. De Genova 2002, 439.

46. Ibid.

47. See Coutin 2003, 55.

48. Csordas 1994, 269.

49. See, e.g., Quesada, Hart, and Bourgois 2011; Larchanché 2012; Castañeda et al. 2015; Holmes 2013; Horton 2016; Willen et al. 2017.

50. Coutin 2003, 30; Yoshikawa 2011; Suárez-Orozco et al. 2011; Bloch, Sigona, and Zetter 2014; Dreby 2015; Gonzales 2016.

Chapter 2

1. At the time, authorized migrant caregivers who had babies in Israel were required to send their newborn "home" to be raised by others. Otherwise, their visa would be terminated, and they would immediately become deportable. Although the Ministry of Interior later amended this requirement slightly, few migrant caregivers who give birth in Israel are

able to continue working with legal authorization (ACRI, HRM, & PHR-IL 2016; Kemp and Kfir 2016).

2. Dieter Grimm, in a cover endorsement of Rosen 2012.

3. Moyn 2015, 26.

4. See, e.g., Benhabib 2011; Dworkin 2011; Kateb 2011; Rosen 2012; Waldron 2012; McCrudden 2014.

5. Schulman 2008, 13.

6. Moyn 2014, 26. Other Christian traditions embrace different interpretations. For the Russian Orthodox Church, anthropologist Jarrett Zigon notes, dignity is at once inherent and also dependent upon human spiritual work and moral responsibility to avoid its potential "darkening" (2013, 62).

7. Rosen 2012, 6.

8. Ibid., 7, emphasis added.

9. Goodale 2009.

10. United Nations General Assembly 1948.

11. Rosen 2012, 41 and 1, quoting Schopenhauer 1965.

12. Jensen 2008, 196.

13. Agamben 1998; Arendt 1973.

14. von Schnitzler 2014, 340.

15. Bennett 2016, 2.

16. See, e.g., S. Kaufman 2000; Lock 2002; Jenkins 2015.

17. Hamdy 2012.

18. Han 2012, 39, 89.

19. Oka 2014.

20. Ibid., 24.

21. Zigon 2014, 752. As he demonstrates ethnographically, sometimes terms like "dignity" or "rights" are the "only concept historically available to try to articulate something about being-in-the-world that exceeds what it is that concept has come to represent, indicate, or mean."

22. Nussbaum 2011, 31.

23. Margalit 1996, 290–91.

24. Rosen 2012, 7.

25. M. Jackson 2005, 64.

26. M. Jackson 2013, 229.

27. M. Jackson 2005, 65, emphasis in original.

28. Zigon 2014, 762.

29. Jackson 2005, 181.

30. De Genova 2002, 439.

31. Jacobson 2012, 193. Mann called for a "taxonomy of dignity violation" to help map the "profoundly important 'terra incognita' of dignity and health" (1998, 32–33).

32. Jacobson 2009a, 1538, emphasis added; cf. Jacobson 2009b, 2012; Jacobson, Oliver, and Koch 2009.

33. Jacobson 2012, 14.

34. Jacobson 2009b.

35. Parekh 2008, 10.

36. Ibid., 166.

37. Ibid., 148.

38. Margalit 1996, 105.

39. Ibid., 121.

40. Ibid., 96.

41. Ibid., 150.

42. Ibid., 274.

43. Ibid., 122.

44. Nigerian, Ghanaian, and other African migrants in Tel Aviv were unlikely to "pass," or even try to "pass," as members of the country's community of 130,000 *olím*—new immigrants—of Ethiopian descent. With exceptions (e.g., in a few Tel Aviv nightclubs), Ethiopian Israelis and unauthorized African migrants interactions' were infrequent, and not necessarily smooth (Dorchin 2017).

45. L. R. Gordon 2005, 16. Subsequent quote is from Fanon 1967, 116.

46. Suárez-Navaz 2004, 127, emphasis added.

47. In fact, Margalit's text (1996, 101, translated from Hebrew into English) misquotes Silk, although he does capture the poet's sentiment. In "Vanishing Trick" (1990), Silk writes, in English, of "invisibility powder."

48. King 1963.

49. Coe 2016, 352.

50. I riff here on Philippe Bourgois's notion of "conjugated oppression." Bourgois characterizes the experience of oppression as "more than merely the sum of its constituent parts." Rather, different forms of domination and exploitation—for example, classism and racism—are social processes that "cannot be thought separately" but rather "define one another" (1988, 330–31). This helpful formulation predates and supports more recent thinking about intersectionality (see, e.g., Crenshaw 1989).

51. Diouf 2005. Following quotations are drawn from this account.

52. But see Willen 2010, 2011, 2015.

53. Goodale 2006, 30.

54. Nyers 2003, 1072–73; cf. Krause 2008.

55. Azoulay 2012. Azoulay develops her argument specifically in relation to the naqba, and to Israeli Jews descended from their state's founders. She writes, "The time has come for Israeli Jews to recognize the constitutive disaster—the Nakba—not only as a Palestinian catastrophe but as a catastrophe in the production of which they are implicated on a daily basis. The time has come for the second generation of perpetrators—descendants of those who expelled Palestinians from their homeland—to claim *our* right, *our* fundamental and inalienable human right: *the right not to be perpetrators*" (emphasis in original). Although I never asked directly, a broad interpretation of this claim would seem relevant to migrant advocacy and activist efforts alike. As for the regional particulars of Azoulay's claims, however, I suspect activists would be inclined to agree with Azoulay, whereas advocates would draw a bright line between obligations toward migrants and toward Palestinians (cf. Redfield [2013] on the "ethic of refusal" motivating Médecins Sans Frontières).

56. Kav La'Oved and Hotline for Migrant Workers 2003.

57. The Passover holiday traditionally is celebrated for seven days in Israel and eight days elsewhere.

58. Rosen 2012, 157.

59. Arendt 2005, 22.

60. Rosen 2012, 157.

61. At his request, and in recognition of his public role, I use his real name here (see also Holdbrook 2002, 2005; Sabar 2008).

62. Parekh 2008, 166.

63. Quoted in Wuhrgaft 2003b.

64. Holdbrook 2002.

65. See, e.g., Aretxaga 1997.

66. Parekh 2008, 166.

67. Wuhrgaft 2004.

68. Holdbrook 2005.

69. Macklin 2003.

70. Rajaram and Grundy-Warr 2004, 35.

Chapter 3

1. In anthropology, for instance, the concept has been employed, with varying degrees of precision, to probe topics as diverse as migration (Fassin 2001, 2005; Watters 2001), medicine (Wendland 2010), access to medications (Redfield 2008; Nguyen 2010), heroin sharing (Bourgois and Schonberg 2009), survival (Prince 2012), and sacrifice (Weiss 2014), among others.

2. Fassin 2009; cf. Daston 1995 as well as Edelman 2012; Friberg and Götz 2015; Siméant 2015.

3. IMPRS Moral Economies, accessed October 24, 2018 at https://www.mpib-berlin.mpg.de /en/research/research-schools/imprs-moral-economies.

4. Kleinman 1997, 327.

5. Kleinman 1998, 365–66.

6. Mattingly 2014, 204.

7. A literal translation ("explanation," from *l'hasbír*, to explain) fails to capture these connotations. Longtime Israeli television journalist Rina Matzliach offered the following explanation: "Hasbara means knowing you are speaking to a hostile audience and knowing how to win their hearts" (quoted in Myre 2004).

8. For more on Israel's internal diversity, see Kimmerling 2001; Shafir and Peled 2002; Dalsheim 2011; Kemp et al. 2014.

9. See, e.g., Kouts et al. 2007.

10. LaCapra 2001, 81.

11. Zertal 2005, 3.

12. C. Gordon 1991, 35; emphasis in original.

13. See, e.g., Rouhana 1997, 57–58.

14. Ochs 2011, 4.

15. In the 2010s, as the entire Israeli political spectrum shifted rightward, left-leaning organizations and activists increasingly came under fire from politicians and groups on the right.

16. See Halbfinger and Kershner 2018 for an analysis of the "Nation-State Law" and its passage. For critical analysis of the tensions between Israel's claims to be both "Jewish" and "democratic," see, e.g., Rouhana 1997; Shafir and Peled 1998; Rabinowitz and Abu-Baker 2005; Yiftachel 2006.

17. Pinkas 1993, 67 cited in Rouhana 1997, 42.

18. Lomsky-Feder and Rapoport 2001, 2.

19. Agamben 1998, 591.

20. A similar argument is developed by legal scholar Tally Kritzman-Amir (2009), who points to Otherness as "the underlying principle in Israel's asylum regime."

21. See, e.g., Chavez 2017.

22. Lustick 1999.

23. Exodus 22:20.

24. Bava Metzia 71a. I include the familiar Hebrew translation of this phrase rather than the Aramaic original.

25. Genesis 1:28.

26. Kanaaneh 2002, 23.

27. Remennick 2000.

28. Berkovitch 1997; see also Ivry 2009; Teman 2010.

29. Kahn 2000, 3.

30. Ibid.; see also Birenbaum-Carmeli and Carmeli 2010.

31. At times, however, those who do *not* count among the state's ratified citizens have seen corollary benefits, including Palestinian citizens (Kahn 2000; Gooldin 2013) and, in limited ways, even unauthorized migrant workers (Willen 2005).

32. Segev 2007, 67.

33. Rouhana 1997, 56.

34. Rabinowitz and Abu-Baker 2005, 59.

35. State of Israel 1948.

36. See, e.g., Rabinowitz and Abu-Baker 2005; Sultany 2012; Monterescu 2015; McKee 2016; Shalev 2016.

37. Peled 1992, 433; Shafir and Peled 1998.

38. Smooha 1990; Yiftachel 2006.

39. Rabinowitz and Abu-Baker 2005, 7.

40. Kanaaneh 2008.

41. Shamir 2005, 210.

42. Fassin 2001, 5.

43. Butler 1997, 104.

44. Tyler 2013, 46.

45. Torstrick 2000, 34.

46. Rabinowitz and Abu-Baker 2005, 131; see also Ochs 2011.

47. Rabinowitz and Abu-Baker 2005, 146; Masalha 2014.

48. See, e.g., the reports and resources produced by Adalah, the Legal Center for Arab Minority Rights in Israel (https://www.adalah.org/).

49. Al-Haj 2005; ACRI and Adalah 2001; Azmi Bishara 2001; Or 2006.

50. A. Kaufman 2014.

51. Hasson and Ettinger 2014.

52. Shpigel, Khoury, and Kubovich 2014.

53. Ibid.

54. Khoury 2014.

55. Basharat 2014.

56. Shpigel, Khoury, and Kubovich 2014.

57. Ibid.

58. Omer-Man 2015.

59. Although social scientific scholarship on the occupation was slow to emerge, a robust body of work has appeared since the mid-1990s, mostly in English, and—for various reasons (see, e.g., Tamari 1994; Furani and Rabinowitz 2011)—only occasionally by Palestinian social scientists. See, e.g., Swedenburg 1995; Weizman 2007; N. Gordon 2008; Allen 2013; Azoulay and Ophir 2012; Atshan 2013; Amahl Bishara 2012. For a critical review of Israeli scholarship on the occupation, see Gazit 2017.

60. Bornstein 2002; Roy 2002; Atshan 2013; Buch Segal 2016; Berda 2017.

61. Fassin and Rechtman 2009; Giacaman et al. 2007; el-Sarraj et al. 1996.

62. Gazit 2015.

63. Caption from photo exhibit on the MachsomWatch website: www.machsomwatch.org (accessed February 8, 2007).

64. See, e.g., Mansbach 2016.

65. Kleinman, Das, and Lock 1997, x.

66. See, e.g., Breaking the Silence 2012; Amnesty International 2017; B'Tselem 2017.

67. B'Tselem 2017.

68. See, e.g., Bergman-Sapir and Stroumsa 2016.

69. Bornstein 2002, 8.

70. Buch Segal 2016.

71. For two notable examples, see Leibowitz 1992; Burg 2008.

72. Weiss 2014.

73. Meir 2005.

74. These were the instructions of her hospital supervisor, she told me.

75. Khosravi 2010.

Chapter 4

1. *Haaretz* 2003a.

2. *Globes* 2003.

3. Freilich and Eichner 2003.

4. Butler 2009.

5. Butler 2004, 17. In fact, Butler distinguishes between grievability and livability, as opposed to bearability, although she tends to blur the line between the latter two. I see bearability and livability as distinct: bearability is about surviving, whereas livability, as developed more fully in the next chapter, is about flourishing and the pursuit of dignity and meaning.

6. Yoman 2003.

7. Zaka is the Hebrew acronym for *Zihúi Korbanót Asón*—identification of disaster victims.

8. Ochs 2011, 70, 73.

9. Chaim, Rabin, and Ben-David 2003; Mozgovaya 2003.

10. *Haaretz* 2003b.

11. Another Ghanaian man injured in the bombing, Henry, showed up at the Open Clinic about a month later and recounted another, more sinister urban legend that kept him

from seeking care. Henry feared doctors might secretly extract his kidney because "I have the correct blood. I don't have HIV blood, you understand?"

12. Stevenson 2014, 13.

13. "Sitting shiva," from the Hebrew word for seven (*shéva*), refers to the Jewish custom of setting aside all usual obligations during the first seven days after burying a loved one to focus exclusively, and communally, on the work of mourning. Shiva rituals, which are intensely social and intersubjective, call upon the extended family and community of the deceased to support the immediate mourners in their grief.

14. After the ceremony, the room quickly emptied out, only to be immediately reorganized for a previously scheduled meeting.

15. See, e.g., Liebelt 2011. This held true for many South Americans in Tel Aviv as well.

16. Ahmed 2010, 97.

17. As early as 1996, *Haaretz* reported, "the Minister of Internal Security urged the Tel Aviv Municipality to cease providing social services to undocumented migrants and 'to make their life in Tel Aviv miserable'" (*Haaretz* September 18, 1996, cited in Rosenhek 2000, 60). See also (Fezehai 2015).

18. Ahmed 2010, 120.

19. Hardly any of the West Africans (or other migrants) I knew were even aware that an official memorial had taken place.

20. I draw here on my own notes as well as the VHS video later available for purchase.

21. He also encouraged community members to follow the news of brewing war with Iraq, which eventually broke out two months later, and contact the embassy if they had questions or concerns.

22. Genesis 12:3.

23. See, e.g., Hage 2003; Asad 2007.

24. Ahmed 2010, 120.

Chapter 5

1. On global migrants' exclusion from Israel's nationalized health care system, see Filc 2009; Gottlieb, Filc, and Davidovitch 2012; Fleischman et al. 2015. On the role of the Israeli AIDS Task Force in caring for migrant patients, see Rosenthal 2007.

2. African women living in Paris *sans papiers* shared similar terrors with anthropologist Miriam Ticktin: "the stigma of AIDS was great enough in their communities that they would rather compromise their bodily integrity than live ostracized and without dignity" (2011, 196).

3. Matters of personal status in Israel (e.g., marriage, divorce, and burial) are governed by religious authorities, and there is no provision for civil marriage or divorce within the country (ACRI, HRM, and PHR-IL 2016).

4. I shared two key pieces of information: (1) biomedical evidence that mother-to-child transmission of HIV can be prevented (if pregnant women receive ARVs during pregnancy; ARVs are administered in the earliest months; and mothers refrain from breast-feeding), and (2) the availability of such treatment, with support from the clinic and task force. Although I

was in no position to offer comprehensive medical explanations, I provided Father Joseph with contact information for medical experts who could.

5. Hirschman 1971; Biehl 2014.

6. Chinn 2007, 316.

7. As noted earlier, all names and identifying details have been changed to protect confidentiality.

8. Cavell 2004; Mattingly 2014.

9. Smith 2004.

10. Hollan 2012, 37, following William James.

11. Kleinig and Evans 2013.

12. M. Jackson 2013, 228.

Conclusion

1. Ben-Zikri 2015. In Hebrew: "*Mevakésh miklát nurá b'shogég ve'huká la'mávet b'zirát ha'pigúa b'Beershéva.*"

2. M. Jackson 1996, 22.

3. Willen 2012b.

4. Csordas 1994, 269.

5. See, e.g., Krieger 2005; Ong, Deshpande, and Williams 2018.

6. See, e.g., Castañeda 2009; Castañeda et al. 2015; Holmes 2013; Horton 2016; Willen et al. 2017; Quesada, Hart, and Bourgois 2011; Larchanché 2012.

7. Geronimus et al. 2006.

8. Arendt 1972, 5; emphasis in original.

9. Zigon 2014, 752.

10. Kleinig and Evans 2013.

11. Mattingly 2014, 10–11.

12. See, e.g., Gottlieb, Filc, and Davidovitch 2012; Kalir 2014; Kemp and Kfir 2016 as well as my own earlier work on the topic (Willen 2010, 2011, 2015).

13. See, e.g., Weiss 2014; Wright 2016.

14. See Kamir 2002 for a discussion of how this distinct formulation has entered contemporary Israeli discourse; see also Lorberbaum 2014 and Heschel 2018.

15. Rosen 2012, 157.

16. Kemp and Raijman 2003, 7; see also Raijman and Kemp 2016.

17. Semyonov and Lewin-Epstein 1987, 112.

18. Eligibility criteria included children's age, duration of residence in the country, Hebrew proficiency, and participation in the educational system, as well as a requirement that parents had entered the country with visas (Kemp and Kfir 2016).

19. Burston 2008. For a fuller discussion of these dynamics, see Willen 2010.

20. Lior and Zarchin 2012; see also Nesher 2012.

21. Brenner 2012.

22. See, e.g., Birger et al 2018; Hotline for Refugees and Migrants 2017.

23. Israeli Population and Immigration Authority 2018.

24. Fishbain 2018.

25. Michal Rozin and Mossi Raz, quoted in Yaron and Landau 2018.

26. Landau 2018.

27. Corin 2012, 104.

28. Foucault 1966, 385, cited in and translated by Corin 2012, 106; emphasis in original. Subsequent quotes in this paragraph are Corin's (110–11).

29. Mattingly 2014, 204, emphasis added.

30. See Chapter 1 as well as Willen and Cook 2016.

BIBLIOGRAPHY

ACRI (Association for Civil Rights in Israel) and Adalah. 2001. "Report on the October 2000 Violence Against Arab Citizens of Israel, 7 January 2001." *Journal of Palestine Studies* 30: 164–66.

ACRI, HRM, and PHR-IL (Association for Civil Rights in Israel, Hotline for Refugees and Migrants, and Physicians for Human Rights–Israel). 2016. *The Labyrinth: Migration, Status and Human Rights.* Tel Aviv: ACRI, HRM, and PHR-IL. Accessed October 25, 2018, at https://www.acri.org.il/en/wp-content/uploads/2016/01/The-Labrynth-English.pdf.

Agamben, Giorgio. 1998. *Homo Sacer.* Stanford, CA: Stanford University Press.

Ahmed, Sara. 2010. *The Promise of Happiness.* Durham, NC: Duke University Press.

Al-Haj, Majid. 2005. "Whither the Green Line? Trends in the Orientation of the Palestinians in Israel and the Territories." *Israel Affairs* 11: 183–206.

Allen, Lori. 2013. *The Rise and Fall of Human Rights: Cynicism and Politics in Occupied Palestine.* Stanford, CA: Stanford University Press.

Amnesty International. 2017. *Amnesty International Report 2016/17: The State of the World's Human Rights.* London: Amnesty International.

Andersson, Ruben. 2014. *Illegality, Inc.* Berkeley: University of California Press.

Arendt, Hannah. 1972. *Crises of the Republic.* New York: Harcourt Brace Jovanovich.

——. 1973. *The Origins of Totalitarianism.* New York: Harcourt Brace Jovanovich.

——. 2005. *The Promise of Politics.* New York: Schocken Books.

Aretxaga, Begoña. 1997. *Shattering Silence: Women, Nationalism, and Political Subjectivity in Northern Ireland.* Princeton, NJ: Princeton University Press.

Asad, Talal. 2007. *On Suicide Bombing.* New York: Columbia University Press.

Atshan, Sa'ed Adel. 2013. "Prolonged Humanitarianism: The Social Life of Aid in the Palestinian Territories." PhD dissertation, Department of Anthropology, Harvard University.

Azoulay, Ariella. 2012. "The Time Has Come." *Verso Blog.* Accessed October 25, 2018, at http://www.versobooks.com/blogs/1199-ariella-azoulay-the-time-has-come.

Azoulay, Ariella, and Adi Ophir. 2012. *The One-State Condition.* Stanford, CA: Stanford University Press.

Bartram, David V. 1998. "Foreign Workers in Israel: History and Theory." *International Migration Review* 32: 303–25.

Basharat, Oudeh. 2014. "If You're an Arab, They Shoot First." *Haaretz.* November 10.

Benhabib, Seyla. 2011. *Dignity in Adversity: Human Rights in Troubled Times.* Cambridge: Polity Press.

Bennett, Gaymon. 2016. *Technicians of Human Dignity.* New York: Fordham University Press.

Ben-Yehuda, Eliezer. 1960. *Milon ha-lashon ha-'Ivrit ha-yeshanah yeha-ḥadashah* [Dictionary of the Old and New Hebrew Language]. New York: Thomas Yoseloff.

Ben-Zikri, Almog. 2015. "Mevakésh miklát nurá b'shogég ve'huká la'mávet b'zirát ha'pigúa b'Beersheva" [Asylum Seeker Shot by Mistake and Beaten to Death at Scene of the Attack in Beersheva.] *Haaretz*. October 15.

Berda, Yael. 2017. *Living Emergency: Israel's Permit Regime in the Occupied West Bank*. Stanford, CA: Stanford University Press.

Bergman-Sapir, Efrat, and Rachel Stroumsa. 2016. *Independent Report to the UN Committee Against Torture Toward the Review of the Fifth Periodic Report on Israel*. Jerusalem: Public Committee Against Torture in Israel.

Berkovitch, Nitza. 1997. "Motherhood as National Mission: The Construction of Womanhood in the Legal Discourse in Israel." *Women's Studies International Forum* 20: 605–19.

Biehl, João. 2014. "The Right to a Nonprojected Future." Paper presented at the American Anthropological Association Annual Meetings, Washington, DC, December.

Bilefsky, Dan. 2015. "17,000 Migrants Stranded in Croatia by Border Crackdown." *New York Times*. September 18.

Birenbaum-Carmeli, Daphna, and Yoram S. Carmeli. 2010. *Kin, Gene, Community: Reproductive Technologies Among Jewish Israelis*. New York: Berghahn.

Birger, Lior, Shahar Shoham, and Liat Bolzman. 2018. *Better a Prison in Israel than Dying on the Way*. Independent report, Berlin and Tel Aviv–Jaffa. Accessed October 25, 2018, at https://drive.google.com/file/d/11bR_8cski2tRDczmQBfTI6GHUuuFK_JZ/view.

Bishara, Amahl. 2012. *Back Stories: U.S. News Production and Palestinian Politics*. Stanford, CA: Stanford University Press.

Bishara, Azmi. 2001. "Reflections on October 2000: A Landmark in Jewish-Arab Relations in Israel." *Journal of Palestine Studies* 30: 54–67.

Bloch, Alice, Nando Sigona, and Roger Zetter. 2014. *Sans Papiers: The Social and Economic Lives of Young Undocumented Migrants*. London: Pluto Press.

Boehm, Deborah A. 2013. *Intimate Migrations: Gender, Family, and Illegality among Transnational Mexicans*. New York: New York University Press.

Bornstein, Avram S. 2002. *Crossing the Green Line Between the West Bank and Israel*. Philadelphia: University of Pennsylvania Press.

Bourgois, Philippe. 1995. *In Search of Respect*. Cambridge: Cambridge University Press.

Bourgois, Philippe, and Jeff Schonberg. 2009. *Righteous Dopefiend*. Berkeley: University of California Press.

Breaking the Silence. 2012. *Our Harsh Logic: Israeli Soldiers' Testimonies from the Occupied Territories, 2000–2010*. New York: Metropolitan Books.

Brenner, Neri. 2012. "Clashes Erupt During South TA Protest; Migrants Attacked." *Ynetnews*. May 24.

Brodkin, Karen. 1998. *How Jews Became White Folks and What That Says About Race in America*. New Brunswick, NJ: Rutgers University Press.

Brubaker, Rogers. 1992. *Citizenship and Nationhood in France and Germany*. Cambridge, MA: Harvard University Press.

B'Tselem. 2017. *Getting off Scot-Free: Israel's Refusal to Compensate Palestinians for Damages Caused by Its Security Forces*. Jerusalem: B'Tselem.

Buchanan, Holly. 2008. "Escape from Darfur: Why Israel Needs to Adopt a Comprehensive Domestic Refugee Law Comment." *Chapman Law Review* 11: 601–32.

Buch Segal, Lotte. 2016. *No Place for Grief: Martyrs, Prisoners, and Mourning in Contemporary Palestine*. Philadelphia: University of Pennsylvania Press.

Burg, Avraham. 2008. *The Holocaust Is Over; We Must Rise from Its Ashes*. New York: Palgrave Macmillan.

Burston, Bradley. 2008. "A Kinship of Genocide." *Haaretz*. November 23.

Butler, Judith. 1997. *The Psychic Life of Power*. Stanford, CA: Stanford University Press.

———. 2004. *Undoing Gender*. New York: Routledge.

———. 2009. *Frames of War: When Is Life Grievable?* London: Verso.

Castañeda, Heide. 2009. "Illegality as Risk Factor: A Survey of Unauthorized Migrant Patients in a Berlin Clinic." *Social Science and Medicine* 68: 1–9.

———. 2019. *Borders of Belonging: Struggle and Solidarity in Mixed-Status Immigrant Families*. Stanford, CA: Stanford University Press.

Castañeda, Heide, Seth M. Holmes, Daniel S. Madrigal, Maria-Elena DeTrinidad Young, Naomi Beyeler, and James Quesada. 2015. "Immigration as a Social Determinant of Health." *Annual Review of Public Health* 36 (1): 375–92.

Castles, Stephen, and Alastair Davidson. 2000. *Citizenship and Migration*. New York: Routledge.

Cavell, Stanley. 2004. *Cities of Words*. Cambridge, MA: Harvard University Press.

Chavez, Leo R. 1998. *Shadowed Lives*. Fort Worth, TX: Harcourt Brace.

———. 2017. *Anchor Babies and the Challenge of Birthright Citizenship*. Stanford, CA: Stanford University Press.

Chetrit, Sami Shalom. 2000. "Mizrahi Politics in Israel: Between Integration and Alternative." *Journal of Palestine Studies* 29 (4): 51–65.

Chinn, Sarah. 2007. "*Undoing Gender* by Judith Butler." *Women's Studies Quarterly* 35: 315–18.

Coe, Cati. 2016. "Longing for a House in Ghana: Ghanaians' Responses to the Dignity Threats of Elder Care Work in the United States." *Ethos* 44 (3): 352–74.

Cohen-Hattab, Kobi, and Noam Shoval. 2007. "Tourism Development and Cultural Conflict: The Case of 'Nazareth 2000.'" *Social and Cultural Geography* 8 (5): 701–17.

Colen, Shellee. 1995. "'Like a Mother to Them': Stratified Reproduction and West Indian Childcare Workers and Employers in New York." In *Conceiving the New World Order: The Global Politics of Reproduction*, edited by Faye D. Ginsburg and Rayna Rapp. Berkeley: University of California Press. 78–102.

Corin, Ellen. 2012. "Commentary: Interdisciplinary Dialogue; A Site of Estrangement." *Ethos* 40: 104–12.

Coutin, Susan Bibler. 2003. *Legalizing Moves*. Ann Arbor: University of Michigan Press.

Crenshaw, Kimberlé. 1989. "Demarginalizing the Intersection of Race and Sex: A Black Feminist Critique of Antidiscrimination Doctrine, Feminist Theory and Antiracist Politics." *University of Chicago Legal Forum* 1(8).

Csordas, Thomas J. 1993. "Somatic Modes of Attention." *Cultural Anthropology* 8: 135–56.

———. 1994. *Embodiment and Experience*. Cambridge: Cambridge University Press.

Dalsheim, Joyce. 2011. *Unsettling Gaza*. Oxford: Oxford University Press.

Das, Veena. 2010. "Moral and Spiritual Striving in the Everyday: To Be a Muslim in Contemporary India." In *Ethical Life in South Asia*, edited by Anand Pandian and Daud Ali. Bloomington: Indiana University Press. 232–52.

Daston, Lorraine. 1995. "The Moral Economy of Science." *Osiris* 10: 2–24.

Deeb, Lara, and Jessica Winegar. 2016. *Anthropology's Politics: Disciplining the Middle East*. Stanford, CA: Stanford University Press.

De Genova, Nicholas. 2002. "Migrant 'Illegality' and Deportability in Everyday Life." *Annual Review of Anthropology* 31: 419–47.

Desjarlais, Robert. 1997. *Shelter Blues: Sanity and Selfhood Among the Homeless*. Philadelphia: University of Pennsylvania Press.

Diabate, Naminata. 2011. "Women's Naked Protest in Africa: Comparative Literature and Its Futures." PhD dissertation, Department of Comparative Literature, University of Texas, Austin.

Diouf, Aziz. 2005. "She Treated Me like Her Cow." *Ha'Ir*. February 10.

Dominguez, Virginia. 1989. *People as Subject, People as Object*. Madison: University of Wisconsin Press.

Dorchin, Uri. 2017. "Afrovision: Rehearsing Diasporic Africanism in a Tel-Aviv Nightclub." *African and Black Diaspora: An International Journal*, November, 1–16.

Dreby, Joanna. 2015. *Everyday Illegal: When Policies Undermine Immigrant Families*. Oakland, CA: University of California Press.

Dworkin, Ronald. 2011. *Justice for Hedgehogs*. Cambridge, MA: Harvard University Press.

Edelman, Marc. 2012. "E. P. Thompson and Moral Economies." In *A Companion to Moral Anthropology*, edited by Didier Fassin. Malden, MA: Wiley-Blackwell. 49–66.

El-Sarraj, Eyad, Raija-Leena Punamäki, Suhail Salmi, and Derek Summerfield. 1996. "Experiences of Torture and Ill-Treatment and Posttraumatic Stress Disorder Symptoms Among Palestinian Political Prisoners." *Journal of Traumatic Stress* 9 (3): 595–606.

Ettinger, Yair. 2009. "Yishai: Deporting Foreign Children Preserves Israel's Jewish Identity." *Haaretz*. October 14.

Fanon, Frantz. 1986[1967]. *Black Skin, White Masks*. London: Pluto Press.

Farmer, Paul. 2003. *Pathologies of Power*. Berkeley: University of California Press.

Fassin, Didier. 2001. "The Biopolitics of Otherness: Undocumented Foreigners and Racial Discrimination in French Public Debate." *Anthropology Today* 17: 3–7.

———. 2005. "Compassion and Repression: The Moral Economy of Immigration Policies in France." *Cultural Anthropology* 20: 362–87.

———. 2009. "Les Économies Morales Revisitées." *Annales* 6: 1237–66.

———. 2012. *Humanitarian Reason*. Berkeley: University of California Press.

Fassin, Didier, and Richard Rechtman. 2009. *The Empire of Trauma: An Inquiry into the Condition of Victimhood*. Princeton, NJ: Princeton University Press.

Feldman-Savelsberg, Pamela. 2016. *Mothers on the Move*. Chicago: University of Chicago Press.

Fezehai, Malin. 2015. "Israel's Chilly Reception for African Asylum Seekers." *New York Times*. October 31.

Filc, Dani. 2009. *Circles of Exclusion: Citizenship, Occupation, and the Americanization of the Israeli Health Care System*. Ithaca, NY: Cornell University Press.

Fischer, Edward F. 2014. *The Good Life: Aspiration, Dignity, and the Anthropology of Wellbeing*. Stanford, CA: Stanford University Press.

Fishbain, Einat. 2018. "Menahél Tiḥón Biálik-Rogózin: Aḥalék Ishurím leHoréi haYeladím kdéi Limnóa et Gerushám" [Principal of Bialik-Rogozin Elementary: I Will Distribute Permits to the Children's Parents to Prevent Their Deportation]. *HaMakóm Haḥí Ham* [The Hottest Place in Hell]. Accessed October 25, 2018 at https://www.ha-makom.co.il/post/fishbain-bialik-pta.

Fleischman, Yonina, Sarah S. Willen, Nadav Davidovitch, and Zohar Mor. 2015. "Migration as a Social Determinant of Health for Irregular Migrants: Israel as Case Study." *Social Science and Medicine* 147: 89–97.

Foucault, Michel. 1966. *Les Mots et les Choses* [The Order of Things]. Paris: Gallimard.

Freilich, Rivka, and Itamar Eichner. 2003. "Netanyahu Solves the Mystery of the Anonymous Patient." *Yediot Acharonot*. January 7.

Friberg, Katarina, and Norbert Götz. 2015. "Introduction to the Thematic Issue 'Moral Economy: New Perspectives.'" *Journal of Global Ethics* 11 (2): 143–46.

Furani, Khaled, and Dan Rabinowitz. 2011. "The Ethnographic Arriving of Palestine." *Annual Review of Anthropology* 40 (1): 475–91.

Galili, Lily. 2002. "A Jewish Demographic State." *Haaretz*. June 28.

Galtung, Johan. 1971. "Structural and Direct Violence: A Note on Operationalization." *Journal of Peace Research* 8: 73–76.

Garcia, Angela. 2010. *The Pastoral Clinic*. Berkeley: University of California Press.

Gardner, Andrew. 2010. *City of Strangers*. New York: Cornell University Press.

Gazit, Nir. 2015. "State-Sponsored Vigilantism: Jewish Settlers' Violence in the Occupied Palestinian Territories." *Sociology* 49 (3): 438–54.

———. 2017. "Sotziológia shel haKibúsh: MiTheória Mosadít leRibonút Fragmentárit" [Sociology of the Occupation: From Institutional Theory to Fragmentary Sovereignty]. Paper presented at the Israeli Sociological Society Annual Meeting, Raanana, Israel, January.

Geronimus, Arline T., Margaret Hicken, Danya Keene, and John Bound. 2006. "'Weathering' and Age Patterns of Allostatic Load Scores Among Blacks and Whites in the United States." *American Journal of Public Health* 96 (5): 826–33.

Giacaman, Rita, Niveen M. E. Abu-Rmeileh, Abdullatif Husseini, Hana Saab, and William Boyce. 2007. "Humiliation: The Invisible Trauma of War for Palestinian Youth." *Public Health* 121: 563–71.

Globes. 2003. "Basár Me'bsaréinu" [Flesh of Our Flesh]. *Globes*. January 9.

Gonzales, Roberto G. 2016. *Lives in Limbo: Undocumented and Coming of Age in America*. Oakland: University of California Press.

Gonzales, Roberto G., and Leo R. Chavez. 2012. "'Awakening to a Nightmare': Abjectivity and Illegality in the Lives of Undocumented 1.5-Generation Latino Immigrants in the United States." *Current Anthropology* 53: 255–81.

Good, Byron J. 1994. *Medicine, Rationality, and Experience*. Cambridge: Cambridge University Press.

Goodale, Mark. 2006. "Ethical Theory as Social Practice." *American Anthropologist* 108: 25–37.

———. 2009. *Surrendering to Utopia*. Stanford, CA: Stanford University Press.

Gooldin, Sigal. 2013. "'Emotional Rights,' Moral Reasoning, and Jewish–Arab Alliances in the Regulation of In-Vitro-Fertilization in Israel." *Social Science and Medicine* 83: 90–98.

Gordon, Colin. 1991. "Governmental Rationality: An Introduction." In *The Foucault Effect*, edited by Graham Burchell, Colin Gordon, and Peter Miller. Chicago: University of Chicago Press. 1–51.

Gordon, Lewis R. 2005. "Through the Zone of Nonbeing: A Reading of *Black Skin, White Masks* in Celebration of Fanon's Eightieth Birthday." *CLR James Journal* 11 (1): 1–43.

Gordon, Neve. 2008. *Israel's Occupation*. Berkeley, CA: University of California Press.

Gottlieb, Nora, Dani Filc, and Nadav Davidovitch. 2012. "Medical Humanitarianism, Human Rights, and Political Advocacy: The Case of the Israeli Open Clinic." *Social Science and Medicine* 74: 839–45.

Gravlee, Clarence C. 2009. "How Race Becomes Biology: Embodiment of Social Inequality." *American Journal of Physical Anthropology* 139 (1): 47–57.

Haaretz. 2003a. "23 Die in TA Bus Station Double Bombing." *Haaretz.* January 6.

———. 2003b. "Foreign Wounded Promised Visas." *Haaretz.* January 6.

Hage, Ghassan. 2003. "'Comes a Time We Are All Enthusiasm': Understanding Palestinian Suicide Bombers in Times of Exighophobia." *Public Culture* 15: 65–89.

Ḥaim, Assaf, Eitan Rabin, and Ami Ben-David. 2003. "Ḥasháshti sheYishtamshú baKtóvet Shelí veYaatzrú Otí Meuḥár Yotér" [I Was Afraid They Would Use My Address and Arrest Me Later]. *Maariv.* January 7.

Halbfinger, David M. and Isabel Kershner. 2018. "Israeli Law Declares the Country the 'Nation-State of the Jewish People.'" *New York Times.* July 19.

Hamdy, Sherine. 2012. *Our Bodies Belong to God.* Berkeley: University of California Press.

Han, Clara. 2012. *Life in Debt.* Berkeley: University of California Press.

Hartman, Ben. 2011. "TA Cinema Packed for Film on Kids of Foreign Workers." *Jerusalem Post.* January 4.

Hasson, Nir, and Yair Ettinger. 2014. "Aharonóvitch: Kol Pigúa Tzaríḥ L'histayém baMávet haMeḥabél baZirá" [Aharonovitch: Every Attack Must End with the Death of the Terrorist at the Scene]. *Haaretz.* November 5.

Heschel, Susannah. 2018. "'Wherever You See the Trace of Man, There I Stand Before You': The Complexities of God and Human Dignity Within Judaism." In *Human Dignity in Context,* edited by Dieter Grimm, Alexandra Kemmerer, and Christoph Möllers. Oxford: Nomos/Hart. 129–62.

Hirsch, Jennifer S. 2003. *A Courtship After Marriage.* Berkeley: University of California Press.

Hirschman, Albert O. 1971. *A Bias for Hope.* New Haven, CT: Yale University Press.

Holdbrook, Naana. 2002. "We, Your Housecleaners." *Haaretz.* September 10.

———. 2005. "It's Good to Be Home, But . . ." *Jerusalem Report.* February 21.

Hollan, Douglas. 2012. "On the Varieties and Particularities of Cultural Experience." *Ethos* 40: 37–53.

Holmes, Seth. 2013. *Fresh Fruit, Broken Bodies.* Berkeley: University of California Press.

Horton, Sarah. 2016. *They Leave Their Kidneys in the Fields.* Oakland: University of California Press.

Hotline for Refugees and Migrants. 2017. "Asylum Seekers from Eritrea and Sudan in Israel—December 2017." Tel Aviv. Accessed October 25, 2018, at http://hotline.org.il/en/asylum-seekers-from-eritrea-and-sudan-in-israel-december-2017/.

IMPRS (International Max Planck Research School for Moral Economies of Modern Societies). 2013. *Detailed Research Statement.* Berlin: Max Planck Institute. Accessed October 25, 2018, at https://www.mpib-berlin.mpg.de/en/research/research-schools/imprs-mems/research/research-statement.

Israeli Ministry of Foreign Affairs. 2000. *Israel 2000: Celebrating 2000 in the Place Where It All Began.* Accessed October 25, 2018, at http://mfa.gov.il/MFA/MFA-Archive/2000/Pages/Israel%202000.aspx.

Israeli Population and Immigration Authority. 2018. "Special Track for Voluntary Departure of Infiltrators from Israel." News release. January 1. Accessed October 25, 2018, at https://www.gov.il/en/Departments/news/voluntary_return_operation.

Ivry, Tsipy. 2009. *Embodying Culture: Pregnancy in Japan and Israel*. New Brunswick, NJ: Rutgers University Press.

Izenberg, Dan. 2003. "Court: Ads Against Illegal Workers Were Hateful." *Jerusalem Post.* December 15.

Jackson, John L. 2013. *Thin Description: Ethnography and the African Hebrew Israelites of Jerusalem*. Cambridge, MA: Harvard University Press.

Jackson, Michael. 1996. *Things As They Are*. Bloomington: Indiana University Press.

———. 2005. *Existential Anthropology*. New York: Berghahn.

———. 2009. "Where Thought Belongs." *Anthropological Theory* 9: 235–51.

———. 2013. *The Wherewithal of Life*. Berkeley: University of California Press.

Jacobson, Nora. 2009a. "Dignity Violation in Health Care." *Qualitative Health Research* 19 (11): 1536–47.

———. 2009b. "A Taxonomy of Dignity: A Grounded Theory Study." *BMC International Health and Human Rights* 9(3).

———. 2012. *Dignity and Health*. Nashville: Vanderbilt University Press.

Jacobson, Nora, Vanessa Oliver, and Andrew Koch. 2009. "An Urban Geography of Dignity." *Health and Place* 15: 725–31.

Jenkins, Janis H. 2015. *Extraordinary Conditions*. Oakland: University of California Press.

Jensen, Steffen. 2008. *Gangs, Politics and Dignity in Cape Town*. Oxford: James Currey.

Jewish Publication Society. 1917. *The New English Translation of the Bible*. Philadelphia: Jewish Publication Society.

Jones, Camara Phyllis. 2000. "Levels of Racism: A Theoretic Framework and a Gardener's Tale." *American Journal of Public Health* 90 (8): 1212–15.

Kahn, Susan Martha. 2000. *Reproducing Jews*. Durham, NC: Duke University Press.

Kalir, Barak. 2010. *Latino Migrants in the Jewish State*. Bloomington: Indiana University Press.

———. 2014. "The Jewish State of Anxiety: Between Moral Obligation and Fearism in the Treatment of African Asylum Seekers in Israel." *Journal of Ethnic and Migration Studies*. 41(4): 580–98.

Kamir, Orit. 2002. "Honor and Dignity Cultures: The Case of Kavod and Kvod Ha-Adam in Israeli Society and Law." In *The Concept of Human Dignity in Human Rights Law*, edited by David Kretzmer and Eckart Klein, 231–62. Amsterdam: Kluwer.

Kanaaneh, Rhoda. 2002. *Birthing the Nation*. Berkeley: University of California Press.

———. 2008. *Surrounded: Palestinian Soldiers in the Israeli Military*. Stanford, CA: Stanford University Press.

Kateb, George. 2011. *Human Dignity*. Cambridge, MA: Harvard University Press.

Kaufman, Ami. 2014. "Netanyahu Government's True Colors Are Shining Through." *+972.* November 10.

Kaufman, Sharon. 2000. "In the Shadow of 'Death with Dignity': Medicine and Cultural Quandaries of the Vegetative State." *American Anthropologist* 102: 69–83.

Kav La'Oved and Hotline for Migrant Workers. 2003. *Immigration Administration or Expulsion Unit?* Tel Aviv: Kav La'Oved and Hotline for Migrant Workers. Accessed October 25,

2018, at https://hotline.org.il/wp-content/uploads/Hotline_and_Kav_Laoved_paper_on
_Immigration_Police_May_2003_Eng.pdf.

Kemp, Adriana. 2004. "Labour Migration and Racialisation: Labour Market Mechanisms and
Labour Migration Control Policies in Israel." *Social Identities* 10: 267–92.

———. 2007. "Managing Migration, Reprioritizing National Citizenship: Undocumented Migrant Workers' Children and Policy Reforms in Israel." *Theoretical Inquiries in Law* 8(2):
663–92.

Kemp, Adriana, and Nelly Kfir. 2016. "Wanted Workers but Unwanted Mothers: Mobilizing
Moral Claims on Migrant Care Workers' Families in Israel." *Social Problems* 63 (3):
373–94.

Kemp, Adriana, David Newman, Uri Ram, and Oren Yiftachel. 2014. *Israelis in Conflict*. Brighton: Sussex Academic Press.

Kemp, Adriana, and Rebeca Raijman. 2003. "'Ovdím Zarím' beYisraél" ["Foreign Workers"
in Israel]. Tel Aviv: Adva Center. Accessed October 25, 2018, at http://adva.org/wp-content
/uploads/2014/09/ovdim-zarim-kamp.pdf.

Keyes, Corey L. M. 2016. "Why Flourishing?" In *Well-Being and Higher Education*, edited by
Donald W. Harward, 99–107. Washington: Association of American Colleges and Universities.

Khosravi, Shahram. 2010. *"Illegal" Traveler: An Auto-ethnography of Borders*. London: Palgrave
Macmillan.

Khoury, Jack. 2014. "When It Comes to Arab Citizens, the Police Are Quick on the Trigger."
Haaretz. November 10.

Kimmerling, Baruch. 2001. *The Invention and Decline of Israeliness*. Berkeley: University of
California Press.

King, Martin Luther, Jr. "Letter from Birmingham Jail." 1963. Accessed October 25, 2018, at
http://okra.stanford.edu/transcription/document_images/undecided/630416-019.pdf.

Kliot, Nurit and Noga Collins-Kreiner. 2010. "Wait for Us—We're Not Ready Yet: Holy Land
Preparations for the New Millenium—The Year 2000." *Current Issues in Tourism* 6(2)
119–49.

Kleinig, John, and Nicholas G. Evans. 2013. "Human Flourishing, Human Dignity, and Human
Rights." *Law and Philosophy* 32: 539–64.

Kleinman, Arthur. 1997. "'Everything That Really Matters': Social Suffering, Subjectivity, and
the Remaking of Human Experience in a Disordering World." *Harvard Theological Review* 90: 315–35.

———. 1998. "Experience and Its Moral Modes: Culture, Human Conditions, and Disorder."
The Tanner Lectures on Human Values 20: 355–420.

———. 2006. *What Really Matters*. New York: Oxford University Press.

Kleinman, Arthur, Veena Das, and Margaret Lock. 1997. *Social Suffering*. Berkeley: University of California Press.

Kleinman, Arthur, and Joan Kleinman. 1994. "How Bodies Remember." *New Literary History*
25: 707–23.

Kouts, Gideon, Jacob Katz, Shmuel Ettinger, Arthur Hertzberg, Moshe Medizini, and Chaim
Yahil. 2007. "Zionism." In *Encyclopedia Judaica*, edited by Michael Berenbaum and Fred
Skolnik. Detroit: Macmillan Reference.

Krause, Monika. 2008. "Undocumented Migrants: An Arendtian Perspective." *European Journal of Public Theory* 7: 331–48.

Krieger, Nancy. 2005. "Embodiment: A Conceptual Glossary for Epidemiology." *Journal of Epidemiology and Community Health* 59: 350–55.

Kritzman-Amir, Tally. 2009. "'Otherness' as the Underlying Principle in Israel's Asylum Regime." *Israel Law Review* 42 (3): 603–27.

Kuperboim, Rona. 2003. "Dlatót Mesumanót" [Marked Doors]. *Ha'Ir.* July 3.

LaCapra, Dominick. 2001. *Writing History, Writing Trauma.* Baltimore: Johns Hopkins University Press.

Landau, Noa. 2018. "Netanyahu Suspends Asylum Seeker Deal with UN After Right-Wing Pushback." *Haaretz.* April 3.

Larchanché, Stéphanie. 2012. "Intangible Obstacles: Health Implications of Stigmatization, Structural Violence, and Fear Among Undocumented Immigrants in France." *Social Science and Medicine* 74 (6): 858–63.

Law, Lisa. 2005. "Home Cooking: Filipino Women and Geographies of the Senses in Hong Kong." In *Empire of the Senses*, edited by David Howes. Oxford: Berg. 224–41.

Leder, Drew. 1990. *The Absent Body.* Chicago: University of Chicago Press.

Leibovich-Dar, Sara. 2003. "Cleaned Out." *Haaretz.* September 17.

Leibowitz, Yeshayahu. 1992. *Judaism, Human Values, and the Jewish State.* Cambridge, MA: Harvard University Press.

Levenkron, Nomi. 2007. *Deported and Dispossessed: Human Trafficking and the State of Israel—Between Economic Struggle and Systemic Dispossession.* Tel Aviv: Hotline for Migrant Workers.

Levy-Barzilai, Vered. 2003. "Unpromised Land." *Haaretz.* June 4.

Liebelt, Claudia. 2011. *Caring for the "Holy Land."* New York: Berghahn.

Lior, Ilan, and Tomer Zarchin. 2012. "Demonstrators Attack African Migrants in South Tel Aviv." *Haaretz.* May 24.

Lock, Margaret. 2002. *Twice Dead.* Berkeley: University of California Press.

Lomsky-Feder, Edna, and Tamar Rapoport. 2001. "Homecoming, Immigration, and the National Ethos: Russian-Jewish Homecomers Reading Zionism." *Anthropological Quarterly* 74: 1–14.

Lorberbaum, Yair. 2014. "Human Dignity in the Jewish Tradition." In *The Cambridge Handbook of Human Dignity*, edited by Marcus Düvell et al. Cambridge: Cambridge University Press, 135–44.

Lucht, Hans. 2011. *Darkness Before Daybreak.* Berkeley: University of California Press.

Luibhéid, Eithne. 2013. *Pregnant on Arrival.* Minneapolis: University of Minnesota Press.

Lustick, Ian S. 1999. "Israel as a Non-Arab State: The Political Implications of Mass Immigration of Non-Jews." *Middle East Journal* 53: 417–33.

Macklin, Ruth. 2003. "Dignity Is a Useless Concept." *BMJ* 327: 1419.

Malkki, Liisa. 2010. "Children, Humanity, and the Infantilization of Peace." In *In the Name of Humanity*, edited by Ilana Feldman and Miriam Ticktin. Durham, NC: Duke University Press, 58–85.

Mann, Jonathan. 1998. "Dignity and Health: The UDHR's Revolutionary First Article." *Health and Human Rights* 3: 30–38.

Mansbach, Daniela. 2016. "Witnessing as Activism: Watching the Other at the Israeli Checkpoints." *Journal of Human Rights* 15 (4): 496–508.

Margalit, Avishai. 1996. *The Decent Society.* Translated by Naomi Goldblum. Cambridge, MA: Harvard University Press.

Markowitz, Fran, Sara Helman, and Dafna Shir-Vertesh. 2003. "Soul Citizenship: The Black Hebrews and the State of Israel." *American Anthropologist* 105: 302–12.

Masalha, Salman. 2014. "Israeli Apartheid Exposed at the Airport." *Haaretz*. June 5.

Matabisi, Lukumu. 1997. "Migrant Workers in Israel: With Insights on Black Africans." MA thesis, Department of Public Policy, Tel Aviv University.

Mathews, Gordon, and Carolina Izquierdo, eds. 2009. *Pursuits of Happiness: Well-Being in Anthropological Perspective*. New York: Berghahn.

Mattingly, Cheryl. 2014. *Moral Laboratories*. Berkeley: University of California Press.

———. 2013. "Moral Selves and Moral Scenes." *Ethnos* 78: 301–27.

McClintock, Anne. 1995. *Imperial Leather*. New York: Routledge.

McCrudden, Christopher. 2014. *Understanding Human Dignity*. Oxford: Oxford University Press.

McKee, Emily. 2016. *Dwelling in Conflict: Negev Landscapes and the Boundaries of Belonging*. Stanford, CA: Stanford University Press.

Meir, Ofer. 2005. "'At Rofá Filipínit? Ma Pitóm, At Ovédet Zará'" ["You're a Filipina Doctor? What Are You Talking About, You're a Foreign Worker"]. *Ynet*. January 16.

Menjívar, Cecilia. 2006. "Liminal Legality: Salvadoran and Guatemalan Immigrants' Lives in the United States." *American Journal of Sociology* 111: 999–1037.

Menjívar, Cecilia, and Daniel Kanstroom. 2014. *Constructing Immigrant "Illegality."* New York: Cambridge University Press.

Mesila. 2007. *Doḥ Mesila 2006* [Mesila Report for 2006]. Tel Aviv: Mesila Aid and Information Center for the Foreign Community.

Monterescu, Daniel. 2015. *Jaffa Shared and Shattered*. Bloomington: Indiana University Press.

Morfix. 2018. "Totzaót Targúm laAnglít avúr: L'hávdil" [English Translation Results for: L'hávdil]. Accessed October 25, 2018, at www.morfix.co.il.

Moyn, Samuel. 2010. *The Last Utopia*. Cambridge, MA: Belknap Press of Harvard University Press.

———. 2014. *Human Rights and the Uses of History*. London: Verso.

———. 2015. *Christian Human Rights*. Philadelphia: University of Pennsylvania Press.

Mozgovaya, Natasha. 2003. "'Paḥádti sheAḥaréi haTipúl haRefuí Yaatzrú Otí'" ["I Was Afraid That After the Medical Care, They Would Arrest Me"]. *Yedioth Aharonoth*. January 7.

Myre, Greg. 2004. "Israeli TV Tackles Hearts and Minds." *New York Times*. November 29.

Nesher, Talila. 2012. "Association for Civil Rights in Israel: Violence Against Migrants in Israel Reaches Record High in 2012." *Haaretz*. December 16.

Ngai, Mae M. 2004. *Impossible Subjects*. Princeton, NJ: Princeton University Press.

Nguyen, Vinh-Kim. 2010. *The Republic of Therapy*. Durham, NC: Duke University Press.

Nussbaum, Martha. 2000. *Women and Human Development: The Capabilities Approach*. Cambridge: Cambridge University Press.

———. 2011. *Creating Capabilities*. Cambridge, MA: Harvard University Press.

Nyers, Peter. 2003. "Abject Cosmopolitanism: The Politics of Protection in the Anti-deportation Movement." *Third World Quarterly* 24: 1069–93.

Ochs, Julianna. 2011. *Security and Suspicion: An Ethnography of Everyday Life in Israel*. Philadelphia: University of Pennsylvania Press.

Office of the State Comptroller. 2013. *Annual Report*. Jerusalem: Office of the State Comptroller.

Oka, Rahul Chandrashekhar. 2014. "Coping with the Refugee Wait: The Role of Consumption, Normalcy, and Dignity in Refugee Lives at Kakuma Refugee Camp, Kenya." *American Anthropologist* 116: 1–15.

Omer-Man, Michael Schaeffer. 2015. "No Charges for Officers Involved in Kafr Kanna Killing." *+972*. May 5.

Omidian, Patricia, and Catherine Panter-Brick. 2015. "Dignity Under Extreme Duress: The Moral and Emotional Landscape of Local Humanitarian Workers in the Afghan-Pakistan Border Areas." In *Medical Humanitarianism*. Philadelphia: University of Pennsylvania Press. 23–40.

Ong, Anthony D., Saarang Deshpande, and David R. Williams. 2018. "Biological Consequences of Unfair Treatment: A Theoretical and Empirical Review." In *The Handbook of Culture and Biology*, edited by Jose M Causadias, Eva H. Telzer, and Nancy A. Gonzales. Newark, NJ: Wiley-Blackwell. 279–315.

Or, Theodor. 2006. "The Report by the State Commission of Inquiry into the Events of October 2000." *Israel Studies* 11: 23–53.

Parekh, Serena. 2008. *Hannah Arendt and the Challenge of Modernity*. New York: Routledge.

Paz, Alejandro. 2018. *Latinos in Israel: Language and Unexpected Citizenship*. Bloomington: Indiana University Press.

Peled, Yoav. 1992. "Ethnic Democracy and the Legal Construction of Citizenship: Arab Citizens of the Jewish State." *American Political Science Review* 86: 432–43.

Peres, Shimon. 1993. *The New Middle East*. New York: Henry Holt.

Physicians for Human Rights–Israel, Israeli Children, and Hotline for Migrant Workers. 2013. *Doḥ Meḥkár: Mipúi Tnaéi haMaatzár vehaKliá shel Yaldéi Mehagréi Avodá vePlitím beYisraél* [Research Report: Survey of Detention and Incarceration Conditions for Children of Migrant Workers and Refugees in Israel]. Tel Aviv: Association for Civil Rights in Israel. Accessed October 25, 2018, at https://www.acri.org.il/he/wp-content/uploads/2013/12/children-research.pdf.

Pinkas, Alon. 1993. "Garrison Democracy: The Impact of the 1967 Occupation of Territories on Institutional Democracy in Israel." In *Democracy, Peace, and the Israeli-Palestinian Conflict*, edited by Edy Kaufman, Shukri B. Abed, and Robert L. Rothstein. Boulder, CO: Lynne Rienner. 61–83.

Pinto, Sarah. 2014. *Daughters of Parvati: Women and Madness in Contemporary India*. Philadelphia: University of Pennsylvania Press.

Prince, Ruth. 2012. "HIV and the Moral Economy of Survival in an East African City." *Medical Anthropology Quarterly* 26: 534–56.

Quesada, James, Laurie Kain Hart, and Philippe Bourgois. 2011. "Structural Vulnerability and Health: Latino Migrant Laborers in the United States." *Medical Anthropology* 30: 339–62.

Rabinowitz, Dan, and Khawla Abu-Baker. 2005. *Coffins on Our Shoulders: The Experience of the Palestinian Citizens of Israel*. Berkeley: University of California Press.

Raijman, Rebeca, and Adriana Kemp. 2007. "Labor Migration, Managing the Ethno-national Conflict, and Client Politics in Israel." In *Transnational Migration to Israel in Global Comparative Context*, edited by Sarah S. Willen. Lanham, MD: Lexington. 31–50.

———. 2016. "The Institutionalization of Labor Migration in Israel." *Arbor* 192 (777): a289.

Rajaram, Prem Kumar, and Carl Grundy-Warr. 2004. "The Irregular Migrant as Homo Sacer." *International Migration* 42 (March): 33–64.

Rapoport, Tamar, and Edna Lomsky-Feder. 2001. "Reflections on Strangeness in Context: The Case of Russian–Jewish Immigrants in the Kibbutz." *Qualitative Sociology* 24: 483–506.

Redfield, Peter. 2008. "Doctors Without Borders and the Moral Economy of Pharmaceuticals." In *Human Rights in Crisis*, edited by Alice Bullard, 129–44. Aldershot, UK: Ashgate.

———. 2013. *Life in Crisis*. Berkeley: University of California Press.

Remennick, Larissa. 2000. "Childless in the Land of Imperative Motherhood: Stigma and Coping Among Infertile Israeli Women." *Sex Roles* 43: 821–41.

Robbins, Joel. 2013. "Beyond the Suffering Subject: Toward an Anthropology of the Good." *Journal of the Royal Anthropological Institute* 19: 447–62.

Rosen, Michael. 2012. *Dignity: Its History and Meaning*. Cambridge, MA: Harvard University Press.

Rosenhek, Zeev. 2000. "Migration Regimes, Intra-state Conflicts, and the Politics of Exclusion and Inclusion: Migrant Workers in the Israeli Welfare State." *Social Problems* 47: 49–67.

Rosenthal, Anat. 2007. "'Illegality' and Illness in the Everyday Struggles of Undocumented HIV+ Migrant Workers in Tel Aviv." *International Migration* 45: 134–56.

Rouhana, Nadim. 1997. *Palestinian Citizens in an Ethnic Jewish State*. New Haven, CT: Yale University Press.

Roy, Sara. 2002. "Ending the Palestinian Economy." *Middle East Policy: Washington* 9 (4): 122–65.

Ruszczyk, Stephen P., and Guillermo Yrizar Barbosa. 2017. "A Second Generation of Immigrant Illegality Studies." *Migration Studies* 5 (3): 445–56.

Sabar, Galia. 2008. *Lo Bánu Lehishaér: Mehagréi Avodá meÁfrika leYisraél uvaḤazará* [We Didn't Come to Stay: Migrant Workers from Africa to Israel and Back]. Tel Aviv: Tel Aviv University Press.

Sargent, Carolyn, and Stéphanie Larchanché. 2007. "The Muslim Body and the Politics of Immigration in France: Popular and Biomedical Representations of Malian Migrant Women." *Body and Society* 13: 79–102.

Schopenhauer, Arthur. 1999. *On the Basis of Morality*. Translated by E. F. J. Payn. Indianapolis: Hackett.

Schulman, Adam. 2008. "Bioethics and the Question of Human Dignity." In *Human Dignity and Bioethics: Essays Commissioned by the President's Council on Bioethics*. Washington, DC: Government Printing Office. 3–18.

Schwartz, Tamar. 2007. *Doḥ Tkufatí laKéren haYedidút Mesilá* [Periodic Report to the Friends of Mesila Fund]. Tel Aviv: Mesila Aid and Information Center for the Foreign Community.

Scott, James C. 1976. *The Moral Economy of the Peasant*. New Haven, CT: Yale University Press.

Seeman, Don. 2009. *One People, One Blood: Ethiopian-Israelis and the Return to Judaism*. New Brunswick, NJ: Rutgers University Press.

Segev, Tom. 2007. *1967: Israel, the War, and the Year That Transformed the Middle East*. New York: Metropolitan Books.

Semyonov, Moshe, and Noah Lewin-Epstein. 1987. *Hewers of Wood and Drawers of Water: Noncitizen Arabs in the Israeli Labor Market*. Ithaca, NY: Cornell University Press.

Shadmi, Haim. 2003. "Ignacius Came Home in Anticipation of the Delivery—and Was Killed with His Wife." *Haaretz*. July 1.

Shafir, Gershon, and Yoav Peled. 1998. "Citizenship and Stratification in an Ethnic Democracy." *Ethnic and Racial Studies* 21: 408–27.

———. 2002. *Being Israeli: The Dynamics of Multiple Citizenship*. Cambridge: Cambridge University Press.

Shalev, Guy. 2016. "The 'P' Word: Hospital Ethics Committees and Palestinian National Identity." *Somatosphere*. Accessed October 25, 2018, at http://somatosphere.net/2016/10/the-p-word-hospital-ethics-committees-and-palestinian-national-identity.html.

Shamir, Ronen. 2005. "Without Borders? Notes on Globalization as a Mobility Regime." *Sociological Theory* 23: 197–217.

Shohat, Ella. 1999. "The Invention of the Mizrahim." *Journal of Palestine Studies* 29 (1): 5–20.

Shpigel, Noa, Jack Khoury, and Yaniv Kubovich. 2014. "Netanyahu Backs Police After Fatal Shooting of Israeli Arab Sparks Clashes in Galilee." *Haaretz*. November 28.

Sigona, Nando. 2012. "'I Have Too Much Baggage': The Impacts of Legal Status on the Social Worlds of Irregular Migrants." *Social Anthropology* 20: 50–65.

Silk, Dennis. 1990. *Catwalk and Overpass: Poems*. New York: Viking.

Siméant, Johanna. 2015. "Three Bodies of Moral Economy: The Diffusion of a Concept." *Journal of Global Ethics* 11 (2): 163–75.

Sinai, Ruth. 2002. "Benizri Reconvenes Long-Dormant Council on Demography Today." *Haaretz*. September 3.

———. 2003. "Foreigners Pay the Price." *Haaretz*. September 23.

———. 2004. "Bimkóm l'Hapés et haShotrím SheHitalelú baOvdím Zarím, Mehapsím et haShtínker" [Instead of Looking for the Officers that Abused Foreign Workers, They're Looking for the Informer]. *Haaretz*. February 10.

Singer, Roni, and Yam Yehoshua. 2003. "Seven Killed, Six Hurt as Building Collapses Following Gas Blast in Southern Tel Aviv." *Haaretz*. July 1.

Smith, Daniel Jordan. 2004. "Contradictions in Nigeria's Fertility Transition: The Burdens and Benefits of Having People." *Population and Development Review* 30: 221–38.

Smooha, Sami. 1990. "Minority Status in an Ethnic Democracy: The Status of the Arab Minority in Israel." *Ethnic and Racial Studies* 13: 389–413.

Soysal, Yasemin N. 1994. *Limits of Citizenship*. Chicago: University of Chicago Press.

State of Israel. 1948. *Declaration of the Establishment of the State of Israel*. Jerusalem: State of Israel.

Stevens, Phillips. 2006. "Women's Aggressive Use of Genital Power in Africa." *Transcultural Psychiatry* 43 (4): 592–99.

Stevenson, Lisa. 2014. *Life Beside Itself*. Berkeley: University of California Press.

Stoller, Paul. 2014. *Yaya's Story: The Quest for Well-Being in the World*. Chicago: University of Chicago Press.

Suárez-Navaz, Liliana. 2004. *Rebordering the Mediterranean*. New York: Berghahn.

Suárez-Orozco, Carola, Hirokazu Yoshikawa, Robert T. Teranishi, and Marcelo M. Suárez-Orozco. 2011. "Growing Up in the Shadows: The Developmental Implications of Unauthorized Status." *Harvard Educational Review* 81: 438–72.

Sultany, Nimer. 2012. "The Making of an Underclass: The Palestinian Citizens of Israel." *Israel Studies Review* 27 (2): 190–212.

Swedenburg, Ted. 1995. *Memories of Revolt*. Minneapolis: University of Minnesota Press.

Tamari, Salim. 1994. "Problems of Social Science Research in Palestine: An Overview." *Current Sociology* 42 (2): 69–86.

Teman, Elly. 2010. *Birthing a Mother*. Berkeley: University of California Press.

Thompson, E. P. 1963. *The Making of the English Working Class*. New York: Pantheon Books.

Throop, C. Jason. 2002. "Articulating Experience." *Anthropological Theory* 3: 219–41.

Ticktin, Miriam. 2011. *Casualties of Care*. Berkeley: University of California Press.

Tormey, Anwen. 2007. "'Everyone with Eyes Can See the Problem': Moral Citizens and the Space of Irish Nationhood." *International Migration* 45: 69–100.

Torstrick, Rebecca. 2000. *The Limits of Coexistence*. Ann Arbor: University of Michigan Press.

Tyler, Imogen. 2013. *Revolting Subjects: Social Abjection and Resistance in Neoliberal Britain*. London: Zed Books.

United Nations General Assembly. 1948. "Universal Declaration of Human Rights." Accessed October 25, 2018, at http://www.un.org/en/udhr/.

UNHCR (United Nations High Commissioner for Refugees). 2017. "UNHCR's Position on the Status of Eritrean and Sudanese Nationals Defined as 'Infiltrators' by Israel." Position paper. November. Accessed October 25, 2018, at http://www.refworld.org/docid/5a5889584.html.

Vogt, Wendy. 2018. *Lives in Transit*. Berkeley: University of California Press.

von Schnitzler, Antina. 2014. "Performing Dignity: Human Rights, Citizenship, and the Techno-Politics of Law in South Africa." *American Ethnologist* 41: 336–50.

Waldron, Jeremy. 2012. *Dignity, Rank, and Rights*. Oxford: Oxford University Press.

Watters, Charles. 2001. "Avenues of Access and the Moral Economy of Legitimacy." *Anthropology Today* 17 (April): 22–23.

Weiss, Erica. 2014. *Conscientious Objectors in Israel*. Philadelphia: University of Pennsylvania Press.

Weizman, Eyal. 2007. *Hollow Land: Israel's Architecture of Occupation*. London: Verso.

Wendland, Claire. 2010. *A Heart for the Work*. Chicago: University of Chicago Press.

Willen, Sarah S. 2005. "Birthing 'Invisible' Children: State Power, NGO Activism, and Reproductive Health Among Undocumented Migrant Workers in Tel Aviv, Israel." *Journal of Middle East Women's Studies* 1: 55–88.

———. 2007a. "Toward a Critical Phenomenology of 'Illegality': State Power, Criminalization, and Abjectivity Among Undocumented Migrant Workers in Tel Aviv, Israel." *International Migration* 45: 8–36.

———. 2007b. "Introduction: Exploring 'Illegal' and 'Irregular' Migrants' Experiences of Law and State Power." *International Migration* 45: 2–7.

———. 2010. "Darfur Through a Shoah Lens: Sudanese Asylum Seekers, Unruly Biopolitical Dramas, and the Politics of Humanitarian Compassion in Israel." In *A Reader in Medical Anthropology*, edited by Byron J. Good, Michael M. J. Fischer, Sarah S. Willen, and Mary-Jo DelVecchio Good, 505–21. Malden, MA: Blackwell.

———. 2011. "Do 'Illegal' Migrants Have a 'Right to Health'? Engaging Ethical Theory as Social Practice at a Tel Aviv Open Clinic." *Medical Anthropology Quarterly* 25 (3): 303–30.

———. 2012a. "How Is Health-Related 'Deservingness' Reckoned? Perspectives from Unauthorized Im/Migrants in Tel Aviv." *Social Science and Medicine* 74: 812–21.

———. 2012b. "Introduction: Migration, 'Illegality,' and Health: Mapping Embodied Vulnerability and Debating Health-Related Deservingness." *Social Science and Medicine* 74: 805–11.

———. 2014. "Plotting a Moral Trajectory, sans Papiers: Outlaw Motherhood as Inhabitable Space of Welcome." *Ethos* 42: 84–100.

———. 2015. "Lightning Rods in the Local Moral Economy: Debating Unauthorized Migrants' Deservingness in Israel." *International Migration* 53 (3): 70–86.

Willen, Sarah S., and Jennifer Cook. 2016. "Health-Related Deservingness." In *Handbook of Migration and Health*, edited by Felicity Thomas. Cheltenham, UK: Edward Elgar. 95–118.

Willen, Sarah S., Michael Knipper, César E. Abadía-Barrero, and Nadav Davidovitch. 2017. "Syndemic Vulnerability and the Right to Health." *Lancet* 389: 964–77.

Willen, Sarah S., and Don Seeman. 2012. "Introduction: Experience and Inquiétude." *Ethos* 40: 1–23.

Williams, Bernard. 1981. *Moral Luck*. Cambridge: Cambridge University Press.

Wright, Fiona. 2018. *The Israeli Radical Left: An Ethics of Complicity*. Philadelphia: University of Pennsylvania Press.

Wuhrgaft, Nurit. 2003a. "Living in Fear Is Exhausting." *Haaretz*. September 30.

———. 2003b. "Our Challenge: To Break the Apathy." *Haaretz*. May 6.

———. 2004. "Shalom. VeTodá al haYáḥas haMashpíl" [Goodbye. And Thanks for the Humiliating Treatment]. *Haaretz*. April 3.

Yaron, Lee, and Noa Landau. 2018. "Israel Reaches Deal with UN to Deport Asylum Seekers to West, Not Africa." *Haaretz*. April 2.

Yiftachel, Oren. 2006. *Ethnocracy*. Philadelphia: University of Pennsylvania Press.

Ynet. 2009. "Yishai: Foreigners Will Bring AIDS, Drugs." *Ynet*. October 31.

Yoman. 2003. "News Broadcast." Israel Broadcasting Authority. January 10.

Yoshikawa, Hirokazu. 2011. *Immigrants Raising Citizens*. New York: Russell Sage Foundation.

Zertal, Idith. 2005. *Israel's Holocaust and the Politics of Nationhood*. Cambridge: Cambridge University Press.

Zigon, Jarrett. 2007. "Moral Breakdown and the Ethical Demand." *Anthropological Theory* 7: 131–50.

———. 2013. "Rights, Responsibility, and Health Services: Human Rights as an Idiomatic Language of Power." In *Assembling Health Rights in Global Context*, edited by Alex Mold and David Reubi. London: Routledge. 65–80.

———. 2014. "An Ethics of Dwelling and a Politics of World-Building: A Critical Response to Ordinary Ethics." *Journal of the Royal Anthropological Institute* 20: 746–64.

Zigon, Jarrett, and C. Jason Throop, eds. 2014. "Special Issue: Moral Experience." *Ethos* 42 (1).

ACKNOWLEDGMENTS

So many years, so many people, so much gratitude. Above all, I thank those who came to Israel seeking the raw materials of a dignified, flourishing life—those I describe in this book as "global migrants"—who chose to trust me. Although I cannot thank you by name, I am indebted to each of you for welcoming me into your life, and for enriching mine.

Many colleagues and friends in Israel helped breathe life into this project, especially Rami Adout, Maskit Bendel, Anat Aviv, Hadas Ziv, Ran Cohen, Sigal Rozen, Shevy Korzen, Ella Keren, Edna Altar-Dembo, Adi Azov-Amon, Sara Ashkenazi, Miri Barbero-Elkayam, Ido Lurie, Zsuzsa Katona, Naana Holdbrook, Noam Ilan, and Uri Naveh. I thank Zeev Rosenhek, Adriana Kemp, Tamar Rapoport, Edna Lomsky-Feder, and Tally Kritzman-Amir, among other Israeli scholars who helped me launch. I thank Dani Filc and especially Nadav Davidovitch for their unflinching critical feedback and perpetual inspiration. My cousins—the Benory women, especially Eidit, and the Handelsmans, including Tova (z"l) and Levi (z"l)—have drawn me close, fed me well, and complicated my view of Israel in important ways. I thank Nomi Levenkron and Irit Elboher for helping me win my first, and hopefully last, legal suit (in small claims court).

A Raoul Wallenberg Fellowship at the Hebrew University of Jerusalem offered a firsthand view of Israel's tumultuous complexity—and the incomparable honor and privilege of working for Naomi Chazan.

At Emory, I was blessed with an extraordinary mentor, Peter Brown, who will always be my role model. Don Seeman has been an indispensable mentor, critic, and collaborator. From the start, Peter and Don, together with Jennifer Hirsch and Bob Desjarlais, pushed me to refine my thinking, unclutter my writing, and claim my voice. I am grateful for their early confidence and, now, for their friendship. From Emory onward, I thank Erin Finley, Svea Closser, Alexa Dietrich, Emily Mendenhall, and Diana Smay Toebbe. Other mentors deserving thanks include Bobby Paul, Marcia Inhorn, Benny

Hary, Mel Konner, Doug Hollan, Leo Chavez, Mark Nichter, Jonathan Sadowsky, Woody Gaines, Catherine Panter-Brick, Caroline Brettell, and David Meltzer.

An NIMH Fellowship in the Department of Global Health and Social Medicine at Harvard Medical School helped this project take longitudinal form. At Harvard, Arthur Kleinman offered vital feedback on an early version of this text. Mary-Jo Delvecchio Good and Byron Good have been unflagging sources of loving encouragement, guidance, and support. I thank Michael Jackson for engaging my work with seriousness, and generosity. Michael M. J. Fischer deserves thanks for his incisive feedback, sage counsel, and overall *menschkeit* (the Yiddish kind). To the multigenerational Friday Morning Seminar community in Harvard's Department of Anthropology—especially Chris Dole, Sarah Pinto, Elizabeth Carpenter-Song, Cheryl Mattingly, Tom Csordas, Janis Jenkins, Linda Garro, Sadeq Rahimi, Amélie Oksenberg Rorty, Antonio Bullon, and Seth Hannah—I am deeply grateful.

Many programs and institutions supported my research, including Fulbright-Hays, the National Science Foundation (No. 0135425), the Social Science Research Council, the Wenner-Gren Foundation for Anthropological Research, the Amy Adina Schulman Memorial Fund, and the Lady Davis Fellowship Trust. Thanks are also due to Emory University's Center for Health, Culture, and Society, Tam Institute for Jewish Studies, and Department of Anthropology; to the Department of Anthropology at Southern Methodist University; and to the University of Connecticut's Humanities Institute (for a year-long Faculty Residential Fellowship), Human Rights Institute, Center for Judaic Studies and Contemporary Jewish Life, Department of Anthropology, Office of Global Affairs, and Scholarship Facilitation Fund, as well as my colleagues in the Research Program on Global Health and Human Rights.

Earlier versions of this work were shared with more audiences in North America, Europe, and Israel than I can enumerate here, but one particularly welcoming community merits mention: the Mind, Medicine, and Culture Seminar in the Department of Anthropology at UCLA. I am grateful to colleagues and friends, there and elsewhere, for critically engaging my ideas over the years, especially Sa'ed Atshan, Adia Benton, Mara Buchbinder, Heide Castañeda, Nadia el-Shaarawi, Roberto Gonzales, Erin Good, Seth Holmes, Michael Knipper, Molly Land, Kathy Libal, Kate Mason, Daniel Monterescu, Nia Parson, Alejandro Paz, Merav Shohet, Carolyn Smith-Morris, Rich Sosis, Jason Throop, William Tootle, Anwen Tormey, and Jarrett Zigon. Particular thanks are due to Shay Cannedy, Anne Kohler, Kristin Yarris, and Anat Rosenthal for commenting on the manuscript in full, and to Yael Maoz Shai and Gerry Krieg for their image and map-related heroics. I thank Daniel Wogenstein for lending his painting (*Untitled*, 2005) for the book's cover. At Penn Press, I am grateful to Peter Agree, to series editors Alma Gottlieb and Kirin Narayan, to Noreen O'Connor-Abel, and to the book's anonymous reviewers for their invaluable feedback.

For their friendship over this long journey, I thank Avigail Rosenzweig, Emily Hecker, and my cousin, Yosafa Deutsch. And for years of stalwart field companionship, transformative conversation, and unparalleled hospitality, I cannot thank Mati Milstein, Anat Rosenthal, or Anat Litvin enough.

The unwavering love and support of my parents, Carol and David Willen, are gifts beyond measure. My sister, Rachel, and brother, Seth, along with their own growing families, have helped keep my feet planted on the ground, as have my uncle, Stuart Kleiner, my in-laws, Wolfgang and Brigitte Wogenstein, and my brother- and sister-in-law, Daniel Wogenstein and Franziska Degendorfer. My grandparents (z"l), Gertude and Carl Kleiner and Lee and Ray Willen, left an ethical and spiritual legacy that I strive to carry forward in this book, and in all I do. Two beautiful beings—Gabriella Hadas and Noam Adin—entered the world before this book could make its way into print. I am humbled by their luminous presence in my life, and by the chance to be their mother. And Sebastian Wogenstein, their father, is my rock, my kindred spirit, my demon editor, my long-awaited love. My gratitude to you is beyond words.

*   *   *

An earlier version of Chapter 1 appeared as "Toward a Critical Phenomenology of 'Illegality': State Power, Criminalization, and Abjectivity Among Undocumented Migrant Workers in Tel Aviv, Israel," *International Migration* 45(3 [2007]). Brief portions of Chapters 1 and 3 appeared in earlier form in "Lightning Rods in the Local Moral Economy: Debating Unauthorized Migrants' Deservingness in Israel," *International Migration* 53(3 [2015]). A brief portion of Chapter 2 appeared in the "Top of the Heap" column at *Somatosphere* (September 12, 2014; accessed October 25, 2018, at http://somatosphere .net/2014/09/top-of-the-heap-sarah-willen.html). An earlier version of Chapter 3 appeared as "Citizens, 'Real' Others, and 'Other' Others: Governmentality, Biopolitics, and the Deportation of Undocumented Migrants from Tel Aviv," in *The Deportation Regime: Sovereignty, Space, and the Freedom of Movement*, ed. Nicholas De Genova and Nathalie Peutz (Durham, NC: Duke University Press, 2010). An earlier version of Chapter 4 was published as "'Flesh of Our Flesh'? Terror and Mourning at the Boundaries of the Israeli Body Politic," in *Transnational Migration to Israel in Global Comparative Context*, ed. Sarah S. Willen (Lanham, MD: Lexington Books, 2007). The conclusion includes a brief excerpt from "Migration, 'Illegality,' and Health: Mapping Embodied Vulnerability and Debating Health-Related Deservingness," *Social Science and Medicine* 74 (6 [2012]). Material published in earlier form is used with permission.